Saturday Afternoon
at the Bijou

SATURDAY

AT THE

by

ARLINGTON HOUSE

AFTERNOON
BIJOU

DAVID ZINMAN

New Rochelle, New York

Library of Congress Catalog Card Number 72–91641

ISBN 0-87000-197-3

MANUFACTURED IN THE UNITED STATES OF AMERICA

For Caz

Introduction

Saturday's heroes were not only the gridiron greats who raced to touchdowns with the roar of the crowd echoing in their ears. They were also the celluloid figures who thrilled us and regaled us with laughter as they showed up larger than life on our neighborhood movie screens.

Perhaps, instead of the Bijou, your picture show was the Olympia or the Grand or the Riverside. The name really doesn't matter. Those unforgettable moments of high adventure and madcap mirth were shared by every youngster who plunked down a dime—later a quarter—for a Saturday matinee double feature.

Many of our idols appeared in low-budget B-movies that showed up as the bottom half of double bills. Low-budget they may have been. But they were a fixture on the national movie scene of the 1930s and 1940s.

Because audiences enjoyed seeing familiar faces, a good many of them evolved into series. Some of them could only loosely be called a series because over the years, they had only one or two continuing characters. And the actors playing these roles, as in the *Frankenstein* series, changed almost from picture to picture. But others, like *Henry Aldrich,* had a substantial number of repeating characters. And studios often tried to keep the cast intact as long as they could.

There was a pleasant feeling about knowing all the people in the picture—like dropping in on old friends for an afternoon visit. In fact, some of the characters seemed so real, fans wrote to them. Andy Hardy (Mickey Rooney) regularly dispensed advice to teen-agers (while he himself was wining and dining starlets). When small-town doctors visited Hollywood, they often went over to RKO to see Dr. Christian (Jean Hersholt).

From Hollywood's standpoint, series films were an integral part of movie economics. In that period of "block booking," theatres were required to take a series in order to get major productions. And so the series movies were either made by the big studios as a necessary part of the twin-feature setup, or by the shoestring boys who couldn't afford a star. But they were a vast proving ground for some key talents. Rita Hayworth, Glenn Ford and Lana Turner are only a few of the many stars who came out of B-movies and series flicks.

Some of the series turned out to be enormously profitable. Production costs were minimal. Sets were used over and over. No expensive salaries were needed because the actors were all contract players. Moreover, a good number of the pictures—like *Tarzan, Sherlock Holmes* and *Charlie Chan*—were based on already popular fictional characters. And so they were pre-sold.

Unfortunately, the studios were lazy. After concentrating their efforts on the opener, many producers allowed their product to deteriorate. Plots became mechanical and predictable. And so, as the series went along, audiences dwindled. Television provided the *coup de grace*.

But while they lasted, they gave us incomparable fantasies in our retreat in the cool darkness. Some buffs count more than 70 different series. For the family trade, there were *Andy Hardy* and *Blondie*. For the western buff, there were *Hopalong Cassidy* and the *Cisco Kid*. For the detective fan, there were *Crime Doctor* and *The Saint* and *Mr. Moto*. For the popcorn set, there were *Henry Aldrich* and *Nancy Drew* and *Our Gang*. And for the horror aficionado, there were *Frankenstein* and the *Mummy* and the *Wolf Man*.

Look for them now in the pages of *Saturday Afternoon at the Bijou*. It's an America gone by.

Author's Note and Acknowledgments

The book contains 30 chapters, each followed by a filmography listing movie title, studio, release year, director, cast and running time.

Most films in this book are series movies from the 1930s and 1940s. They are personal favorites from what now seems like a more innocent era. But a few are too new to have played at the old Bijou. And so they were included for other reasons.

James Bond and *Planet of the Apes* were picked to illustrate how studios handled a series in the 1960s, and how series films fared when backed by a major budget. The *Doctor in the House* series, filmed in the 1950s, was chosen to point up how physicians were portrayed in British pictures in contrast to the way they showed up in such U.S. movies as *Dr. Kildare* and *Dr. Christian.*

Gene Autry? Why is he included in a section with three cowboy series? But Autry was a series. He always played the same character—himself—in all but two of his 93 pictures. Chalk this one up to poetic license.

As for the many people who were kind enough to help me, there are three who must be singled out—John Cocchi, Monty Arnold and Nick Williams. Cocchi, a B-film expert, checked my copy for accuracy and helped me identify bit players in the stills. He also did the Gene Autry filmography, and arranged for screenings of rarely shown films. Arnold, a dedicated researcher, compiled most of the filmographies—a tedious job but a worthwhile effort for film buffs and scholars. Williams, a western fan, provided me with voluminous reference material for the cowboy chapters. He did the filmography on the *Three Mesquiteers,* and lent me most of the stills for the western section from his personal collection.

For research help, I am also indebted to the staff of the Theatre Collection of the New York Public Library—Astor, Lenox and Tilden Foundations—in Lincoln Center. I owe thanks to Paul Myers, its curator, and his professional staff of Donald Fowle, Rod Bladel, Monty Arnold, Maxwell Silverman, Dorothy Swerdlove and Betty Wharton. I am also grateful to Don Madison of Photographic Services.

For helping me locate stills, I am thankful to Movie Star News, Kier's Celebrity Photos of New York, Kenneth G. Lawrence, the Movie Memorabilia Shop of Hollywood and the Nostalgia Book Club.

For lending me stills from their collections, I am grateful to: Harry Wilkinson of Marblehead, Mass.; Mike Dobbs of Granby, Maine; James Murray of Landsdowne, Pa.; Gordon Samples of San Diego, Calif.; John Cocchi of Brooklyn,

N.Y.; Ivan Maule of El Monte, Calif.; James A. Stringham of Lansing, Mich.; Max Terhune of Cottonwood, Ariz.; Morris Everett, Jr., of Cleveland; John Stoginski of Chicago; and Bernie Velleman of Long Island City, N.Y.

The *Hopalong Cassidy* filmography was largely based on one compiled by Don Miller of Staten Island, N.Y., in *Captain George's Whizzbang* magazine number nine. For permission to use it, thanks to Captain George Henderson of *The New Captain George's Whizzbang.*

Thanks also to Michael Pointer of London and Dr. Julian Wolff, Commissionaire of the Baker Street Irregulars, for help on the *Sherlock Holmes* chapter; to D. Peter Ogden of Tampa, Fla.; Paul C. Allen of Rochester, N.Y.; Vernell Coriell of Kansas City, Mo.; and Robert M. Hodes and Hulbert Burroughs of Tarzana, Calif., for help on the *Tarzan* chapter; and to Alan G. Barbour for permission to use John Cocchi's filmography from *Screen Facts* No. 5, 1963 (which has been expanded for this book).

Finally, I am most grateful to Bob Everroad of New York City for showing me films in his home; to Jim Ward of Nashville, Tenn., for helping me identify characters in stills; and to Martin Gross, a first-rate editor and friend who helped me far beyond the call of duty.

DAVID ZINMAN

Point Lookout, L.I., New York
June, 1972

Photo Credits

Contents

Saturday Afternoon
at the Bijou

How it all began. And now you'd pay $100 for a copy of the 1912 *All-Story* magazine with the first *Tarzan* tale.

TARZAN

Tarzan, The Ape Man
(1932)

Based on the novels by Edgar Rice Burroughs. Scenarist, Cyril Hume. Dialogue, Ivor Novello. Editors, Ben Lewis and Tom Held. Camera, Harold Rosson and Clyde DeVinna. Directed by W. S. Van Dyke. Released by Metro-Goldwyn-Mayer. 90 minutes.

Tarzan	JOHNNY WEISSMULLER
Harry Holt	NEIL HAMILTON
James Parker	C. AUBREY SMITH
Jane Parker	MAUREEN O'SULLIVAN
Mrs. Cutten	DORIS LLOYD
Beamish	FORRESTER HARVEY
Riano	CURTIS NERO

A few years ago, Maureen O'Sullivan was reminiscing about the genesis of perhaps the most famous line of movie dialogue.

It came from *Tarzan the Ape Man* (1932), the first feature-length talking *Tarzan* film. "I was deathly afraid of height," Miss O'Sullivan said. "And one day, Johnny Weissmuller and I had to cower in the high branches of a tree for one of our scenes. Johnny was a practical joker. He knew I was afraid of height. So he began to shake our branch and I screamed."

"As I shrieked, Johnny smiled," she recalled. It occurred to him that she was, in a sense, stealing his thunder. After all, he was the one who was supposed to boom out with the blood-chilling, bull-ape call. So, with dry sarcasm, Weissmuller said sternly:

"*ME* . . . Tarzan. *YOU* . . . Jane."

Everyone on the lot broke up. Miss O'Sullivan said, "It was so funny, it was kept in the script. As far as I know, Johnny never got a penny for his contribution. Nor did I."

But memory plays tricks on us. That line actually never was said in the film although a similar line, without the pronouns, was spoken. Nevertheless, the apocryphal quotation has somehow been handed down through the years and become the butt of countless camp jokes.

Ironically, this item of movie trivia probably would not have seemed a bit humorous to Tarzan's creator, Edgar Rice Burroughs. It was in 1912 that Burroughs' first Tarzan story appeared in a pulp magazine. The jungle lord became an instant hit and went on to appear in books, movies, radio serials, comics and newspaper strips. All these enterprises earned more than $20 million for Burroughs and made Tarzan possibly the world's best-known fictional hero.

But most adventure buffs remember the ape-man best from his films. And it was this medium that gave Burroughs one of his most bitter disappointments. The movies virtually ignored the dialogue and plots of his books.

"My father was never able to understand why the *Tarzan* motion pictures would not follow his stories more closely," Burroughs' daughter, Joan Burroughs Pierce, said. "Instead, Hollywood writers changed the stories and created their own version of Dad's hero."

For example, far from being a monosyllabic caveman, Burroughs' Tarzan was actually a self-educated, titled Englishman. He was the son of John Clayton, Lord Greystoke,* who was stranded with his wife on the West African coast by a mutinous crew. Lady Alice lost her mind and then her life a year after giving birth to a son. Soon afterward, a band of great apes killed Lord Greystoke. But the gentle she-ape, Kala, who had lost her own newborn, adopted the strange white baby. She nursed him, and called him Tarzan. "Tar" means white and "zan" means skin in the language Burroughs' fictional apes spoke.

As he grew up, Tarzan taught himself to read and write from books discovered at his parents' cabin. Later, he learned French, German and Italian as well as Bantu and the so-called native dialects. Tarzan eventually returned to civilization

*Marlon Brando sometimes uses the name Lord Greystoke in signing a hotel register.

Tarzan's creator, Edgar Rice Burroughs, dictating a story in his Tarzana, California, office in 1935. The apeman, perhaps the most popular fictional character of all time, earned more than $20 million for ERB.

The most famous of all Tarzan combos—Cheta, Johnny Sheffield, Johnny Weissmuller and Maureen O'Sullivan.

where he mixed in upper-class circles in London and Paris. But he eventually left because he preferred the jungle.

"One time, we saw a movie together," Burroughs' daughter recalled. "After it was all over, although the audience seemed enthusiastic, my father remained in his seat and kept shaking his head sadly."

Just why this aristocrat-turned-noble-savage did not appeal to Hollywood remains a mystery. The Burroughs version won a huge following from the day the author's first ape-man story appeared in *All-Story* magazine when he was 37 years old. It was the turning point of his life.

The son of wealthy parents, ERB, as his fans called him, had been unsuccessful in everything he tried. As a youth, he had flunked out of a succession of prep schools including the exclusive Phillips Academy in Andover, Massachusetts. West Point rejected him and so did Teddy Roosevelt's Rough Riders.

He worked for his father's firm, the American Storage Battery Company, for a while, then decided to try it on his own. He drifted from job to job. He was a cattle-driver, miner, railroad cop, salesman, accountant. For a time, he was head of a stenographic department for Sears, Roebuck in Chicago. Then he failed in several business ventures, including an advertising agency he managed into bankruptcy in less than a year. Some say he was the type of person who expected to make a fortune at everything he did, then quit when he did not get quick results.

At 35, a failure in all he had attempted, Burroughs turned to writing. In his despondency, he would escape from his setbacks in the real world by daydreaming, conjuring up fanciful adventures. One day, reading some pulp magazine, he became convinced he could do better. "I . . . made up my mind," said Burroughs, "that if people were paid for writing rot such as I read, I could write stories just as rotten."

That year, he sold his first effort, a science fiction novella called *Under the Moons of Mars* to *All-Story* for $400. But it was his second published work, *Tarzan of the Apes* (for which he got $700), that captured the public's fancy. It became possibly the most popular story any U.S. magazine has ever published.

Tarzan, the virile, God-like lord of a jungle empire, was a masculine hero with whom every man could identify. He offered a unique escape to an exotic world offering one hair-raising adventure after another. "Tarzan," wrote Russell Nye in *The Unembarrassed Muse,* "was science fiction, combining the super-being theme, the lost world theme, the Utopian theme and the time-warp device."

Critics have said Burroughs probably found his inspiration in the Romulus and Remus legend, *The Jungle Book* of Rudyard Kipling and H. Rider Haggard's *She* and *King Solomon's Mines.* What is certain is that Burroughs did not draw on his own experiences. He never set foot in Africa. His description of that exotic continent came in large part from H. M. Stanley's *In Darkest Africa* and other books he found in the Chicago Public Library. Once he used Sabor, the tiger, as

Burroughs with Elmo Lincoln, the first movie Tarzan on the set of *Tarzan of the Apes* (1918), the original *Tarzan* movie.

Glenn Morris, Tarzan number nine, with Olympic swim champ Eleanor Holm in *Tarzan's Revenge* (1938). "He took himself very seriously," said Miss Holm. "He thought he *was* Tarzan."

a leading character—although tigers, of course, roam the wilds of India.

Burroughs never claimed to be a classical writer. But he had a gift for spellbinding narrative and a boundless imagination. His editor, Thomas Metcalf of *All-Story* magazine, knew he had a pulp classic as soon as he put down that first Tarzan tale. "If you will stop and realize how many thousands and thousands of stories an editor has to read, day in, day out," Metcalf wrote in an introduction to the piece, "you will be impressed when we tell you that we read this yarn at one sitting and had the time of our young lives. It is the most exciting story we have seen in a blue moon, and about as original as they make 'em." Collectors pay $100 and more today for that 15-cent issue published in October, 1912.

The original Tarzan created an immediate sensation. An avalanche of letters demanded a sequel. Soon, Burroughs was turning out one Tarzan tale after another. They were translated into 31 languages—including Chinese, Esperanto, Hebrew, Serbo-Croatian, and Urdu. He became a hero of the Russians—even the Germans until World War I, when Tarzan took on the Huns in one of his adventures.

In all, Burroughs wrote 26 *Tarzan* books. One estimate is that 36 million copies have been sold. But Robert M. Hodes, vice president of Edgar Rice Burroughs Inc., in Tarzana, California, which continues to manage ERB's properties, puts the total at from 50 to 100 million.

Tarzana is something of a story in itself. Burroughs died in 1950 at the age of 75. But a four-man company continues to manage his properties from a small one-story office building ERB built in 1927 in the San Fernando Valley. Although it has its own post office, it is now situated on Ventura Boulevard within the Los Angeles city limits.

"When my father got the property in 1919," said 64-year-old Hulbert Burroughs, one of the corporation owners, "he bought the 550-acre estate from Harrison Gray Otis, founder of the *Los Angeles Times.* Burroughs made it a ranch and the town that grew up around it was called Tarzana."

Today, the ERB corporation owns only about 10 acres of the original land, and its office building, built along the Spanish-style architecture, which was in vogue then, looks more like a mission or a church. So there really isn't much there for summer visitors who make the pilgrimage. But they come anyway because they want to see where it all began. They get a cordial welcome and a tour through the corporation's three office rooms and one storage room. And they are shown the original *Tarzan* books and illustrations. Some of the loyal buffs belong to fan clubs—the Burroughs Bibliophiles, Erbana, the Barsoomian* —and they read *ERB-dom Magazine.*

*The name "Barsoomian" comes from ERB's John Carter tales of Martian adventure. The inhabitants of Mars called their planet Barsoom. Hence, "Barsoomian" is equivalent to "Martian."

Tarzan number four, James H. Pierce, in *Tarzan and the Golden Lion* (1927). Pierce, ERB's son-in-law, was also a radio Tarzan whose Jane was his wife, Joan Burroughs Pierce.

Lex Barker, one of Lana Turner's ex-husbands, gets set to let fly an arrow. He was Tarzan number 10.

The first blond Tarzan, UCLA basketball star Denny Miller. He was ape-man number 12.

TV's Tarzan, Ron Ely, jungle lord number 15.

Tarzan probably reached the height of his popularity in the 1930s. Burroughs had extensive merchandising arrangements then. Tarzan's image appeared on bread wrappers, ice cream cups and in promotions for gasoline. "Drive with the power of Tarzan," billboards read. There were also Tarzan statuettes, Tarzan knives and Tarzan loincloths. Though these business ventures have long since faded, kids of today can still see Tarzan in comic strips in about 100 papers, comic books, TV reruns and second-run movie houses. Europe has replaced the United States as the jungle lord's commercial stamping grounds. Hulbert Burroughs says Tarzan books are enjoying a revival there. They were best-sellers in France last year, he said. And they're going great guns in Italy now.

Ironically, the 26 *Tarzan* novels comprise less than half the 68 books Burroughs turned out in his lifetime. Many of his science fiction works deal with life on other worlds. They include eleven Martian adventures, seven tales from the Inner World (the earth's core) and five Venusian fantasies. He also wrote a Hollywood exposé, a book on slum youth in Chicago, historical novels, two Apache novels (from the Indian's viewpoint) and several detective and humorous books. None matched the sales of his Tarzan stories.

Still, as popular as Tarzan was in books and pulp magazines, he undoubtedly reached an even wider audience on the screen. The first to portray him was Elmo Lincoln, a 200-pound, barrel-chested actor who had featured roles in D. W. Griffith's *Birth of a Nation* (1915—as a blacksmith) and *Intolerance* (1916—as Belshazzar's bodyguard). In 1918, Lincoln appeared in *Tarzan of the Apes,* one of the first silent films to gross more than $1 million.*

Over the years, 15 actors and athletes have played the jungle lord. Tarzan No. 2 was Gene Pollar, a New York City fireman; (3) P. Dempsey Tabler, a flabby, balding, former Tennessee athlete and later a silent film actor who, at the age of 41, played the ape-man under a shaggy, ill-fitting wig; (4) James H. Pierce, Burroughs' son-in-law and also a radio Tarzan with his wife, Joan Burroughs Pierce, as Jane; (5) Frank Merrill, a champion gymnast and the first who shod his feet with sandals, and (6) Weissmuller.

Then (7) Buster Crabbe, another Olympic swimming champ who later starred in the *Flash Gordon* serials; (8) Herman Brix, an Olympic shot-putter whose acting name became Bruce Bennett; (9) Glenn Morris, 1936 decathlon champion; (10) Lex Barker, an adventure film actor who would marry and divorce such Hollywood beauties as Arlene Dahl and Lana Turner; (11) Gordon Scott, a Las Vegas lifeguard; (12) Denny Miller, UCLA basketball star and the first blond Tarzan; (13) Jock Mahoney, stuntman and stepfather of Sally Field, the Flying

*Technically, Lincoln was the first *adult* Tarzan. Silent screen buffs fastidiously point out that the first Tarzan was actually 10-year-old Gordon Griffith, who played the ape-man as a boy in *Tarzan of the Apes* (1918).

Tarzan learns to count on the toes of his pretty jungle mate in *Tarzan the Ape Man*. Monkeys gave Miss O'Sullivan some rough times. "I always had one fresh bite, one about half-healed, and one scar," she said.

Miss O'Sullivan and Weissmuller, whose screen romance was never legitimized by clergy or by city hall. The famous line, "Me Tarzan, You Jane," came from their *Tarzan, the Ape Man* (1932), the first feature-length talking *Tarzan* film. Only it wasn't said that way in the movie.

Mike Henry, Tarzan number 14, in *Tarzan and the Valley of Gold* (1966). He was a pro-football player.

Nun of television; (14) Mike Henry, Los Angeles Rams linebacker, and (15) Ron Ely, the first TV Tarzan.

Enid Markey was the original Jane. Among those who followed were Julie Bishop, Dorothy Hart, Vanessa Brown, Virginia Huston, Brenda Joyce, Joyce MacKenzie and swim star Eleanor Holm.* Other actresses who appeared in the films but did not play Jane included Linda Christian, Denise Darcel, Frances Gifford, Nancy Kelly, Vera Miles, Monique Van Vooren, Evelyn Ankers, Acquanetta and Patricia Morison.

Weissmuller and Miss O'Sullivan were easily the most famous pair. They teamed in six jungle epics from 1932 to 1942. A lithe, pretty, Irish-born colleen (who 30 years later would become better known as Mia Farrow's mother), Miss O'Sullivan gave the part a delicate blend of femininity, spunk and sophistication. But she had no great love for the role, which offered her few lines and fewer clothes. In *Tarzan and His Mate* (1934), she wore only a bra and loin cloth. "She is practically nude," gasped critic P. S. Harrison of *Harrison's Reports,* a reviewing service for theater owners. In fact, one underwater sequence showed Jane bare-breasted for an instant.** PTA groups howled. The scene was subsequently cut from the film.

However, this was the least of Miss O'Sullivan's worries. "I was never more consistently sick and miserable in all my life," she said later. " . . . I was never without an ache or a pain. I was never completely or comfortably warm. And I was never without a bite from one of those monkeys. I always had the same average—one fresh bite, one about half-healed and one scar." She was also pregnant a good deal of the time and had to get used to saying her lines half-hidden behind props.***

Weissmuller wasn't exactly thrilled with his parts either. Tarzan had a vocabulary of only 60 words. "My lines read like a backward 2-year-old talking to his nurse." he once said. But he took his share of lumps, too. "Once I was following my elephant by vine when he stopped," Weissmuller said. "I ran into his ass and broke my nose."

*Miss Holm played Jane in *Tarzan's Revenge* (1938). "I was an awful actress," she said in a 1972 interview. "*Time* magazine put me on a cover. In the review inside, they said, 'In a love scene, Miss Holm looks like she's going to spit in Tarzan's eye.' And that's the kind of actress I was." Glenn Morris played opposite her. "He was very dull," she recalled. "He took himself very seriously. He thought he *was* Tarzan. I would cut the ropes and he'd go flying on his fanny. Yeah, there were alligators. But their jaws were all shut."

**It was actually a double filmed in profile.

***Although she never achieved stardom, Miss O'Sullivan did become an accomplished actress. Brought to the United States without dramatic experience, she learned her trade well enough to give memorable performances in such films as *The Barretts of Wimpole Street* (1934), *The Thin Man* (1934), *David Copperfield* (1935), *Anna Karenina* (1935) and *Pride and Prejudice* (1940). She married director John Farrow in 1936 and they had seven children. Miss O'Sullivan resumed her acting career in the 1960s, appearing in both stage and screen versions of *Never Too Late*. Her husband died in 1963 but she continued her career, scoring a success in the hit play, "The Subject Was Roses," opposite Chester Morris.

High on a mountain ledge, Tarzan takes firm hold of Tom Conway, who would later become the Falcon. From *Tarzan's Secret Treasure* (1941).

Former Las Vegas lifeguard Gordon Scott, Tarzan number II, argues with a tribal chief in *Tarzan The Magnificent* (1960). Betta St. John is on right.

However, Weissmuller was content with his lot because he never considered himself an actor. In fact, he was a superlative swimmer. Representing the United States in the 1924 and 1928 Olympic Games, he won five gold medals. For years, he was unbeatable in races from 50 yards to a half-mile. During his long and glorious career, he set 67 world swimming records. His 100-yard freestyle mark (51 seconds) stood from 1927 to 1944. In 1953, the Associated Press named him the greatest swimmer of the half-century.

So in 1932, it was not totally unexpected when, at the peak of his career, MGM picked the six-foot three-inch, 190-pound Olympic champion to play the first talking Tarzan. The studio had decided to do a Tarzan picture after its success with *Trader Horn* (1931), a jungle thriller about a white goddess brought back to civilization. William S. Van Dyke, its director and *Tarzan*'s as well, began a meticulous search for the ape-man. He tested scores of actors, college men and athletes. He thought Clark Gable wasn't built well enough. Johnny Mack Brown wasn't tall enough. "I want someone like Jack Dempsey, only younger," Van Dyke said. "Tom Tyler is the best so far. But he's not muscular enough."

Van Dyke was ready to settle for Herman Brix. But Brix broke a shoulder filming *Touchdown* (1931). Then one day, screenwriter Cyril Hume happened to spot Weissmuller swimming at his hotel pool. Impressed by his physique, Hume brought Weissmuller to Van Dyke. The director asked the big guy to strip to his shorts. He did. Van Dyke hired him without a screen test.

As it turned out, Van Dyke couldn't have made a better choice. Weissmuller's voice was strangely high pitched, but his broad chest, ample crop of dark hair, cat-like walk and powerful swim style fit the role perfectly.

The studio pulled out all stops for its first talking *Tarzan* film, *Tarzan the Ape Man*. Production costs mounted to a cool $1 million, and the publicity department launched a spectacular promotion campaign. It overlooked no angle. "Girls," the ads said, "would you live like Eve if you found the right Adam?"

In fact, Weissmuller's sex appeal had a lot to do with the picture's success. Crowds filing out of the Stanley Theatre at the Baltimore premiere in 1932 were enthralled by Weissmuller's manliness. The *Baltimore Sun*'s inquiring photographer turned up these typical reactions: "If all of us could handle the women like Johnny Weissmuller, the world would be a wonderful place," said H. Raymond Grove of 6216 Baltimore Avenue. "Tarzan," said Miss Bea Knighton of 735 East 21 Street, "is certainly the ideal lover that every girl would love to have—if she only dared."

The movie, besides being a dandy adventure yarn, is memorable for at least three reasons. First, it introduced Cheta, the chimpanzee who became Tarzan's jungle buddy. Second, the picture showed us how Tarzan and Jane met. Finally, it gave us Weissmuller's famous yodel, "aaah—eee—aaaah" or was it "eh-wa-au-wau-aooow"? Tarzan used it as a victory cry or a danger shout to summon help from elephants and other animal pals. Actually, Merrill, Tarzan No. 5, developed the ape-call in a 1929 semi-sound serial. But the jungle lord's triumphant cry as we know it today was a creation of the Metro-Goldwyn-Mayer sound department.

To produce it, technicians ingeniously blended a whole series of unconnected sounds. They reportedly mixed a camel's bleat, a hyena's yowl played backward, the pluck of a violin string, a soprano's high-C and Weissmuller's bellowing at the top of his lungs. Then, they played them a fraction of a second after one another, thus creating a weird jungle call that became Weissmuller's trademark. Amazingly, Weissmuller learned to imitate it. At Saturday matinees, kids often greeted the ape-man's yowl with cheers.

The picture begins with Jane Parker (Miss O'Sullivan) joining her father (C. Aubrey Smith) and his young associate Harry Holt (Neil Hamilton) on a dangerous African safari. They are bound for the unexplored land beyond the Mutia Escarpment, a wall-like barrier of mountains. The safari is searching for an elephant burial ground where a fortune in tusks lies buried.

"Enough ivory to supply the world," Parker tells Jane. "There's a million pounds for the man who finds it."

During their trek through the wilderness, Harry becomes keenly aware of Jane's beauty and personal charm. "If we get through this all right," he asks her, "is there any chance for me?" But Jane is noncommittal.

Days later, they reach the escarpment and begin a tortuous climb. "A bit tricky here," Harry says, leaping across a crevice. Moments afterward, a native carrier makes the same leap, misses a narrow ledge and plunges to his death. Still, the safari goes on over sun-baked cliffs, through crocodile-infested waters, sleeping at night with animals baying just beyond their campfire. One night, just before they are going to sleep, they hear a long, animal-like cry.

"Aaaah–ee–aaah."

"What was that?" Jane asks.

"Bwana—maybe hyena," says Riano (Curtis Nero), one of the native men. Again, the call sounds, this time nearer.

"That was a human cry," Parker says. Concerned about Jane, Parker considers turning back. The natives become restless, too. But Jane won't hear of quitting.

The next morning, they break camp and forge ahead. They pick up the tracks of an elephant herd and follow them to a turbulent stream. There they build two rafts. But as they set out, a herd of hippopotami wallow into the water and capsize one of the rafts. Holt and Parker drag most of the struggling natives aboard their craft. But crocodiles pull two men to the river bottom before they can swim ashore.

Some of the beasts follow the party up the river bank. Then, from overhead, that strange, fearful cry booms out again. As if in obedience to a command, the hippos back off and wade into the water. Moments later, the tall figure of a wild man appears in the trees. He makes no response to any questions. Nor does he answer Riano's Swahili dialect.

Just for an instant, Parker's and Holt's attention is diverted. And in that instant, Jane disappears.

The jungle man has whisked her away, swinging her up into the overhanging branches to his tree home among a group of apes. Terrified, she tries to escape. But one of them pushes her down. She shrinks back. "Let me go," she screams hysterically. When she looks up at the white man, it's clear that he doesn't understand.

Suddenly, the ape approaches her again and tries to grab her arm. This time the ape-man does understand. He sternly motions the ape off.

"Thank you," Jane says more calmly. There is no response. She adds, "Thank you for protecting me."

"Me—," the giant repeats, pointing to Jane.

"No," Jane answers. Then, like a schoolteacher, she points to herself. "It's only 'me' for me."

Tarzan still does not comprehend.

Jane pauses, trying to figure out how to make it plain. "I'm Jane Parker—understand? Jane. Jane."

"Jane—Jane," Tarzan says, at last understanding her. "Jane," he says, pointing to her.

"Yes, Jane. And you? You?"

"Tarzan," he says, stabbing his chest proudly. "Tarzan."

Then, Tarzan points enthusiastically to her and back to him. "Jane—Tarzan."

He continues like a child with a new toy, poking her harder each time he says her name, delightedly repeating his and her names faster and faster like a train gathering speed.

"Jane—Tarzan. Jane—Tarzan. Jane—Tarzan. Jane—Tarzan. Jane—Tarzan. Jane—Tarzan."

"Oh, please stop it," Jane says, exasperated and on the verge of tears. She suddenly realizes she is separated from her hunting party, thousands of miles from civilization with a wild man who speaks no English. "Let me go," she screams. "I can't stand this."

And so that immortal line—"Me Tarzan, you Jane"—was never spoken. Such is the reality from which one Hollywood myth was born.*

*Tarzan and Jane had a more breathless first encounter in the Burroughs version. Tarzan saves Jane from Terkoz, a giant anthropoid ape. When she goes to thank him with open arms, what does Tarzan do? "He did what no red-blooded man needs lessons in doing," Burroughs wrote in *Tarzan of the Apes*. "He took his woman in his arms and smothered her upturned, panting lips with kisses. For a moment, Jane lay there with half-closed eyes. For a moment—the first in her young life—she knew the meaning of love."

That night, Jane sleeps in Tarzan's simple tree home. He spreads a leopard skin, draws a screen of vines around her and stretches his huge form outside on a big bough.

Days later, Parker hears Jane's voice as he and his party search the jungle. He calls her and she runs to him.

"Were you very frightened?" he asks, embracing his daughter, whom he had given up for dead.

"At first, I thought he was a savage," Jane says, "But I found out he wasn't."

"Oh, my dear, he's not like us . . ." Parker says—in what must be the movie's most unique use of that cliché.

But it's obvious from Jane's changed attitude that her experience in the wilderness with Tarzan has affected her deeply. For one thing, she has lost her fear of the ape-man's animal friends. She has begun to sense the beauty of the untamed jungle. And Tarzan's protectiveness and gentleness has kindled a growing affection. When Tarzan joins the safari, she takes notice of his magnificent body. "I wonder what you'd look like dressed," she muses. And then answers herself, "Pretty good."

As Tarzan leads the expedition through the unmapped wilderness, movie audiences of the 1930s got their first glimpse of his jungle prowess. He swims up a storm, commands an army of loyal jungle animals, and glides from vine to vine with the ease and agility of a trapeze artist. Cheta accompanies Tarzan on many of his exploits. The chimp, who appears as comic relief, became one of Hollywood's all-time favorite animal characters.

One day, when Tarzan is frolicking with his animal friends, a savage tribe of pygmies attack the party, captures them and begins lowering them one by one to a giant gorilla in a pit. Tarzan rushes to the rescue with a herd of elephants, stampedes the pygmies and kills the gorilla with his knife.

After the battle royal, a wounded elephant leads the safari through a waterfall to the elephants' graveyard. Tusks and skeletons of hundreds of pachyderms are scattered across an immense plateau. "It's beautiful," says Jane. "Solemn and beautiful. We shouldn't be here."

Holt sees things differently. "It's riches. Millions," he says, looking greedily over the ivory-strewn landscape.

But the exhausting journey has been too hectic for the elderly Parker. After finally reaching his goal, he collapses and dies. "He found what he was looking for," Jane says. Then, anticipating mourners in thousands of B-films to come, she adds, "I know that somewhere—wherever great hunters go—he's happy."

After the party has buried Parker in the elephant graveyard, they retrace their steps through the waterfall and back toward civilization. Jane has decided to stay with Tarzan. Holt, she feels, can only give her worldly things that no longer have

With a knife his only weapon, Tarzan readies for combat in *Tarzan and His Mate* (1934).

Tarzan's New York Adventure (1942) took him to the big city and put him in civvies for the first time. From left, Virginia Grey, Eddie Kane, Weissmuller and Miss O'Sullivan.

meaning for her—money, civilization, clothes. Tarzan, the animals and the rich warm earth of the jungle have become her new natural life.

"You'll be coming back, Harry," Jane says consolingly. "I can see a huge safari with you at the head bearing ivory down to the coast. Only this time, there'll be no danger. Because we'll be there to protect you every step of the way."

As the safari moves on, Holt looks back, There in the distance, Tarzan and Jane stand side by side on a hill waving. Behind them the African sun is setting, its rays bathing the jungle in long, deepening shadows. The sound track fades out with Tchaikowsky's plaintive Theme from *Romeo and Juliet.*

The second Weissmuller-O'Sullivan movie, *Tarzan and His Mate,* appeared two years later in 1934. Critics said the sequel had the rare attribute of being even better than the original. From then on, the *Tarzan* movies came out about every two or three years right through the 1960s. Though they were never mentioned in Academy Award circles, they became tremendous money-makers, particularly in foreign markets, where they earned 75 percent of their gross. In some Western European and Asian countries, they opened with the pomp and circumstance of a Hollywood premiere—including white tie and tails and evening gowns. Producer Sol Lesser, who bought the Tarzan story rights from MGM and eventually Weissmuller's contract, estimated that the silent and talking *Tarzan* movies grossed more than $500,000,000 and played to more than two billion people.

There were many anecdotal footprints left along that endless, gold-paved jungle trail:

• Burroughs had invented an ape language with which Tarzan talked with his animal friends. "Kambu" was jungle, "gree-ah" love and "gomangani" Negro. In the movies screenwriters added to the dialect. "Umgawa" was Weissmuller's favorite expression. He translated it as "Let's get the hell out of here."

• None of the Weissmuller movies was made in Africa. The early films picked up much of the leftover footage from *Trader Horn.* The studios shot the rest in a thickly wooded area in North Hollywood, augmenting natural scenery with imported fruit trees, tropical plants and lush vegetation.

• In the early Tarzans, the natives were American Negroes, many of whom were hired off the streets of Los Angeles. "One day my friend and I were walking down Central Avenue in L.A.," said Rudy Morgan, who played a native in six Weissmuller pictures. "This big bus pulls up with quite a few colored actors. They started honking their horn and asked us if we wanted to work in pictures. I saw the MGM sign on the bus. I said 'Sure.' We got in and went to the studio and they lined us up. There were about 75 of us. And since I'm one of the few actors born with natural makeup, I think I was No. 3 chosen. They told me I looked more like the natives than the natives." Morgan said he got about $12 a day in those nonunion times, double pay if he came in contact with animals. But Morgan said he was never afraid. The animals were well-trained and a trainer was always nearby with a whip and a gun, he said. And most of them, especially the alligators, didn't have any teeth.

- One of the most publicized incidents connected with *Tarzan* movies happened in 1961. Parents in Downey, California, objected on moral grounds to the Burroughs books in a school library. They accused the jungle pair of living together in sin. While Tarzan and Jane were having a swinging time in the trees, they allegedly had never gotten married. But the scandalous accusation proved false. Tarzan and his mate had indeed been married by a minister—Jane's father. Anybody who read the second of Burroughs' jungle books, *The Return of Tarzan*, would have known that the great jungle couple steered clear of monkey business.

- However, it is true that the Weissmuller-O'Sullivan team were never formally married in their films. When MGM decided to give them a son, they had Tarzan and Jane adopt him. It seemed the simplest way to avoid criticism from the Legion of Decency. So in *Tarzan Finds a Son!* (1939), the script called for a young couple to be killed in a jungle plane crash. Tarzan rescues their youngster. He calls the lad "Boy" and he and Jane raise him. Weissmuller himself picked five-year-old Johnny Sheffield for the role.

Weissmuller went on to do 12 *Tarzan* pictures—more than any other actor. Then, his waistline ballooned. Columbia Pictures simply put clothes on him, made him a hunter and started a new series called *Jungle Jim* (1948). Weissmuller liked doing these pictures. He owned a share in them and made a small fortune. He lost most of it, though, through high living, bad investments and expensive divorce settlements. He married five times—wife No. 3 was actress Lupe Velez, the Mexican Spitfire.

But he aged gracefully and remained active in his golden years. In 1972, with a full mane of hair at age 68, he was actively promoting swimming pools, mail-order vitamins and health foods. However, his Tarzan image is indelible. In restaurants, at conventions—wherever he goes—children and even adults ask him to boom out with just one more bull-ape call. He usually obliges.

He throws his head back and cups his hand around his mouth. And for an instant in time, we are back with Weissmuller in the primeval jungle, swinging from tree to tree with Jane, riding the back of swimming hippos, barking orders to great anthropoid apes, fighting lions and tigers barehanded, throwing a water buck with one mighty twist of the neck. "Aaaah—eee—aaaaah." The voice of Tarzan echoes again in the land.

TARZAN SERIES

1. *Tarzan of the Apes.* National Film Corp., 1918, Scott Sidney.
   Elmo Lincoln (as Tarzan), Enid Markey (as Jane), True Boardman, Kathleen Kirkham, George French, Gordon Griffith (as young Tarzan), Colin Kenny. Eight reels.

2. *The Romance of Tarzan.* National Film Corp., 1918, Wilfred Lucas.
   Elmo Lincoln, Enid Markey, Thomas Jefferson, Cleo Madison. Seven reels.

3. *The Revenge of Tarzan.* Goldwyn Pictures Corp., 1920, Harry Revier.
   Gene Pollar (as Tarzan), Karla Schramm (as Jane). Seven reels.

4. *The Son of Tarzan.* National Film Corp., 1920, Harry Revier.
   P. Dempsey Tabler (as Tarzan), Karla Schramm, Gordon Griffith (as the son of Tarzan), Kamuela C. Searle (as the son of Tarzan grown up). Fifteen episodes and a prologue.

5. *The Adventures of Tarzan.* Numa Picture Corp., 1921, Robert F. Hill.
   Elmo Lincoln (as Tarzan), Louise Lorraine (as Jane). Fifteen episodes and a prologue.

6. *Tarzan and the Golden Lion.* F.B.O. Gold Bond, 1927, J. P. MacGowan.
   James Pierce (as Tarzan), Dorothy Dunbar (as Jane), Edna Murphy, Harold Goodwin. Six reels.

7. *Tarzan the Mighty.* Universal, 1928, Ray Taylor and Jack Nelson.
   Frank Merrill (as Tarzan), Al Ferguson, Natalie Kingston, Bobby Nelson, Lorimer Johnston. Fifteen episodes.

8. *Tarzan the Tiger.* Universal, 1929, Henry McRae.
   Frank Merrill (as Tarzan), Natalie Kingston, Al Ferguson. Fifteen episodes.

9. *Tarzan the Ape Man.* MGM, 1932, W. S. Van Dyke.
   Johnny Weissmuller (as Tarzan), Maureen O'Sullivan (as Jane), Neil Hamilton, C. Aubrey Smith, Doris Lloyd, Forrester Harvey, Ivory Williams. 99 minutes.

10. *Tarzan the Fearless.* Principal, 1933, Robert F. Hill.
    Buster Crabbe (as Tarzan), Jacqueline Wells (who later changed her movie name to Julie Bishop), Mischa Auer, Philo McCullough, Matthew Betz, Frank Lackteen, Eddie Woods, E. Alyn Warren. Twelve episodes of which the first episode was initially released as a full-length feature.

11. *Tarzan and His Mate.* MGM, 1934, Cedric Gibbons.*
Johnny Weissmuller, Maureen O'Sullivan, Neil Hamilton, Paul Cavanagh, Forrester Harvey, Nathan Curry, William Stack, Desmond Roberts, Paul Porcasi. 105 minutes.

12. *The New Adventures of Tarzan.* Burroughs-Tarzan Enterprises, 1935, Edward Kull. Herman Brix (as Tarzan; Brix later changed his movie name to Bruce Bennett), Ula Holt, Don Castello, Frank Baker, Louis Sargent, Dale Walsh, Merrill McCormick, Jiggs the Monkey. Twelve episodes (released as both feature and serial).

13. *Tarzan Escapes.* MGM, 1936, Richard Thorpe.
Johnny Weissmuller (as Tarzan), Maureen O'Sullivan (as Jane), John Buckler, Benita Hume, William Henry, Herbert Mundin, E. E. Clive, Darby Jones, Cheta. 90 minutes.

14. *Tarzan and the Green Goddess.* Principal, 1938, Edward Kull.
Herman Brix (as Tarzan), Ula Holt, Frank Baker, Lew Sargent, Jack Mower, Don Castello, Frank Baker, Merrill McCormick, Jiggs the Monkey. 72 minutes. (Feature version of the last half of *The New Adventures of Tarzan.*)

15. *Tarzan's Revenge.* Fox, 1938, D. Ross Lederman.
Glenn Morris (as Tarzan), Eleanor Holm, George Barbier, Hedda Hopper, George Meeker, C. Henry Gordon, Joseph Sawyer, Gordon (Bill) Elliott. 70 minutes.

16. *Tarzan Finds a Son!* MGM, 1939, Richard Thorpe.
Johnny Weissmuller (as Tarzan), Maureen O'Sullivan (as Jane), Johnny Sheffield (as Boy), Ian Hunter, Henry Stephenson, Frieda Inescort, Henry Wilcoxon, Laraine Day, Morton Lowry, Gavin Muir. 90 minutes.

17. *Tarzan's Secret Treasure.* MGM, 1941, Richard Thorpe.
Johnny Weissmuller, Maureen O'Sullivan, Johnny Sheffield, Reginald Owen, Barry Fitzgerald, Tom Conway, Philip Dorn, Cordell Hickman. 82 minutes.

18. *Tarzan's New York Adventure.* MGM, 1942, Richard Thorpe.
Johnny Weissmuller, Maureen O'Sullivan, Johnny Sheffield, Virginia Grey, Charles Bickford, Paul Kelly, Chill Wills, Cy Kendall, Russell Hicks, Howard Hickman, Charles Lane, Miles Mander, Eddie Kane, Mantan Moreland, Anne Jeffreys, Elmo Lincoln. 70 minutes.

19. *Tarzan Triumphs!* RKO, 1943, William Thiele.
Johnny Weissmuller, Frances Gifford, Johnny Sheffield, Stanley Ridges, Sig Ru-

*Gibbons is credited as director although Jack Conway replaced him for most of the shooting.

mann, Rex Williams, Pedro de Cordoba, Philip van Zandt, Stanley Brown, Cheta. 78 minutes.

20. *Tarzan's Desert Mystery.* RKO, 1943, William Thiele.
Johnny Weissmuller, Nancy Kelly, Johnny Sheffield, Otto Kruger, Joe Sawyer, Lloyd Corrigan, Robert Lowery. 70 minutes.

21. *Tarzan and the Amazons.* RKO, 1945, Kurt Neumann.
Johnny Weissmuller, Brenda Joyce (as Jane), Johnny Sheffield, Henry Stephenson, Maria Ouspenskaya, Barton MacLane, Don Douglas, J. M. Kerrigan, Shirley O'Hara, Steven Geray. 76 minutes.

22. *Tarzan and the Leopard Woman.* RKO, 1946, Kurt Neumann.
Johnny Weissmuller, Brenda Joyce, Johnny Sheffield, Acquanetta (as Lea, the Leopard Woman), Edgar Barrier, Tommy Cook, Dennis Hoey, Anthony Caruso, George J. Lewis, Iris Flores, Lillian Molieri, Helen Gerald, Kay Solinas. 72 minutes.

23. *Tarzan and the Huntress.* RKO, 1947, Kurt Neumann.
Johnny Weissmuller, Brenda Joyce, Johnny Sheffield, Patricia Morison (as Tanya the huntress), Barton MacLane, John Warburton, Wallace Scott, Charles Trowbridge, Maurice Tauzin, Ted Hecht, Mickey Simpson. 72 minutes.

24. *Tarzan and the Mermaids.* RKO, 1948, Robert Florey.
Johnny Weissmuller, Brenda Joyce, Johnny Sheffield, Linda Christian (as Mara, a mermaid), John Laurenz, Fernando Wagner, Edward Ashley, George Zucco, Andrea Palma, Gustavo Rojo, Matthew Boulton. 68 minutes.

25. *Tarzan's Magic Fountain.* RKO, 1949, Lee Sholem.
Lex Barker (as Tarzan), Brenda Joyce, Albert Dekker, Evelyn Ankers, Charles Drake, Alan Napier, Henry Brandon, Ted Hecht, Henry Kulky, David Bond. 73 minutes.

26. *Tarzan and the Slave Girl.* RKO, 1950, Lee Sholem.
Lex Barker, Vanessa Brown (as Jane), Robert Alda, Denise Darcel, Hurd Hatfield, Arthur Shields, Robert Warwick, Tony Caruso, Tito Renaldo, Mary Ellen Kay, Shirley Ballard, Rosemary Burton, Gwen Cauldwell, Martha Clements, Mona Knox, Josephine Parra, Jackee Waldron. 74 minutes.

27. *Tarzan's Peril.* RKO, 1951, Byron Haskin.
Lex Barker, Virginia Huston (as Jane), George Macready, Douglas Fowley, Glenn Anders, Alan Napier, Edward Ashley, Dorothy Dandridge, Walter Kingsford, Frederick O'Neal. 79 minutes.

28. *Tarzan's Savage Fury.* RKO, 1952, Cyril Endfield.
Lex Barker, Dorothy Hart (as Jane), Patric Knowles, Charles Korvin, Tommy Carlton (as Joey, a takeoff on Boy). 81 minutes.

29. *Tarzan and the She-Devil.* RKO, 1953, Kurt Neumann.
Lex Barker, Joyce MacKenzie (as Jane), Raymond Burr, Monique Van Vooren (as Lyra, the She-Devil), Tom Conway, Henry Brandon, Michael Granger, Robert Bice, Mike Ross, Cheta. 75 minutes.

30. *Tarzan's Hidden Jungle.* RKO, 1955, Harold Schuster.
Gordon Scott (as Tarzan), Vera Miles, Peter Van Eyck, Jack Elam, Charles Fredericks, Richard Reeves, Don Beddoe, Ike Jones, Jester Hairston, Madie Norman, Rex Ingram. 72 minutes.

31. *Tarzan and the Lost Safari.* MGM, 1957, Bruce Humberstone.
Gordon Scott (as Tarzan), Robert Beatty, Yolande Donlan, Betta St. John, Wilfrid Hyde-White, George Coulouris, Peter Arne, Orlando Martins, Cheta. 80 minutes. (First *Tarzan* in color.)

32. *Tarzan's Fight for Life.* MGM, 1958, Bruce Humberstone.
Gordon Scott, Eve Brent (as Jane), Rickie Sorenson (as Tartu, their adopted son), Jil Jarmyn, James Edwards, Carl Benton Reid, Harry Lauter, Woody Strode, Roy Glenn, Cheta. 89 minutes.

33. *Tarzan's Greatest Adventure.* Paramount, 1959, John Guillermin.
Gordon Scott, Anthony Quayle, Sara Shane, Niall MacGinnis, Sean Connery, Al Mulock, Scilla Gabel. 90 minutes.

34. *Tarzan the Ape Man.* MGM, 1959, Joseph Newman.
Denny Miller (as Tarzan), Cesare Danova, Joanna Barnes (as Jane), Robert Douglas, Thomas Yangha, Leon Anderson. 82 minutes.

35. *Tarzan the Magnificent.* Paramount, 1960, Robert Day.
Gordon Scott, Jock Mahoney, Betta St. John, John Carradine, Lionel Jeffries, Alexandra Stewart, Gary Cockrell, Earl Cameron, Charles Tingwell, Al Mulock. 82 minutes.

36. *Tarzan Goes to India.* MGM, 1962, John Guillermin.
Jock Mahoney (as Tarzan), Jai (as the Elephant Boy), Leo Gordon, Mark Dana, Feroz Khan, Simi, Murad, Jagdish Raay, G. Raghaven, Aaron Joseph, Abas Khan, Pehelwan Ameer, K. S. Tripathi. 88 minutes.

37. *Tarzan's Three Challenges.* MGM, 1963, Robert Day.
Jock Mahoney, Woody Strode, Tsu Kobayashi, Earl Cameron, Salah Jamal, Anthony Chinn, Robert Hu, Christopher Carlos, Ricky Der. 92 minutes.

38. *Tarzan and the Valley of Gold.* American International, 1966, Robert Day.
Mike Henry (as Tarzan), David Opatoshu, Manuel Padilla Jr., Nancy Kovack, Don Megowan, Frank Bandstetter, Eduardo Noriega, Enrique Lucero. 90 minutes.

39. *Tarzan and the Great River.* Paramount, 1967, Robert Day.
Mike Henry (as Tarzan), Jan Murray, Manuel Padilla, Jr., Diana Millay, Rafer Johnson, Paulo Grazindo. 88 minutes.

40. *Tarzan and the Jungle Boy.* Paramount, 1968, Robert Day.
Mike Henry, Rafer Johnson, Alizia Gur, Steve Bond, Ed Johnson, Ronald Gans. 90 minutes.

41. *Tarzan's Jungle Rebellion.* National General, 1970, William Witney.
Ron Ely (as Tarzan), Manuel Padilla, Jr. (as Jai, the elephant boy), Ulla Stromstedt, Sam Jaffe, William Marshall, Harry Lauter, Jason Evers, Lloyd Haynes, Chuck Wood. 95 minutes. (Taken from the Tarzan TV series.)

42. *Tarzan's Deadly Silence.* National General, 1970, Robert L. Friend and Larry Dobkin.
Ron Ely, Manuel Padilla, Jr., Jock Mahoney, Woodrow (Woody) Strode, Gregorio Acosta, Rudolph Charles, Michelle Nichols, Robert Do Qui, Kenneth William Washington, Lupe Garnica, Jose Chaves, Virgil Richardson. 89 minutes. (Taken from the Tarzan TV series.)

The Wolf Man (Lon Chaney, Jr.) in all his mangy glory. His story traces back to Greek legends.

THE WOLF MAN

The Wolf Man
(1941)

A screenplay by Curt Siodmak. Camera, Joseph Valentine. Makeup, Jack Pierce. Assistant director, Vernon Keays. Produced and directed by George Waggner. Presented by Universal Pictures. 71 minutes.

Sir John Talbot	CLAUDE RAINS
Dr. Lloyd	WARREN WILLIAM
Captain Paul Montford	RALPH BELLAMY
Frank Andrews	PATRIC KNOWLES
Bela	BELA LUGOSI
Twiddle	FORRESTER HARVEY
Maleva	MARIA OUSPENSKAYA
Jenny Williams	FAY HELM
Gwen Conliffe	EVELYN ANKERS
Charles Conliffe	J. M. KERRIGAN
Lawrence Talbot (The	
Wolf Man)	LON CHANEY, JR.
Kendall	LEYLAND HODGSON
Gypsy	KURT KATCH

Mrs. Williams	DORIS LLOYD
Reverend Norman	HARRY STUBBS
Wykes	HARRY CORDING

Even a man who is pure in heart
And says his prayers by night
May become a wolf when the wolfsbane blooms
And the autumn moon is bright.

—Gypsy Folk Rhyme
from *The Wolf Man*

A full moon drifts across a cold, forbidding sky. Its white light transforms the countryside into a shadow-strewn wilderness. There is stark, still silence.

Suddenly, little sounds come from the forest—soft, quick sounds, like those of an animal running. For an instant, scudding clouds mask the moon. In the darkness, the very trees, the very shrubs, seem to stiffen into a wirebrush of tension. Now the sounds are closer. Twigs snap. Leaves crackle.

And then the moon plunges back with all its brilliance. And with a chilling, deep-throated growl, a creature springs into the silver light—half-man, half-beast. The Wolf Man. It was in 1941—ten years after Dracula and the Frankenstein creation's debut and nine years after the Mummy—that the Wolf Man made his late arrival on the horror scene. Monster buffs agree he was worth waiting for. He had the special quality of being the only one to take the form of an animal to claim his victims.* His fierce hairy face, long jagged teeth and savage strength send cascades of chills down the spine. But what also captured the imagination of Hollywood horror movie writers was the possibility of turning the man-beast into a tragic creature with whom audiences would still empathize even while they were repelled.

As he appeared in films, the Wolf Man is a reluctant victim of his macabre condition. He is cursed because he has been bitten by a werewolf. When he changes under a full moon, he kills without knowing what he is doing. Later, he retains a vague memory of his slaughters. He agonizes over them and longs for an end to his own life, an end that would free him from his torment. So he is consumed by a death wish and his search for release from his fate turns him into a figure of sympathy.

No one is sure just where the werewolf legend originated. One theory is that it goes back to the days of cannibalism. As tribes evolved, the more civilized in them shunned those who continued to devour human flesh. Eventually, the more

*Dracula at times assumes the guise of a bat. But it is only when he takes his true form as Count Dracula that he drains the blood of those who will later join him in the world of the undead.

If Bela (Bela Lugosi), the gypsy fortune-teller, seems distraught, it isn't heartburn. He has seen the mark of the pentagram—the sign of the werewolf's next victim—in Jenny's (Fay Helm) palm. From *The Wolf Man* (1941).

Henry Hull in *Werewolf of London* (1935), the original werewolf of sound films. *The Werewolf,* a silent movie made in 1913, was the grandwolf of them all.

Maleva (Maria Ouspenskaya), Bela's mother, tells the stunned Larry Talbot he has inherited the curse of the Wolf Man.

highly developed likened their more primitive brothers to beasts and cast them into the wilds. The next step was to believe that the ostracized ones had actually transformed themselves into animals.

The only certainty, though, is that the belief got its name from the Greeks. They called it lycanthropy—the transformation of man into an animal. "Lukos" means wolf and "anthropos" man. However, the superstition exists in the folklore of every continent and so the term applies to transformation into any animal shape. For instance, in regions where there are no wolves, the fiercest animal takes its place. In India and parts of Asia, there is the weretiger. In Russia, the bear. In South America, the jaguar. In Africa, the leopard.

In some areas, legend had it that the man physically became an animal at night and roamed the countryside. In other places, the belief was that only his spirit entered the animal. His body remained unchanged. Whatever version persisted, it is clear that werewolfism was everywhere a kind of primitive Jekyll and Hyde theme, an embodiment of the belief that both good and evil exists in man. And that he could make of these qualities what he would.

Despite the widespread superstition there seems to have been no equivalent of a *Dracula* novel to set the standards for a movie werewolf. So film writers had to make the ground rules themselves.

A Balkan legend relating lycanthropy to flowers caught their fancy at the outset. The first werewolf picture of the talking era, *Werewolf of London* (1935), had Henry Hull as the ill-fated hero. He played an English botanist searching Tibet for a rare flower, called marifasa, which blooms only in moonlight. A werewolf (Warner Oland) bites Hull and so Hull becomes one himself. Later, Hull and Oland return to London to battle for the mysterious flower. Its juice squeezed onto the skin is the only known antidote for their cursed affliction.

The film had some good moments. But it failed to sustain interest, in part, because Hull wasn't frightening enough. He reportedly refused to submit to the long hours of makeup under the expert hands of Jack Pierce, creator of the Frankenstein monster. Instead, Pierce devised a light facial workup that, at best, gave Hull the disconcerting appearance of an unshaven Aborigine.

It was the second werewolf film, in 1941, which convinced Universal to begin a series. *The Wolf Man,* which bore little resemblance to its predecessor, set down all the laws of lycanthropy and became the definitive werewolf film.

Lon Chaney, Jr., son of the greatest of the silent-day bogeymen, played the title role. His father, known as the man of a thousand faces, had created classic portrayals in *The Hunchback of Notre Dame* (1923) and *The Phantom of the Opera* (1925). Movie-goers were naturally eager to make a comparison. But the six-foot, three-inch Chaney, Jr. was a hulking, unimaginative actor, and he recognized that he was but a pale shadow of his father. "He [the elder Chaney] could do things with his eyes and even with his facial muscles that I'll never be able to duplicate," Chaney said.

So in the beginning, the younger Chaney was careful to stay away from horror roles. For the first seven years of his acting career, the craggy-faced Chaney played a hectic schedule of serials, westerns and B-movies. "I was in a new picture practically every two weeks, always a heavy," Chaney said. "I'll swear I spoke the line, 'So you won't talk, eh?' at least 50 times. I'd rather not think about the times I had to say, 'Don't shoot him now. I have a better plan.' "

Then in 1939, Chaney was cast as the huge, feeble-minded Lennie in *Of Mice and Men* in a stage version of the John Steinbeck novel. He endowed the role with sympathy and understanding and got 13 curtain calls on opening night. That same year, he went on to score a personal triumph in the film version with Burgess Meredith. After that, it was just a matter of time before Chaney made the transition to horror films. But *The Wolf Man* would always remain his favorite. In 1963, nearly a quarter century later, Chaney said: "I've played them all. Most of them were the second time around—Frankenstein, the Mummy, Dracula. But the Wolf Man was mine, all alone. I played him six times."*

He had his own philosophy about what set the Wolf Man apart from modern horror figures. "All the best of the monsters played for sympathy," he said. "That goes for my father, Karloff, myself and all the others. They all won the audience's sympathy. The Wolf Man didn't want to do all those bad things. He was forced into them.

"The trouble with most of the monster pictures today is that they go after horror for horror's sake. There's no motivation for how the monsters behave. There's too much of that science-fiction baloney."

As *The Wolf Man* opens, Sir John Talbot (Claude Rains), a research scientist and wealthy landowner, welcomes his son back to Talbot Castle, the family estate in the Welsh village of Llanwelly. Larry (Chaney) has been to college in the United States and then stayed on for some years before returning. And so he has forgotten the superstitions of his hometown.

But within the first 24 hours, Larry becomes acquainted again with the village's old werewolf legend. In an antique store, he meets Gwen Conliffe (Evelyn Ankers), the shopkeeper's winsome daughter. To make conversation, he decides to buy a walking stick. He picks a rare silver-tipped cane mounted with the head of a wolf and a five-pointed star. Curious, he asks about its meaning. Gwen tells him the star is called the pentagram. "Every werewolf is marked with that," she says lightheartedly. "He sees it in the palm of his next victim's hand." Then she offhandedly recites a poem about the werewolf folklore.

*Five movies, once on TV's "Route 66."

> Even a man who is pure in heart
> And says his prayers by night
> May become a wolf when the wolfsbane blooms
> And the autumn moon is bright.

Larry says she isn't scaring him away and invites her to take a walk to the gypsy camp that night to have her fortune told.

Later, when Larry shows his father the cane, the elder Talbot doesn't dismiss the werewolf story easily. Every legend must have a basis in fact, Sir John says. And then he quotes the same rhyme that Gwen recited.

That night, when Larry arrives for his date, there are two girls waiting. To make things respectable, Gwen has brought along a girl friend, Jenny (Fay Helm). They set out together and as they approach the gypsy camp, Jenny sees a bush blooming by the roadside. "Oh, look, wolfsbane,"* she says. And then, she, too, recites the strange werewolf rhyme.

At the camp, Larry and Gwen take a stroll while Jenny goes into the tent of Bela (Bela Lugosi), the fortune teller. "Your hands, please," Bela says. "Your left hand shows your past. Your right hand shows your future." Jenny opens her right hand. Suddenly, Bela shuts his eyes and looks away. "Go quickly," he says. "Go . . . I can't tell you anything tonight . . . Go quickly." He has seen the mark of the pentagram.

The camera cuts to the woods. Larry and Gwen hear an animal howl and then a woman's startled scream. As Larry dashes to the source of the sound, a wolf springs at him and sinks its fangs into his chest. Larry has his sturdy silver-tipped walking stick. Using it as a club, he stuns the snarling beast. Then, again and again, he smashes at its skull. As he deals the last fatal blow, Larry sinks exhausted to the ground.

But when police come on the scene, there is no wolf to be seen. Instead, they find the bodies of Jenny and Bela. The gypsy, whose feet are bare, has had his head crushed. Jenny's throat has been slashed and her jugular severed.

Police Captain Paul Montford (Ralph Bellamy) is skeptical of Larry's story, particularly since he can find no wound. But Dr. Lloyd (Warren William) tells the captain that Larry is suffering from shock and must have rest. Instead, Larry slips off and goes to Maleva (Maria Ouspenskaya),** the mother of the slain

---

*A wild flowering herb that grows in cool, damp, mountainous regions. Since ancient days, it has been known that the plant exerts a strong effect on the body's physiological functions. If eaten or ingested, it is poisonous and so it was considered the "bane" of "wolves." The Chinese, Gauls and hill tribes of India used various species to prepare arrow poison. Because it induces a slowing of the heart beat, it was later used medicinally as a heart and nerve sedative. Wolfsbane is also called "monkshood" and "friarscap" because its beautiful white or yellow flowers, which hang clustered around its stalk, resemble helmets or hoods.

**This tiny Russian character actress, famed for her portrayals of villainesses and grandmothers, settled in the United States in 1924 after touring the country with the Moscow Art Theater. Her stage

gypsy fortune teller. She tells Larry her son Bela was a werewolf. Larry has now become one himself. "Whoever is bitten by a werewolf and lives becomes a werewolf himself," Maleva says. "A werewolf can be killed only with a silver bullet or a silver knife or a stick with a silver handle." Larry shrugs this off as superstition. But she dares him to show her his wound. Without hesitation, he tears open his shirt. There, over his heart, he is astonished to see a five-pointed star—the pentagram.

"Go now," Maleva says. "Heaven help you."

That night the moon is full and Larry becomes aware of strange forces taking possession of him. In the film's most memorable moments, his body begins to change. Thick, bristly hair sprouts on his legs. His toes shorten to stumps until they become the blunt paws of an animal. Coarse hair gradually covers his body and his fingers curl into sharp pointed claws.

Most dreadful of all are the changes in his face. The eyes narrow. His hairline moves down over his forehead. His beard becomes bushy and grows over his cheeks. The nose widens into a broad snout, glistening with moisture, and sharp white fangs push up over his lips. He is no longer human. He is an animal. Standing in a crouch, his nostrils quivering, his red eyes dart about the room. His burly body leaps to the window. Then out he runs into the night.

The next morning, Captain Montford follows the wolf tracks from a gravedigger's torn body back to Talbot Castle. There, Larry has changed back to his normal self. Confused and uncertain as to how to face the tragedy that has befallen him, he asks his father what he knows about the werewolf belief.

"It's an old legend," Sir John says. "You'll find something like it in the folklore of nearly every nation. The scientific name for it is lycanthropy. It's a variety of schizophrenia."

"That's all Greek to me," Larry says.

"It *is* Greek. It's a technical explanation for something simple. There's good and evil in every man's soul. In this case, evil takes the name of an animal."

But does Sir John believe werewolves really exist, Larry wants to know. No, his father says. However, he does believe almost anything can happen to a man in his own mind. Confused and still searching for a way out, Larry asks Dr. Lloyd the same question.

"I believe that a man lost in the mazes of his mind may imagine he's anything," the doctor replies. "Science has found many examples of the mind's power over the body. The case of the stigmata appearing in the skin of zealots."

"Self hypnotism," Sir John says, scoffing.

career began on Broadway but shifted to Hollywood. She got an Oscar nomination in her Hollywood debut—a supporting role as the Baroness von Obersdorf in *Dodsworth* (1936). Her Tartar features and intriguing accent appeared in scores of pictures thereafter, including *The Mortal Storm (1940), Kings Row (1941)* and *A Kiss in the Dark (1949).* She died in 1949 at the age of 82.

Gwen Conliffe (Evelyn Ankers) shows Larry Talbot a werewolf charm she wears around her neck. In a moment, he will see the pentagram in her hand.

The werewolf has been done in by a silver-tipped cane swung by his father, Sir John Talbot (Claude Rains). And now, transformed in death, Larry lies tranquil. Bending over him are Dr. Lloyd (Warren William) and Rains. Ralph Bellamy, playing Police Captain Montford, stands to the right in plaid jacket.

"But if a man isn't ever thinking about such things," Larry asks, isn't even interested in it, how could he hypnotize himself?"

"Might be a case of mental suggestion plus mass hypnotism," Dr. Lloyd says, vaguely. He urges Larry to leave the castle. The doctor thinks Larry has received a shock that has set off problems in his mind. But Sir John won't listen.

That night, the police set traps in the forest. When the full moon rises, Larry again undergoes a transformation and plunges into the woods. But as he prowls through the bushes, he runs into a trap. He struggles vainly to free himself, then collapses and undergoes a retransformation. Before police arrive, Maleva, the gypsy woman, rides by and frees him.

Driven to desperation, Larry limps to the antique store and tells Gwen he is a werewolf. She doesn't take him seriously. When he says he's leaving, she asks to go with him. Then, half jokingly, she shows him a werewolf charm she wears around her neck. When she extends her hands, Larry sees the sign of the pentagram in her palm.

Desperate, Larry goes to his father and shows him the starlike brand on his chest. But Sir John still thinks his son is merely distraught.

"That scar could be made by any animal," he says. ". . . Larry, Larry, how can I help you get rid of this fear, this mental quagmire you've gotten into?"

To convince Larry it's all in his mind, Sir John straps Larry to a chair and locks him in his room that night.

"Dad," Larry says, "Take the cane."

The elder Talbot is puzzled. But he does take the silver-tipped walking stick as he joins police in the woods.

Back in his room, Larry has changed into a werewolf. He easily breaks his bonds and plunges out into the night. Within minutes, he comes across Gwen in the woods and attacks her. But her screams bring Sir John. Swinging the heavy stick, he strikes the wolf man. It stuns the beast. Again, Sir John crashes the cane down upon the monster's head. Time after time, he sends the silver handle down until he has crushed the werewolf's skull.

Limp with exhaustion, Sir John pulls himself away. As he does, the creature undergoes a transformation. Before Sir John's eyes, it turns into his dead son.

When the police arrive, they are astonished to see Sir John standing over Larry's body. But Captain Montford tries to console the grief-stricken father. A wolf must have attacked Gwen and Larry came to her rescue, he says.

Maleva, the old gypsy woman is there, too, and she adds her mystic thoughts to the tragic scene.

"As the rain enters the soil, the river enters the sea. So tears run to a predestined end."

Looking at Larry's face, serene and tranquil in death, she adds, "Your suffering is over. Now you will find peace for eternity."

THE WOLF MAN SERIES

1. *Werewolf of London.* Universal, 1935, Stuart Walker.
    Henry Hull (as the Werewolf and Dr. Glendon), Warner Oland, Valerie Hobson, Lester Mathews, Lawrence Grant, Spring Byington, Clark Williams, J. M. Kerrigan, Charlotte Granville, Ethel Griffies. 75 minutes.

2. *The Wolf Man.* Universal, 1941, George Waggner.
    Claude Rains, Warren William, Ralph Bellamy, Patric Knowles, Bela Lugosi, Forrester Harvey, Maria Ouspenskaya, Fay Helm, Evelyn Ankers, J. M. Kerrigan, Lon Chaney, Jr. (as the Wolf Man and Larry Talbot). 71 minutes.

3. *Frankenstein Meets the Wolf Man.* Universal, 1943, Roy William Neill.
    Lon Chaney, Jr. (as the Wolf Man and Larry Talbot), Bela Lugosi (as the Monster), Patric Knowles, Ilona Massey, Dennis Hoey, Maria Ouspenskaya, Lionel Atwill, Rex Evans, Don Barclay, Dwight Frye, Beatrice Roberts, Harry Stubbs. 72 minutes.

4. *The Return of the Vampire.* Columbia, 1943, Lew Landers.
    Bela Lugosi (as Armand Tesla, a vampire), Frieda Inescort, Nina Foch, Roland Varno, Miles Mander, Matt Willis (as Andreas Obry, the Wolf Man), Ottola Nesmith, Gilbert Emery, Leslie Denison, William Austin, Jeanne Bates, Billy Bevan, Donald Dewar, Shirlee Collins, Nelson Leigh, George McKay, Olaf Hytten, Stanley Logan. 69 minutes.

5. *Cry of the Werewolf.* Columbia, 1944, Henry Levin.
    Nina Foch (as the Werewolf and Celeste), Stephen Crane, Osa Massen, Blanche Yurka, Barton MacLane, Ivan Triesault, John Abbott, Fred Graff, John Tyrrell, Robert Williams, Fritz Leiber, Milton Parsons. 63 minutes.

6. *House of Frankenstein.* Universal, 1944, Erle C. Kenton.
    Boris Karloff, J. Carrol Naish, Lon Chaney, Jr. (as the Wolf Man and Larry Talbot), John Carradine (as Dracula), Anne Gwynne, Peter Coe, Lionel Atwill, George Zucco, Elena Verdugo, Sig Rumann, William Edmunds, Charles Miller, Phillip Van Zandt, Julius Tannen, Glenn Strange (as the Monster). 71 minutes.

7. *House of Dracula.* Universal, 1945, Erle C. Kenton.
    Lon Chaney, Jr. (as the Wolf Man and Larry Talbot), John Carradine (as Dracula), Martha O'Driscoll, Lionel Atwill, Jane Adams, Onslow Stevens, Ludwig Stossel, Glenn Strange (as the Monster), Skelton Knaggs, Joseph E. Bernard, Dick Dickinson, Fred Cordova, Carey Harrison. 67 minutes.

8. *She-Wolf of London.* Universal, 1946, Jean Yarbrough.
    June Lockhart, Don Porter, Sara Haden, Jan Wiley, Dennis Hoey, Lloyd Corrigan, Eily Malyon, Martin Kosleck, Frederic Worlock, Clara Blandick. 61 minutes.

9. *Abbott and Costello Meet Frankenstein.* Universal, 1948, Charles Barton.
    Bud Abbott, Lou Costello, Lon Chaney, Jr. (as the Wolf Man and Larry Talbot), Bela Lugosi (as Dracula), Glenn Strange (as the Monster), Lenore Aubert, Jane Randolph, Frank Ferguson, Charles Bradstreet, Howard Negley, Joe Kirk, Helen Spring, Paul Stader, Vincent Price (as the voice of the Invisible Man). 92 minutes.

10. *The Werewolf.* Columbia, 1956, Fred F. Sears.
    Steven Rich (as the werewolf and Duncan Marsh), Don Megowan, Joyce Holden, Eleanore Tanin, Kim Charney, Harry Lauter, Larry J. Blake, Ken Christy, James Gavin, S. John Launer, George M. Lynn. 78 minutes.

11. *I Was a Teenage Werewolf.* American International, 1957, Gene Fowler, Jr.
    Michael Landon (as the Werewolf and Tony), Yvonne Lime, Whit Bissell, Tony Marshall, Dawn Richard, Barney Phillips, Ken Miller, Cindy Robbins, Michael Rougas, Robert Griffin, Joseph Mell, Malcolm Atterbury. 76 minutes.

12. *The Curse of the Werewolf.* Universal, 1961, Terence Fisher.
    Clifford Evans, Oliver Reed (as the Werewolf and Leon), Yvonne Romain, Catherine Feller, Anthony Dawson, Josephine Llewellyn, Richard Wordsworth, Hira Talfrey, John Gabriel, Warren Mitchell, Anne Blake, George Woodbridge, Michael Ripper, Ewen Solon, Peter Sallis. 91 minutes.

13. *Werewolf in a Girl's Dormitory.* MGM, 1963, Richard Benson.
    Barbara Lass, Carl Schell, Curt Lowens (as the Werewolf and Mr. Swift), Maurice Marsac, Maureen O'Connor, Mary McNeeran, Grace Neame, Alan Collins, Ann Steinert. 82 minutes.

Through the dungeon door lumbers the Monster. Karloff's jacket had shortened sleeves to make his arms appear longer. Electrodes—plugs for the lightning that gave him life—protrude from his neck. On his feet are 18-pound, lead-weighted boots to make his movements awkward.

FRANKENSTEIN'S MONSTER

Son of Frankenstein

(1939)

A screenplay by Willis Cooper based on characters created by Mary Shelley. Camera, George Robinson. Assistant Director, Jack Otterson. Directed and produced by Rowland V. Lee. Presented by Universal Pictures. 80 minutes.

Baron Wolf von Frankenstein	BASIL RATHBONE
The Monster	BORIS KARLOFF
Ygor	BELA LUGOSI
Inspector Krogh	LIONEL ATWILL
Elsa von Frankenstein	JOSEPHINE HUTCHINSON
Amelia	EMMA DUNN
Peter von Frankenstein	DONNIE DUNAGAN
Benson	EDGAR NORTON

Putty hoods the deep and sunken eyes. Painted-on surgical scars streak the gaunt, elongated face. A matted wig tops off the box-like, double-domed forehead.

In the sides of the neck are two electrodes—inlets for the lightning that gave him life. To add massive proportions to the body, padded undergarments broaden the shoulders. They flesh out the chest and fill the arms, which seem enormous because they hang from shortened sleeves. Finally, a sheepskin jerkin reaches below the waist, and 18-pound lead-weighted boots—to make walking appear awkward and unnatural—cover the feet.

This was the ingenious makeup that created the Frankenstein monster. In the process, it turned Boris Karloff into an overnight star. Without uttering a word —depending solely on his grotesque appearance and his consummate pantomime skill—Karloff played the superstrong artificial man to perfection.

At the same time, he typed himself forever in a genre he helped popularize— the horror movie of the sound era. And yet, he always felt that "horror" was the wrong word.

> Horror means something revolting (Karloff said). Anybody can show you a pailful of innards. But the object of the roles I played is not to turn your stomach —but merely to make your hair stand on end. It (the descriptive word) should have been "terror." They are bogey stories, that's all. Bogey stories with the same appeal as thrilling ghost stories or fantastic fairy tales that entertain and enthral children in spite of being so hokey.
>
> Actually, *Jack and the Beanstalk* is shocking. And *Grimm's Fairy Tales* are appalling. I suppose films like *Frankenstein* remain popular because they have such deep, deep roots.

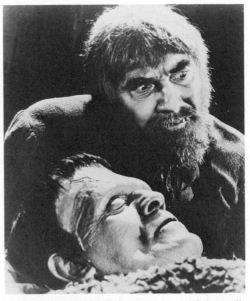

The face that haunted a thousand dreams. Boris Karloff as the Monster in the original *Frankenstein* (1931).

The two greatest horror genre actors of them all. Bela Lugosi as the hunchback Ygor watches over the unconscious Monster in *Son of Frankenstein* (1939). The movie marked the third and last time Karloff played the Monster.

Unquestionably, *Frankenstein* has become the greatest shock movie of all time. Yet, despite its amazing longevity, Karloff's brilliant performance originally all but went unnoticed. He was billed fourth in the cast. The studio reportedly did not even invite him to the Hollywood premiere. When the movie opened in the East, *New York Times* reviewer Mordaunt Hall disposed of Karloff perfunctorily. "Boris Karloff," wrote Hall, "undertakes the Frankenstein creature and his make-up can be said to suit anybody's demand."

However, once the public began turning out in numbers, it was obvious that Hollywood had created something unusual. The idea of a scientist creating life in the laboratory—man playing God—fascinated audiences. When the monster's face flashed on the screen for the first time, movie-goers were scared stiff. Cold reptilelike eyes darted from scarred and depraved features. Wrote one reviewer: "Many laughed to cover their true emotions."

Karloff had set the standards for hundreds of chillers to come. The roster of monsters would include vampires, werewolves, mummies, ghouls, zombies, giant apes, wasp women, cat people, voodoo women, and she-demons. But unlike his successors, Karloff did more than just raise goose flesh. He infused his role with pathos. There is, for example, a moving sequence where the monster sees light for the first time. With guttural cries, he gropes heavenward, his long, corpselike hands trying to grasp the golden sunshine.

In another scene—cut from the original because it was thought too violent— he comes upon a little girl (Marilyn Harris) tossing flowers in a lake. She is not repelled and invites him to play. When all the flowers are gone, the monster, thinking the child will float as well, throws her in. Moments later, he staggers away, wringing his hands in agony as he perceives the terrible thing he has done. It is this touch of remorse that gives poignancy and dimension to the character. And this is what makes the monster unforgettable.

There was an avalanche of mail for Karloff. It continued all his life, although he played the monster only twice more—in *Bride of Frankenstein* (1935) and *Son of Frankenstein* (1939). Most of the letters came from children, who, Karloff said, always showed insight into the monster's character. "They seemed to understand that he was the victim of something beyond his control. He was bewildered and afraid. It was his great strength and panic which made him dangerous . . . They [the children] always expressed great compassion."

Karloff became firmly cemented in the Hollywood horror mold. But he never complained about the many grotesque roles that were to follow—grave robbers, mad scientists, executioners, a mummy, Fu Manchu. "Certainly, I was typed," he said. "But what is typing. It is a trademark, a means by which the public recognizes you. Actors work all their lives to achieve that. I got mine with just one picture. It was a blessing."

Nevertheless, playing the role was far from easy. He had to be at the studio

The Monster picks flowers with a little girl (Marilyn Harris) by a lakeside in one of *Frankenstein*'s most poignant and horrifying scenes. They toss the flowers in the water, watching them float. When the flowers are all picked, the Monster throws in the little girl—thinking she, too, will float. The studio thought the scene too shocking and cut it from the original.

The climactic moment from *Bride of Frankenstein* (1935). To the Monster's utter chagrin, the artificial woman created to be his mate is repelled and rejects him. Note Elsa Lanchester's far-out, frizzled hair-do.

at 5:30 every morning and spend nearly four hours with makeup specialist Jack Pierce. He became 18 inches taller and 60 pounds heavier. During the filming of *Frankenstein,* Karloff, a six-footer who weighed 175 pounds, lost 20 pounds.

Universal copyrighted the makeup process, preventing other studios from creating an artificial man in the same likeness. But in 1939, Pierce told how he went about fashioning the monster:

> There are six ways a surgeon can cut the skull, and I figured Dr. Frankenstein, who was not a practicing surgeon, would take the easiest. That is, he would cut the top of the skull off straight across like a pot lid, hinge it, pop the brain in, and clamp it tight. That's the reason I decided to make the monster's head square and flat like a box and dig that big scar across his forehead and have two metal clamps hold it together. The two metal studs that stick out the sides of his neck are inlets for electricity—plugs. Don't forget, the monster is an electrical gadget and that lightning is his life force . . .
>
> The lizard eyes were made of rubber, as was his false head. I made the arms look longer by shortening the sleeves of his coat. His legs were stiffened by steel struts and two pairs of pants. His large feet were the boots asphalt-spreaders wear. His fingernails were blackened with shoe polish. His face was coated with blue-green greasepaint, which photographs gray (in black-and-white film).

This frightening guise notwithstanding, Karloff was in private life a gentle, cultured Englishman, about as far removed from mayhem and brutality as a civil servant. In fact, he was pointed toward a career in that very profession. He was born William Henry Pratt in 1887, youngest of nine sons of a member of Britain's Indian civil service. (His stage name came from his mother's family. He added Boris to keep the Slavic flavor.)

But when he played the part of a demon in his parish's annual Christmas pantomime, he was sold on an acting career. He attended the University of London before leaving for Canada in 1909. Success didn't come easily. He had to work as a farmhand, logger, ditchdigger, and truck driver before landing a job with a touring stock company.

In 1919, he appeared in his first Hollywood movie as an extra, a swarthy Mexican soldier, in *His Majesty, the American,* starring Douglas Fairbanks. He went on to bit parts and character roles but he remained an obscure actor until 1931, the year Universal produced *Frankenstein.*

Actually, Karloff got the monster role only because Bela Lugosi had turned it down after making film rushes. Lugosi, who had just created a sensation in *Dracula,* rejected it because the heavy makeup made him unrecognizable. He also objected to the fact that the monster had no lines.

Searching for another actor, director James Whale remembered a fellow Britisher at Universal who had impressed him playing a murderer in the gangster movie *Graft.* That was Karloff, who was then 44.

Whale tested him. The rest is history.*

Whale, a brilliant stage craftsman, directed the first two *Frankenstein* movies and they have become the most discussed films in retrospective articles. But in my opinion, the third in the series, *Son of Frankenstein,* also deserves a niche among memorable horror movies. Its mood is unrelenting, its sets brooding, its dialogue crisp. And it contains the mirror scene, one of Karloff's greatest.

The picture opens 25 years after the death of Henry Frankenstein. His son, Baron Wolf von Frankenstein (Basil Rathbone), the baron's wife (Josephine Hutchinson), and their son Peter (Donnie Dunagan) return to the tiny village of Frankenstein, home of the family's ancestral castle. As Frankenstein steps off the train in a night rainstorm, hundreds of villagers, huddled under umbrellas, are there to see him. But it is not a cheerful encounter. "We come to meet you, not to greet you," the burgomeister says. The townsfolk still remember vividly those who lost their lives at the hands of the creation of Frankenstein's father.

"I can't undo the wrongs you have suffered," Frankenstein says. "But I beg of you, let the dead past remain buried." The crowd groans, then rudely walks away while Frankenstein is talking.

At the massive stone castle—whose somberness is suggested by "psychological sets" of criss-crossing shadow arrays—Frankenstein discovers his father's notes about creating life. But police inspector Krogh (Lionel Atwill) calls to warn him against continuing work in his father's field. Krogh has a wooden arm and uses it to snap off salutes and hold his monocle. However, Frankenstein is not much impressed by Krogh or his admonitions.

"Do you honestly know of one criminal act this poor creature committed?" Frankenstein asks "Did you ever even see him?"

"The most vivid recollection of my life," the inspector replies, responding to Frankenstein's challenge with a chilling tale. "I was a child at the time . . . One night, he burst into our house. My father took a gun and fired at him. The savage brute sent him crashing to the corner. Then, he grabbed me by the arm. One doesn't easily forget, Herr Baron, an arm torn out by the roots . . ."

Krogh adds that his life-long ambition was to have been a soldier. "But for this, I, who command seven gendarmes in a little mountain village, might have been a general."

The one-armed inspector goes on to tell Frankenstein about a rash of recent murders—six, all unsolved, all prominent men of the village. In each case, an autopsy points to death by violent concussion.

---

*Ironically, Karloff got only $125 a week for his work in *Frankenstein,* which grossed $14 million for Universal.

The next day, as Frankenstein inspects his father's old laboratory in a tower near the castle, he discovers Ygor (Lugosi), a deformed, crazed shepherd living there. Ygor has been sent to the gallows for stealing bodies. Somehow he has survived. "They hanged me once," he tells Frankenstein. "They broke my neck. They said I was dead. Then, they cut me down."

Ygor leads Frankenstein past a bubbling sulphur pit at the bottom of the tower. He takes the scientist to the family crypt where he shows Frankenstein the monster, lying in a coma, the result of a bolt of lightning.

"But he's supposed to have been destroyed," the astonished Frankenstein says.

"No," Ygor says. "Cannot be destroyed. Cannot die. Your father made him live for always. Now he's sick. Make him well, Frankenstein."

When the young scientist is reluctant to follow his father's experimental work, Ygor points out that the younger Frankenstein and the monster have the same father.

"You mean to imply that he is my brother?" Frankenstein says, faintly amused.

Ygor nods. "But," he adds, "his [the monster's] mother is lightning."

With scientific fervor, Frankenstein rebuilds his father's lab, and, using electricity produced by a generator, attempts to revive the monster. Weeks go by without any results. Frankenstein thinks he has failed until one day his son tells him that a giant has visited his bedroom.

One of the memorable scenes occurs as Frankenstein rushes to the lab and the monster confronts the son of his creator. The synthetic man puts his great hands on Frankenstein's neck. But only for an instant. A mirror distracts his attention and suddenly fascinated, he explores his reflection. He stares at his face, then groans despairingly. He touches his hideous features and tries to rub them away. He pulls Frankenstein over and compares the baron's aristocratic features with his own pathetically ugly face. He makes Frankenstein look, too. Finally, with a deep-throated growl, the brute pushes the mirror away.

Frankenstein, in time, learns that Ygor has been using the monster to carry out a systematic murder plan. One by one, the monster has killed the jurors who had sentenced Ygor to death. Only two remain alive. Bent on stopping Ygor, Frankenstein takes a gun to the lab. Ygor lunges at him with a hammer, misses, and Frankenstein fires three shots into him.

Meanwhile, the monster has taken the lives of the remaining two jurors. And the townspeople, suspecting the truth, march on the castle with torchlights. Trying to head off violence, Inspector Krogh rushes to the castle. Frankenstein refuses to confide in him, but the inspector won't leave. Each waiting for the other to crack, they play darts, the inspector sticking the extra missiles in his wooden arm while taking aim. Finally, losing patience, the inspector bluntly tells Frankenstein he is sure the monster is loose again. "There's a murderer afoot and you know it," Krogh says. ". . . By heaven, I think you're a worse fiend than your

Ygor is delighted to see his old pal revived after years of preservation in a sulphur pit—ready to stalk the world of horror again. Scene is from *The Ghost of Frankenstein* (1942). Cowboy villain Glenn Strange plays the Monster.

Torch-carrying villagers close in as the Monster (Strange) lugs Dr. Frankenstein from his castle in *House of Frankenstein* (1944).

Christopher Lee in *The Curse of Frankenstein* (1957). Universal's copyright prevented Hammer Studios from imitating the Monster's makeup. So Hammer created its own artificial man.

father. Where is it, monster? Where is he? I'll stay by your side until you confess. And if you don't, I'll feed you to the villagers like the Romans fed Christians to the lions."

Suddenly they learn the monster has kidnapped Frankenstein's boy. Together with the inspector, Frankenstein dashes to the lab. But Krogh is the first to reach the giant. The monster, standing over the boiling sulphur, puts down the child and goes after the inspector, ripping off his wooden arm. But before he can make another move, Frankenstein, standing on a balcony overlooking the scene, grabs a rope. Using it for a swing, he soars down and kicks the monster into the bubbling pit.

But you can't keep a good monster down. Preserved by sulphur, the monster rose again in *Ghost of Frankenstein* (1942), only to go up in flames at the end. In *Frankenstein Meets the Wolf Man* (1943), the monster was found frozen in a block of ice only to drown with the Wolf Man as the townspeople blow up the village dam. Next came *House of Frankenstein* (1944). Thawed from another frozen limbo, he ended by sinking into a quicksand bog. In *House of Dracula* (1945), flames devoured him and in *Abbott and Costello Meet Frankenstein* (1948), he fell into the sea.

That ended the Universal cycle. However, in 1957, the British Hammer Studios revived the series with *The Curse of Frankenstein*. Unable to use the monster-style makeup because of Universal's copyright, Hammer devised a new monster which it called the "creature"—more recognizable as a human but hideous in his own fashion. It also added color, reducing the psychological impact of lights and darks by achieving the more immediate fright of showing blood in all its gory detail.

A host of other actors went on to play the resurrected monster in these seemingly endless revivals. They included Lugosi, second-string bogeyman Lon Chaney, Jr., veteran western villain Glenn Strange (later seen as Sam the bartender in TV's "Gunsmoke") and Britain's Christopher Lee.

But no one approached Karloff's penetrating characterization. When he died in 1969 at the age of 81, newspapers around the world remembered his frightening but moving performances in the *Frankenstein* movies. Obituaries hailed him as "the acknowledged king of Hollywood horror films."

FRANKENSTEIN SERIES

1. *Frankenstein.* Universal, 1931, James Whale.
   Colin Clive (as Henry Frankenstein), Mae Clarke, John Boles, Boris Karloff (as the Monster), Frederick Kerr, Edward Van Sloan, Dwight Frye, Lionel Belmore, Marilyn Harris, Michael Mark, Arletta Duncan, Pauline Moore, Francis Ford. 71 minutes.

2. *Bride of Frankenstein.* Universal, 1935, James Whale.
   Boris Karloff (as the Monster), Colin Clive (as Henry Frankenstein), Valerie Hobson, Elsa Lanchester (as the Mate and Mary Shelley), O. P. Heggie, Ernest Thesiger, Dwight Frye, E. E. Clive, Una O'Connor, Anne Darling, Douglas Walton (as Percy Shelley), Gavin Gordon (as Lord Byron), Neil Fitzgerald, Gunnis Davis, Reginald Barlow, Mary Gordon, Ted Billings, Lucien Prival, John Carradine, Walter Brennan. 80 minutes.

3. *Son of Frankenstein.* Universal, 1939, Rowland V. Lee.
   Basil Rathbone (as Baron Wolfgang von Frankenstein), Boris Karloff (as the Monster), Bela Lugosi, Lionel Atwill, Josephine Hutchinson, Emma Dunn, Donnie Dunagan, Edgar Norton. 95 minutes.

4. *The Ghost of Frankenstein.* Universal, 1942, Erle C. Kenton.
   Sir Cedric Hardwicke (as Dr. Ludwig Frankenstein), Lon Chaney, Jr., (as the Monster), Lionel Atwill, Ralph Bellamy, Evelyn Ankers, Bela Lugosi, Janet Ann Gallow, Barton Yarborough, Doris Lloyd, Leyland Hodgson, Olaf Hytten, Holmes Herbert, Lawrence Grant, Brandon Hurst, Dwight Frye, Michael Mark. 68 minutes.

5. *Frankenstein Meets the Wolf Man.* Universal, 1943, Roy William Neill.
   Lon Chaney, Jr. (as Larry Talbot and the Wolf Man), Bela Lugosi (as the Monster), Patric Knowles, Ilona Massey, Dennis Hoey, Maria Ouspenskaya, Lionel Atwill, Rex Evans, Don Barclay, Dwight Frye, Beatrice Roberts, Harry Stubbs. 72 minutes.

6. *House of Frankenstein.* Universal, 1944, Erle C. Kenton.
   Boris Karloff, J. Carrol Naish, Lon Chaney, Jr. (as Larry Talbot and the Wolf Man), John Carradine (as Dracula), Anne Gwynne, Peter Coe, Lionel Atwill, George Zucco, Elena Verdugo, Sig Rumann, William Edmunds, Charles Miller, Philip Van Zandt, Julius Tannen, Hans Herbert, Dick Dickinson, George Lynn, Michael Mark, Olaf Hytten, Frank Reicher, Brandon Hurst, Belle Mitchell, Edmund Cobb, Charles Wagenheim, Glenn Strange (as the Monster). 70 minutes.

7. *House of Dracula.* Universal, 1945, Erle C. Kenton.
Lon Chaney, Jr. (as Larry Talbot and the Wolf Man), John Carradine (as Dracula), Martha O'Driscoll, Lionel Atwill, Jane Adams, Onslow Stevens, Ludwig Stossel, Glenn Strange (as the Monster), Skelton Knaggs, Joseph E. Bernard, Dick Dickinson, Fred Cordova, Carey Harrison, Harry Lamont, Gregory Muradian, Beatrice Gray. 67 minutes.

8. *Abbott and Costello Meet Frankenstein.* Universal, 1948, Charles T. Barton.
Bud Abbott, Lou Costello, Lon Chaney, Jr. (as Larry Talbot and the Wolf Man), Bela Lugosi (as Dracula), Glenn Strange (as the Monster), Lenore Aubert, Jane Randolph, Frank Ferguson, 92 minutes.

9. *The Curse of Frankenstein.* Hammer Pro./Warner, 1957, Terence Fisher.
Peter Cushing (as Baron Victor Frankenstein), Christopher Lee (as the Creature), Hazel Court, Robert Urquhart, Valerie Gaunt, Noel Hood, Marjorie Hume, Melvin Hayes, Sally Walsh, Paul Hardtmuth, Fred Johnson, Claude Kingston, Henry Caine, Michael Mulcaster, Patrick Troughton, Joseph Behrman, Hugh Dempster, Anne Blake, Raymond Rollett, Alex Gallier, Ernest Jay, J. Trevor Davis, Bartlett Mullins, Eugene Leahy. 82 minutes.

10. *I Was a Teenage Frankenstein.* American International, 1957, Herbert L. Strock.
Whit Bissell (as Professor Frankenstein), Phyllis Coates, Robert Burton, Gary Conway (as the teen-age monster), George Lynn, John Cliff, Marshall Bradford, Claudia Bryar, Angela Blake, Russ Whiteman, Charles Seel, Paul Keast, Gretchen Thomas, Joy Stoner, Larry Carr, Pat Miller. 72 minutes.

11. *The Revenge of Frankenstein.* Hammer Pro. / Columbia, 1958, Terence Fisher.
Peter Cushing (as Baron Frankenstein), Francis Matthews, Eunice Gayson, Michael Gwynn, John Welsh, Lionel Jeffries, Oscar Quitak, Richard Wordsworth, Charles Lloyd Pack, John Stuart. 89 minutes.

12. *Frankenstein—1970.* Allied Artists, 1958, Howard W. Koch.
Boris Karloff (as Baron Frankenstein), Tom Duggan, Jana Lund, Donald Barry, Charlotte Austin, Irwin Berke, Rudolph Anders, John Dennis, Norbert Schiller, Mike Lane (as the Monster). 83 minutes.

13. *Frankenstein's Daughter.* Astor, 1958, Richard Cunha.
John Ashley, Sandra Knight (as a Nighttime Monster), Donald Murphy, Sally Todd, Harold Lloyd Jr., Felix Locher, Wolfe Barzell. 85 minutes.

14. *The Evil of Frankenstein.* Hammer Pro. / Universal, 1964, Freddie Francis.
Peter Cushing (as Baron Frankenstein), Peter Woodthorpe, Sandor Eles, Duncan Lamont, Katy Wild, David Hutcheson, Caron Gardner, Tony Arpino, James

Maxwell, Alister Williamson, Frank Forsyth, Kenneth Cove, Michele Scott, Howard Goorney, Anthony Blackshaw, David Conville, Timothy Bateson, Derek Martin, Robert Flynn, Anthony Poole, James Garfield, Kiwi Kingston (as the Creature). 85 minutes.

15. *Frankenstein Meets the Space Monster*. Allied Artists, 1966, Robert Gaffney.
Robert Reilly (Col. Frank Saunders and Frankenstein), James Karen, David Kerman, Nancy Marshall, Marilyn Hanold, Lou Cutell.

16. *Jesse James Meets Frankenstein's Daughter*. Embassy, 1966, William Beaudine.
John Lupton, Estelita (Estelita Rodriguez), Cal Bolder (The Monster), Narda Onyx, Steven Geray, Rayford Barnes, Jim Davis, Felipe Turich, Rosa Turich, Page Slattery, Nestor Paiva, Dan White, Roger Creed, Fred Stromsoe, William Fawcett, Mark Norton.

17. *Frankenstein Created Woman*. Hammer Pro. / Twentieth Century-Fox, 1967, Terence Fisher.
Peter Cushing (as Baron Frankenstein), Susan Denberg (as the "Woman"), Thorley Walters, Robert Morris, Peter Blythe, Barry Warren, Derek Fowlds, Alan MacNaughton, Peter Madden, Stuart Middleton, Duncan Lamont, Collin Jeavens, Ivan Beavis, John Maxim, Phillip Ray, Kevin Flood. 92 minutes.

18. *Frankenstein Must Be Destroyed*. Hammer Pro. / Warner Bros., 1969, Terence Fisher.
Peter Cushing (as Baron Frankenstein), Veronica Carlson, Freddie Jones, Simon Ward, Thorley Walters, Maxine Audley, George Pravda, Geoffrey Bayldon, Colette O'Neil, Harold Goodwin, Frank Middlemass, Norman Shelley, Michael Gover, George Belbin, Peter Copley. 97 minutes.

19. *The Horror of Frankenstein*. Hammer Pro. / American Continental Films, 1970, Jimmy Sangster.
Ralph Bates (as Victor Frankenstein), Graham James, Kate O'Mara, Veronica Carlson, Dennis Price, Bernard Archard, James Hayter, James Cossins, Jon Finch, Stephen Turner, Neil Wilson, C. Lethbridge Baker, Dave Prowse (as the Monster; Prowse also played the muscle-man in *A Clockwork Orange*). 94 minutes.

20. *Dracula Vs. Frankenstein*. Independent-International Pictures, 1971. Al Adamson.
J. Carrol Naish, Lon Chaney, Jr., Russ Tamblyn, Jim Davis, Regina Carrol, Anthony Eisley, Angelo Rossitto, Greydon Clark, Anne Morrell, William Bonner, Bruce Kimball, Forrest J. Ackerman, Maria Lease, Albert Cole, Irv Saunders, Gary Kent, Connie Nelson, Lu Dorn, Shelly Weiss, John Bloom (as the

Monster), Zandor Vorkov (as Dracula). The picture was formerly called *Satan's Blood Freaks* and *Blood of Frankenstein.* 90 minutes.

There were also a Japanese-produced film—*Frankenstein Conquers the World* (1966)—and a Spanish-produced film—*Frankenstein's Bloody Terror* (1971).

Claude Rains as Jack Griffin, a young scientist who has discovered a chemical that makes him invisible—and also mad—in *The Invisible Man* (1933). Rains, whose face was seen only at the end, made his screen debut in this picture.

THE
INVISIBLE MAN

The Invisible Man

(1933)

A screen drama adapted by R. C. Sherriff from the novel by H. G. Wells. Art director, Charles B. Hall. Film editor, Ted Kent. Cameraman, Arthur Edeson. Special effects, John B. Fulton. Makeup, Jack Pierce. Produced by Carl Laemmle, Jr. Directed by James Whale and presented by Universal. 71 minutes.

Jack Griffin	CLAUDE RAINS
Flora Cranley	GLORIA STUART
Dr. Kemp	WILLIAM HARRIGAN
Dr. Cranley	HENRY TRAVERS
Jenny Hall	UNA O'CONNOR
Herbert Hall	FORRESTER HARVEY
Chief of Police	HOLMES HERBERT
Jaffers	E. E. CLIVE
Chief of Detectives	DUDLEY DIGGES
Inspector Bird	HARRY STUBBS
Inspector Lane	DONALD STUART
Milly	MERLE TOTTENHAM
Doctor	JAMESON THOMAS

Reporter	DWIGHT FRYE
Bicycle Owner	WALTER BRENNAN
Informer	JOHN CARRADINE

A man stands alone in a room. He has the macabre appearance of a living mummy. Bandages mask his face. Dark goggles hide his eyes. Gloves fit over his hands. A dark suit covers every inch of his body.

Suddenly he tears off his goggles and strips the bandages from his face. Piece by piece, he pulls off his clothing. Underneath, one can see neither flesh nor blood nor bone. There is only . . . thin air . . . emptiness . . . nothingness.

Is there anyone who has ever dreamed the impossible dream of becoming invisible? Is there anyone who has not yearned to disappear—to become as one with nature? What would it mean, we all have wondered, to know the secret of invisibility?

To a criminal, it holds out the possibility of stealing without fear of being caught. To a general, it means commanding invincible troops. To a peeping tom, it offers incomparable opportunities. And to Jack Griffin, the chemist who actually does become invisible in *The Invisible Man,* it brings the exquisite madness of possessing unlimited power. "Power to walk into the gold vaults of nations," Griffin laughs, "and into the secrets of kings, into the holy of holies. Power to make monsters run squealing in terror at the touch of my invisible finger. Even the moon is frightened of me . . ."

In 1897, H. G. Wells conceived the idea of turning an invisible man loose in England in his remarkable pseudo-scientific novel. Three decades later in 1933, Universal bought the movie rights and assigned the picture to James Whale, a British stage director who came to Hollywood to direct *Journey's End* (1930). He stayed to produce two first-rate thrillers—*Frankenstein* (1931) and *The Old Dark House* (1932). Then he turned his stylistic talent to the Wells fantasy. The famed English biologist and later social philosopher had created a taut, gripping story tinged with psychological insights.

But Whale saw in it elements of humor—albeit a black humor—and he infused the film with weird sight gags. Such as, for example, scenes where the invisible man scares the daylights out of villagers—stripping off his clothes to fade out of sight as people chase him. Or riding off on a bike which then seems to be going by itself.

Unquestionably, one of the great fascinations with the film was its technical wizardry. Movie invisibility was then new to audiences. How does one go about photographing an unseen man? One way is to use "spirit" wires to move books and other objects and create the illusion. Another is to suspend a hat and coat over a wire and move them around. But Universal made a great mystery out of the process. Press releases said the studio had discovered the possibilities of using

A constable (E. E. Clive) and curious villagers break into Griffin's inn room, where he has been trying to discover an antidote to restore him to visibility.

In *The Invisible Man Returns* (1940), Vincent Price's bandages and dark goggles shock a constable (Harry Stubbs) and a second man (Forrester Harvey). At left is Nan Grey.

small mirrors arranged, as magicians employ them, to create optical illusions. Of course, this was pure hokum. Actually, special effects man John B. Fulton achieved most of his dazzling ends using double exposure, negative masking and other film processing techniques.

Still, as good as the trick photography was, the magnificent voice of Claude Rains contributed as much toward establishing the picture as a classic of its genre. Because he was never seen—except when he wore clothes and in the final scene —he was, in effect, playing a radio part. He created his characterization by voice —a voice that was enormously wide-ranging. It could be sonorous, raging, resonant, tender, menacing, world-weary, suave—even at times maniacal, especially when he laughed wildly and shrilly at his own jokes.

Ironically, Rains failed his screen test. But Whale wanted him anyway. "I don't care what he looks like," the director said. "That's the voice I want."

Rains, who projected a dominant personality—despite the fact that he was only five feet, seven inches tall and sometimes played scenes standing on a ramp—had spent half his lifetime on the stage before making *The Invisible Man.* The picture, which was the 44-year-old Rains' film debut, catapulted him to fame. In 1935, when he divorced his third wife—he married six times in all—tabloid headline writers wrote, "Invisible Man Rains Divorces Stage Wife."

He went on to do 56 movie roles before his death in 1967. Few of his parts were starring roles. He played mostly shrewd, aristocratic villains. But Rains earned a reputation as an actor who never gave a bad performance. Although he did not win an Academy Award, he was nominated four times. They were for playing a crooked senator in *Mr. Smith Goes to Washington* (1939), a sympathetic police captain in *Casablanca* (1942), a banker and financial genius in *Mr. Skeffington* (1944), and a post-war Nazi collaborator in *Notorious* (1946). He became the first British film star to earn $1 million for a single movie. That was in 1945 for playing Julius Caesar in *Caesar and Cleopatra.*

But it is in his first role, as the mad scientist who nearly throws all England into a panic, that many film buffs remember him best. Curiously, Rains never made another *Invisible Man* picture. Vincent Price and Jon Hall were among the others who stepped into the role in later movies. Some say the best of the sequels was *The Invisible Man Returns* (1940), in which Price becomes invisible to try to prove his innocence in a murder. But no other actor approached Rains' *bravura* performance.

Actually, Rains thought *The Invisible Man* would be a flop. He left Hollywood right after the shooting ended. A few months later, *The Invisible Man* scored a rousing success. Reviewers hailed the picture for its brilliant inventiveness, technical ingenuity and first-rate acting. It broke box office records at its opening run at the Roxy in New York City. In one four-day period, 80,000 persons saw the picture at the famous movie palace. In the then six-year history of the huge house,

Jon Hall, invisible man number three, stops John Carradine from summoning help in *The Invisible Man's Revenge* (1944).

Leon Errol, third from left, a supporting player in *The Invisible Man's Revenge*, hears Leyland Hodgson, right, accuse him of blackmail. At left are Evelyn Ankers and Alan Curtis.

only four other movies had played to larger audiences. Ads said: "Suppose you loved a man who could feel and hear and sense. But whom it was impossible to see . . . what would you do?"

The movie opens during a snow storm as a bizarre-looking stranger (Rains) arrives in the English village of Iping. The man, his features hidden behind thick bandages and dark goggles, enters the Lion's Head Tavern. All conversation breaks off. The piano stops. A dart game ends.

"I want a room and a fire," the stranger says, shaking snow from his coat.

And so begins his mysterious stay at the local inn. In the next few days, boxes of chemicals arrive and he works feverishly, closeted in his room. But he soon runs short of cash and has a row with the owner. The villagers inevitably become curious about what he is doing. "If you ask me,"says one man, "he's a criminal flying from justice." They call the local constable and barge into his room. Infuriated, the stranger rages at them. "You're crazy to know who I am, aren't you? All right, I'll show you. There's a souvenir for you and one for you." He rips off a stage nose and false hair. Then, he unwinds the bandages from his face.

"Look," the constable exclaims. "'E's all eaten away."

A headless figure dances before them. Before they can catch him off comes his shirt, hat, underwear, shoes and socks. In front of their startled eyes, he has disappeared.

"It's easy, really, if you're clever," a voice says. "A few chemicals mixed together, that's all. And flesh and blood and bone just fade away. A little of this injected under the skin of the arm for a month . . . An invisible man can rule the world. Nobody will see him come. Nobody will see him go. He can hear every secret. He can rob the rich and kill." The voice breaks into a hysterical laugh.

The scene dissolves to the home of Dr. Cranley (Henry Travers), a scientist. The sudden disappearance of Jack Griffin, Cranley's young associate, has puzzled the doctor as well as his daughter Flora (Gloria Stuart), and Dr. Kemp (William Harrigan), another medical colleague. Griffin, who has been conducting secret experiments, has left behind only one clue—a scrap of paper with the word "monocaine." Cranley tells Flora that it is a little-known but powerful Indian drug that draws color from everything it touches. However, it also drives its user mad and Griffin does not know this.

Griffin, of course, is the invisible man. He had secluded himself in the country inn in an attempt to discover an antidote to the drug and return to visibility. But the villagers have interrupted his experiment. He has had to flee and seek help elsewhere.

That evening, while Kemp is listening to radio reports of the strange occurrence at Iping, Griffin visits him and explains all that has happened. Kemp is, at first, sympathetic. But as he listens to Griffin rage on about a scheme for world domination, Kemp realizes that his colleague has lost his mind.

"It was just a scientific experiment at first," the invisible man says. "That's all. To do something no other man in the world had done. But there's more to it than that, Kemp . . . The drugs I took seemed to light up my brain. Suddenly, I realized the power I held. The power to rule. To make the world grovel at my feet. Hahahaha. We'll soon put the world right now, Kemp. You and I."

Griffin says he needs a partner. A dozen little things can expose him. He must always stay in hiding for an hour or two after meals. Food can be seen inside him until it is digested. He can only work on clear days. Rain can be seen on his head and shoulders. In a fog, he looks like a bubble. In smoky cities, soot settles on him until a dark outline is visible. Kemp must always be close by to wipe off his feet. Even dirt between his fingernails can give him away.

Kemp is revolted. But Griffin is so carried away, he doesn't notice. "We'll begin with a reign of terror," the invisible man says. "A few murders here and there. Murders of great men. Murders of little men—just to show we make no distinction. We might even wreck a train or two. Just these fingers around a signalman's throat. That's all."

Terrorized, Kemp drives Griffin back to the village so he can retrieve his notebooks. Once there, Griffin cannot resist murdering a police captain who tells the villagers their invisible man must be a hoax. The killing arouses the country. Radio newscasts and papers carry the story across Britain. Police in every hamlet begin searching for a fugitive they cannot see.

Flora Cranley (Gloria Stuart) warns Griffin that his experiment has affected his brain and pleads with him to let her help him.

One night while Griffin sleeps, Kemp calls Dr. Cranley and then the police. When Flora learns the truth from her father, she rushes to Griffin. She warns him that monocaine has warped his mind. She pleads with him to let her father help him. But he only boasts of the new power that he has.

"I shall offer my secret to the world . . ." he tells her. "The nations of the world will bid for it—thousands, millions. The nation that wins my secret can sweep the world with invisible armies."

While they are talking, police surround the house. But Griffin easily slips past them after warning Kemp he will kill him for his treachery. The time will be precisely at 10 o'clock the next evening. Meanwhile, Griffin starts a campaign of terror. He derails a train. He robs a bank and scatters the money on the streets.

That night, Kemp, disguised as a policeman, drives off alone to the mountains. He is sure he has escaped. But exactly at 10, a voice commands him to stop. The invisible man has been inside the car. He ties up Kemp, shoves him in the back seat and sends the car over a precipice.

All attempts to capture Griffin appear hopeless. Weeks pass. Then one day, a heavy snow blankets England. And the invisible man, forced to stay indoors, falls asleep in a barn. While he is snoring, a farmer enters, hears him, sees his impression in the hay and calls the police. They quickly encircle the barn and set fire to it.

The scene takes place at night. Huge searchlights light up the area. Suddenly, the barn door flies open and footsteps appear in the snow. A pistol fires twice. The tracks stop. And the outline of a man appears in the snow.

The scene cuts to a hospital. A doctor tells Cranley and Flora that the bullets have passed through both lungs. It's impossible to treat wounds that cannot be seen. With his life ebbing and his chemically induced invisibility weakening, Griffin's ferocity fades, too. Flora moves close to his bed.

"I knew you'd come to me," Griffin says softly. "I wanted to come back to you, my darling. I failed." And then he adds a classic line that would find its way into scores of pseudo-science films in decades to come. "I meddled in things that man must leave alone."

And so Griffin dies. But he has still one more surprise for us. Gradually, an opaque mist forms on the pillow, shifting into shadows and then to substance. And on the bed, where there was only an empty impression, lies the head of a young and handsome man. His eyes are closed. His face is serene and peaceful in death.

THE INVISIBLE MAN SERIES

1. *The Invisible Man.* Universal, 1933, James Whale.
    Claude Rains (as Jack Griffin, "the invisible man"), Gloria Stuart, William Harrigan, Henry Travers, Una O'Connor, Forrester Harvey, Holmes Herbert, E. E. Clive, Dudley Digges, Harry Stubbs, Donald Stuart, Merle Tottenham. 71 minutes.

2. *The Invisible Man Returns.* Universal, 1940, Joe May.
    Sir Cedric Hardwicke, Vincent Price (as Geoffrey Radcliffe, "the invisible man"), Nan Grey, John Sutton, Cecil Kellaway, Alan Napier, Forrester Harvey, Ivan Simpson, Edward Fielding, Frances Robinson. 81 minutes.

3. *The Invisible Woman.* Universal, 1941, A. Edward Sutherland.
    Virginia Bruce (as Kitty Carroll, "the invisible woman"), John Barrymore, John Howard, Charles Ruggles, Oscar Homolka, Edward Brophy, Donald MacBride, Margaret Hamilton, Shemp Howard, Anne Nagel, Kathryn Adams, Maria Montez, Charles Lane, Mary Gordon, Thurston Hall, Eddy Conrad. 70 minutes.

4. *Invisible Agent.* Universal, 1942, Edwin L. Marin.
    Ilona Massey, Jon Hall (as Frank Raymond, "the invisible agent"), Peter Lorre, J. Edward Bromberg, Sir Cedric Hardwicke, Albert Basserman, John Litel, Holmes Herbert, Keye Luke. 81 minutes.

5. *The Invisible Man's Revenge.* Universal, 1944, Ford Beebe.
    Jon Hall (as Robert Griffin, "the invisible man"), Alan Curtis, Evelyn Ankers, Leon Errol, John Carradine, Doris Lloyd, Ian Wolfe, Gray Shadow (as himself), Gale Sondergaard, Lester Mathews, Halliwell Hobbes, Leyland Hodgson, Billy Bevan, Cyril Delevanti, Harry Stubbs, Forrester Harvey. 78 minutes.

6. *Abbott and Costello Meet the Invisible Man.* Universal, 1951, Charles Lamont.
    Bud Abbott, Lou Costello, Nancy Guild, Arthur Franz (as Tommy Nelson, "the invisible man"), Adele Jergens, Sheldon Leonard, William Frawley, Gavin Muir, John Day. 82 minutes.

Tom Tyler came shuffling into our hearts a generation ago in *The Mummy's Hand* (1940). And, hoo-boy, were we scared. If you're seeing more horror movies lately but enjoying them less, it all goes to prove they're not making monsters the way they used to.

THE MUMMY

The Mummy's Hand

(1940)

Screen play by Griffin Jay and Maxwell Shane from a story by Jay. Camera, Elwood Bredell. Editor, Phil Cahn. Music director, H. J. Salter. Associate producer, Ben Pivar. Directed by Christy Cabanne. A Universal release. 67 minutes.

Steve Banning	DICK FORAN
Marta Solvani	PEGGY MORAN
Babe Jenson	WALLACE FORD
The High Priest	EDUARDO CIANNELLI
Andoheb	GEORGE ZUCCO
Solvani, the Great	CECIL KELLAWAY
Dr. Petrie	CHARLES TROWBRIDGE
The Mummy	TOM TYLER
The Beggar	SIEGFRIED ARNO
Egyptian	EDDIE FOSTER
Bartender	HARRY STUBBS
Bazaar Owner	MICHAEL MARK
Girl	MARA TARTAR
Ali	LEON BELASCO

Priest
Priest

FRANK LACKTEEN

MURDOCK MACQUARRIE

Scenes from *The Mummy* (1932) with Boris Karloff and James Crane (as the Pharaoh).

> *Who shall defile the temples of the ancient gods, a cruel and violent death shall be his fate and never shall his soul find rest until eternity. Such is the curse of Amon-Ra, king of all the gods.*
>
> *—The High Priest of Karnak*
> *in* The Mummy's Hand

Outside the tent, you can hear the shuffling footsteps. They plod heavily through the Sahara sand. There is a slight jarring sound at the doorway flap. Suddenly, it tears away. And there he stands, his eyes gleaming like stars, his face a mask shriveled by the ages, his body a nightmare in tattered shrouds.

Your hand finds your revolver. Your finger tightens on the trigger. You fire one, two, three shots. But on he comes, moving with the stiffness of centuries in the tomb. You look on—frozen to the spot, paralyzed with fear—as he lumbers forward. Not a word does he say as his fingers grip your throat, tightening like steel bands. You gasp for breath. Slowly the tent vanishes, slowly the world turns black. Night is everywhere. And so is death.

Such is the vicarious fate movie-goers suffer when the living mummy plods across the silver screen. As a figure of fright, the mummy has always been overshadowed by the Frankenstein monster, Dracula, and even the Wolf Man. But for some horror buffs, no terror can match that which comes from an ancient grave. And no spectre that stalks the night is as terrifying as the creature in shrouds.

Of course, we all know it's Hollywood make-believe at its bogeyman best. But what adds an intriguing dimension to the mummy movies are the ancient Egyptian burial rites upon which these films are loosely based. The pharaohs preserved themselves because they thought their souls would return and would need their bodies. And this life-after-death belief, dating back more than 40 centuries, retains a fascination.

In ancient days, the process—essentially a drying-out—was as amazing as the result. First, embalmers removed all the internal organs, which decayed most easily—except the heart, the core of life. Much like fish-dealers salting their wares to preserve them, embalmers soaked the organs in a solution of ordinary carbonate of soda. Meanwhile, they filled the body cavity with spices, which acted as a preservative. Then, they wrapped the organs separately, replaced them and

Those who remember mummy single out Boris Karloff as the pioneer of sound movie mummies. He alternated between archeologist and a 3,000-year-old mummy in *The Mummy* (1932).

Karloff, seen here as priest in *The Mummy*, tries to convince an English girl (Zita Johann) that she is the reincarnation of his long-dead Egyptian love.

wound the body in fine linen bandages. Finally, they enclosed the mummy in a series of splendid coffins—the innermost sometimes of pure gold.

Despite all these intricate preparations, modern scientists have come to believe it was the intense dry desert heat that did most to preserve mummies.

Though commoners were also mummified (through a cheaper, less careful process), the most elaborate burial rites were reserved for a nobleman or king. With him, the royal one took his treasure and left food and drink so his soul could eat. In fact, he made contracts with priests to supply him with food and drink for centuries. The contracts seldom were carried out beyond one or two generations.

The ancient Egyptians also believed that eternal life was assured only if their bodies remained inviolate. So through the ages, pharaohs' remains have lain in rock-cut chambers or within great pyramids whose inner walls bear inscriptions threatening trespassers with the vengeance of the gods. To protect their wealth and immortality, they built passages leading to dead ends. Tons of stone covered the burial chamber. The entrance to the pyramid was so carefully blocked, it defied detection.

Yet, all these devices proved to be in vain. Tomb robbers managed to plunder nearly all the pyramids. The sole exception was the Tomb of Tutankhamen (King Tut), a minor, 18-year-old pharaoh who died in 1352 B.C. and whose burial chamber had lain untouched below that of a later king. In 1922, when British archeologist Howard Carter and his patron Lord Carnarvon opened Tutankhamen's tomb, they found the most dazzling treasure the ruins of Egypt had ever yielded.

Their discovery gave rise to the myth of the "Pharaoh's Curse." Within six months, Carnarvon died suddenly from an infected mosquito bite complicated by pneumonia. According to newspaper stories, an inscription in Tutankhamen's tomb warned that death would come on swift wings to violators of the tomb. Thereafter, Sunday supplement writers kept track of the fate of the members of the expedition, often reporting sensational deaths of people who were not actually members of the party. One man, in fact, was a suicide. But most lived to old age and died natural deaths.

Nevertheless, when Universal made *The Mummy* in 1932, there was ancient history, mysticism and a modern adventure story to whet the public's taste. Boris Karloff, fresh from his triumph as the Frankenstein monster, played the title role. As Im-Ho-Tep, Karloff portrayed a 3,000-year-old mummy restored to life when an English archeologist inadvertently read the sacred words from the Scroll of Thoth.

Karloff produced some unforgettable sequences in this first talking mummy film. Audiences shivered when his parchment-like eyes flickered open, when he strangled his victims with the awesome power of a robot, and when he crumbled into dust at the end. Karloff appeared only briefly as the mummy. Most of the time, he was seen as a wizened-faced Egyptian archeologist, Ahdet Bey. Nevertheless, the film became a minor classic of its genre and Karloff's performance insured his succession to Lon Chaney, Sr. as Hollywood's crown prince of horror.

Still, Karloff never achieved much fame for this role because he played it only once. The actor who appeared most as the mummy was Lon Chaney, Jr., a mechanical and uninspired horror star despite his famous surname. One-eyed and appropriately ugly, he took the title part in *The Mummy's Tomb* (1942), *The Mummy's Ghost* (1944) and *The Mummy's Curse* (1945)—except when stuntman Edwin Parker filled in. In 1959, Britain's Hammer Studios began a technicolor cycle of mummy films with Christopher Lee assuming the role convincingly. In one chilling scene, a sword runs through his entrails without even slowing him down. But the horror of the Egyptian night raises more goose bumps in somber black and white.

And so it was Tom Tyler, a little-known B-picture actor, who, in my judgment, emerges as the king of the mummies. His choice was somewhat accidental.

In 1940, Universal began looking over old properties for a low-cost production and found it could use stock footage from the Karloff *Mummy* in a sequel. This meant finding an actor who looked like a younger Karloff. In a surprising bit of casting, the studio picked Tyler, a veteran cowboy star who had once been an Olympic weight-lifter.* His magnificent physique was part of his appeal.

Born Vincent Marko, Tyler had used his six-foot four-inch stature to help get him his first bit parts in silent cowboy pictures and then in the 1926 silent film spectacular *Ben Hur.* Dark and strapping, he went on to play in over 100 westerns, including the classic *Stagecoach* (1939) with John Wayne, the popular Republic *Three Mesquiteers* B-series with Bob Steele and Rufe Davis, and the memorable *Red River* (1948) with Wayne and Montgomery Clift. Although he was indelibly typed in horse operas, Tyler longed to try more demanding roles. And, before he died in 1954, he did manage a few non-cowboy appearances. He was a commanding officer during the evacuation of Atlanta in *Gone With the Wind* (1939). And he played the superhero title roles in the adventure serials *Captain Marvel* (1941) and *The Phantom* (1943). But it was in his only monster role, in *The Mummy's Hand,* that Tyler achieved his most off-beat characterization.

Even though he never approached the fame that Karloff achieved, Tyler nonetheless had to endure a similar makeup ordeal. It took long hours each morning to turn him into a mummy. Then, he was so uncomfortable he could work only three hours before the cameras.

Jack Pierce, who created the Frankenstein monster makeup, thought an Egyptian mummy's skin ought to be somewhat like the texture and color of a hip-

---

*Tyler won three National Amateur Athletic Union heavyweight weight-lifting championships and competed in the 1928 Olympics at Amsterdam.

popotamus—but more wrinkled. "So," Pierce said, "I covered all of Mr. Tyler's face, neck and hands with thin slivers of cotton. Then I saturated it with spirit gum. When it dried, it wrinkled like his own skin—only the wrinkles were bigger and deeper." Next, Pierce covered face, neck and hands with a grisly-gray paint and flecked them with particles of clay.

So far so good. But what about his shroud? Pierce used a roll of two-inch bandage gauze for this. When the mummy was wrapped, he sloshed him all over with gray paint. Then Tyler shut his eyes and Pierce showered him with brown dust. Finally for Tyler's hair, which looked like it had just undergone a cement hair spray, Pierce rubbed on a mixture of glue and clay.

After each day's filming, it took an hour-and-a-half to get the makeup off. Pierce said he saturated head, face and hands with acetone. Then, he soaked the mummy all over with hot oil and rubbed. "It hurts like the devil," Tyler said. "Just stings a little, is all," said Pierce.

The movie that made all these laborious goings-on necessary opens on the dark theme of death. The elderly High Priest of Karnak (Eduardo Ciannelli), member of an ancient Egyptian sect that has kept alive the mummy Kharis (Kar-eés), is passing on the torch to his son and disciple (George Zucco).

Intoning in the sacrificial chamber, the High Priest says: "Who shall defile the temples of the ancient gods, a cruel and violent death shall be his fate, and never shall his soul find rest until eternity. Such is the curse of Amon-Ra, king of all the gods."

In the mummy's tomb, the languishing priest recounts the secret guarded by the high priests. (As he talks, the film flashes back to footage of the old Karloff picture.) Ten centuries before Christ, the old mystic says, Princess Ananka died. Kharis, a prince of the royal house who loved her, refused to believe she was lost to him. He broke into the sacred altar room of Isis to steal the secret of eternal life—the forbidden tanna leaves. With this mysterious elixir, he knew he could bring Ananka back to life. But guards caught him. And for his sacrilege, the Pharaoh had Kharis' tongue cut out and buried him alive. However, priests secretly removed him from his unholy grave and placed his body in a cave near Ananka's tomb.

"There, he has waited for over 3,000 years to bring death to whoever tries to defile Ananka's tomb," the priest says. "Kharis has never really died!"

The priest tells his astonished disciple to open a copper box beneath the idol of Isis. It holds the long, thin tanna leaves.

"Three of the leaves will make enough fluid to keep Kharis' heart beating," the old man says. "Once each night during the cycle of the full moon, you will dissolve three tanna leaves and give the fluid to Kharis."

Far away on the desert, a jackal bays at the moon. The high priest looks up.

"Nine tanna leaves," says the High Priest of Karnak (Zucco) to archeologist Dr. Petrie (Charles Trowbridge). "That wouldn't mean anything to you. But watch . . ."

Chaney takes a firm grip on another victim in *The Mummy's Curse* (1945). As a three-time mummy, he was the most prolific of the mummy players.

"Children of the night,"* he says. "They howl among the Hill of the Seven Jackals when Kharis must be fed."

Above all, the dying priest instructs his disciple, the tomb must be kept inviolate. "If unbelievers seek to desecrate the tomb of Ananka, you will use nine leaves each night to give life and movement to Kharis," the priest says. "Thus, you will enable him to bring vengeance on the heads of those who try to enter."

The film dissolves to a native bazaar in Cairo where Steve Banning (Dick Foran), an archeologist, and his Brooklyn sidekick Babe Jenson (Wallace Ford), find an ancient vase. From its hieroglyphics and map, Banning thinks he's on to something. They take it to the Cairo museum where its director, Dr. Petrie (Charles Trowbridge), examines it. The markings translate to the "Hill of the Seven Jackals," Petrie says, and the map locates the famous, jewel-laden Tomb of Ananka.

"If we're right and we find it . . . ," Banning says.

"Your place in archeology is assured," Petrie says, excitedly. "It's as important a find as the Tomb of Tutankhamen."

They go down the hall to consult with fez-topped Professor Andoheb, a formal, stodgy man with an imposing reputation as an Egyptologist and relic expert. He is also the disciple who has just become the High Priest of Karnak. And so Andoheb immediately pronounces the vase a fake.

"The Cairo bazaar does a thriving business for tourists," he says, rudely impugning the scholarship of his colleagues. "The desert is paved with the good intentions of many enthusiastic but mistaken archeologists."

When Banning takes issue with him, the professor drops the vase, smashing it to bits. But his clumsy trick backfires. Banning becomes even more determined to find the tomb. He mounts an expedition with the financial help of a traveling magician (Cecil Kellaway). Then, accompanied by the magician and his pretty daughter Marta (Peggy Moran), Banning, his sidekick, and Dr. Petrie push into the interior of Egypt. Andoheb awaits them.

At first, the party finds only the bones of other expeditions that failed in similar efforts. Then, they dynamite into the side of a slope and excavate a cave with the seal of the Seven Jackals. Inside, they discover the mummified corpse of a man. It is, of course, Kharis, and Banning and Dr. Petrie are astonished by his remarkable state of preservation.

Dr. Petrie is left alone for a moment and Professor Andoheb suddenly appears. "You knew about this tomb. And yet you insisted the vase was an imitation," says Petrie, curiously feeling it more important to upbraid the professor for his pedantic deceit than to find out what he's doing here in the middle of the desert.

---

*The line is reminiscent of *Dracula* (1931). The Count, hearing wolves cry outside his castle, remarks, "Children of the night. What music they make."

"There are some things in science that should be brought to light," Andoheb responds coolly. "And others that should be left alone."The professor asks Petrie to feel the mummy's wrist. Petrie feels a pulse. "Absurd . . . fantastic," he exclaims. Andoheb takes nine tanna leaves. "Nine tanna leaves . . . That wouldn't mean anything to you. But watch."

The mummy stirs, his dried, withered face shows no expression. But in a moment, his hand is around Petrie's throat. In a few seconds, he has squeezed the life from the scientist.

Now the camera backs away and we see Kharis in full form. He is tall and powerfully built. The right arm is paralyzed and held across his chest. When he kills, it is with the brute strength of his one good arm.

Andoheb has hidden tanna leaves in the tents of the expedition party. Vowing to see everyone killed who entered the tomb, the professor tells Kharis that only the tanna fluid will help him regain the use of his arm and leg. The monster shuffles off into the desert night. It is in Tyler's creation of the mummy's walk that he best realizes the creature's potential for horror. Kharis' left leg is lame. So when he walks, he takes a long, slow stride, dragging his crippled leg. He moves relentlessly, inexorably. His victims could easily outrun him. But they are too frightened to flee. And this underscores the silent terror of his deliberate pursuit.*

Kharis kills a native guide, Ali (Leon Belasco), then kidnaps Marta and carries her to Andoheb. The professor, for reasons unexplained, drops his mass murder plan and instead decides to seek immortality for Marta and himself via the tanna leaves. He straps her to a sacrificial table.

But a noise distracts the professor. When he steps outside to investigate, he finds Banning's assistant, Babe. The two are standing fez to fez near the top of the pyramid. "What are you doing out in the mountains here—selling real estate?" Babe says.

He pulls a gun and demands that Andoheb lead him to Marta. Andoheb refuses. The professor is hiding a gun in the folds of his cloak.

"I'll give you three to tell me where she is," Babe warns. "One."

"You wouldn't shoot an unarmed man in cold blood," Andoheb says calmly. "Two."

The professor suddenly seems less assured. He tries to frighten Babe. "If you shot me, you would leave at large a monster that only I could control."

But Andoheb's ploy doesn't work.

"Three," says Babe, opening fire. Stunned and mortally wounded, the professor

*There is another side to Kharis—his everlasting devotion to a lost love. But by making him speechless and turning him into a total horror figure, Universal overlooked the poignancy inherent in his character. It is this extra dimension of humanity that adds breadth to all the great fictional monsters. For more on this theme, see the *Frankenstein* chapter.

rolls down the full flight of pyramid steps. "Mighty Isis," he gasps. "Forgive me."

Meanwhile, Banning has found Marta and untied her. Suddenly, Kharis shuffles into the tomb. The mummy is after the tanna fluid burning in a nearby urn. Banning empties his gun into the corpse—but to no avail. Kharis smashes Banning aside and goes for the life-giving fluid. As he raises it to his lips, Babe bursts in and shoots the urn out of his hand. Kharis falls to his knees and frantically starts licking the floor. Before he can reinvigorate himself, Banning tips a flaming brazier on him and the mummy goes up in flames.

And so the tomb of Ananka has lost its defender. It will be opened and plundered. And after 30 centuries, Ananka's other worldly glory will be no more.

But who knows what lies ahead for those who dare disturb the final resting place of the royal house of Egypt? Outside the jackals howl. In the cold Sahara, their mournful cries ring eerily over the endless sand. Do those voices say that Amon-Ra, king of all the gods, is watching?

THE MUMMY SERIES

1. *The Mummy.* Universal, 1932, Karl Freund.
   Boris Karloff (as Im-Ho-Tep), Zita Johann, David Manners, Edward Van Sloan, Arthur Byron, Bramwell Fletcher, Noble Johnson, Leonard Mudie, Katherine Byron, Eddie Kane, Tony Merlo, James Crane, Arnold Grey, Henry Victor. 78 minutes.

2. *The Mummy's Hand.* Universal, 1940, Christy Cabanne.
   Dick Foran, Peggy Moran, Wallace Ford, Eduardo Ciannelli, George Zucco, Cecil Kellaway, Charles Trowbridge, Tom Tyler (as the Mummy), Siegfried Arno, Eddie Foster, Harry Stubbs, Michael Mark, Mara Tartar, Leon Belasco. 67 minutes.

3. *The Mummy's Tomb.* Universal, 1942, Harold Young.
   Lon Chaney, Jr. (as the mummy Kharis), Dick Foran, Elyse Knox, John Hubbard, Mary Gordon, Virginia Brissac, Turhan Bey, Wallace Ford, George Zucco, Cliff Clark, Paul E. Burns, Frank Reicher, Eddy Waller, Emmett Vogan, Janet Shaw, Pat McVey, Glenn Strange, Walter Byron. 61 minutes.

4. *The Mummy's Ghost.* Universal, 1944, Reginald Le Borg.
   Lon Chaney, Jr. (as the mummy Kharis), John Carradine, Robert Lowery, Ramsay Ames, Barton MacLane, George Zucco, Frank Reicher, Harry Shannon, Emmett Vogan, Lester Sharpe, Claire Whitney, Oscar O'Shea, Stephen Barclay, Dorothy Vaughan, Mira McKinney, Bess Flowers, Eddy Waller, Anthony Warde, Ivan Triesault, Martha Vickers. 60 minutes.

5. *The Mummy's Curse.* Universal, 1945, Leslie Goodwins.
   Lon Chaney, Jr. (as the Mummy), Peter Coe, Virginia Christine, Kay Harding, Martin Kosleck, Kurt Katch, Addison Richards, Holmes Herbert, Napoleon Simpson, Charles Stevens, William Farnum, Ann Codee. 61 minutes.

6. *Abbott and Costello Meet the Mummy.* Universal, 1955, Charles Lamont.
   Bud Abbott, Lou Costello, Marie Windsor, Michael Ansara, Dan Seymour, Richard Deacon, Kurt Katch, Richard Karlan, Mel Welles, George Khoury, Edwin Parker (as the Mummy), Mazzone-Abbott Dancers, Chandra Kaly Dancers, Peggy King. 79 minutes.

7. *The Mummy.* Universal, 1959, Terence Fisher.
   Peter Cushing, Christopher Lee (as the mummy Kharis), Yvonne Furneaux, Eddie Byrne, Felix Aylmer, Raymond Huntley, George Pastell, John Stuart, Harold Goodwin, Dennis Shaw. 86 minutes.

8. *The Curse of the Mummy's Tomb.* Columbia, 1964, Michael Carreras.
   Terence Morgan, Fred Clark, Ronald Howard, Jeanne Roland, George Pastell, John Paul, Jack Gwillim, Bernard Rebel, Dickie Owen, Michael McStay, Jill Mai Meredith, Vernon Smythe. 80 minutes.

9. *The Mummy's Shroud.* 20th Century-Fox, 1967, John Gilling.
   Andre Morell, John Phillips, David Buck, Elizabeth Sellars, Maggie Kimberley, Michael Ripper, Tim Barrett, Richard Warner, Roger Delgado, Catherine Lacey, Dickie Owen, Bruno Barnabe, Toni Gilpin, Toolsie Persaud (as the mummy Kah-To-Bey), Eddie Powell, Andreas Malandrinos. 90 minutes.

10. *Blood from the Mummy's Tomb.* Hammer Prod./American International, 1972, Seth Holt.
    Andrew Keir, Valerie Leon (as Margaret and the mummy Tera), James Villiers, Hugh Burden, George Coulouris, Mark Edwards, Rosalie Crutchley, Aubrey Morris, David Markham, Joan Young, James Cossins, David Jackson, Jonathan Burn, Graham James, Tamara Ustinov. 94 minutes.

Behind Dr. Zira's intense simian features is Kim Hunter, accomplished Broadway actress who won a 1951 Oscar in *Streetcar Named Desire*.

PLANET OF THE APES

Escape from the Planet of the Apes

(1971)

Written by Paul Dehn based on characters created by Pierre Boulle. Director of photography, Joseph Biroc. Music, Jerry Goldsmith. Film editor, Marion Rothman. Creative makeup design, John Chambers. Makeup supervision, Dan Striepeke. Makeup artist, Jack Barron. Assistant director, Pepi Lenzi. Directed by Don Taylor. Associate producer, Frank Capra, Jr. Produced by Arthur P. Jacobs. Released by 20th Century-Fox. 98 minutes.

Cornelius	RODDY MCDOWALL
Zira	KIM HUNTER
Dr. Lewis Dixon	BRADFORD DILLMAN
Dr. Stephanie Branton	NATALIE TRUNDY
Dr. Otto Hasslein	ERIC BRAEDEN
The President	WILLIAM WINDOM
Milo	SAL MINEO
E-1	ALBERT SALMI
E-2	JASON EVERS
Chairman	JOHN RANDOLPH
Armando	RICARDO MONTALBAN

General Brody	STEVE ROBERTS
Aide-Captain	M. EMMET WALSH
Lawyer	ROY E. GLENN, SR.
Cardinal	PETER FORSTER
Army Officer	NORMAN BURTON
Naval Officer	WILLIAM WOODSON
Orderly	TOM LOWELL
TV Newscaster	BILL BONDS
Curator	DONALD ELSON

A spaceship, sailing through intergalactic infinity, crash-lands on an unfamiliar planet apparently beyond the solar system. The craft had taken off from Cape Kennedy some 20 centuries earlier. But since it has traveled at the speed of light and its astronauts have sealed themselves in airtight bunks, the crew has lived in a kind of suspended animation. They have aged only 18 months.

Aging turns out to be the least of their worries. They have landed in a strange simian world where Earth's evolutionary processes have been reversed. Man is a brute—wild, unintelligent, naked. The ape is civilized—capable of speech, clothed, cultured. It is the ape who rules over man. He cages man, dissects him for research, stuffs him for museum display. He is careful to see that humans do not grow in numbers and strength and ultimately overrun and destroy ape society.

And so begins the engrossing saga of *Planet of the Apes,* a film based on a novel that ironically had everything going against its becoming a movie. For openers, Pierre Boulle, author of *Bridge on the River Kwai,* did not write *Planet* with the screen in mind. "I didn't think a picture could be made of it," he said. Producer Arthur Jacobs—a former public relations executive who once represented Marilyn Monroe—thought otherwise.

He bought the screen rights when *Planet* was still in manuscript form and in French (Boulle's native language). But for a while, it looked like he had purchased a white elephant. Every movie company he contacted in Europe and the United States turned it down. Their reaction: "How can you put a bunch of talking chimps in a serious drama?"

Jacobs refused to give up. He had Rod Serling write a screenplay. He persuaded Charlton Heston and Edward G. Robinson to make a 15-minute test in full simian makeup, and got Franklin Schaffner to join the package as director. Twentieth Century-Fox finally agreed to do the film.

But once the project was underway, Jacobs faced an undertaking of enormous proportions. He had to create a cast in which all the leading characters but one appear as apes. They would have to come through not as masquerading actors but as if they were living, breathing chimpanzees, gorillas and orangutans. This meant that despite an elaborate disguise, a player's face would have to show the subtlest emotional reaction. He would have to be able to move facial muscles and change expression for camera closeups. The audience would have to accept the character as an intelligent being, capable of thought, speech, even scientific and artistic achievement.

Out of his $6 million shooting budget, Jacobs allocated a cool $1 million to makeup. Nearly 80 makeup artists—possibly the largest such force in movie history—worked under John Chambers, Fox's makeup specialist and a former surgical technician who had helped repair the faces of wounded soldiers.

The production had an impact all over Hollywood. When large-scale scenes involving 200 or more apes went before the camera, so many makeup men were pulled in that other film and TV shows found their productions paralyzed.

Makeup artists weren't all the talent needed. *Planet* called in chemists, sculptors, wigmakers. The chemists experimented with new rubber compounds to develop materials that permitted full facial mobility. At the same time, the new substances allowed the actors' skin to breathe inside the heavy outer layer of ape makeup.

"At first," a studio spokesman explained, "this makeup required six to seven hours to apply. It took three hours to remove. Obviously, no actor can be asked to show up for work at two in the morning and work through until ten at night —nobody could survive such a schedule five days a week for several months. So new techniques had to be invented to speed up putting on and taking off the disguises. Ultimately, a small army of specialists was trained to apply the makeup in three to four hours. They took one to two hours to remove it."

Each morning when they reported for work, actors spent hours in makeup chairs as foam rubber, plastic noses, anthropoid jaws and hair were applied. They had an extra set of teeth set in their jaws that protruded beyond their own facial bones. Eating was a problem. The actors had to use mirrors to guide their forks or long chopsticks past their false mandibles and into their mouths. Somehow they got used to it. "After a while, you forget you look like an ape," said Maurice Evans, who played the skeptical orangutan Dr. Zaius in *Planet*. For supervising all these efforts, makeup chief Chambers won a special Oscar—only the second award for original makeup in Academy history.

Despite the ingenious makeup job, the real key to *Planet*'s success is its biting irony. It is true that, at times, the film's attempts at satire went askew. For example, an ape's eulogy at a funeral recalls Will Rogers. It goes: "The dear departed told me, 'I never met an ape I didn't like.' " A monkey says, "Human see. Human do." A three-judge tribunal strikes a pose resembling see no evil, hear no evil, tell no evil.

But overriding these hokey gags is a first-rate science fiction fantasy embellished with penetrating commentary on human values. The picture strikes out against suppression—a timely subject in the 1960s—the intransigence of estab-

George Taylor (Charlton Heston), held in captivity along with his fellow wild humans, tries to get the attention of Zira and Dr. Zaius (Maurice Evans), talking outside his cage. That's Nova (Linda Harrison) alongside Taylor.

Determination etched in their fearsome features, ape guards charge en masse after Taylor, who has temporarily broken free from captivity.

lished authority and the vanity of ambition. And it provides a chilling allegorical prophecy about man's destiny—if he persists in rushing pell-mell toward nuclear holocaust.

Some of its morals are even quite plain to children. *Life* critic Richard Schickel says it taught his young daughter that "animals, and by implication all creatures different from her, are capable of feeling. It taught her, she tells me in her own way, that they can be scared of the unfamiliar and therefore be as foolish and as prejudiced as more familiar beings can be."

Charlton Heston, the godlike movie hero who has played Ben Hur, Moses, and John the Baptist, was the ideal choice to play George Taylor, the astronaut visitor to a subhuman world. "He represents American power . . . he has the profile of an eagle . . . he is the perfect American Adam," said Pauline Kael in the *New Yorker*. Heston, president of the Screen Actors Guild, came to Hollywood in repertory stock, where he made his debut with Katharine Cornell in "Antony and Cleopatra." After he appeared in such network television shows as "Playhouse 90" and "Studio One," Hal Wallis brought him to Hollywood to star in *Dark City* (1950). Cecil B. DeMille then put him in *The Greatest Show on Earth* (1952). But Heston's career was really launched after he won an Oscar for *Ben Hur* (1959).

As Heston is inevitably linked to the epic film, Roddy McDowall, who plays the ape archeologist Cornelius in the first and third pictures, will always be remembered as a child star. The British-born actor scored a personal triumph as the Welsh miner's son in *How Green Was My Valley* (1941). He went on to become a box office favorite with *My Friend Flicka* (1943) and *Lassie Come Home* (1943). Still later, McDowall broadened his career to photography and the theatre, appearing in such Broadway hits as "Misalliance," "No Time for Sergeants" and "Compulsion."

But the only character to play in the first three *Planet* pictures* was Kim Hunter, who portrayed the sympathetic ape scientist, Dr. Zira. A seasoned actress, she nevertheless had to endure the same arduous makeup demands as the smallest bit player. It meant getting up at 4:00 A. M. for a three-and-a-half hour makeup session, then a 90-minute dressing room ritual at night. Miss Hunter played Stella in the original Broadway production of "A Streetcar Named Desire" opposite Marlon Brando. She won an Academy Award for her screen version of the same role in 1951. But her Oscar failed to lure her to Hollywood permanently. Although she continued her film career, she returned to Broadway for such plays as "Darkness at Noon," "The Children's Hour" and "The Tender Trap."

*Roddy McDowall has also appeared in three *Planet* pictures—the first, third and fourth films. So has Natalie Trundy—a mutant in the second, a human scientist in the third, and an ape in the fourth. But none has been in all five movies.

Collared and on a leash, Taylor goes on trial for his freedom before a three-judge tribunal. Zira and Cornelius (Roddy McDowall), right foreground, are sympathetic.

In *Beneath the Planet of the Apes* (1970), astronaut Brent (James Franciscus), who has followed Taylor into space years later, finds he is in the subterranean remains of New York City after a nuclear war that destroyed civilization.

Even with three such first-rate actors heading the cast, no one at first had thought of *Planet of the Apes* in terms of a series. But when the domestic box office returns came in, they showed that *Planet* had earned a hefty $25 million—more than four times the studio's investment. The film became the second-biggest-grossing non-road show picture in 20th Century-Fox's history. So, reacting to the public's response, the studio went on to do a sequel and then a series—two's a sequel, three's a series.* And in 1972, Fox released a fourth film, *Conquest of the Planet of the Apes.*

In the original *Planet,* Taylor wins his freedom through the help of Zira and Cornelius. With Nova (Linda Harrison), a beautiful but mute cavewoman, Taylor departs for the Forbidden Zone—a kind of no man's land on the planet of the apes. In the surprise ending, they ride down a beach on horseback. Suddenly, we see the spiked crown of the Statue of Liberty looming in the foreground. So the spaceship's long voyage has taken Taylor not to a faraway world but back to his own globe. Mankind has destroyed his own civilization and become a creature inferior to the apes.

The follow-up adventure takes us to a subterranean land beneath the planet of the apes. Here, a race of super-intelligent human mutants—survivors of a nuclear war—live in the buried ruins of New York City. They communicate by thought projection, take control of people by capturing their minds, and worship an atom bomb intact on an altar in what is left of St. Patrick's Cathedral. In a moment of terror, they pull off the lifelike rubberized masks that hide their features, revealing a colored network of veins—ugly to us, but beautiful to themselves. The climax pits the simian forces in a horrendous struggle against the mutants. They battle to the death as a doomsday chain of nuclear explosions incinerates the world.

Escape from the Planet of the Apes begins after Zira, Cornelius and a third simian scientist, Milo (Sal Mineo), have found the crashed U.S. spacecraft. They blast off into space moments before the atomic catastrophe. Flying backward 20 centuries through a bend in time, they return to the present, splashing down off the California coast. Thus, they bring with them the knowledge of mankind's impending destruction.

But they are returning to a world where apes are still jungle beasts. And so when they lumber out of their spaceship and lift their helmets, they remain silent.

A shocked military welcoming group quickly dump the apes in a zoo where an angry gorilla kills Milo. Nevertheless, Cornelius and Zira continue to stay mute. "Apes at this instant cannot yet talk," Cornelius cautions Zira. "For the moment, we shall follow their example." However, when animal psychiatrists Drs. Lewis Dixon (Bradford Dillman) and Stephanie Branton (Natalie Trundy,

---

*All were moneymakers. By 1972, *Beneath the Planet of the Apes,* which cost $4.5 million to shoot, had earned $15 million. And *Escape* had grossed over $10 million.

Taylor and Nova exchange a searching look before they flee deep into the forbidden zone. "What will he find there?" Zira asks. "His destiny," replies Zauis.

In *Escape from Planet of the Apes* (1971), Milo (Sal Mineo), Zira and Cornelius, left to right, have splashed down off California and are being taken to a zoo.

Zira quickly confounds humans with her intelligence. Watching in skeptical amazement is animal psychiatrist Dr. Lewis Dixon (Bradford Dillman), while colleague Dr. Stephanie Branton (Natalie Trundy, wife of producer Arthur P. Jacobs), smiles. A zoo attendant is in background.

the wife of producer Jacobs) test them with colored blocks, the temptation to speak proves irresistible. The psychiatrist cannot understand why Zira won't eat a banana. "Because I loathe bananas," Zira tells the astonished humans.

The President is notified. He appoints an inquiry commission to find out where they came from. "We came from your future," Zira tells the astonished panel. It fails to comprehend her meaning. But the commission frees Zira and Cornelius after seeing the apes are intelligent and peaceful.

Zira and Cornelius emerge as world celebrities. They are taken to the plush Beverly Wilshire Hotel in Los Angeles and given a suite packed with cellophane-wrapped fruits and flowers. Cornelius is taken to a boxing match. He calls it "beastly." Zira appears before women's clubs, lecturing on women's liberation. "A marriage bed is meant for two," she says. "But every damn morning, it's the woman who has to make it. We have heads as well as hands. I call on man to let us use them."

The next day it is discovered that Zira is pregnant. And everything changes.

Dr. Otto Hasslein (Eric Braeden), the President's science advisor, warns that the ability of these intelligent apes to breed might eventually pose a threat to mankind and the civilization he has created.

"We have evidence," he tells the President (William Windom), "that one day talking apes will dominate the earth and destroy it by 3950." Hasslein thinks he can forestall man's downfall by stopping Zira and Cornelius from breeding. Then a searching philosophical dialogue occurs.

"Given the power to alter the future," the President asks somberly, "have we the right to use it?"

"I don't know," Hasslein says. ". . . If I urge the destruction of these apes, am I defying God's will or obeying it?"

"Do you approve of assassination?"

"Mr. President, we condoned the attempted assassination of Hitler because he was evil."

"Yes," the President replies. "But would we have approved killing him in babyhood when he was still innocent? Or killing his mother when she was still in her womb? Or slaughtering his remote ancestors?"

Eventually, Hasslein prevails on the President to convene another inquiry, this one in secret, to see if the apes have withheld vital information.

Zira and Cornelius are brought to a military base and it is at this point that we learn the strange story of man's future fall from grace. The simians tell their interrogators that what has led to the ape's domination was a plague that wiped out the world's dogs and cats.

"Man was without pets," Cornelius explains. "To man, this was intolerable . . . So humans took primitive apes as pets, primitive and dumb but 20 times more intelligent than dogs and cats. They were quartered in cages. But they lived and moved freely in human homes. They became responsive to human speech. In the course of less than three centuries, they progressed from performing mere tricks to performing mere services."

"Nothing more and less than a well-trained sheep dog can do?" Cornelius is asked.

"Can a sheep dog cook?" Cornelius says, "Or clean the house? Or do the marketing for the groceries for his mistress? Or wait on tables? Or, after three more centuries, turn the tables on his owners? Then they became alert to the concept of slavery. And when their numbers grew they became alert to slavery's antidote, which, of course, is unity. At first, they began assembling in small groups. Then, they learned the art of corporate and militant action. They learned to refuse. Of course, they just grunted their refusal. But then on an historic day which is commemorated by my species and which is fully documented in the sacred scrolls, there came Aldo. He did not grunt. He articulated. He spoke a word . . . He said 'No.' "

So the commission has learned how the apes rose to power. Now the questioning becomes tougher. The panel wants to know how the apes treated humans when they became the dominant species. Zira is reluctant to say more. But under truth serum, she reveals to her startled questioners that gorillas hunted humans for sport. The survivors were put in cages. The army used some for target practice. The rest were given to her and other doctors to dissect in the interest of medical science and perform experimental brain surgery.

In its report, the Presidential Commission finds that Zira committed actions against the human race of a sort which, if they had been committed today, would be called "atrocities." On the other hand, the commission concedes that "atrocities" might be too strong a term to apply to actions 2,000 years hence, when, it is alleged, humans will be dumb brutes. After all, humans are now using beasts for precisely the same type of medical experimentation. Nevertheless, the commission is persuaded that the ancestors of these apes could be a threat to the human race. Therefore, it recommends an abortion for Zira and sterilization for Zira and Cornelius.

The commission's decision is the beginning of the end for the apes. While they are held incommunicado in military custody, Cornelius becomes enraged when an orderly calls Zira "monkey," He knocks the orderly down, accidentally killing him. They flee from the base and Drs. Dixon and Branton hide them with Armando (Ricardo Montalban), a sympathetic circus animal trainer. Near the cage of a chimpanzee who has just had a child, Zira gives birth. Armando, proud to have helped bring Zira's baby into the world, puts a St. Christopher's medal around his neck. Then, there is a brief but touching scene when Zira goes into the chimp's cage and the two mothers and babies stare at each other over centuries of evolving time.

The serenity is short-lived. With police and the army in pursuit, Zira and Cornelius leave the circus with their baby. Drs. Dixon and Branton give Cornelius a gun and take him and his family to a mothballed tanker in a deserted shipyard. But police quickly pick up their trail and as they begin closing in, Hasslein reaches the ship first. He has taken a revolver, determined to kill the apes—despite the commission's more merciful decision.

Slowly, carefully, the scientist stalks down the corridors. Cornelius has left Zira to go to the bridge. And so, when Hasslein encounters Zira and her baby on deck, she is alone.

"I see you have your baby, Zira," Hasslein says. "The Presidential Commission has empowered me to take it in my care."

She turns to run. Hasslein draws his gun and shoots her in the back. The baby, swaddled in a blanket, falls to the deck and Hasslein opens fire again.

High on the bridge, Cornelius has looked down at this slaughter of the innocents. With the gun his psychiatrist friends have given him, he fires two bullets into Hasslein's chest. Then police guns explode. As their bullets rip into him, Cornelius reels over the railing and crashes onto the deck near the dying Zira. With her last strength, Zira throws her baby overboard into the water, staggers over to Cornelius' body and topples across him.

But the movie is not over. There is one last surprise. The film cuts to the circus,

In *Conquest of the Planet of the Apes* (1972), Caesar (Roddy McDowall) is the intelligent ape who leads a revolt of his enslaved fellows.

where trainer Armando is admiring a baby chimpanzee. It seems to be mumbling something. Armando smiles. "You're an intelligent creature," he says. "But then so were your mother and father." The little chimp, wearing a St. Christopher's medal around his neck mutters, "Mama, mama, mama."*

*In *Conquest,* the child becomes a man. The chimp (Roddy McDowall), called Caesar, joins his fellow simians and leads them in an uprising against their human oppressors—an obvious attempt to ape the black revolution. The picture got a mixed reception. Some critics said it was "fun." Others panned it, calling it a "shoddy, witless" film. In the New York City area, five reviewers liked it, three turned thumbs down, and four said it was not bad but not good either.

PLANET OF THE APES SERIES

1. *Planet of the Apes.* 20th Century-Fox, 1968, Franklin J. Schaffner.
    Charlton Heston (as George Taylor), Roddy McDowall (as Cornelius), Kim
    Hunter (as Zira), Maurice Evans (as Dr. Zaius), James Whitmore, James Daly,
    Linda Harrison (as Nova), Robert Gunner, Lou Wagner, Woodrow Parfrey, Jeff
    Burton, Buck Kartalian, Norman Burton, Wright King, Paul Lambert. 112 minutes.

2. *Beneath the Planet of the Apes.* 20th Century-Fox, 1970, Ted Post.
    James Franciscus, Kim Hunter, Maurice Evans, Linda Harrison, Paul Richards,
    Victor Buono, James Gregory, Jeff Corey, Natalie Trundy, Thomas Gomez,
    David Watson (as Cornelius), Don Pedro Colley, Tod Andrews, Gregory Sierra,
    Eldon Burke, Lou Wagner, Charlton Heston. 93 minutes.

3. *Escape from the Planet of the Apes.* 20th Century-Fox, 1971, Don Taylor.
    Roddy McDowall, Kim Hunter, Bradford Dillman, Natalie Trundy, Eric Bra-
    eden, William Windom, Sal Mineo, Albert Salmi, Jason Evers. John Randolph,
    Ricardo Montalban, Steve Roberts, M. Emmet Walsh, Roy E. Glenn, Sr., Peter
    Forster, Norman Burton, William Woodson, Tom Lowell, Bill Bonds, Donald
    Elson. 98 minutes.

4. *Conquest of the Planet of the Apes.* 20th Century-Fox, 1972, J. Lee Thompson.
    Roddy McDowall (as Caesar), Don Murray, Natalie Trundy (as Lisa), Hari
    Rhodes, Severn Darden, Lou Wagner, John Randolph, Asa Maynor, H. M.
    Wynant, David Chow, Buck Kartalian, John Dennis, Gordon Jump, Dick Span-
    gler, Joyce Haber, Hector Soucy, Paul Comi, Ricardo Montalban (as Armando).
    87 minutes.

Gene Autry, the singing cowboy with the oil baron's income, doffs his hat atop his stallion, Champion, "the world's wonder horse."

GENE AUTRY

Public Cowboy Number One
(1937)

Screenplay by Oliver Drake based on a story by Bernard McConville. Camera, Jack Marta. Editors, Lester Orlebeck and George Heid. Songs: "Wanderers of the Waste Land," "The West Ain't What It Used to Be," "I Picked up the Trail," "Defective Detective from Brooklyn" and "Old Buckaroo." Songs by: Felix Bernard, Paul Francis Webster, Oliver Drake and Fleming Allen. Music director, Raoul Kraushaar. Directed by Joseph Kane. A Republic production and release. 69 minutes.

Gene Autry	GENE AUTRY
Frog Millhouse	SMILEY BURNETTE
Helen Morgan	ANN RUTHERFORD
Sheriff Matt Doniphon	WILLIAM FARNUM
Eustace Quackenbush	JAMES C. MORTON
Justice	FRANK LARUE
Thad Slaughter	MASTON WILLIAMS
Jack Shannon	ARTHUR LOFT
Stubby	FRANKIE MARVIN
Jim Shannon	HOUSE PETERS, JR.

Ezra	MILBURN MORANTE
Steve	KING MAJAVE
Bidwell	HAL PRICE
Larry	JACK INGRAM
Collins, pilot	RAY BENNETT
Townsmen	FRANK ELLIS
	GEORGE PLUES
Henchman	JAMES MASON
Radio Announcer	DOUGLAS EVANS
Extra	BOB BURNS

It all started, Gene Autry recalls, on a rainy night in the Chelsea, Oklahoma, railroad station. He was then a 22-year-old relief telegraph operator. On quiet nights, he used to while away the hours strumming a guitar and singing to himself. One night, an older man happened by to send a wire. He stayed to listen to the young man.

"You belong in Hollywood, boy, playing the guitar—not that telegraph instrument," the older man said. "Your heart ain't in it. Why don't you get yourself a job singing on the radio?"

Autry took the remark casually—as an offhand compliment. That is, until he read the stranger's signature on the telegram. The older man was Will Rogers.

If that sounds suspiciously like a tale concocted by Horatio Alger or Bill Stern, Autry to this day swears it's true. In fact, he says, it gave him all the encouragement he needed.

Rogers did not know it, but he had put up an invisible ladder for Autry to climb. Few men have ever made a swifter ascent to success.

Within a few years, Autry's name would be as well known as Rogers' in the small towns of America—first as a radio balladeer, then as the singing cowboy of the movies. The sandy-haired, blue-eyed, gum-chewing vocalist soon became the top box office star of his field. Personal appearances in rodeos and a string of hit records broadened his national following. With his ever-increasing income, he built a vast financial empire that ranged from oil wells to radio stations to a major league baseball team. By 1950, his holdings were estimated at $4–7 million. By 1970, his worth was figured at over $100 million.

Yet, his fans knew him only as the homespun, straight-shooting cowboy of the plains. In private life, he may have had a tycoon's income. But to the millions of kids who saw him atop his magnificent horse Champion at Saturday matinees, he was Gene Autry, the tough but oh-so-gentle range rider.

Many adults never understood his meteoric rise. They found his acting weak, his personality colorless, his voice lackluster. But youngsters were taken by his friendly, natural, honest manner. They admired his manliness tempered by just

Autry strums his guitar and sings along with Frances Grant in *Red River Valley* (1936). The Texas-born Autry, whose records have sold more than 20 million copies, has cut such western classics as "Mexicali Rose," "Tumbling Tumbleweeds" and "South of the Border."

The Sons of the Pioneers join Autry in a tune from *The Big Show* (1936). That's Smiley Burnette on the left. Do you recognize the guitarist standing on the right? It's Roy Rogers (under the name Dick Weston), who would become Autry's movie rival after World War II.

enough shyness. Still, the quesion of why Autry made it has always intrigued writers.

- William Everson and George N. Fenin, co-authors of *The Western,* thought his popularity was due, in part, to his ability to keep any hard-nosed capitalist tendencies in his personality from showing up on the screen or in public. "He had the happy knack," they wrote, "of being able to hide his shrewdness behind the amiable facade of the hillbilly singer."

- Archer Winsten, the *New York Post*'s movie reviewer, credited his rise to his appealing ordinariness. Said Winsten: "He was a true representation of the common man with a nasal twang."

- Alva Johnson, a free-lancer for the *Saturday Evening Post,* said Autry's poor acting ability was only a negligible flaw, later an asset. "Like Gary Cooper and Jimmy Stewart," said Johnson, "Autry has the kind of awkwardness and embarrassment that audiences like."

- Mary Braggiotti, a feature writer for the *New York Post,* thought that Autry, unlike other heroes, never appeared out of reach. "He seemed," she wrote, "an understandable, understanding man, almost an attainable dream."

Autry himself was somewhat mystified by his rise to fame. But he always remembered where the source of his great appeal lay. "I know that I owe about all I have to the devotion and support of the kids," Autry said. ". . . To young-

In this uncharacteristic pose, Gene seems to be right at home with Adele Mara. Oh, how the kids would groan if they ever found out. Scene is from *Twilight on the Rio Grande* (1947).

sters, Gene Autry is not simply a human being, but a kind of superman. They accept anything he does or says as the right thing. That's why Gene Autry has to be so careful about the way he handles himself."

So, to preserve his spotless reputation, Autry adopted what he called his cowboy's code. In 93 movies from 1934 to 1953, he never shot first, hit first, hit a smaller man, took a drink, or smoked. He never took unfair advantage of anyone, never broke his word, rarely kissed a leading lady.*

"I think the image was good for me," he said. "My movies were always clean . . . Parents didn't need a baby sitter. For 50 cents, they could send their kids down to see my pictures and know they would be entertained wholesomely." It was estimated that his movies were seen by 40 million persons in 10,000 theatres in the United States and Canada.

But Autry had something else going for him besides his Mr. Clean character. He added a new dimension to the grade-B western. Recognized as the first successful singing cowboy,** he sprinkled ballads between the action and comedy scenes. The tunes—some of them simple but haunting prairie melodies like "Tumbling Tumbleweeds" and "Back in the Saddle," and other romantic ballads like "Mexicali Rose" and "South of the Border"—found a welcome reception. Autry's unique pictures became so popular, they gave rise to a caravan of imitators—Dick Foran, Tex Ritter, Bob Baker, Jack Randall and later Jimmy Wakely, Eddie Dean and Rex Allen. But none could match the magic that Autry made.

In his later years, with characteristic modesty, he tossed it all off to the happy accident of timing. "I happened to come along in an era when movies were changing," he said. "That was about 1934. There was a break between the great silent screen stars—Buck Jones, Tom Mix and Hoot Gibson—and the new crop that was to come along. I was the first of the singing cowboys. If I'd come into the picture five years earlier or five years later, I might not have succeeded . . . As I look over my life, I'd say the most important thing is to be at the right place at the right time."

For a cowboy actor, Autry certainly was at the right place at the right time when he was born. Movie fans are often disappointed to find out that their saddle hero really came from the east. Autry, though not a cowhand, was a true son of the west. Born in Tioga, Texas, in 1907, Orvon Gene Autry was the child of

*There were exceptions. He kissed Hope Manning in one of his earlier pictures. "Thereafter," said film historian William Everson, "he saw to it that any such activity took place off screen or quite inadvertently—as when he and his leading lady would be pushed into an embrace by the nudging of an obliging, match-making horse."

**A number of actors actually put songs into westerns before Autry—most notably Ken Maynard. Some say John Wayne was first because of a dubbed effort in a western series called *Singing Sandy*. Bob Steele also sang briefly as early as 1930. And Warner Baxter crooned in *In Old Arizona* (1929), the first talking picture filmed outdoors. But movie historians usually credit Autry for adding songs to cowboy films because he was the first to stress or exploit the musical aspect of his movies. Nevertheless, it is probably more accurate to call him the first "successful" singing cowboy.

parents of French-Irish descent. His father was a cattle buyer, tenant farmer and non-denominational circuit-riding preacher. After the family moved to Oklahoma, young Autry learned to ride horses and he sang at the local entertainments, with a traveling medicine show and at his father's church services.

At 16, he went to work as a railroad baggage hustler, then graduated to a job as relief telegrapher on the Frisco line. One day, he bought a guitar for $1 down and 50 cents a month and learned to sing and yodel to his own accompaniment. It was after his brief but inspirational meeting with Will Rogers that ambition hit Autry. He quit the railroad and headed east.

In New York, recording executives told him to go back home and get some radio experience. He did and he was a local sensation for KVOO Tulsa as "Oklahoma's Yodeling Cowboy." With a year's work under his belt, he returned to New York and recorded "That Silver-Haired Daddy of Mine," a song he wrote with a friend—Jimmy Long, a train dispatcher—during his railroad days. It was an immediate hit—it has since sold 5 million records—and led to weekly appearances on the "National Barn Dance Hour" over Chicago's WLS. That was 1931. His network (NBC) radio show gave him national exposure and within four years, he was Hollywood-bound. He made his film debut in *In Old Santa Fe* (1934) starring Ken Maynard. Then, in 1935, he sang in *Tumbling Tumbleweeds,* his first starring feature movie. Audiences responded enthusiastically to the idea of seeing the hero take time out from chasing outlaws to sing a song. The movie became so popular that Republic Pictures producer Nat Levine signed Autry to a long-term contract. And so began the musical western.

With Smiley Burnette* as his sidekick, Autry, who cast himself as "Gene Autry,"** appeared with a wide range of stars. They included Buster Crabbe, Kermit Maynard, Jimmy Durante, Chill Wills, Jack Holt, Clayton Moore, Max Terhune (Autry's M.C. on "the National Barn Dance") and George (Gabby) Hayes. There were badmen Glenn Strange, Lon Chaney, Jr. and Roy Barcroft. There were actresses Jane Withers, Barbara Pepper, Ann Miller, Ann Rutherford and Mary Beth Hughes. And, of course, there were the Sons of the Pioneers and

*Lester Alvin (Smiley) Burnette, who made his film debut with Autry, was an old pal from the "National Barn Dance" show. In fact, it was Autry who got Burnette on the program. He offered Burnette a job after hearing him on a Tuscola, Illinois, radio station. He lured Burnette away for $35 a week, twice as much as Burnette was getting to run the one-man station. Burnette's talent ranged from playing 52 musical instruments (he was a one-man band) to composing songs (he wrote more than 350 tunes including "It's My Lazy Day," "Hominy Grits," and "Riding Down the Canyon"). But movie fans knew him best as the chubby, sloppily dressed, happy-go-lucky Frog Millhouse, whose voice ranged from a deep bass to a high-pitched treble. Even as Autry's sidekick, he became so popular he made the top-ten cowboy list in 1940 and stayed on for 12 straight years. Later, he played comedy relief for Roy Rogers, and Charles Starrett in the *Durango Kid* series. When his film career ended, he played the railroad engineer in TV's "Petticoat Junction." Burnette died of leukemia in 1967 at the age of 56.
**Except in *Mystery Mountain* (1934), a serial, and *Shooting High* (1940), in which he played a movie star.

The hombre with the bullet belt across his chest is Noah Beery, Wallace's brother and one of the silent screen's most celebrated heavies. Here he cuts up with Autry and Burnette in *Mexicali Rose* (1939).

"Oh, wow!" Smiley Burnette howls as Joe Stauch, Jr. tightens a press in *Under Fiesta Stars* (1941).

the Cass County Boys. Even Elmo Lincoln, who created Tarzan on the silent screen in 1918, played in two films *(Colorado Sunset* and *Blue Montana Skies* in 1939).

With each picture, more emphasis was given to the musical scenes until they sometimes dominated and slowed down the action. One classic gag tells how Autry, facing disaster in a movie, starts talking out loud to himself. "Them bandits," Gene says, "have beaten mah mother, ravished mah girl, burned down mah house, killed mah best friend and stolen all mah prize cattle. Ah'm gonna get 'em if'n it's the last thing ah do. But first, folks, ah'm gonna sing ya a little song."

But usually there was a good balance, and the musical horse operas packed the movie houses. From 1937 until he enlisted in the Army Air Force in 1942, theatre-owners named him the top box office star of western pictures.* He was voted among the first ten box office stars in the entire industry, becoming the first western actor to be in this group. All the while Autry kept busy in other areas. Singing for Columbia Records, his discs outsold Crosby's three to one. He had his own radio show, "The Melody Ranch." He toured the country with his Gene Autry Rodeo each year. His fan mail of 40,000 letters a month—60 percent of it from females—exceeded Garbo's, Gable's and Shirley Temple's.

To add to his international fame, he made trips to England and Ireland, where few had ever seen a cowboy. Throngs cheered as he rode his handsome chestnut stallion Champion** through the streets of London and Dublin.

In his troupe were six American Indians and Autry is fond of telling about the unique way they worked out paying their bills in an unfamiliar foreign currency.

"We all had a lot of trouble keeping track of the exchange rates," Autry said. "But those boys didn't even bother. They just filled their pockets with shillings —a shilling then was about 15 cents. Well, whenever they'd take a taxi ride or go into a shop to buy something, they'd just pay the bill with a shilling. And when the cabby or merchant would protest, they'd add another shilling or so on until the protests stopped."

In 1942, Autry's career took a three-year hiatus. Over the protest of his studio, he joined the service, selling bonds, recruiting and putting on radio shows for the troops. Later, determined to play a more direct role in the war, he got into the Air Ferry Command. To do it, Autry learned to fly on his own time. His job was

*From 1946 to 1954, Autry ranked second to Roy Rogers. ("Top box office star," by the way means most money earned for exhibitors—rather than for the actor.)

**Billed as "the world's wonder horse," Champion became almost as famous as his rider. Actually, there were three Champions—all Tennessee walking horses from the same strain and the same farm near Nashville. The original was a horse named Lindy because he was foaled on the day Lindbergh flew the Atlantic. Before Autry got him, Tom Mix had used him in his movies.

Autry swaps stories with Jimmy Durante in *Melody Ranch* (1940). The brunette in riding togs is Ann Miller.

Autry disarms a scowling Denver Pyle as Gail Davis watches in *Goldtown Ghost Riders* (1953).

co-piloting giant cargo planes hauling men and supplies to far-flung bases in China, Burma and India.

After the war, he found that Republic was now featuring Roy Rogers, who had played bit parts in Autry's pictures. So in 1947, he formed his own company, Flying A Productions. He began making his own movies and released them through Columbia Pictures.

Autry himself would be hard-pressed to pick a favorite from the long list of films he made over his 19-year movie career. But one that typically contrasted pretty tunes with a lively plot and comedy scenes was *Public Cowboy Number One* (1937). The title has no connection with the story. But it's worth looking at to recapture some of the flavor of the early Autry pictures.

The movie opens with a sequence showing big city crooks bringing modern cattle rustling techniques to the prairies. In a scene that must have seemed then like a sophisticated James Bond caper, we see rustlers operating a mobile slaughter house. A plane spots the herd and radios its location to trucks hauling men and horses. Riders quickly round up the cattle and butchers clout them over the head as they come through a chute. They remove their hides, quarter them and load the beef aboard refrigerated trucks for shipping to a packing house. Then, it's a quick fadeout before Sheriff Matt Doniphon (William Farnum) and Gene Autry, his first deputy, come to the scene.

The slick operation has brought mounting headaches to the sheriff. The raids, combined with a rancher's killing, have brought a storm of protests. Headlines in the *Prairie County Courier* blare: "Rustlers Strike Again. Another Herd Vanishes Overnight." "Reign of Terror Sweeps Prairie County." "Sheriff Doniphon No Match for Modern Rustlers."

Newspaper editor Helen Morgan (Ann Rutherford) thinks the sheriff's old-time methods are outmoded. She is campaigning to have him ousted.

"Maybe I am getting too old," the sheriff mutters after reading her articles. But Autry won't hear of his boss quitting. "If the town would only give us modern equipment to work with," Gene says, "we could get results. You can't catch high-speed trucks and airplanes with a horse and buggy."

Fuming, Autry storms into the tiny newspaper office. "Where's that editor who's been writing those things about Sheriff Doniphon?" he asks.

"Why?" asks editor Morgan.

"Because I'm going to poke him right in the nose," Autry says.

"Go ahead and poke," Miss Morgan says. "I'm the editor."

That takes Gene down a notch or two. "Well, I'm sorry," Autry says, changing his tune. "But you've been printing some pretty mean things about the sheriff . . . You've been unfair."

"Have the thieves been caught?" Miss Morgan asks. "Is rustling still going on?" Silence from Autry. "Very well, then," she says. "The *Courier* prints facts."

Autry tries to cool Miss Morgan off by crooning a tune—"The West Ain't What It Used to Be." But this fiery newshen won't be sidetracked.

"Why don't you try that on the rustlers," she suggests. "You might sing them to sleep."

With that sarcastic remark ringing in his ears, Autry starts investigating the packing houses. His less than brilliant sidekick Frog (Smiley Burnette) thinks he has found an important clue when he discovers blood on the floor. But packing house boss Jack Shannon (Arthur Loft) quickly enlightens Frog. "What do you think you'll find around a packing house—milk?"

Nevertheless, Autry demands to see the cattle hides. Their brands would show what ranch they came from and prove they were stolen. Shannon tells Autry the hides are in his warehouse, some miles away.

Before he can get there, Shannon warns his pals via a shortwave set. They toss the hides on a truck. As they leave, a gun battle breaks out and the sheriff takes a bullet in the shoulder. But Frog has spotted the assailant and when Frog later sees him in town, Autry arrests him.

Gene rushes to the newspaper office to see the paper gets the story. But Miss Morgan is one step ahead of him and she shows him the next day's headline already set in type: "Rustling Suspect Arrested." That immediately starts Autry breaking into song again—"I Picked Up the Trail / When I Found You . . ."

"That was lovely," says Miss Morgan, dropping her guard for the moment.

"Sounds a little bit better under the moon," says Autry.

"Yes," Miss Morgan says, regaining her iceberg demeanor, "where you wouldn't be disturbing anyone."

Meanwhile, the rustlers are concerned that their arrested pal might talk. They slip up to the jail, call him to his barred window and club him to death.

The killing is the last straw as far as the ranchers are concerned. They demand that the sheriff resign. And they call in a nationally famous private detective agency run by Eustace P. Quackenbush (James Morton).

Quackenbush, a kind of poor man's W.C. Fields, arrives to a great ceremonious welcome. Carrying signs reading "Law and Order Forever," most of the county's citizens turn out to greet him. Those who can't come stay close to their radios to hear Quackenbush's arrival address.

"My friends, ranchers and citizens," the distinguished sleuth says. "I deem it a great honor to be chosen to bring law and order to Prairie County. My aides are all trained in scientific criminology . . . Under my generalship, they have solved crimes that baffled the police departments of all nations. And I promise to rid this part of the country of outlaws and raiders. In fact, the news of my men and I being here in Prairie County has probably caused half of them to flee in fear of their lives. Remember, my friends, the Quackenbush motto—bad news for bad men."

Then, Frog adds a light touch to the reception with a ditty called "Defective Detective from Brooklyn," during which he makes lightning costume changes to become Sherlock Holmes and Charlie Chan.

Even while the ceremonies are going on, the rustlers are taking advantage of the fact that there isn't a cowboy on the range. That is, all except one. After his song, the underestimated Frog slips off to the prairie, disguises himself as a cow and joins a herd. Then, as the crooks move in, Frog uses a portable shortwave set to warn Autry. Gene races to the microphone to send an SOS. "This is Gene Autry—calling all cowboys." He warns them that rustlers are on the loose.

Quackenbush joins the pursuit. But his car and motorcycle men quickly get bogged down trying to cross a stream. Their tear gas bombs are jarred loose and they disappear behind great clouds of gas as the sheriff, Autry and their riders gallop by. With the help of an army of cowboys converging from all directions, they quickly round up the rustlers—except for their boss, Shannon. He kidnaps Miss Morgan to use her as a hostage and speeds off in his car. But Sheriff Doniphon, relying on his tried and trusted ability as a marksman, shoots out the tires. Shannon, using Miss Morgan as a shield, forces Doniphon to drop his gun. But as he is about to shoot the lawman, Autry rushes onto the scene and fires a bullet into his arm.

"Looks like pretty good teamwork for a couple of old timers," Doniphon says. And so the sheriff has proven that old-fashioned ways still have their place on the range. Autry, with Miss Morgan riding side saddle with him, canters off singing "Wanderers of the Wasteland." As the riders pass Quackenbush, still mired in the stream with gas bombs going off, Frog quips, "As a detective, you'd make a good bartender."

Autry made his final starring movie,* *Last of the Pony Riders,* in 1953. Convinced of the rising popularity of television, he adapted his movie unit to produce his television series. Using an old-time movie ranch he bought as a locale, Autry made 91 half-hour westerns, including a group in color. He also produced several series in which he did not star. They included "The Range Rider," "Annie Oakley," "Buffalo Bill Jr.," "The Adventures of Champion," "Cavalcade of America" and the first 39 episodes of "Death Valley Days."

At the same time, he started devoting more time to other business ventures. He acquired the major interest in California's Golden West Broadcasting Company (four radio stations and a TV station). He bought a 10 percent interest in two Phoenix newspapers–the *Gazette* and the *Arizona Republic*–and 25 oil wells in Texas. His Midas touch became legendary. Two movie friends drilled for oil in Texas. They got only dry wells. Autry sank 17 wells within 10 miles. All struck oil.

*Autry guest-starred in *The Silent Treatment* (1968), but it was never released.

Diverting his holdings, he bought interests in a 100,000-acre ranch at Winslow, Arizona, a cattle ranch at Florence, Arizona, a 3,200-acre spread at Dublin, Texas, and another of 2,300 acres at Berwyn, Oklahoma. In a gesture of hospitality toward its new neighbor, Berwyn changed its name to Gene Autry.

Autry's empire was just beginning. He bought controlling stock in the Madison Square Garden Rodeo, music publishing companies, motels and hotels, including the Gene Autry Hotel in Phoenix. Royalties poured in from a million Gene Autry comic books sold each year and from nearly 50 products bearing his name—jeans, hats, boots, billfolds, lassoes. By 1965, he controlled eight corporations. Perhaps his most famous holdings are his majority interest in the California Angels baseball team* and his minority interest in the Los Angeles Rams professional football team.

While he wheeled and dealed, Autry kept making records. Nine of his tunes sold over a million discs and earned a gold record for him. They are: "Tumbling Tumbleweeds," "South of the Border," "Mexicali Rose," "Back in the Saddle Again," "Silver-Haired Daddy," "You Are My Sunshine," "Here Comes Santa Claus," "Peter Cottontail" and "Rudolph the Red-Nosed Reindeer." "Rudolph," which has gone over the 10 million mark, is his all-time best-seller.

With all his vast wealth, he is still happily married to Ina Mae Spivey of Duncan, Oklahoma. The couple, who have no children, recently celebrated their fortieth wedding anniversary on their 125-acre "Melody Ranch" overlooking the San Fernando Valley.

Today, Autry no longer sings or appears before the camera. But even in his mid-60s, he still seems fit in the western style clothes and boots he always wears. Looking back on it all, a reporter once asked, is there any nostalgic moment that stands out from his early days? It was not something from his Hollywood days or his radio or record career, but an incident in Ireland that Autry recalled:

I think the greatest thrill I ever had, came to me during my trip to the British Isles in 1939. There was a large balcony outside the room I had in Dublin. In the evening when I returned to the hotel after the show there would usually be a crowd below in the square. They'd call up and ask me to come out and sing a song. And I always did.

The last night of my stay, the crowd was especially big—must have been about 7,500 or so. And when they called to me, I went out and, as usual, sang a song. Afterward, I made a little speech about how much I enjoyed being there and so on.

---

*Autry once said that his unrealized ambition was playing big league baseball. As a young man, he played semi-pro ball in Oklahoma. But he had to give it up for telegraphy, which paid him $125 a month to the $50 he could get on the diamond.

Well, for a moment, there was dead silence. And then, all of a sudden, a couple of people started to sing. Then, more and more joined them until the whole square was filled with the sound.

They were serenading *me*. And their song was "Come Back to Erin. " I can tell you I still get a lump when I remember that.

GENE AUTRY FILMS

1. *In Old Santa Fe.* Mascot, 1934. David Howard.
   Ken Maynard, Evalyn Knapp, H. B. Warner, Kenneth Thomson, Wheeler Oakman, George (Gabby) Hayes, George Chesebro, Smiley Burnette, Gene Autry, George Burton, Edward Hearn, Stanley Blystone, Horace B. Carpenter, Jack Kirk, Jack Rockwell, Frank Ellis, Jim Corey, Tarzan (Maynard's horse). 63 minutes.

2. *Mystery Mountain.* Mascot, 1934. Otto Brower and B. Reeves Eason.
   Ken Maynard, Verna Hillie, Edmund Cobb, Sid Saylor, Alan Bridge, Edward Earle, Hooper Atchley, Edward Hearn, Lynton Brent, Bob Kortman, Tom London, George Chesebro, Lafe McKee, Frank Ellis, Art Mix, Wally (Hal Taliaferro) Wales, Philo McCullough, Smiley Burnette, Gene Autry. Serial 12 chapters. 25 reels.

3. *The Phantom Empire.* Mascot, 1935. Otto Brower and B. Reeves Eason.
   Gene Autry, Lester (Smiley) Burnette, Champion, Frankie Darro, Betsy King Ross, Dorothy Christy, Wheeler Oakman, J. Frank Glendon, Bill Moore (later Peter Potter), Warner Richmond, Edward Piel, Sr., Charles K. French, Hal Taliaferro, Stanley Blystone, and the Scientific City of Murania, Jack Carlyle, Don Brodie, Henry Hall, Buffalo Bill, Jr. (Jay Wilsey), George Magrill, Tracy Layne, Bruce Mitchell, Bob Card, Bob Burns, Frank Ellis. Serial 12 chapters. 25 Reels. Feature version released in 1940 as *Radio Ranch* and *Men with Steel Faces.*

4. *Tumbling Tumbleweeds.* Republic, 1935. Joseph Kane.
   Gene Autry, Smiley Burnette, Lucile Browne, Norma Taylor, George Hayes, Edward Hearn, Jack Rockwell, Frankie Marvin, George Chesebro, Eugene Jackson, Charles King, Tom London, Slim Whittaker, Cornelius Keefe, Cliff Lyons, Tracy Layne. 57 minutes.

5. *Melody Trail.* Republic, 1935, Joseph Kane.
   Gene Autry, Smiley Burnette, Ann Rutherford, Wade Boteler, Alan Bridge, Willy Castello, Marie Quillan, Fern Emmett, Gertrude Messinger, Tracy Layne, Jane Barnes, Ione Reed. 60 minutes.

6. *The Sagebrush Troubadour.* Republic, 1935, Joseph Kane.
   Gene Autry, Barbara Pepper, Smiley Burnette, Fred Kelsey, Hooper Atchley, J. Frank Glendon, Tom London, Julian Rivero, Denny Meadows (Dennis Moore). 54 minutes.

7.　*The Singing Vagabond.* Republic, 1935, Carl Pierson.
Gene Autry, Ann Rutherford, Smiley Burnette, Barbara Pepper, Niles Welch, Frank LaRue, Warner Richmond, Charles King, Henry Roquemore, Grace Goodall, Bob Burns, Chief Big Tree, Chief Thundercloud, Elaine Shepherd. 52 minutes.

8.　*Red River Valley* (TV title: *Man of the Frontier*). Republic, 1936, B. Reeves Eason.
Gene Autry, Smiley Burnette, Frances Grant, Boothe Howard, Jack Kennedy, Champion, Sam Flint, George Chesebro, Charles King, Eugene Jackson, Edward Hearn, Frank LaRue, Lloyd Ingraham, Hank Bell. 56 minutes.

9.　*Comin' Round the Mountain.* Republic, 1936, Mack V. Wright.
Gene Autry, Ann Rutherford, Smiley Burnette, LeRoy Mason, Champion, Raymond Brown, Ken Cooper, Tracy Layne, Robert McKenzie, John Ince, Frank Lackteen, Steve Clark, Frank Ellis, Hank Bell, Dick Botiller. 55 minutes.

10.　*The Singing Cowboy.* Republic, 1936, Mack Wright.
Gene Autry, Smiley Burnette, Lois Wilde, Lon Chaney, Jr., Ann Gillis, Champion, John Van Pelt, Earle Hodgins, Earl Eby, Ken Cooper, Wes Warner, Snowflake (Fred Toones), Jack Rockwell, Tracy Layne, Jack Kirk, Frankie Marvin, Oscar Gahan, Harvey Clark, Harrison Greene, Audrey Davis, George Pearce, Charlie McAvoy, Alfred P. James, Pat Caron. 56 minutes.

11.　*Guns and Guitars.* Republic, 1936. Joseph Kane.
Gene Autry, Dorothy Dix, Smiley Burnette, Tom London, Charles King, Champion, J. P. McGowan, Earle Hodgins, Frankie Marvin, Eugene Jackson, Jack Rockwell, Ken Cooper, Tracy Layne, Wes Warner, Jim Corey, Pascale Perry, Bob Burns, Jack Kirk, Frank Stravenger, Harrison Greene, Jack Don, Audrey Davis, Al Taylor, George Morrell, Sherry Tansey, Jack Evans, George Plues, Denver Dixon. 56 minutes.

12.　*Oh, Susannah!* Republic, 1936, Joseph Kane.
Gene Autry, Smiley Burnette, Frances Grant, Clara Kimball Young, Earle Hodgins, Donald Kirke, Boothe Howard, Carl Stockdale, Frankie Marvin, Ed Piel, Sr., The Light Crust Doughboys Band. 59 minutes.

13.　*Ride, Ranger, Ride.* Republic, 1936, Joseph Kane.
Gene Autry, Smiley Burnette, Kay Hughes, Monte Blue, George Lewis, Max Terhune, Robert E. Homans, Lloyd Whitlock, Chief Thundercloud, Tennessee Ramblers, Iron Eyes Cody, Sunny Chorre, Sky Eagle, Shooting Star, Arthur Singley, Greg Whitespear, Robert Thomas, Frankie Marvin, Bud Pope, Nelson McDowell. 63 minutes.

14.　*The Big Show.* Republic, 1936, Mack V. Wright.
Gene Autry, Smiley Burnette, Kay Hughes, Sally Payne, Roy Rogers, Sons of the

Pioneers; Charles Judels, Max Terhune, William Newell, The Jones Boys, The Beverly Hills Billies, The Light Crust Doughboys Band, Rex King, Harry Worth, Antrim Short, June Johnson, Grace Durkin, Mary Russell, Christine Maple, Jack O'Shea, Art Mix, I. Stanford Jolley, Vic Lacardo, Jeanne Lafayette, Richard Beach, Frances Morris, Helen Servis, Horace Carpenter, Martin Stevenson, Southern Methodist University 50, Governor Scholz of Florida, Capt. Leonard Pack, Lady Godiva, Sally Rand. 70 minutes.

15. *The Old Corral.* Republic, 1936, Joseph Kane.
Gene Autry, Smiley Burnette, Hope Manning, Roy Rogers, Sons of the Pioneers, Champion, Lon Chaney, Jr., Cornelius Keefe, John Bradford, Milburn Morante, Abe Lufton, Merrill McCormick, Charles Sullivan, Buddy Roosevelt, Oscar and Elmer, Lynton Brent, Frankie Marvin. 56 minutes.

16. *Round-up Time in Texas.* Republic, 1937, Joseph Kane.
Gene Autry, Smiley Burnette, Maxine Doyle, The Cabin Kids, Champion, LeRoy Mason, Earle Hodgins, Dick Wessel, Buddy Williams, Cornie Anderson, Frankie Marvin. 58 minutes.

17. *Git Along, Little Dogies.* Republic, 1937, Joseph Kane.
Gene Autry, Smiley Burnette, Maple City Four, Judith Allen, Weldon Heyburn, William Farnum, Willie Fung, Carleton Young, Will and Gladys Ahearn, The Cabin Kids, G. Raymond Nye, Frankie Marvin, George Morrell, Horace B. Carpenter, Rose Plummer, Earl Dwire, Lynton Brent, Jack Kirk, Al Taylor, Frank Ellis, Jack C. Smith, Murdock Mac Quarrie, Oscar Gahan, Monte Montague, Sam McDaniel, Eddie Parker, Bob Burns. 62 minutes.

18. *Rootin' Tootin' Rhythm.* Republic, 1937, Mack V. Wright.
Gene Autry, Smiley Burnette, Armida, Monte Blue, Al Clauser and his Oklahoma Outlaws, Hal Taliaferro, Ann Pendleton, Max Hoffman, Jr., Charles King, Frankie Marvin. 60 minutes.

19. *Yodelin' Kid from Pine Ridge.* Republic, 1937, Joseph Kane.
Gene Autry, Betty Bronson, Smiley Burnette, LeRoy Mason, Charles Middleton, Russell Simpson, Tennessee Ramblers, Jack Dougherty, Guy Wilkerson, Frankie Marvin, Henry Hall, Snowflake, Jack Kirk, Bob Burns, Al Taylor, George Morrell, Lew Meehan, Jim Corey, Jack Ingram, Art Dillard, Art Mix, Bud Osborne, Oscar Gahan. 62 minutes.

20. *Public Cowboy No. 1.* Republic, 1937, Joseph Kane.
Gene Autry, Smiley Burnette, Ann Rutherford, William Farnum, Arthur Loft, Frankie Marvin, House Peters, Jr., James C. Morton, Maston Williams, Frank LaRue, Milburn Morante, King Majave, Hal Price, Jack Ingram, Ray Bennett, Frank Ellis, George Plues, James Mason (not the British star), Douglas Evans, Bob Burns. 59 minutes.

21. *Boots and Saddles.* Republic, 1937. Joseph Kane.
Gene Autry, Smiley Burnette, Ra Hould, Judith Allen, Guy Usher, Gordon (William) Elliott, John Ward, Frankie Marvin, Chris Pin Martin, Stanley Blystone, Bud Osborne. 59 minutes.

22. *Manhattan Merry-Go-Round.* Republic, 1937. Charles F. Riesner.
Gene Autry, Phil Regan, Leo Carrillo, Ann Dvorak, Tamara Geva, Ted Lewis and Orchestra, Cab Calloway and Cotton Club Orchestra, Joe DiMaggio, Louis Prima, Henry Armetta, Max Terhune, Smiley Burnette, Jimmy Gleason, Kay Thompson and Ensemble, Selmer Jackson, Moroni Olsen, Eddie Kane, Nellie V. Nichols, Gennaro Curci, Sam Finn, Jack Jenny and Orchestra, the Lathrops, Rosalean and Seville, Luis Alberni, Robert E. Perry, Jack Adair, Ralph Edwards. 84 minutes.

23. *Springtime in the Rockies.* Republic, 1937, Joseph Kane.
Gene Autry, Smiley Burnette, Polly Rowles, Ula Love, Ruth Bacon, Jane Hunt, George Chesebro, Alan Bridge, Tom London, Edward Hearn, Frankie Marvin, William Hole, Edmund Cobb, Fred Burns, Jimmy's Saddle Pals (featuring Art Davis), Frank Ellis, Jack Kirk, Robert Dudley, George Letz (Montgomery), Lew Meehan, Jack Rockwell. 60 minutes.

24. *The Old Barn Dance.* Republic, 1938, Joseph Kane.
Gene Autry, Smiley Burnette, Helen Valkis, Sammy McKim, Dick Weston (Roy Rogers), Sons of the Pioneers, Ivan Miller, Earl Dwire, Hooper Atchley, Ray Bennett, Carleton Young, Frankie Marvin, Maple City Four, Stafford Sisters, Earle Hodgins, Gloria Rich, Walter Shrum and his Colorado Hillbillies, Denver Dixon. 60 minutes.

25. *Gold Mine in the Sky.* Republic, 1938, Joseph Kane.
Gene Autry, Smiley Burnette, Carol Hughes, Craig Reynolds, Cupid Ainsworth, LeRoy Mason, Frankie Marvin, Robert Homans, Benny Corbett, Milburn Morante, Stafford Sisters, J. L. Frank's "Golden West Cowboys" of WSM (radio), Nashville, Eddie Cherkose, Jim Corey, George Guhl, Jack Kirk, Snowflake, George Montgomery, Charles King, Earl Dwire, Lew Kelly, Maudie Prickett, Al Taylor, Art Dillard. 60 minutes.

26. *Man from Music Mountain.* Republic, 1938, Joe Kane.
Gene Autry, Smiley Burnette, Carol Hughes, Sally Payne, Ivan Miller, Edward Cassidy, Lew Kelly, Howard Chase, Frankie Marvin, Earl Dwire, Lloyd Ingraham, Jose Yrigoyen, Polly Jenkins and her Plowboys. 58 minutes.

27. *Prairie Moon.* Republic, 1938, Ralph Staub.
Gene Autry, Smiley Burnette, Shirley Deane, Tommy Ryan, Walter Tetley, Da-

vid Gorcey, Stanley Andrews, William Pawley, Warner Richmond, Ray Bennett, Tom London, Bud Osborne, Jack Rockwell, Peter Potter. 58 minutes.

28. *Rhythm of the Saddle.* Republic, 1938, George Sherman.
Gene Autry, Smiley Burnette, Pert Kelton, Peggy Moran, LeRoy Mason, Arthur Loft, Ethan Laidlaw, Eddie Hart, Eddie Acuff, Selmer Jackson, Walter de Palma, Archie Hall, Bucko the Trained Horse (Douglas Wright and Company), Alan Gregg, Rudy Sooter, Emmett Vogan, Jack Kirk, James Mason. 58 minutes.

29. *Western Jamboree.* Republic, 1938, Ralph Staub.
Gene Autry, Smiley Burnette, Jean Rouverol, Esther Muir, Joe Frisco, Frank Darien, Margaret Armstrong, Harry Holman, Ray Teal, Bentley Hewlett, Jack Ingram, Frank Ellis, Kermit Maynard, Jack Perrin, Eddie Dean. 56 minutes.

30. *Home on the Prairie.* Republic, 1939, Jack Townley.
Gene Autry, Smiley Burnette, June Storey, George Cleveland, Jack Mulhall, Walter Miller, Gordon Hart, Hal Price, Earle Hodgins, Ethan Laidlaw, John Beach, Jack Ingram, Bob Woodward, Sherven Brothers. 58 minutes.

31. *Mexicali Rose.* Republic, 1939, George Sherman.
Gene Autry, Smiley Burnette, Noah Beery, Sr., Luana Walters, William Farnum, William Royle, LeRoy Mason, Wally Albright, Roy Barcroft, Kathryn Frye, John Beach, Dick Botiller, Vic Demourelle, Henry Otho, Joe Dominguez, Al Haskel, Merrill McCormick, Snowflake, Sherry Hall, Al Taylor, Josef Swickard, Tom London, Jack Ingram, Eddie Parker. 58 minutes.

32. *Blue Montana Skies.* Republic, 1939, B. Reeves Eason.
Gene Autry, Smiley (Frog) Burnette, June Storey, Harry Woods, Tully Marshall, Al Bridge, Glenn Strange, Dorothy Granger, Edmund Cobb, Robert Winkler, Jack Ingram, Augie Gomez, John Beach, Walt Shrum and his Colorado Hillbillies, Allan Cavan, Buffalo Bill, Jr., Elmo Lincoln. 59 minutes.

33. *Mountain Rhythm.* Republic, 1939, B. Reeves Eason.
Gene Autry, Smiley Burnette, June Storey, Maude Eburne, Ferris Taylor, Walter Fenner, Jack Pennick, Hooper Atchley, Edward Cassidy, Jack Ingram, Tom London, Roger Williams, Frankie Marvin, Bernard Suss. 59 minutes.

34. *Colorado Sunset.* Republic, 1939, George Sherman.
Gene Autry, Smiley Burnette, June Storey, Buster Crabbe, Elmo Lincoln, Barbara Pepper, Robert Barrat, Patsy Montana, Purnell Pratt, William Farnum, Kermit Maynard, Jack Ingram, Frankie Marvin, The CBS-KMBC Texas Rangers. 64 minutes.

35. *In Old Monterey.* Republic, 1939, Joseph Kane.
Gene Autry, Smiley Burnette, George "Gabby" Hayes, June Storey, Stuart Hamblen, The Ranch Boys including Ken Carson, Billy Lee, Jonathan Hale, Robert Warwick, Hoosier Hot Shots, Eddy Conrad. Sarie and Sallie, William Hall, Fred Burns, James Mason, Dan White, Frank Ellis, Jim Corey, Edward Earle, Rex Lease, Jack O'Shea, Tom Steele, Hal Price, Bob Wilke. 73 minutes.

36. *Rovin' Tumbleweeds.* Republic, 1939, George Sherman.
Gene Autry, Smiley Burnette, Mary Carlisle, Douglass Dumbrille, William Farnum, Lee "Lasses" White, Ralph Peters, Gordon Hart, Victor Potel, Jack Ingram, Sammy McKim, Reginald Barlow, Eddie Kane, Guy Usher, Pals of the Golden West, Horace Murphy, Jack Kirk, Bob Burns, Horace B. Carpenter, Snowflake, Frank Ellis, Fred Burns, Ed Cassidy, Forrest Taylor, Tom Chatterton, Maurice Costello, Charles K. French, Bud Osborne, Chuck Morrison, Harry Semels, Lee Shumway, Crauford Kent, Dave Sharpe, Rose Plummer, Art Mix. 64 minutes.

37. *South of the Border.* Republic, 1939, George Sherman.
Gene Autry, Lupita Tovar, Smiley Burnette, Duncan Renaldo, June Storey, Mary Lee, William Farnum, Frank Reicher, Alan Edwards, Claire DuBrey, Sheila Darcy, Rex Lease, Selmer Jackson, Dick Botiller, Julian Rivero, Hal Price, Slim Whitaker, Jack O'Shea, Curley Dresden, Reed Howes, Charles King. 75 minutes.

38. *Rancho Grande.* Republic, 1940, Frank McDonald.
Gene Autry, Smiley Burnette, June Storey, Mary Lee, Dick Hogan, Ellen E. Lowe, Ferris Taylor, Roscoe Ates, Rex Lease, Ann Baldwin, Roy Barcroft, Joseph De Stefani. 68 minutes.

39. *Shooting High.* 20th Century-Fox, 1940, Alfred E. Green.
Gene Autry, Jane Withers, Marjorie Weaver, Robert Lowery, Kay Aldridge, Hobart Cavanaugh, Jack Carson, Tom London, Charles Middleton, Ed Brady, Eddie Acuff, Frank M. Thomas, Hamilton MacFadden, Pat O'Malley, George Chandler, Harold Goodwin, Lee Moore, LeRoy Mason, Carl Stockdale, Lew Kelly, Ivan Miller, Emmett Vogan, Kathryn Sheldon, Paul E. Burns, Georgia Simmons. 65 minutes.

40. *Gaucho Serenade.* Republic, 1940, Frank McDonald.
Gene Autry, Smiley Burnette, June Storey, Mary Lee, Duncan Renaldo, Clifford Severn, Jr., Lester Matthews, Smith Ballew, Joseph Crehan, William Ruhl, Ted Adams, Wade Boteler, Fred Burns, Julian Rivero, Joe Dominguez, George Lloyd, Olaf Hytten, Snowflake, Ed Cassidy, Gene Morgan, Jack Kirk, Harry Strang, Hank Worden, Ralph Sanford, Kernan Cripps, Tom London, Jim Corey, Walter Miller. 71 minutes.

41.　*Carolina Moon.* Republic, 1940, Frank McDonald.
Gene Autry, Smiley Burnette, June Storey, Mary Lee, Eddy Waller, Hardie Albright, Frank Dae, Jim Lewis, Robert Fiske, Etta McDaniel, Fred Ritter, Paul White, Ralph Sanford. 65 minutes.

42.　*Ride, Tenderfoot, Ride.* Republic, 1940, Frank McDonald.
Gene Autry, Smiley Burnette, June Storey, Mary Lee, Warren Hull, Joe Frisco, Isabel Randolph, Forbes Murray, Joe McGuinn, Si Jenks, Mildred Shay, The Pacemakers. 56 minutes.

43.　*Melody Ranch.* Republic, 1940, Joseph Santley.
Gene Autry, Jimmy Durante, Ann Miller, Barton MacLane, George "Gabby" Hayes, Jerome Cowan, Barbara Jo Allen (Vera Vague), Mary Lee, Joe Sawyer, Horace McMahon, Dick Elliott, Billy Benedict, Clarence Wilson, Veda Ann Borg, Billy Bletcher, Horace Murphy, Jack Ingram, Art Mix, George Chandler, Tiny Jones, Herman Hack, Jack Kirk, Tom London, Merrill McCormick, Lloyd Ingraham, Edmund Cobb, Slim Whitaker, John Merton, Curley Dresden, Wally West, Bob Wills Orchestra. 84 minutes.

44.　*Ridin' on a Rainbow.* Republic, 1941, Lew Landers.
Gene Autry, Smiley Burnette, Mary Lee, Carol Adams, Ferris Taylor, Georgia Caine, Byron Foulger, Ralf Harolde, Jimmy Conlin, Anthony Warde, Guy Usher, Forrest Taylor, Ed Cassidy, Ben Hall, Tom London, Walter Long. 79 minutes.

45.　*Back in the Saddle.* Republic, 1941, Lew Landers.
Gene Autry, Smiley Burnette, Mary Lee, Edward Norris, Jacqueline Wells (Julie Bishop), Addison Richards, Arthur Loft, Edmund Elton, Edmund Cobb, Robert Barron, Joe McGuinn. 71 minutes.

46.　*The Singing Hill.* Republic, 1941, Lew Landers.
Gene Autry, Smiley Burnette, Virginia Dale, Mary Lee, Spencer Charters, Gerald Oliver Smith, George Meeker, Wade Boteler, Harry Stubbs, Cactus Mack Peters, Jack Kirk, Monte Montague, Hal Price, Herman Hack, Jack O'Shea. 75 minutes.

47.　*Sunset in Wyoming.* Republic, 1941, William Morgan.
Gene Autry, Smiley Burnette, George Cleveland, Maris Wrixon, Robert Kent, Sarah Edwards, Monte Blue, Dick Elliott, John Dilson, Stanley Blystone. 65 minutes.

48.　*Under Fiesta Stars.* Republic, 1941, Frank McDonald.
Gene Autry, Smiley Burnette, Carol Hughes, Frank Darien, Joseph Strauch, Jr., Pauline Drake, Ivan Miller, Sam Flint, John Merton, Jack Kirk, Inez Palange, Elias Gamboa. 64 minutes.

49. *Down Mexico Way*. Republic, 1941, Joseph Santley.
Gene Autry, Smiley Burnette, Fay McKenzie, Harold Huber, Sidney Blackmer, Joe Sawyer, Andrew Tombes, Murray Alper, Arthur Loft, Paul Fix, Julian Rivero, Duncan Renaldo. 78 minutes.

50. *Sierra Sue*. Republic, 1941, William Morgan.
Gene Autry, Smiley Burnette, Fay McKenzie, Frank Thomas, Robert Homans, Earle Hodgins, Dorothy Christy, Jack Kirk, Budd Buster, Rex Lease, Kermit Maynard, Eddie Dean, Hugh Prosser, Sammy Stein, Eddie Cherkose, Roy Butler, Syd Saylor, Bob McKenzie, Hal Price, Marin Sais, Vince Barnett, Bud Brown, Gene Eblen, Buel Bryant, Ray Davis, Art Dillard, Frankie Marvin. 64 minutes.

51. *Cowboy Serenade*. Republic, 1942, William Morgan.
Gene Autry, Smiley Burnette, Fay McKenzie, Cecil Cunningham, Addison Richards, Rand Brooks, Tristram Coffin, Lloyd "Slim" Andrews, Johnnie Berkes, Melinda Leighton, Otto Han, Forrest Taylor, Lorin Raker, Bud Wolfe, Bud Geary, Forbes Murray, Hal Price, Si Jenks, Hank Worden, Frankie Marvin, Tom London, Ethan Laidlaw, Ken Terrell, Ken Cooper, Rick Anderson, Roger Kirby. 68 minutes.

52. *Heart of the Rio Grande*. Republic, 1942, William Morgan.
Gene Autry, Smiley Burnette, Fay McKenzie, Edith Fellows, Pierre Watkin, Joe Strauch, Jr., William Haade, Sarah Padden, Jean Porter, Jimmy Wakely Trio, Gloria and Gladis Gardner, Jan Lester, Patsy Fay Northrup, Betty Jane Graham, Kay Frye, Jeanne Herbers, Frankie Marvin, Budd Buster, George Reed Porter, Harry Depp, Ira "Buck" Woods, Mady Laurence, Nora Lane, Allan Wood, Howard Mitchell, Edmund Cobb, Milton Kibbee, Frank Mills. 70 minutes.

53. *Home in Wyomin'*. Republic, 1942, William Morgan.
Gene Autry, Smiley Burnette, Olin Howland, Chick Chandler, Joseph Strauch, Jr., Forrest Taylor, James Seay, George Douglas, Charles Lane, Hal Price, Fay McKenzie, Bud Geary, Ken Cooper, James McNamara, Roy Butler, Kermit Maynard, Ted Mapes, Jack Kirk, Billy Benedict, Cyril Ring, Betty Farrington, Tom Hanlon, Rex Lease, Bill Kellogg, Lee Shumway. 67 minutes.

54. *Stardust on the Sage*. Republic, 1942, William Morgan.
(remake of *Git Along Little Dogies* [1937].)
Gene Autry, Smiley Burnette, Edith Fellows, Bill Henry, Louise Currie, Emmett Vogan, George Ernest, Betty Farrington, Roy Barcroft, Tom London, Frank Ellis, Vince Barnett, Ed Cobb, George MacQuarrie, Monte Montague, Ed Cassidy, Rex Lease, George De Normand, Bert Le Baron, Jerry Jerome, Bud Jamison, Jimmy Fox, Franklyn Farnum, George Sherwood, Bill Nestell, Frank O'-Connor, Frank LaRue, Griff Barnett, Lee Shumway, Fred Burns, Merrill McCormick. 65 minutes.

55. *Call of the Canyon.* Republic, 1942, Joseph Santley.
Gene Autry, Smiley Burnette, Sons of the Pioneers, Ruth Terry, Thurston Hall, Joseph Strauch, Jr., Cliff Nazarro, Dorothea Kent, Edmund MacDonald, Marc Lawrence, John Harmon, John Holland, Eddy Waller, Red Knight, Edna Johnson, Budd Buster, Frank Jaquet, Charles Flynn, Lorin Raker, Charles Williams, Fred Santley, Carey Harrison, Broderick O'Farrell, Anthony Marsh, Joy Barlowe, Frank L. Ward, Freddie Walburn, Earle Hodgins, Jimmy Lucas, Ray Bennett, Al Taylor, Bob Burns, Johnny Duncan. 71 minutes.

56. *Bells of Capistrano.* Republic, 1942, William Morgan.
Gene Autry, Smiley Burnette, Virginia Grey, Lucien Littlefield, Morgan Conway, Claire DuBrey, Charles Cane, Joe Strauch, Jr., Marla Shelton, Tristram Coffin, Jay Novello, Al Bridge, Eddie Acuff, Bill Telaak, Ken Christy, Dick Wessel, Ed Jauregui, Guy Usher, Ralph Peters, Joe McGuinn, Howard Hickman, Bill Kellogg, Teresita Osta, Carla and Fernando Ramos, William Forrest, Julian Rivero, Peggy Satterlee. 73 minutes.

57. *Sioux City Sue.* Republic, 1946, Frank McDonald.
Gene Autry, Lynne Roberts, Sterling Holloway, Richard Lane, Ralph Sanford, Ken Lundy, Helen Wallace, Pierre Watkin, Cass County Boys, Edwin Mills, Minerva Urecal, Frank Marlowe, Kenne Duncan, Tex Terry, LeRoy Mason, Harry V. Cheshire, George Carleton, Sam Flint, Michael Hughes, Tristram Coffin, Frankie Marvin, Forrest Burns, Tommy Coats. 69 minutes.

58. *Trail to San Antone.* Republic, 1947, John English.
Gene Autry, Peggy Stewart, Sterling Holloway, William Henry, John Duncan, Tristram Coffin, Dorothy Vaughan, Edward Keane, Ralph Peters, The Cass County Boys. 67 minutes.

59. *Twilight on the Rio Grande.* Republic, 1947, Frank McDonald.
Gene Autry, Sterling Holloway, Adele Mara, Bob Steele, Charles Evans, Martin Garralaga, Howard J. Negley, George J. Lewis, Nacho Galindo, Tex Terry, The Cass County Boys, Champion, Jr., Barry Norton, Gil Perkins, Nena Campana, Kenne Duncan, Tom London, Alberto Morin, Keith Richards, Ana Camargo, Donna de Mario (Martell), Jack O'Shea, Steve Soldi, Bud Osborne, Frank MacCarroll, Bob Wilke, Alex Montoya, Connie Menard, Joaquin Elizondo, Frankie Marvin, Enrique Acosta, Bob Burns, George Magrill. 71 minutes.

60. *Saddle Pals.* Republic, 1947, Lesley Selander.
Gene Autry, Lynne Roberts, Sterling Holloway, Irving Bacon, Demian O'Flynn, Charles Arnt, Jean Van, Tom London, The Cass County Boys, Champion, Jr., Charles Williams, Francis McDonald, George Chandler, Ed Gargan, Paul E. Burns, Joel Friedkin, LeRoy Mason, Larry Steers, Edward Keane, Maurice Cass, Nolan Leary, Minerva Urecal, John S. Roberts, James Carlisle, Sam Ash, Frank

O'Connor, Frank Henry, Neal Hart, Ed Piel, Bob Burns, Joe Yrigoyen, Johnny Day. 72 minutes.

61. *Robin Hood of Texas.* Republic, 1947, Lesley Selander.
Gene Autry, Lynne Roberts, Sterling Holloway, Adele Mara, James Cardwell, John Kellogg, Ray Walker, Michael Branden (Archie Twitchell), Paul Bryar, Dorothy Vaughan, Stanley Andrews, Alan Bridge, The Cass County Boys, Champion, Jr., James Flavin, Hank Patterson, Edmund Cobb, Bill Bailey, Lester Dorr, Irene Mack, Opal Taylor, Eva Novak, Norma Brown, Frankie Marvin, Billy Wilkerson, Duke Green, Ken Terrell, Joe Yrigoyen. 71 minutes.

62. *The Last Round-Up.* Columbia, 1947, John English.
Gene Autry, Jean Heather, Ralph Morgan, Carol Thurston, Mark Daniels, Bobby Blake, Russ Vincent, George Fisher, Trevor Bardette, Lee Bennett, Roy Gordon, Silverheels Smith (Jay Silverheels), Frances Ray, Bob (John) Cason, Texas Rangers, John Halloran, Sandy Sanders, Dale Van Sickel, William P. Wilkerson, George Carleton, Don Kay Reynolds, Nolan Leary, Jack Baxley, Ted Adams, Steve Clark, Ed Piel, Chuck Hamilton, Bud Osborne, Frankie Marvin, Kernan Cripps, Jose Alvarado, Arline Archuletta, Louis Crosby, Virginia Carroll, Brian O'Hara, Rodd Redwing, J. W. Cody, Iron Eyes Cody, Alex Montoya, Blackie Whiteford, Bob Walker. 77 minutes.

63. *The Strawberry Roan.* Columbia, 1948, John English.
Gene Autry, Gloria Henry, Jack Holt, Dickie Jones, Pat Buttram, Rufe Davis, John McGuire, Eddy Waller, Rodd Harper, Jack Ingram, Eddie Parker, Ted Mapes, Sam Flint. In Cinecolor. 79 minutes.

64. *Loaded Pistols.* Columbia, 1949, John English.
Gene Autry, Barbara Britton, Chill Wills, Jack Holt, Russell Arms, Robert Shayne, Vince Barnett, Leon Weaver, Fred Kohler, Jr., Clem Bevans, Sandy Sanders, Budd Buster, John R. McKee, Stanley Blystone, Hank Bell, Slim Gaut, Felice Richmond, Dick Alexander, Frank O'Connor, Reed Howes, William Sundholm, Snub Pollard, Heinie Conklin. 79 minutes.

65. *The Big Sombrero.* Columbia, 1949. Frank McDonald.
Gene Autry, Elena Verdugo, Stephen Dunne, George J. Lewis, Vera Marshe, William Edmunds, Martin Garralaga, Gene Roth, Bob Cason, Rian Valente, Neyle Morrow, Pierce Lyden, Antonio Filauri, Sam Bernard, Joseph Palma, Jose Alvarado, Robert Espinosa, Cosmo Sardo, Alex Montoya, Jose Portugal, Joe Kirk, Artie Ortego, Joe Dominguez. In Cinecolor. 82 minutes.

66. *Riders of the Whistling Pines.* Columbia, 1949, John English.
Gene Autry, Patricia White (Pat Barry), Jimmy Lloyd, Douglass Dumbrille, Damian O'Flynn, Clayton Moore, Jason Robards, Sr., Britt Wood, Leon Weaver,

Loie Bridge, Roy Gordon, Len Torrey, Cass County Boys, Harry V. Cheshire, Lynn Farr, Al Thompson, Virginia Carroll, Nolan Leary, Steve Benton, Lane Chandler, Emmett Vogan. 70 minutes.

67. *Rim of the Canyon.* Columbia, 1949, John English.
Gene Autry, Nan Leslie, Jock O'Mahoney (Jock Mahoney), Thurston Hall, Clem Bevans, Walter Sande, Francis McDonald, Amelita Ward, John R. McKee, Alan Hale, Jr., Denver Pyle, Bobby Clark, Boyd Stockman, Sandy Sanders, Lynn Farr, Rory Mallinson, Frankie Marvin. 70 minutes.

68. *The Cowboy and the Indians.* Columbia, 1949, John English.
Gene Autry, Sheila Ryan, Frank Richards, Hank Patterson, Jay Silverheels, Clayton Moore, Claudia Drake, George Nokes, Charles Stevens, Frank Lackteen, Chief Yowlachie, Lee Roberts, Nolan Leary, Maudie Prickett, Charles Quigley, Alex Fraser, Harry Mackin, Gilbert Alonzo, Roy Gordon, Jose Alvarado, Ray Beltran, Felipe Gomez, Shooting Star, Ro Mere Darling, Iron Eyes Cody. 70 minutes.

69. *Riders in the Sky.* Columbia, 1949, John English.
Gene Autry, Gloria Henry, Robert Livingston, Pat Buttram, Mary Beth Hughes, Steve Darrell, Alan Hale, Jr., Tom London, Hank Patterson, Ben Welden, Dennis Moore, Joe Forte, Kenne Duncan, Frank Jaquet, Roy Gordon, Loie Bridge, Boyd Stockman, Vernon Johns, Pat O'Malley, John Parrish, Bud Osborne, Lynton Brent, Isabel Withers, Sandy Sanders, Kermit Maynard, Denver Dixon, Bob Walker. 70 minutes.

70. *Sons of New Mexico.* Columbia, 1950, John English.
Gene Autry, Gail Davis, Robert Armstrong, Dick Jones, Frankie Darro, Irving Bacon, Clayton Moore, Russell Arms, Marie Blake, Sandy Sanders, Roy Gordon, Frank Marvin, Pierce Lyden, Paul Raymond, Kenne Duncan, Harry Mackin, Bobby Clark, Gaylord (Steve) Pendleton, Billy Lechner. 71 minutes.

71. *Mule Train.* Columbia, 1950, John English.
Gene Autry, Pat Buttram, Sheila Ryan, Robert Livingston, Frank Jaquet, Vince Barnett, Syd Saylor, Sandy Sanders, Gregg Barton, Kenne Duncan, Roy Gordon, Stanley Andrews, John Miljan, Robert Hilton, Bob Wilke, Robert S. Carson, Pat O'Malley, John R. McKee, George Morrell, George Slocum, Frank O'Connor, Norman Leavitt, Eddie Parker. 70 minutes.

72. *Cow Town.* Columbia, 1950, John English.
Gene Autry, Gail Davis, Harry Shannon, Jock O'Mahoney, Clark "Buddy" Burroughs, Harry Harvey, Steve Darrell, Sandy Sanders, Ralph Sanford, Bud Osborne, Robert Hilton, Ted Mapes, Chuck Roberson, House Peters, Jr., Holly Bane (Mike Ragan), Herman Hack, Felice Richmond, Frank MacCarroll, Frank

O'Connor, Pat O'Malley, Walt LaRue, Kenny Cooper, Blackie Whiteford, Frankie Marvin. 70 minutes.

73. *Beyond the Purple Hills.* Columbia, 1950, John English.
Gene Autry, Pat Buttram, Jo Dennison, Don Beddoe, James Millican, Don Kay Reynolds, Hugh O'Brian, Roy Gordon, Harry Harvey, Gregg Barton, Bob Wilke, Ralph Peters, Frank Ellis, Sandy Sanders, John Cliff, Pat O'Malley, Herman Hack, Curt Barrett, Frank O'Connor, Joseph Minitello, Frankie Marvin, Bobby Clark, Boyd Stockman, Lynton Brent, Jerry Ambler, Victor Cox, Maudie Prickett, Fenton Jones, Tex Terry, Merrill McCormick. 70 minutes.

74. *Indian Territory.* Columbia, 1950, John English.
Gene Autry, Pat Buttram, Gail Davis, Kirby Grant, James Griffith, Philip Van Zandt, G. Pat Collins, Roy Gordon, Charles Stevens, Robert S. Carson, Boyd Stockman, Sandy Sanders, Frank Ellis, Frankie Marvin, John McKee, Bert Dodson, Nick Rodman, Wes Hudman, Robert Hilton, Roy Butler, Kenne Duncan, Chief Yowlachie, Frank Lackteen, Chief Thundercloud, Chief Thunder Sky. 79 minutes.

75. *The Blazing Hills* (also known as *The Blazing Sun*). Columbia, 1950, John English.
Gene Autry, Pat Buttram, Lynne Roberts, Anne Gwynne, Edward Norris, Kenne Duncan, Alan Hale, Jr., Gregg Barton, Tom London, Steve Darrell, Sandy Sanders, Frankie Marvin, Bob Woodward, Boyd Stockman, Lewis Morphy, Virginia Carroll, Sam Flint, Chris Allen, Charles Colean, Pat O'Malley, Almira Sessions, Nolan Leary. 70 minutes.

76. *Gene Autry and the Mounties.* Columbia, 1951, John English.
Gene Autry, Pat Buttram, Elena Verdugo, Carleton Young, Herbert Rawlinson, Jody Gilbert, Richard Emory, Trevor Bardette, Gregg Barton, Nolan Leary, Jim Frasher, House Peters, Jr., Francis McDonald, Boyd Stockman, Bruce Carruthers, Robert Hilton, Teddy Infuhr, Billy Gray, John McKee, Roy Butler, Stephen Elliott, Gilbert Alonzo, Chris Allen. 70 minutes.

77. *Texans Never Cry.* Columbia, 1951, Frank McDonald.
Gene Autry, Pat Buttram, Mary Castle, Russell Hayden, Gail Davis, Richard Powers (Tom Keene), Don C. Harvey, Roy Gordon, Michael Ragan (Holly Bane), Frank Fenton, Harry Tyler, Minerva Urecal, Richard Flato, Roy Butler, Sandy Sanders, John R. McKee, Harry Mackin, I. Stanford Jolley, Duke York. 70 minutes.

78. *Whirlwind.* Columbia, 1951, John English.
Gene Autry, Smiley Burnette, Gail Davis, Thurston Hall, Harry Lauter, Dick Curtis, Harry Harvey, Gregg Barton, Tommy Ivo, Kenne Duncan, Al Wyatt,

Gary Goodwin, Pat O'Malley, Bud Osborne, Boyd Stockman, Frankie Marvin, Stan Jones, Leon DeVoe. 70 minutes.

79. *Silver Canyon*. Columbia, 1951, John English.
Gene Autry, Dick Alexander, Stanley Andrews, Eugene Borden, Pat Buttram, Steve Clark, Gail Davis, James Davis, Edgar Dearing, Terry Frost, Peter Mamakos, Bob Steele, Duke York, Bobby Clark, Frank Marvin, Boyd Stockman, Sandy Sanders, Kenne Duncan, Bill Hale, Jack O'Shea, Frank Matts, Stanley Blystone, John Merton, Gary Goodwin, Jack Pepper, Pat O'Malley, Martin Wilkins, Jim Magill, John McKee. 70 minutes.

80. *Hills of Utah*. Columbia, 1951, John English.
Gene Autry, Pat Buttram, Elaine Riley, Onslow Stevens, Donna Martell, Harry Lauter, Tom London, Kenne Duncan, Denver Pyle, Harry Harvey, William Fawcett, Sandy Sanders, Teddy Infuhr, Lee Morgan, Billy Griffith, Tommy Ivo, Bob Woodward, Boyd Stockman, Stanley Price. 70 minutes.

81. *Valley of Fire*. Columbia, 1951, John English.
Gene Autry, Pat Buttram, Gail Davis, Russell Hayden, Riley Hill, Terry Frost, Gregg Barton, Harry Lauter, Margie Liszt, Christine Larson, Barbara Stanley, Teddy Infuhr, Victor Sen Yung, Bud Osborne, Fred Sherman, Sandy Sanders, Duke York, James Magill, Frank Marvin, Pat O'Malley, Wade Crosby, William Fawcett, Syd Saylor, John "Skins" Miller. 63 minutes.

82. *The Old West*. Columbia, 1952, George Archainbaud.
Gene Autry, Gail Davis, Pat Buttram, Lyle Talbot, House Peters, Jr., House Peters, Sr., Louis Jean Heydt, Dick Jones, Don Harvey, Tom London, James Craven, Kathy Johnson, Ray Morgan, Frank Marvin, Dee Pollock, Bob Woodward, Syd Saylor, Pat O'Malley, Tex Terry, Bobby Clark, Robert Hilton, John Merton, Frank Ellis, Buddy Roosevelt. 61 minutes.

83. *Night Stage to Galveston*. Columbia, 1952, George Archainbaud.
Gene Autry, Pat Buttram, Virginia Huston, Robert Livingston, Frank Sully, Thurston Hall, Judy Nugent, Clayton Moore, Harry Cording, Robert Bice, Harry Lauter, Steve Clark, Robert Peyton, Lois Austin, Frank Rawls, Kathleen O'Malley, Riley Hill, Duke York, Dick Alexander, Boyd Stockman, Bob Woodward, Sandy Sanders, Ben Welden, Gary Goodwin. 61 minutes.

84. *Apache Country*. Columbia, 1952, George Archainbaud.
Gene Autry, Pat Buttram, Carolina Cotton, Francis X. Bushman, Tom London, Harry Lauter, Gregg Barton, Mary Scott, Sydney Mason, Byron Foulger, Mickey Simpson, Frank Matts, Cass County Boys, Tony Whitecloud's Jemez Indians. 63 minutes.

85. *Barbed Wire*. Columbia, 1952, George Archainbaud.
Gene Autry, Pat Buttram, Anne James, Clayton Moore, Terry Frost, Eddie Parker, Leonard Penn. William Fawcett, Michael Vallon, Sandy Sanders, Stuart Whitman, Zon Murray, Frankie Marvin, Alan Bridge, Victor Cox, Bobby Clark, Pat O'Malley, Bud Osborne, Bob Woodward, Wes Hudman, Duke York, Harry Harvey. 61 minutes.

86. *Wagon Team*. Columbia, 1952, George Archainbaud.
Gene Autry, Pat Buttram, Gail Davis, Dick Jones, Gordon Jones, Harry Harvey, Henry Rowland, George J. Lewis, John Cason, Gregg Barton, Carlo Tricoli, Cass County Boys (Fred S. Martin, Bert Dodson, Jerry Scoggins), Piecre Lyden, Sandy Sanders, Syd Saylor. 61 minutes.

87. *Blue Canadian Rockies*. Columbia, 1952, George Archainbaud.
Gene Autry, Pat Buttram, Gail Davis, Carolina Cotton, Ross Ford, Tom London, John Merton, Don Beddoe, Gene Roth, Mauritz Hugo, David Garcia, Cass County Boys. 58 minutes.

88. *Winning of the West*. Columbia, 1953, George Archainbaud.
Gene Autry, Smiley Burnette, Gail Davis, Robert Livingston, Richard Crane, House Peters, Jr., Gregg Barton, William Forrest, Ewing Mitchell, Rodd Redwing, Frank Jaquet, George Chesebro, Charles Delaney, Bob Woodward, Boyd "Red" Morgan, James Kirkwood, Terry Frost, Eddie Parker, Charles Soldani. 87 minutes.

89. *On Top of Old Smoky*. Columbia, 1953, George Archainbaud.
Gene Autry, Smiley Burnette, Gail Davis, Sheila Ryan, Kenne Duncan, Grandon Rhodes, Robert Bice, Zon Murray, Cass County Boys, Pat O'Malley, Jack Gargan, Cass County Boys (Fred S. Martin, Bert Dodson and Jerry Scoggins). 89 minutes.

90. *Goldtown Ghost Riders*. Columbia, 1953, George Archainbaud.
Gene Autry, Smiley Burnette, Gail Davis, Kirk Riley, Carleton Young, Denver Pyle, John Doucette, Steve Conte, Neyle Morrow. 57 minutes.

91. *Pack Train*. Columbia, 1953, George Archainbaud.
Gene Autry, Smiley Burnette, Gail Davis, Sheila Ryan, Kenne Duncan, Tom London, Harry Lauter, Melinda Plowman, B. G. Norman, Louise Lorimer, Frank Marvin, Tex Terry, Wes Hudman, Norman E. Wescoatt, Kermit Maynard, Frank Ellis, Frank O'Connor, Dick Alexander, Jill Zeller, Herman Hack. 57 minutes.

92. *Saginaw Trail*. Columbia, 1953, George Archainbaud.
Gene Autry, Connie Marshall, Smiley Burnette, Eugene Borden, Ralph Reed,

Henry Blair, Myron Healey, Mickey Simpson, John War Eagle, Rodd Redwing, Billy Wilkerson, Gregg Barton, John Parrish, Charlie Hayes, John Merton. 56 minutes.

93. *Last of the Pony Riders*. Columbia, 1953, George Archainbaud.
Gene Autry, Smiley Burnette, Buzz Henry, Harry Hines, Johnny Downs, Dick Jones, Gregg Barton, Arthur Space, Howard Wright, Harry Mackin, Kathleen Case. 80 minutes.

Warner Baxter, the original Cisco Kid of the talking film era, smiles as he looks into the dark, flashing eyes of Conchita Montenegro. Edmund Lowe makes it a threesome in *The Cisco Kid* (1931), second sound Cisco movie.

THE CISCO KID

Beauty and the Bandit
(1946)

Screenplay by Charles S. Belden based on a character created by O. Henry. Music director, Edward J. Kay. Editor, Fred Maguire. Photography, Harry Neumann. Songs: "Blow the Man Down," Glenn Strange (dubbed) and barflies; "Viens Cher Cher Ton Baiser" (by Gordon Clark), Ramsay Ames in French; "Ride, Amigo, Ride," chorus at end. Assistant director, Eddie Davis. Directed by William Nigh. Produced by Scott R. Dunlap. Released by Monogram. 71 minutes.

Cisco Kid	GILBERT ROLAND
Jeanne DuBois	RAMSAY AMES
Captain	GEORGE J. LEWIS
Doctor Juan Valegra	MARTIN GARRALAGA
Baby	FRANK YACONELLI
Rosita	VIDA ALDANA
Doc Welles	WILLIAM GOULD
Farmer	DIMAS SOTELLO
Sick farmer	FELIPE TURICH
Bill, a sailor	GLENN STRANGE
Cisco's men	ALEX MONTOYA
	ARTIE ORTEGO

The Cisco Kid is riding to a rendezvous with Tonia, his love of the moment. As he approaches her prairie home, he hears noises. Quietly, he dismounts. Slowly, he creeps through the night shadows. She is in the arms of Lt. Sandridge, a ranger out to capture Cisco.

Tonia, his treacherous sweetheart, is telling the lawman she will send him a letter by messenger when Cisco arrives. Cisco's eyes narrow. His moustache curls toward his chin.

The next night, a messenger rushes into the ranger's camp. The letter says Cisco has come. But, it adds, he knows the ranger is near. So to fool him, Cisco plans to switch clothes. He will slip out at dawn disguised as a woman.

In the dim light of a half-moon, the ranger waits outside Tonia's simple home. An hour later, two figures emerge. The man quickly mounts a horse and gallops off. Then, as the woman steps into the pale moonlight, the ranger opens fire. One —two—three bullets he pumps into the quick-turning figure. Then two more. For you can never be too sure of bringing down the Cisco Kid. Moments later, a shriek of discovery echoes through the silent mesquite land. While Tonia was asleep, Cisco had written the letter.

This is the Cisco Kid as conceived by the master of the short story with the surprise ending, O. Henry.* The Kid is ruthless, cunning, resourceful, a wily bandit who killed for the love of it.

But as he was later developed in films and TV, these hard qualities disappeared. He became a noble rider of the plains, a western Robin Hood. Hollywood also stressed the amorous side of his nature. They made him a gay caballero, a charming brigand who prized a beautiful woman as a gourmet savored a vintage wine.

When his sidekick Pancho asks why a ship is called "she," Cisco has a ready answer. "Because she has a slender body. Because she is graceful. And because she goes through the roughest seas with a smile."

His propensity for affairs of the heart turned him into a unique western charac-ter. While other cowboys shrank from a kiss as if they were running from the plague, Cisco pursued the ladies as avidly as he sought the gold of a wealthy landowner. He put the lie to the theory that range heroes couldn't mix rough-riding and romance.

For him, it was love that made the world turn. He was just as ready to test the danger in a señorita's eyes as he was to face the guns of his enemies. "To rob a bank, to hold up a stagecoach is play for a child," says Cisco. "But to make love to two señoritas, ah, that is a job for a man."

Of course, from the feminist point of view, the Kid was a plain and simple cad.

---

*O. Henry (William Sydney Porter) created the Cisco Kid in 1907 in the story "The Caballero's Way." It is part of a short story collection called *Heart of the West.*

With the charm of a gallant gentleman of the west, Cisco (Baxter) introduces himself to Lynn Bari in *The Return of the Cisco Kid* (1939).

That's Cesar Romero, left, looking uncharacteristically unkempt as Lopez in *The Return of the Cisco Kid.* Chris-Pin Martin plays Cisco's sidekick Gordito. Baxter is at right.

His intentions were strictly dishonorable. He would say anything to disarm a señorita. He gave away fake engagement rings like they were Fuller brushes. Even while he was dancing with one señorita, he was ogling another. In the end, this cow-country Casanova could be counted on to ride off on his handsome steed Diablo, leaving his lady-love in the lurch.

Fittingly, all the actors who played Cisco—Warner Baxter (three films, 1929–39), Cesar Romero (six films, 1939–41), Duncan Renaldo (eight films, 1945 and 1949–50) and Gilbert Roland (six films, 1946–47)—were pretty fair ladies men in their own right.

Baxter, who created the Kid in sound movies,* was a matinee idol of the silent days. He made his first *Cisco* film, *In Old Arizona,* in 1929. And his performance was so highly regarded that it won him an Oscar. Baxter went on to play Cisco twice more. But his advanced years eventually threatened his credibility as a convincing lover. (For more on Baxter, see the chapter on *Crime Doctor.*)

And so Romero, an actor who had rescued Baxter from a firing squad in *The Return of the Cisco Kid* (1939), became his successor. It was no secret that Romero's private life rivaled the amorous affairs of the character he played. Born in New York City in 1907 to a Cuban mother and Spanish father, he became one of the movie industry's best-known perennial bachelors. The six-foot three-inch, 200-pound Romero escorted such screen beauties as Joan Crawford, Virginia Bruce, Loretta Young, Ann Sothern, Barbara Stanwyck and Jane Wyman.

Romero arrived in Hollywood when he was 27. He had started in show business as a ballroom dancer. Dancing led to musical comedy—the road company of "Strictly Dishonorable." That, in turn, led to movies. One of his first roles was in *The Thin Man* (1934). His dark good looks led to more movies—*The Devil Is a Woman* (1935), *Orchestra Wives* (1942), *Captain From Castile* (1947), *Vera Cruz* (1954) and *Batman* (1966), among many others.

But he became equally famous for his extracurricular activities as a gay blade. And Hollywood columnists delighted readers with interviews with Romero on the secrets of his success with women. In one story by reporter Lou Gerand, Romero's advice to young men with serious designs on a lady was—don't rush her. Women, Romero explained, like the outer trappings of love-making. There are many women who get a greater kick out of "what we men call the preliminaries" than they do out of the "main event."

A would-be Don Juan's greatest asset, therefore, is patience. If you bide your time, Cesar said, you'll set off certain thought processes in the female mind.

To wit:

*Western movie expert Nick Williams points out that there were at least two silent *Cisco Kid* films: *The Caballero's Way* (1914) and *The Border Terror* (1919). There was also a half-hour radio series with Jackson Beck as the Kid. Jack Mather also played the Kid. The program was heard on Friday nights at 8:30 (EST).

Gilbert Roland sits tall in the saddle astride his horse Diablo. Roland portrayed the kid six times, was the only native Mexican to play him, and, some say, seemed closest of all to O. Henry's original character.

Cisco (Renaldo) pays a call on an ailing William Lester in *The Girl from San Lorenzo* (1950), last feature-length *Cisco* movie to be made. Looking on are Leo Carrillo and Jane Adams.

1. "You'll confuse her. She's so accustomed to the fast pitch, that she won't be able to figure you."

2. "You'll pique her curiosity. She'll wonder just why the hell you're going through all the romantic motions without making the ultimate pass."

3. "You'll alarm her. She'll begin to wonder if maybe all you want, after all, is some occasional feminine company. And that would be a definite slap at her charms and desirability."

4. "As a result of number three, she is challenged to put forth *her* efforts to see if she can entice *you.*"

It turned out the dashing Romero was ideally cast. He brought to the part a humorous casual style that lent a certain coolness and grace to the character. Also, the fact that he spoke Spanish added to his realistic portrayal.

There was a four-year lull in the series during the World War II years. And then Renaldo stepped into the role. His Latin appearance made him seem a natural also, but Renaldo was really a Romanian. In fact, his foreign birth led to one of the great tragedies of his life.

Renaldo came to the United States as a coal stoker on a temporary 90-day seaman's permit. Without bothering to apply for alien status or acquire citizenship, he married, went to Hollywood and scored a success in the African spectacle *Trader Horn* (1931) with Edwina Booth. But Renaldo's wife thought the movie love-making wasn't just restricted to scenes before the cameras. She slapped Miss Booth with a $50,000 alienation of affections suit—which Mrs. Renaldo subsequently lost—then cooperated with the government in prosecuting Renaldo for making false statements on his passport. In going to the Dark Continent for the filming of *Trader Horn,* he swore he was an American citizen born in Camden, New Jersey. Renaldo lost the court battle and, incredibly, served two years for passport perjury in federal prison on McNeil Island in the Pacific Ocean off the state of Washington. He was then faced with deportation, but a last-minute pardon by President Roosevelt saved him.

However, Renaldo refused to let this setback ruin his career. Although he never achieved stardom, he returned to the movies in character roles, including a part in *For Whom the Bell Tolls* (1943), and westerns. Talented and versatile, he also tried his hand at writing, portrait painting, languages (he learned 11) and producing.

Although he appeared as the Cisco Kid more than any other actor (eight movies), he became best known for the role when he played the Kid on television in the 1950s. With Leo Carrillo as his sidekick Pancho, Renaldo made 176 half-hour episodes. During their original run, they earned over $10 million—the highest grossing performance of any syndicate series in that era.

While many so-called adult westerns were emphasizing gunplay and violence, Renaldo's "Cisco" series played down killing. Instead, they focused on stories that pointed up the danger of breaking the law, greed and prejudice. In time, Renaldo became a campaigner for intelligent television entertainment, and took sharp issue with the shoot-'em-up westerns:

> We've taken all our fine western lore and splashed it with criminality and barbarism. The whole idea of these adult westerns is a fallacy. Nowhere did they ever shoot five or six men before breakfast. That quick-draw business, too, is all a fake. Nobody can shoot accurately following a quick draw.
>
> Why bring the kids up on this stupid craze? Nowadays, you frequently read where some kid has shot off his kneecap or wounded a friend trying to perfect a quick draw. A gun has become a plaything.
>
> Ours is the oldest half-hour show of its kind in the country. And we've never killed anybody in any of our shows. We shoot in self-defense. We shoot the guns out of bandits' hands. But we don't kill. We have action and entertainment, but not murder or gore or vengeance.

Gilbert Roland, Cisco number four, is the only genuine article—if Mexican birth is considered the hallmark of authenticity. He was born in Chihuahua in 1905, the son of a famous bull fighter who had migrated from Spain. Roland's early ambition was to be a matador. But one day he saw his first movie, in El Paso,

Romero, looking more like his sartorially resplendent self, exchanges banter with a deputy sheriff played by Robert Sterling in *The Gay Cabellero* (1940).

where his family had settled after fleeing to escape Pancho Villa's Mexican Revolution. ("He was our enemy because we were of Spanish descent," Roland explained.) He stayed in the theatre all day, leaving only after the lights came on. From then on, he wanted to be an actor.

Born Luis Antonio Damaso Alonso, he adopted his movie name by combining the names of his favorite stars—John Gilbert and Ruth Roland. His nickname, though, is "Amigo," because that's what he calls everybody.

Roland, five feet, eleven inches tall and athletic—he was one of Hollywood's top tennis players—started as an extra. But he got his big break in 1927 when he played opposite Norma Talmadge in *Camille.* Roland went on to play Latin lovers and leading-man roles in the early sound movies, then switched to westerns as he grew older, and eventually to character roles.

Some of his films include *She Done Him Wrong* (1933), *The Bull Fighter and The Lady* (1951), *My Six Convicts* (1952), and *The French Line* (1953). Ironically, though Roland made over 80 movies, he had one of the shortest stage careers on record. It stemmed from the fact that he had trouble understanding English as a young actor. He was named to play the young lover Armand Duval in a touring version of "Camille." In the third act, he was supposed to make an entrance and discover Camille, played by that great lady of the theatre, Jane Cowl, seated at a desk. A single spotlight was to be playing on her as they had their last meeting.

"The effect was most dramatic in the tryout." Roland said. "I made my entrance with the line, 'What are you doing, my dear, writing a letter?' And then went into the rest. Then we opened in Los Angeles. Everybody was out front—Louis B. Mayer, Norma Talmadge, Doug Fairbanks, Mary Pickford, Marion Davies—the whole town. I could hear the sniffles in the audience as I waited for the light to go on. That was my cue. I waited and waited. But no light. I couldn't sweat any more. So I went on stage. Jane wasn't seated at the desk. Apparently, she had been carried away with playing the scene before such a distinguished audience. Instead, she was pacing the stage, wringing her hands. My English wasn't so good in those days. And I wasn't ready for ad libs yet. I had my line memorized. So I said, 'What are you doing, my dear, writing a letter?' It got the biggest laugh I've ever heard in a theater. Everybody howled—but Miss Cowl. She ordered the curtain down immediately, and then gave me the damnest tongue-lashing I've ever had. I haven't been on the stage since."

If his theatre debut was less than memorable, he was far from a flop in Hollywood's social scene. Like Romero, he earned a reputation as a ladies' man. Among others, he was seen dancing with Doris Duke, the world's richest woman. The first thing he notices about a woman, he told columnist Sidney Skolsky, are her eyes and walk. "Her voice can destroy all illusion," Roland added.

Roland's first wife was Constance Bennett and they had two daughters. His second and current spouse is Guillermina Cantu, a Mexican tennis champion. They met in an informal doubles match in 1954 and have kept the team together ever since.

Of the four Ciscos, some western buffs think Romero was the best. But others choose Roland for being closest, perhaps, to O. Henry's characterization. So let's look at one of the pictures that point up the adventurous and amorous aspects of Cisco's personality—Roland's third series film, *Beauty and the Bandit* (1946).

As the story opens, Cisco and his men are riding for San Marino, a California coastal town where he is wanted by the authorities. Even so, Cisco is headed that way because he has seen a French ship sailing into the harbor. And he has a feeling someone aboard is carrying a rich cargo. Sure enough, his hunch is confirmed when he meets an old sailor friend (Glenn Strange) at a seaport bar.

"There's a young Frenchman aboard with a chestful of silver," the sailor says. "He's headed for San Marino."

At the pier, Cisco arranges to get on the same stagecoach as the young man (Ramsay Ames). Cisco tries to strike up a conversation. But the young man is reserved and aloof. A closeup shows us that the Frenchman is really a young lady, Jeanne DuBois, disguised because she is traveling alone. Before Cisco can learn this, his men swoop down from the hills. They stop the coach and during a gunfight, they switch the Frenchman's silver chest with one filled with stones.

The camera cuts to the stagecoach's destination—a San Marino inn. There we meet our villains—Doc Welles (William Gould), a former medicine showman and his henchman Juan Valegra (Martin Garralaga), a doctor who has run afoul of the law. Welles has become a land speculator, of late. And he has been fortunate because prices have steadily dropped to rock bottom. Crop failure and the mysterious death of livestock have prompted many farmers to sell their land and leave. As Welles has accumulated vast holdings, he has offered to sell the entire parcel to a French real estate man named DuBois. But DuBois has died and so his daughter has come in his place.

When the coach arrives, Welles receives young DuBois graciously. He puts DuBois' strongbox in his safe and gives her the inn's best room. Unfortunately, there is nothing left for Cisco. So he blithely suggests he share DuBois' room. DuBois, of course, icily rejects the idea. But Cisco at least persuades her to have a drink. "That's good," Cisco smiles after downing a tequila at the hotel bar. He orders one for her, too. "It puts hair on your chest."

Screenwriter Charles S. Belden thought the mistaken sex ploy would titillate Saturday matinee small fry. And so he next has Cisco trying to interest his young friend in their waitress. "Hey," Cisco says. "The little barmaid. She's making eyes at you. If you make a date, maybe she has a little friend."

When DuBois shows no interest, the puzzled Cisco thinks his friend's tendencies are a little too unmasculine for him. "Hey, what's the matter with you? You have no spirit. Don't you like pretty girls? Maybe you're sick?" But Cisco changes his mind when DuBois, tired of listening to Cisco, tells the barmaid to bring dinner to her room. "Ah, say," Cisco says, brightening, "that's a very good technique. You do not need my help."

Later that night, Doc Welles pays a visit to DuBois' room. He tells DuBois there is no money in her strongbox—only rocks. Thinking fast, DuBois tells him she figured he might open it without her permission. So she has made a substitution. "I'll give you the money when I find all is in order," she says.

The next day, Cisco sees a child crying because his goat is sick. When Cisco pays a call on Dr. Valegra, the doctor offers to sell him medicine. But he says the medicine is costly.

"What do you call this [animal] sickness?" Cisco asks.

"We have not completed our diagnosis," the doctor says.

"Ah, you do not know the sickness. But you know the remedy," Cisco says. He takes the medicine without paying.

Back at the inn, DuBois decides to put her hair down and disclose her identity. Cisco is so delighted when he arrives that he has breakfast with her. "You are as beautiful as a butterfly," Cisco says.

"Are you always so sure of yourself?" Jeanne asks.

Cisco leans across the breakfast table and kisses her. "Always."

Instead of slapping his face as a thousand other leading ladies might have done, Jeanne simply smiles back. This is one heroine who doesn't need to be asked twice about love.

Just then, an army captain (George J. Lewis), searching for Cisco, shows up.

"Lots of people, they tell me I look like him," Cisco says coolly. However, he says, his name is Luis Antonio Damaso Alonso Gonzales. The captain suspects Cisco. But he doesn't arrest him. He has another idea, instead. He takes two of Cisco's men to jail. As the captain suspects, Cisco rescues them and, in doing so, reveals his true identity. But, with Jeanne riding with him, Cisco outgallops the captain's pursuing soldiers and takes her to his mountain hideout.

"So this is home," she says. "You'll have to carry me over the threshold." Jeanne is one woman who seems to be Cisco's match in the aggressiveness department. If her forwardness surprises him, Cisco doesn't show it.

Later that night, Jeanne tells Cisco she has no illusions about his character. She tells him she knows he has stolen her money. But he has also stolen her heart.

"I never loved anybody before," she says. "Keep the money. But keep me too."

Cisco asks her why she came to buy the land. To sell it at a big profit in Europe, she says. She knew Doc Welles stole the land from the poor, she admits. In fact, her father was in on the scheme. She is merely carrying out their agreement.

"There is ugliness in your heart," Cisco tells her. He urges her to give the land back to the poor. She only laughs and calls him a "second-class bandit." When Cisco and his men are asleep, she rides off with her silver chest.

The next day, Cisco finds a farmer dying from poisoned grain. When he rushes the man to Dr. Valegra, the physician says he has no antidote. Cisco finds some bottles of chemicals in a back room and forces the doctor to drink.

"It's poison," Valegra gasps. "Doc Welles makes it up. He puts it in the grain." Cisco leaves, not bothering to tell the panicked doctor that he has really given him castor oil.

The camera cuts to the inn where Jeanne has turned over her silver in return for all the deeds Welles has. To Welles' surprise, she strikes a match and burns them. "I'll let the people keep the land," she says, suddenly showing a streak of nobility that has escaped Cisco. But when Jeanne tries to leave, Welles blocks her. He tells her he suspects she's partners with Cisco. Welles insists that she wait at the inn until the soldiers capture Cisco or he returns to the inn.

"If he does, I'll kill him and collect the reward myself," Welles says.

Sure enough, when the sun goes down, Cisco shows up. Welles has all the lights out. As Cisco enters with drawn gun, Welles laughs and challenges Cisco to find him. Cisco fires in the general direction of Welles' voice. He only hears more laughter. "Just an old medicine showman," Welles says. "Used to do a ventriloquist act. Hard to hit a voice, eh, Cisco?"

Now Welles takes the offensive. He starts taking pot shots at Cisco. But Welles has forgotten one thing. The moon is out. And its light floods through the windows. There, on a second story balcony, is Welles' shadow. Cisco rushes Welles and the two go to the floor. A shot sounds through the inn. One man rises and walks toward Jeanne—Welles. He booms out in loud laughter. But a moment later, his laughter suddenly subsides. A terror-filled expression spreads across his face. And he keels over, dead.

And so it is time for Cisco to move on again. He can only ride alone, he tells Jeanne. "Hasta la vista, beautiful one," he says, mounting his horse. "Maybe someday I'll see you again." And off he goes into the land of the mesquite, where adventure and perhaps another señorita await him.

Watching him disappear in the distance is a tearful, broken-hearted maiden. Ah, but Cisco never looks back.

THE CISCO KID SERIES

1. *In Old Arizona.* Fox Film Corp, 1929, Raoul Walsh and Irving Cummings. Edmund Lowe (as Sergeant Mickey Dunn), Warner Baxter (as the Cisco Kid), Dorothy Burgess, J. Farrell MacDonald, Ivan Linow, Soledad Jiminez, Fred Warren, Henry Armetta, Frank Campeau, Frank Nelson, Tom Santschi, Duke Martin, Pat Hartigan, James Marcus, Roy Stewart, Alphonse Ethier, James Bradbury, Jr., John Dillon, Joe Brown, Lola Salvi, Edward Piel, Sr., Helen Lynch. 95 minutes.

2. *The Cisco Kid.* Fox Film Corp., 1931, Irving Cummings. Warner Baxter, Edmund Lowe, Conchita Montenegro, Nora Lane, Frederick Burt, Willard Robertson, James Bradbury, Jr., Jack Dillon, Charles Stevens, Chris-Pin Martin (as Gordito), Douglas Haig, Marilyn Knowlden. 61 minutes.

3. *The Return of the Cisco Kid.* 20th Century-Fox, 1939, Herbert I. Leeds. Warner Baxter, Lynn Bari, Cesar Romero, Henry Hull, Kane Richmond, C. Henry Gordon, Robert Barrat, Chris-Pin Martin, Adrian Morris, Soledad Jiminez, Harry Strang, Arthur Aylesworth, Paul Burns, Victor Kilian, Eddy Waller, Ruth Gillette, Ward Bond. 70 minutes.

4. *The Cisco Kid and the Lady.* 20th Century-Fox, 1939, Herbert I. Leeds. Cesar Romero (as the Cisco Kid), Marjorie Weaver, Chris-Pin Martin, Robert Barrat, Virginia Field, Harry Green, Gloria Ann White, John Beach, Ward Bond, J. Anthony Hughes, James Burke, Harry Hayden, James Flavin, Ruth Warren. 73 minutes.

5. *Viva Cisco Kid.* 20th Century-Fox, 1940, Norman Foster. Cesar Romero, Jean Rogers, Chris-Pin Martin, Minor Watson, Stanley Fields, Nigel de Brulier, Harold Goodwin, Francis Ford, Charles Judels. 70 minutes.

6. *Lucky Cisco Kid.* 20th Century-Fox, 1940, H. Bruce Humberstone. Cesar Romero, Mary Beth Hughes, Dana Andrews, Evelyn Venable, Chris-Pin Martin, Willard Robertson, Joseph Sawyer, John Sheffield, William Royle, Francis Ford, Otto Hoffman, Dick Rich. 68 minutes.

7. *The Gay Caballero.* 20th Century-Fox, 1940, Otto Brower. Cesar Romero, Sheila Ryan, Robert Sterling, Chris-Pin Martin, Janet Beecher, Edmund MacDonald, Jacqueline Dalya, Montague Shaw, Hooper Atchley. 57 minutes.

8.   *Romance of the Rio Grande.* 20th Century-Fox, 1941, Herbert I. Leeds.
     Cesar Romero, Patricia Morison, Lynne Roberts, Ricardo Cortez, Chris-Pin
     Martin, Aldrich Bowker, Joseph McDonald, Pedro De Cordoba, Inez Palange,
     Raphael Bennett, Trevor Bardette, Tom London, Eva Puig. 73 minutes.

9.   *Ride On, Vaquero.* 20th Century-Fox, 1941, Herbert I. Leeds.
     Cesar Romero, Mary Beth Hughes, Lynne Roberts, Chris-Pin Martin, Robert
     Lowery, Ben Carter, William Demarest, Robert Shaw, Edwin Maxwell, Paul
     Sutton, Don Costello, Arthur Hohl, Irving Bacon, Dick Rich, Paul Harvey, Joan
     Woodbury. 64 minutes.

10. *The Cisco Kid Returns.* Monogram, 1945, John P. McCarthy.
     Duncan Renaldo (as the Cisco Kid), Martin Garralaga (as Pancho), Cecilia
     Callejo, Roger Pryor, Anthony Warde, Fritz Leiber, Vicky Lane, Jan Wiley,
     Sharon Smith, Cy Kendall, Eva Puig, Bud Osborne, Bob Duncan, Elmer Napier,
     Carl Mathews, Jerry Fields, Neyle Marx, Cedric Stevens. 64 minutes.

11. *The Cisco Kid in Old New Mexico.* Monogram, 1945, Phil Rosen.
     Duncan Renaldo, Martin Garralaga, Gwen Kenyon, Pedro de Cordoba, Aurora
     Roche, Lee White, Norman Willis, Edward Earle, Donna Dax, John Laurence,
     Richard Gordon, Frank Jaquet, James Farley, the Car-Bert Dancers. 62 minutes.

12. *South of the Rio Grande.* Monogram, 1945, Lambert Hillyer.
     Duncan Renaldo, Martin Garralaga, Armida, George J. Lewis, Lillian Molieri,
     Francis McDonald, Charles Stevens, Pedro Regas, Soledad Jiminez, Tito
     Renaldo, the Guadalajara Trio. 62 minutes.

13. *The Gay Cavalier.* Monogram, 1946, William Nigh.
     Gilbert Roland (as the Cisco Kid), Martin Garralaga, Nacho Galindo, Ramsay
     Ames, Helen Gerald, Drew Allen, Tristram Coffin, Iris Flores, Gabriel Peralta,
     Pierre Andre, Iris Bocignon, John Merton. 65 minutes.

14. *South of Monterey.* Monogram, 1946, William Nigh.
     Gilbert Roland, Martin Garralaga, Frank Yaconelli, Marjorie Riordan, Iris
     Flores, George J. Lewis, Harry Woods, Terry Frost, Rosa Turich, Wheaton
     Chambers. 63 minutes.

15. *Beauty and the Bandit.* Monogram, 1946, William Nigh.
     Gilbert Roland, Ramsay Ames, Martin Garralaga, George J. Lewis, Frank Yaco-
     nelli, Vida Aldana, William Gould, Dimas Sotello, Felipe Turich, Glenn Strange,
     Alex Montoya, Artie Ortego. 71 minutes.

16. *Riding the California Trail.* Monogram, 1947, William Nigh.
     Gilbert Roland, Frank Yaconelli, Teala Loring, Martin Garralaga, Inez Cooper,

Ted Hecht, Eve Whitney, Marcelle Grandville, Frank Marlowe, Alex Montoya, Gerald Echeverria, Rosa Turich, Julia Kent. 59 minutes.

17. *Robin Hood of Monterey.* Monogram, 1947, Christy Cabanne.
Gilbert Roland, Chris-Pin Martin, Evelyn Brent, Jack La Rue, Travis Kent, Donna De Mario (Martell), Ernie Adams, Pedro De Cordoba, Nestor Paiva, Thornton Edwards, Julian Rivero, Alex Montoya, Fred Cordova, Felipe Turich. 55 minutes.

18. *King of the Bandits.* Monogram, 1947, Christy Cabanne.
Gilbert Roland, Chris-Pin Martin, Angela Greene, Anthony Warde, Laura Treadwell, William Bakewell, Rory Mallinson, Pat Goldin, Cathy Carter, Boyd Irwin, Antonio Filauri, Jasper Palmer, Bill Cabanne, Jack O'Shea. 66 minutes.

19. *The Valiant Hombre.* United Artists, 1949, Wallace Fox.
Duncan Renaldo (as the Cisco Kid), Leo Carrillo (as Pancho), John Litel, Stanley Andrews, John James, Barbara Billingsley, Lee "Lasses" White. 60 minutes.

20. *The Gay Amigo.* United Artists, 1949, Wallace Fox.
Duncan Renaldo, Leo Carrillo, Armida, Joe Sawyer, Walter Baldwin, Fred Kohler, Jr., Kenneth MacDonald, George DeNormand, Clayton Moore, Fred Crane, Helen Servis, Beverly Jons, Bud Osborne, Sam Flint. 62 minutes.

21. *The Daring Caballero.* United Artists, 1949, Wallace Fox.
Duncan Renaldo, Leo Carrillo, Kippee Valez, Charles Halton, Pedro De Cordoba, Stephen Chase, David Leonard, Edmund Cobb, Frank Jaquet, Mickey Little. 60 minutes.

22. *Satan's Cradle.* United Artists, 1949, Ford Beebe.
Duncan Renaldo, Leo Carrillo, Ann Savage, Douglas Fowley, Byron Foulger, Buck Bailey, George De Normand, Wes Hudman. 60 minutes.

23. *The Girl From San Lorenzo.* United Artists, 1950, Derwin Abrahams.
Duncan Renaldo, Leo Carrillo, Jane Adams, Bill Lester, Byron Foulger, Don Harvey, Lee Phelps, Edmund Cobb, Leonard Penn, David Sharpe, Wes Hudman. 59 minutes.

That's Robert Mitchum behind those whiskers, stalking Hoppy (William Boyd) in *Riders of the Deadline* (1943).

HOPALONG CASSIDY

Border Vigilantes

(1941)

Screenplay by J. Benton Cheney based on characters created by Clarence E. Mulford. Photography, Russell Harlan. Editor, Carrol Lewis. Song "Is This Our Last Night Together" by Sam Coslow and Pauline Bouchard, sung by Frances Gifford. Produced by Harry Sherman. Directed by Derwin Abrahams. Released by Paramount. 63 minutes.

Hopalong Cassidy	WILLIAM BOYD
Lucky Jenkins	RUSSELL HAYDEN
California Carlson	ANDY CLYDE
Henry Logan	VICTOR JORY
Dan Forbes	MORRIS ANKRUM
Helen Forbes	FRANCES GIFFORD
Aunt Jenifer Forbes	ETHEL WALES
Jim Yager	TOM TYLER
Ed Stone	HAL TALIAFERRO
Henry Weaver	JACK ROCKWELL
Lafe Willis	BRITT WOOD
Wagon Driver	HANK WORDEN

Banker Stevens	EDWARD EARLE
Liveryman	HANK BELL
Bank Guard	CURLEY DRESDEN
Gambler	AL HASKEL
Wagon Driver in brawl	CHUCK MORRISON
Henchman	TED WELLS

He never branded a cow, lassoed a pony or bulldogged a steer. He learned to ride well enough but he couldn't break a bronc. Nor could he strum a guitar or croon a prairie tune. He was really just a fun-loving, good ole boy from Ohio who went into B-westerns because his movie career was on the skids.

This was William Boyd at age 40. As Hopalong Cassidy, he turned out 66 low-budget horse operas from the mid-1930s to the late 1940s. Then, all but forgotten, he suddenly parlayed them into a multimillion-dollar empire via television and product endorsement. He became the 1950s' public hero number one—a hero with the Midas touch.

It was one of the strangest of all Hollywood success stories. Stranger still was the way Boyd reacted to the overnight adulation. The actor disappeared—some fans couldn't even remember his name—and he emerged as Hopalong Cassidy incarnate. He spoke of himself in the third person—as "Hoppy" or "the character." He wouldn't say, "I'm going to Chicago." He would say, "Hoppy's going to Chicago."

Said writer Adela Rogers St. John: "Never before in movies has a star become the character he plays on the screen to the extent that he himself no longer exists separately."

In public, Boyd wore a ten-gallon hat and cowboy boots all the time. On tours, he added his famous black Hoppy outfit, and never smoked while he wore it.

Crowds flocked to see him wherever he went. In 1950, the year *Time* magazine did a cover story on him, an estimated 350,000 people came to see him at the *Daily News* Building in New York City. He stayed nearly five hours, greeting them one by one. "Sometimes I can feel hands all over me when I get home," Boyd said. "But they do it because they're Hoppy's friends."

At times, he seemed as fervently devoted to his fans as they were to him. Once, on a personal appearance tour, a department store manager hinted to Cassidy's followers that they ought to repay the store for Cassidy's appearance by buying things. Hoppy got so mad, *Time* reported, he hauled off and socked the manager.

Another audience surrounded him at intermission when he went to see "Call Me Madam" in New York. When the theatre manager tried to pull Cassidy away, Hoppy roared: "Hey—you. Let go my sleeve. These are my friends, my friend, and I'll come into your theatre in good time." The crowd cheered.

He was both awed and flattered by the adulation. He couldn't help thinking he had an enormous influence on youth. And he took his obligations seriously.

"I've tried to make Hoppy a plain and simple man in manners and dress," he said. "Hoppy isn't a flashy character. He isn't illiterate. Nor is he smart alecky. He doesn't use big words or bad words."

Nor did Cassidy use slang—although in some of the early films he did say "reckon" and "ain't" occasionally. But as the years went on Boyd cut out using the vernacular altogether. "After all," he said, "I felt that Hoppy might be looked up to and that children might try to pattern their lives after the man . . . If Hoppy said 'ain't' and 'reckon' and 'that-a-way,' all the kids might start saying the same things."

In his early days, no one—not even Cassidy himself—could have predicted he would become the idol of the cap pistol set. Born in Cambridge, Ohio, in 1895, the son of a day laborer, he moved to Tulsa, Oklahoma, when he was seven. He wanted to be a construction engineer. But he had to quit school in his early teens after his parents died. He held a variety of jobs—grocery clerk, surveyor, tool dresser in the oil fields—before he came to Hollywood in 1919 at the height of the silent era.

Broad-shouldered, blue-eyed with wavy, prematurely gray hair, he got his first film role as an extra in Cecil B. DeMille's *Why Change Your Wife?* (1920). He bought an expensive wardrobe, caught DeMille's eye and won the romantic lead in epics like *The Volga Boatman* (1926). He became a matinee idol. Soon he was earning $100,000 a year.

This was in the day of low, low taxes and high, high spending in the movie colony, and Boyd joined the free-wheelers. He bought three homes—a Beverly Hills mansion, a beach house at Malibu and a ranch—and he married and divorced three times,* and became a fixture in the cocktail party set. Once he reportedly bought a yacht during a party just because his pals wanted to go for a spin in the ocean.

But in the early 1930s, his career came to an abrupt halt. The silent era ended and the depression began. Like many silent screen stars, he found himself without a contract.** Years went by and Boyd saw his fortune dwindle. Then, one day in 1935, Harry Sherman, a veteran producer of horse operas, offered Boyd the lead in a low-budget western based on Clarence Mulford's pulp stories. The hero, Hop-Along Cassidy of the Bar 20 Ranch, got his nickname from a bullet wound that made him limp—at least for the first picture. He was a hard-bitten, ornery

---

*However, his 1937 marriage to actress Grace Bradley was a lasting one. The two were still man and wife in 1972.

**A quirk of fate contributed to his career's demise. Police arrested another actor named William Boyd during a wild party and charged him with possession of illegal whiskey and gambling equipment. Newspapers ran the better-known Boyd's picture by mistake. (The other Boyd—usually identified as William "Stage" Boyd—was a Broadway actor who played villains in the movies. He died in 1935.)

Hoppy and his pals Andy Clyde, left, and Russell Hayden draw a bead on some unfriendly hombres in *Three Men from Texas* (1940). The series started the idea of the three-man team of heroes.

Lola Lane, winged by a bullet, gets sympathy from Hoppy and Herbert Rawlinson in *Lost Canyon* (1942). The picture was a remake of *Rustlers' Valley* (1937), twelfth in the series.

cuss who smoked, swore, chewed tobacco, gambled and shot up people. But Boyd persuaded Sherman to let him play Cassidy as a clean-living, congenial cowpoke. As Boyd portrayed him, Cassidy didn't smoke, drank nothing stronger than sarsaparilla and rarely kissed a girl.* He tried to capture villains rather than kill them. In any case, he always let the villain draw first.

Boyd hit on the right formula. Sherman began a series and the movies, called "Hoppies" by theatre owners, made a 100 percent profit or better—more, percent-age-wise, than most first-line productions. Movie audiences as far apart as Roundup, Montana, Conway, South Carolina, and New York City loyally lined up on Saturday afternoons. They were drawn by the fast-riding action, authentic outdoor scenery, detective-type plots and the eventual triumph of good over evil. The Mulford stories provided plots for the first 19 films. Thereafter, scenarists did original screenplays.

The Hoppies gave exposure to many young players and character actors. These included Sidney Toler, Lee J. Cobb, Robert Mitchum, James Craig, George Reeves (who later played Superman), Evelyn Venable, Evelyn Brent, Ellen Drew, Lola Lane and Barbara Britton.

The series also started the idea of a three-man team of heroes, a formula called the "Trio Westerns," later brought to the height of its popularity by the Three Mesquiteers. Because Boyd was already forty when the series started, Hoppy got a younger partner to play the romantic leads. Jimmy Ellison was Hoppy's original junior partner. He was followed by Russell Hayden, Brad King, Jay Kirby, Jimmy Rogers and Rand Brooks. A second partner was added for comic relief. George (Gabby) Hayes was the first, followed by Britt Wood and Andy Clyde.**

Of them all, probably the most colorful was scrubby, gray-bearded Hayes, a hard-chewing, hard-drinking but lovable vagabond veteran of almost 200 west-erns. "Yur durn tootin', Hoppy," he was fond of saying in his gravel voice.

In the Cassidy films, he played Windy Halliday and called himself George (Windy) Hayes in line with the character's garrulous nature. Later, when he changed studios, he found that a copyright prevented him from taking along the nickname. So he chose the next best thing—Gabby. Mail soon came to him addressed simply—"Gabby."

Hayes, who started as a burlesque and vaudeville comic and came to Holly-wood after the stock market crashed, went on to become sidekick to such cowboy stars as Gene Autry, Roy Rogers and Randolph Scott. The grizzled, cantanker-

---

*In one movie, he kissed Evelyn Brent on the forehead as she was dying. His fans howled. To kids, who had not yet felt the attraction of the opposite sex, such carryings-on seemed effeminate. So one of Boyd's partners usually took on the romantic burden. And there was a different leading lady in each picture.

**Clyde also appeared with Boyd on the "Hopalong Cassidy" radio show. Edgar Buchanan was in the television half-hour sequences during 1951 and 1952.

Hoppy steps between Hayes and John Powers, who played a stuttering cook in *Hills of Wyoming* (1937). Hoppy's all-black outfit reversed the tradition of western heroes wearing white.

Brooks, Hoppy and Clyde in *Silent Conflict* (1948), one of the last films of the series.

ous veteran, who grew his beard in 1934 and shaved it off only once thereafter, wore flat-heeled boots to make the heroes look taller.

When his Hollywood days were over, he had an afternoon television program on which he introduced biographical stories from American history—figures like Daniel Boone, Kit Carson and Abraham Lincoln—and told tall tales to youngsters. One of his favorites went like this:

"A relative of mine, Uncle Pickax, dug for gold in Arizona. He dug for 10 years. No gold. He dug 20 years, then 30 years. Still no gold. Pickax finally died. But it made no difference. He went down in history as one of the greatest men who ever lived. You see, the hole he dug is—the Grand Canyon."

Many fans thought Hayes was a down-to-earth real rancher. But he really came from Wellsville, New York. He never rode a horse until he was nearly 50. In fact, he had no great love for westerns. "I hate 'em—really can't stand 'em," he said in a newspaper interview after he had retired at the age of 73.* "They always are the same. You have so few plots—the stagecoach holdup, the rustlers, the mortgage gag, the mine setting and the retired gunslinger."

TV westerns were even worse. "At least we had action in our pictures," Hayes said. "We used 100 horses in one of them. Nowadays, you're lucky to see four or five. Besides, they don't spend enough time on these TV westerns. They can't and stay within their budget. All they do on TV in the westerns is talk, talk, talk," said Gabby Hayes.

By 1943, Boyd had made 54 *Cassidy* pictures. Then, with production costs rising, Sherman bowed out. Boyd made 12 more on his own through 1948 before the last roundup came for him, too. So for the second time, Boyd's career was at a standstill.

Then, along came TV. Taking an all-or-nothing gamble, Boyd gathered up all his money to buy the TV rights to his pictures. He sold his ranch, borrowed and came up with $350,000. The complex project involved 1,500 separate contracts. Many of his friends thought he had bought a white elephant. But in 1948, when TV suddenly became the rising new medium, he was ready. The NBC television network leased the films and ran them on Saturday mornings. The thundering, action-packed adventures seemed just right for a new generation. Boyd found he had struck a video goldmine.

Capitalizing on his fame, Boyd immediately started Hopalong Cassidy Enterprises, which put his magic name on everything from cowboy outfits to bread—138 articles in all. Royalties also poured in from comic books, comic strips, radio and records. "If I wasn't so darned old," Boyd said, "the whole thing would frighten me."

What were the movies like that made this jackpot possible? Their locales varied

*Hayes died in 1969 at age 83.

In one of the series' more exotic locales, Hoppy rides with sheiks in Arabia. From left, Clyde, George J. Lewis and Boyd. Scene is from *Outlaws of the Desert* (1941).

Hoppy has the draw on veteran western villain Roy Barcroft in *False Colors* (1943). Jimmy Rogers, son of Will Rogers, and Clyde look on.

from the familiar Bar 20 Ranch to stories set in the High Sierras, lumber camps, Mexico, Argentina, and Arabia. Their plots were a mixed bag, too—ranging from exciting, fast-paced action pictures with handsome outdoor scenery to dull, unimaginative efforts with second-rate photography and third-rate acting.

One that stands a bit below the high-water mark but well above the low-water mark is *Border Vigilantes,* a 1941 picture whose all-star western cast includes Andy Clyde (Hayes' successor), Victor Jory, Frances Gifford, Russell Hayden and Tom Tyler. Like most Hoppies, it follows a simple formula—slow beginning, a few minor skirmishes, then building to an all-out climax.

As the movie opens, outlaw raids on the miners of the border district have kept on despite the formation of a vigilante committee in Silver Center. The raids have scared many of the miners. Some have quit. Others have sold their claims.

"I'm convinced there's something wrong around here," rancher Dan Forbes (Morris Ankrum) tells businessman Henry Logan (Victor Jory).

Logan is the vigilantes' leader. But he is secretly the outlaws' boss. "These bandits have anticipated every move we've made . . . Each time we've found their mule hideout and tried to surprise them, they've surprised us instead . . . Only us vigilantes knew when and where we'd strike. I'm convinced someone among us is talking to the wrong people."

"It does look that way, Dan," says Logan, managing to keep a straight face. "You got any ideas who it is?"

"No. But I will. I'm sending for a friend of mine from Arizona to join us and ferret out the weasel. Name's Hopalong Cassidy."

"Hopalong Cassidy. Who is he? Never heard of him."

"You will . . ."

When the rancher leaves, Logan calls in his henchmen, Jim Yager (Tyler) and Ed Stone (Hal Taliaferro). "I don't like this, boss," Stone says. "I tangled with Cassidy when he was marshal of Santa Fe. He's bad medicine."

"Keep your shirt on, Ed," Yager says, not impressed. "We shouldn't have any trouble taking care of just one man."

"That's what my old outfit thought. But they're dead. And he's still alive."

So Logan tries to upset rancher Forbes' new idea right at its inception. As he is leaving town, Yager shoots Forbes in the back. But he succeeds only in wounding him. Meanwhile, Stone rides to Gunsight Pass to ambush Cassidy.

The scene cuts to three riders—Hopalong and his partners, California (Clyde) and Lucky Jenkins (Hayden)—approaching the pass. As they separate to find the best trail, gunman Stone gets a bead on Cassidy and fires. Hopalong falls off his white horse, Topper, and rolls into the underbrush. When Stone goes to finish him off, Hopalong suddenly emerges from behind a boulder. "An old Indian trick," Hoppy says. When Stone draws, Hoppy shoots him. So even before he has arrived at Silver Center, Cassidy has had an auspicious welcome.

William Boyd as Hopalong Cassidy, whom many consider the king of the series western heroes. When television came in, Boyd bought the rights to his 66 movies and parlayed them into a fortune. He is seen here atop his mount, Topper.

"Not so fast," says Hoppy, suspecting a stacked deck from Kermit Maynard in *Stick to Your Guns* (1941). Looking on, from left, are Weldon Heyburn, Andy Clyde, Jack Rockwell, Dick Curtis and Herman Hack (on bunk).

"Did anyone know you'd sent for me?" Cassidy asks Forbes.

"Henry Logan," Forbes says. "President of the Miners Association and head of the vigilantes."

"That's interesting," Cassidy says. However, before anyone jumps to conclusions, Cassidy adds, he wants to get proof of Logan's duplicity.

Now we see the first of a number of subplots involving Cassidy's partners. For romantic interest, Lucky flirts with Forbes' daughter, Helen (Frances Gifford), who sings to him. For comedy, California does his best to keep one step away from aggressive spinster Aunt Jenifer (Ethel Wales.)

The next day, Hopalong goes into town and visits the local saloon. The piano stops. All conversation breaks off as Cassidy sidles slowly to the bar, eyeing everyone, and then orders sarsaparilla.

Minutes later, Logan's men hold up the bank but Cassidy and his pals manage to save the silver supply. Then, Cassidy sets a trap. He secretly arranges for the silver to be shipped out on the mule train and sees that the vigilantes are told about the route. Instead, Hoppy loads the mules with iron bars. The real shipment is to go out on another wagon. Sure enough, the outlaws intercept the mule train and almost start a shootout among themselves when they learn they've been tricked.

Then things go bad for Hoppy. First, the real shipment that arrives at the railroad turns out to be phony. And the miners, convinced that Cassidy has kept the silver for himself, capture Lucky and start to string him up. Meanwhile, six of Logan's henchmen surround Cassidy in the saloon. Their attention is diverted for an instant as California bursts in to get help for Lucky. Cassidy, shooting like lightning, guns down all the badmen. Then he rides to the hanging party just in time to shoot the rope from Lucky's neck. Cassidy, getting to the bottom of the mixup, finds that the absent-minded California has mistakenly left the real silver in a warehouse. Now, with the miners on his side, Hopalong is ready for a showdown.

He sends all of Logan's men the same note. It reads: "Logan switched the silver and hid it in the shaft at the old Clement's Mine." The ploy works. At the mine, Yager and Stone, each convinced that the other is in cahoots with Logan, kill each other in a shootout. Then, Logan and his boys arrive with Cassidy and the miners in hot pursuit. A massive gunfight erupts with Logan's men battling Cassidy and the miners from a shack. Logan wings Hoppy in the shoulder. But he shakes it off, "I'll take care of it later," he says. Then, he flushes the bandits out by setting fire to a case of shells that pop off like a machine gun.

As Logan goes off to jail, Hoppy remarks, "Don't believe everything you read." And with that, he and his two comrades in the saddle ride off to yet another adventure.

Boyd retired in 1953 and moved to Palm Desert, Calif., where he and his wife,

Grace, lived quietly. He made a few public appearances. But in 1968, he underwent surgery for removal of a tumor from a lymph gland. From then on, he refused all interviews and photographs. "I'm not the man people remember as Hopalong Cassidy," Boyd said. "They'd be shocked at the difference. I don't want to tamper with their memories."

Those memories ended for Boyd on Sept. 12, 1972. After a four-month hospitalization, he died from complications of Parkinson's disease and congestive heart failure. The good guy in black was 77.

HOPALONG CASSIDY SERIES

1. *Hop-Along Cassidy.* Paramount, 1935, Howard Bretherton.
    William Boyd (as Hopalong Cassidy), Jimmy Ellison (as Johnny Nelson), Paula Stone, Robert Warwick, Charles Middleton, Frank McGlynn, Jr., Kenneth Thomson, George Hayes, James Mason, Frank Campeau, Ted Adams, Willie Fung. 63 minutes. (Reissued by Screen Guild as *Hopalong Cassidy Enters.*)

2. *The Eagle's Brood.* Paramount, 1935, Howard Bretherton.
    William Boyd, Jimmy Ellison, William Farnum, Addison Richards, George Hayes, Joan Woodbury, Frank Shannon, Dorothy Revier, Paul Fix, Al Lydell, John Merton. 65 minutes.

3. *Bar 20 Rides Again.* Paramount, 1935, Howard Bretherton.
    William Boyd, Jimmy Ellison, Jean Rouverol, George Hayes (as Windy), Harry Worth, Frank McGlynn, Jr., Howard Lang, Ethel Wales, Paul Fix, J. P. McGowan, Joe Rickson, Al St. John, John Merton, Frank Layton, Chill Wills and his Avalon Boys. 65 minutes.

4. *Call of the Prairie.* Paramount, 1936, Howard Bretherton.
    William Boyd, Jimmy Ellison, Muriel Evans, George Hayes, Chester Conklin, Al Bridge, Hank Mann, Willie Fung, Howard Lang, Al Hill, John Merton, Jim Mason, Chill Wills and his Avalon Boys. 65 minutes.

5. *Three on the Trail.* Paramount, 1936, Howard Bretherton.
    William Boyd, Jimmy Ellison, Onslow Stevens, Muriel Evans, George Hayes, Claude King, William Duncan, Clara Kimball Young, Ernie Adams, Ted Adams, John St. Polis, Al Hill, John Rutherford, Lita Cortez. 67 minutes.

6. *Heart of the West.* Paramount, 1936, Howard Bretherton.
    William Boyd, Jimmy Ellison, George Hayes, Lynn Gabriel, Sydney Blackmer, Charles Martin, John Rutherford, Warner Richmond, Walter Miller, Ted Adams, Fred Kohler, Robert McKenzie. 63 minutes.

7. *Hopalong Cassidy Returns.* Paramount, 1936, Nate Watt.
    William Boyd, George Hayes, Gail Sheridan, Evelyn Brent, Stephen Morris (Morris Ankrum), William Janney, Irving Bacon, Grant Richards, John Beck, Ernie Adams, Al St. John, Joe Rickson, Ray Whitley, Claude Smith. 71 minutes.

8. *Trail Dust.* Paramount, 1936, Nate Watt.
    William Boyd, James Ellison, George Hayes, Stephen Morris, Gwynne Shipman,

Britt Wood, Earl Askam, John Beach, Ted Adams, Al St. John, Tom Halligan, Emmett Daly, Dan Wolheim, George Chesebro, Robert Drew, Harold Daniels, Kenneth Harlan. 77 minutes.

9. *Borderland.* Paramount, 1937, Nate Watt.
William Boyd, James Ellison, George Hayes, Stephen Morris, Charlene Wyatt, Nora Lane, Trevor Bardette, Al Bridge, George Chesebro, Earle Hodgins, John Beach, Ed Cassidy. 82 minutes.

10. *Hills of Old Wyoming.* Paramount, 1937, Nate Watt.
William Boyd, George Hayes, Russell Hayden (as Lucky Jenkins), Gail Sheridan, Morris Ankrum, Clara Kimball Young, Earle Hodgins, Steve Clemento, Chief Big Tree, John Beach, George Chesebro, Paul Gustine, Leo MacMahon, John Powers. 78 minutes.

11. *North of the Rio Grande.* Paramount, 1937, Nate Watt.
William Boyd, George Hayes, Russell Hayden, Stephen Morris, Bernadene Hayes, John Rutherford, Lorraine Randall, Walter Long, Lee (J.) Cobb, John Beach, Al Ferguson, Lafe McKee. 70 minutes.

12. *Rustlers' Valley.* Paramount, 1937, Nate Watt.
William Boyd, George Hayes, Russell Hayden, John St. Polis, Lee (J.) Cobb, Stephen Morris, Muriel Evans, Ted Adams, Al Ferguson, John Beach. 60 minutes.

13. *Hopalong Rides Again.* Paramount, 1937, Lesley Selander.
William Boyd, George Hayes, Russell Hayden, William Duncan, Lois Wilde, Billy King, Nora Lane, Harry Worth, John Rutherford, Ernie Adams, Frank Ellis. 65 minutes.

14. *Texas Trail.* Paramount, 1937, David Selman.
William Boyd, George Hayes, Russell Hayden, Judith Allen, Alexander Cross, Robert Kortman, Billy King, Raphael (Ray) Bennett, Karl Hackett, Jack Rockwell, Philo McCullough, John Beach, John Judd, Ben Corbett, Clyde Kinney, Leo MacMahon. 58 minutes.

15. *Heart of Arizona.* Paramount, 1938, Lesley Selander.
William Boyd, George Hayes, Russell Hayden, John Elliott, Billy King, Natalie Moorhead, Dorothy Short, (Stephen) Alden Chase, John Beach, Lane Chandler, Leo MacMahon. 68 minutes.

16. *Bar 20 Justice.* Paramount, 1938, Lesley Selander.
William Boyd, George Hayes, Russell Hayden, Paul Sutton, Gwen Gaze, Pat O'Brien, Joseph DeStefani, William Duncan, Walter Long, H. Bruce Mitchell, John Beach. 70 minutes.

17. *Pride of the West.* Paramount, 1938, Lesley Selander.
William Boyd, George Hayes, Russell Hayden, Charlotte Field, Earle Hodgins, Billy King, Kenneth Harlan, Glenn Strange, James Craig, Bruce Mitchell, Willie Fung, George Morrell. 56 minutes.

18. *In Old Mexico.* Paramount, 1938, Edward D. Venturini.
William Boyd, George Hayes, Russell Hayden, Paul Sutton, Allan Garcia, Jan Clayton, Trevor Bardette, Betty Amann, Anna Demetrio, Glenn Strange, Tony Roux. 62 minutes.

19. *Sunset Trail.* Paramount, 1938, Lesley Selander.
William Boyd, George Hayes, Russell Hayden, Charlotte Wynters, Jan Clayton, Robert Fiske, Kathryn Sheldon, Maurice Cass, Anthony Nace, Kenneth Harlan, Alphonse Ethier, Glenn Strange, Jack Rockwell, Tom London, Claudia Smith. 60 minutes.

20. *The Frontiersman.* Paramount, 1938, Lesley Selander.
William Boyd, George Hayes, Russell Hayden, Evelyn Venable, William Duncan, Clara Kimball Young, Charles A. (Tony) Hughes, Dickie Jones, Roy Barcroft, Emily Fitzroy, John Beach, St. Brendan Boys' Choir (led by Robert B. Mitchell). 74 minutes.

21. *Partners of the Plains.* Paramount, 1938, Lesley Selander.
William Boyd, Harvey Clark, Russell Hayden, Gwen Gaze, Hilda Plowright, John Warburton, Al Bridge, Al Hill, Earle Hodgins, John Beach. 70 minutes.

22. *Cassidy of Bar 20.* Paramount, 1938, Lesley Selander.
William Boyd, Russell Hayden, Frank Darien, Nora Lane, Robert Fiske, John Elliott, Margaret Marquis, Gertrude W. Hoffman, Carleton Young, Gordon Hart, Edward Cassidy. 56 minutes.

23. *Range War.* Paramount, 1939, Lesley Selander.
William Boyd, Russell Hayden, Willard Robertson, Matt Moore, Pedro de Cordoba, Betty Moran, Britt Wood (as Speedy MacGinnis). 64 minutes.

24. *Law of the Pampas.* Paramount, 1939, Nate Watt.
William Boyd, Russell Hayden, Steffi Duna, Sidney Toler, Sidney Blackmer, Pedro de Cordoba, William Duncan, Anna Demetrio, Eddie Dean, Glenn Strange, Jo Jo La Savio, Tony Roux, Martin Garralaga. 72 minutes.

25. *Silver on the Sage.* Paramount, 1939, Lesley Selander.
William Boyd, George Hayes, Russell Hayden, Stanley Ridges, Frederick Burton, Ruth Rogers, Jack Rockwell, Roy Barcroft, Ed Cassidy, Jim Corey, Sherry Tansey, Bruce Mitchell. 68 minutes.

26. *The Renegade Trail.* Paramount, 1939, Lesley Selander.
William Boyd, George Hayes, Russell Hayden, Charlotte Wynters, Russell Hopton, Sonny Bupp, Jack Rockwell, Roy Barcroft, John Merton, Bob Kortman, The King's Men. 58 minutes.

27. *Santa Fe Marshal.* Paramount, 1940, Lesley Selander.
William Boyd, Russell Hayden, Marjorie Rambeau, Bernadene Hayes, Earle Hodgins, Britt Wood, Kenneth Harlan. 68 minutes.

28. *The Showdown.* Paramount, 1940, Howard Bretherton.
William Boyd, Russell Hayden, Britt Wood, Morris Ankrum, Jan Clayton, Wright Kramer, Donald Kirke, Roy Barcroft, Kermit Maynard, Walter Shumway, The King's Men. 65 minutes.

29. *Hidden Gold.* Paramount, 1940, Lesley Selander.
William Boyd, Russell Hayden, Britt Wood, Ruth Rogers, Roy Barcroft, Minor Watson, Ethel Wales, Lee Phelps, George Anderson, Jack Rockwell, Eddie Dean, Raphael Bennett. 61 minutes.

30. *Stagecoach War.* Paramount, 1940, Lesley Selander.
William Boyd, Russell Hayden, Julie Carter, Harvey Stephens, J. Farrell MacDonald, Britt Wood, Rad Robinson, Eddy Waller, Frank Lackteen, Jack Rockwell, Eddie Dean, The King's Men. 63 minutes.

31. *Three Men from Texas.* Paramount, 1940, Lesley Selander.
William Boyd, Russell Hayden, Andy Clyde (as California), Morris Ankrum, Morgan Wallace, Thornton Edwards, Esther Estrella, Davison Clark, Dick Curtis, George Lollier, Glenn Strange, Neyle Marx. 76 minutes.

32. *Doomed Caravan.* Paramount, 1941, Lesley Selander.
William Boyd, Russell Hayden, Andy Clyde, Minna Gombell, Morris Ankrum, Georgia Hawkins, Trevor Bardette, Pat J. O'Brien, Raphael Bennett, Jose Luis Tortosa. 62 minutes.

33. *In Old Colorado.* Paramount, 1941, Howard Bretherton.
William Boyd, Russell Hayden, Andy Clyde, Margaret Hayes, Morris Ankrum, Sarah Padden, Cliff Nazarro, Stanley Andrews, James Seay, Morgan Wallace, Weldon Heyburn, Glenn Strange, Eddy Waller, Philip Van Zandt. 66 minutes.

34. *Border Vigilantes.* Paramount, 1941, Derwin Abrahams.
William Boyd, Russell Hayden, Andy Clyde, Victor Jory, Morris Ankrum, Frances Gifford, Ethel Wales, Tom Tyler, Hal Taliaferro, Jack Rockwell, Britt Wood, Hank Worden, Edward Earle, Hank Bell. 63 minutes.

35.   *Pirates on Horseback*. Paramount, 1941, Lesley Selander.
William Boyd, Russell Hayden, Andy Clyde, Eleanor Stewart, Morris Ankrum, William Haade, Dennis Moore, Henry Hall, Britt Wood. 69 minutes.

36.   *Wide Open Town*. Paramount, 1941, Lesley Selander.
William Boyd, Russell Hayden, Andy Clyde, Evelyn Brent, Victor Jory, Morris Ankrum, Bernice Kay (Cara Williams), Kenneth Harlan, Roy Barcroft, Glenn Strange, Ed Cassidy, Jack Rockwell. 79 minutes.

37.   *Outlaws of the Desert*. Paramount, 1941, Howard Bretherton.
William Boyd, Andy Clyde, Brad King (as Johnny Nelson), Duncan Renaldo, Forest Stanley, Luli Deste, Alberto Morin, Jean Phillips, Nina Guilbut, George Woolsley, George Lewis, Jean Del Val, Mickey Eissa, Jamiel Hasson. 66 minutes.

38.   *Riders of the Timberline*. Paramount, 1941, Lesley Selander.
William Boyd, Brad King, Andy Clyde, J. Farrell MacDonald, Eleanor Stewart, Anna Q. Nilsson, Edward Keane, Hal Taliaferro, Tom Tyler, Victor Jory, Mickey Eissa, The Guardsmen. 59 minutes.

39.   *Secret of the Wastelands*. Paramount, 1941, Derwin Abrahams.
William Boyd, Brad King, Andy Clyde, Barbara Britton, Douglas Fowley, Keith Richards, Soo Yong, Gordon Hart, Hal Price, Lee Tung Foo, Earl Gunn, Ian MacDonald, John Rawlings, Richard Loo, Roland Got, Jack Rockwell. 66 minutes.

40.   *Stick to Your Guns*. Paramount, 1941, Lesley Selander.
William Boyd, Brad King, Andy Clyde, Jacqueline Holt, Henry Hall, Joe White-head, Bob Card, Jimmy Wakely, Johnny Bond, Dick Rinehart, Jack Smith, Jack Trent, Homer Holcomb, Tom London, Mickey Eissa, Weldon Heyburn, Dick Curtis, Kermit Maynard, Herman Hack, Jack Rockwell, The Jim Wakely Trio. 63 minutes.

41.   *Twilight on the Trail*. Paramount, 1941, Howard Bretherton.
William Boyd, Brad King, Andy Clyde, Jack Rockwell, Wanda McKay, Norman Willis, Robert Kent, Tom London, Frank Austin, Clem Fuller, Johnny Powers, The Jim Wakely Trio. 58 minutes.

42.   *Undercover Man*. United Artists, 1942, Lesley Selander.
William Boyd, Andy Clyde, Jay Kirby, Antonio Moreno, Chris-Pin Martin, Nora Lane, Esther Estrella, Alan Baldwin, Eva Puig, Jack Rockwell, John Vosper, Tony Roux, Pierce Lyden, Ted Wells, Martin Garralaga, Joe Dominguez, Earle Hodgins. 68 minutes.

43. *Lost Canyon.* United Artists, 1942, Lesley Selander.
William Boyd, Jay Kirby, Andy Clyde, Lola Lane, Douglas Fowley, Herbert Rawlinson, Guy Usher, Karl Hackett, The Sportsmen. 61 minutes. (Remake of *Rustlers' Valley* [No. 12]).

44. *Colt Comrades.* United Artists, 1943, Lesley Selander.
William Boyd, Andy Clyde, Jay Kirby, George Reeves, Gayle Lord, Earle Hodgins, Victor Jory, Douglas Fowley, Herb Rawlinson, Bob Mitchum. 67 minutes.

45. *Bar 20.* United Artists, 1943, Lesley Selander.
William Boyd, Andy Clyde, George Reeves, Dustine Farnum, Victor Jory, Douglas Fowley, Betty Blythe, Bob Mitchum, Francis McDonald, Earle Hodgins. 54 minutes.

46. *Hoppy Serves a Writ.* United Artists, 1943, George Archainbaud.
William Boyd, Andy Clyde, Jay Kirby, Victor Jory, George Reeves, Jan Christy, Hal Taliaferro, Forbes Murray, Bob Mitchum, Byron Foulger, Earle Hodgins, Roy Barcroft, Ben Corbett. 67 minutes.

47. *Border Patrol.* United Artists, 1943, Lesley Selander.
William Boyd, Andy Clyde, Jay Kirby, Russell Simpson, Claudia Drake, Cliff Parkinson, George Reeves, Duncan Renaldo, Pierce Lyden, Bob Mitchum. 65 minutes.

48. *The Leather Burners.* United Artists, 1943, Joseph Henabery.
William Boyd, Andy Clyde, Jay Kirby, Victor Jory, George Givot, Shelley Spencer, Bobby Larson, George Reeves, Hal Taliaferro, Forbes Murray. 58 minutes.

49. *False Colors.* United Artists, 1943, George Archainbaud.
William Boyd, Andy Clyde, Jimmy Rogers (as Jimmy Rogers), Tom Seidel, Claudia Drake, Douglass Dumbrille, Bob Mitchum, Glenn Strange, Pierce Lyden, Roy Barcroft, Sam Flint, Earle Hodgins, Elmer Jerome, Tom London, Dan White, George Morrell. 65 minutes.

50. *Riders of the Deadline.* United Artists, 1943, Lesley Selander.
William Boyd, Andy Clyde, Jimmy Rogers, Richard Crane, Frances Woodward, William Halligan, Tony Warde, Bob Mitchum, Jim Bannon, Hugh Prosser, Herbert Rawlinson, Montie Montana, Earle Hodgins, Bill Beckford, Pierce Lyden. 70 minutes.

51. *Mystery Man.* United Artists, 1944, George Archainbaud.
William Boyd, Andy Clyde, Jimmy Rogers, Don Costello, Francis McDonald, Forrest Taylor, Eleanor Stewart, Jack Rockwell, Pierce Lyden, John Merton, Bill

Hunter, Bob Burns, Ozie Waters, Art Mix, George Morrell, Bob Baker, Hank Bell. 58 minutes.

52. *Forty Thieves.* United Artists, 1944, Lesley Selander.
William Boyd, Andy Clyde, Jimmy Rogers, Douglass Dumbrille, Louise Currie, Kirk Alyn, Herbert Rawlinson, Robert Frazer, Glenn Strange, Jack Rockwell, Bob Kortman. 60 minutes.

53. *Texas Masquerade.* United Artists, 1944, George Archainbaud.
William Boyd, Andy Clyde, Jimmy Rogers, Mady Correll, Don Costello, Russell Simpson, Nelson Leigh, Francis McDonald, J. Farrell MacDonald, June Pickerell, John Merton, Pierce Lyden, Robert McKenzie, Bill Hunter, George Morrell. 58 minutes.

54. *Lumberjack.* United Artists, 1944, Lesley Selander.
William Boyd, Andy Clyde, Jimmy Rogers, Herbert Rawlinson, Ellen Hall, Ethel Wales, Douglass Dumbrille, Francis McDonald, John Whitney, Hal Taliaferro, Henry Wills, Charles Morton, Frances Morris, Jack Rockwell, Bob Burns. 65 minutes.

55. *The Devil's Playground.* United Artists, 1946, George Archainbaud.
William Boyd, Andy Clyde, Rand Brooks (as Lucky Jenkins), Elaine Riley, Robert Elliott, Joseph J. Greene, Francis McDonald, Ned Young, Earle Hodgins, George Eldredge, Everett Shields, John George. 65 minutes.

56. *Fool's Gold.* United Artists, 1946, George Archainbaud.
William Boyd, Andy Clyde, Rand Brooks, Jane Randolph, Robert Emmett Keane, Stephen Barclay, Harry Cording, Earle Hodgins, Forbes Murray, William Davis, Benny Corbett, Fred (Snowflake) Toones, Bob Bentley, Glen B. Gallagher. 63 minutes.

57. *Unexpected Guest.* United Artists, 1947, George Archainbaud.
William Boyd, Andy Clyde, Rand Brooks, Una O'Connor, John Parrish, Earle Hodgins, Robert B. Williams, Patricia Tate, Ned Young, Joel Friedkin. 61 minutes.

58. *Dangerous Venture.* United Artists, 1947, George Archainbaud.
William Boyd, Andy Clyde, Rand Brooks, Fritz Leiber, Douglas Evans, Harry Cording, Betty Alexander, Francis McDonald, Neyle Morrow, Patricia Tate, Bob Faust, Ken Tobey, Jack Quinn, Bill Nestell. 59 minutes.

59. *Hoppy's Holiday.* United Artists, 1947, George Archainbaud.
William Boyd, Andy Clyde, Rand Brooks, Andrew Tombes, Jeff Corey, Mary

Ware, Leonard Penn, Donald Kirke, Hollis Bane (Mike Ragan), Gil Patric, Frank Henry. 60 minutes.

60. *The Marauders.* United Artists, 1947, George Archainbaud.
William Boyd, Andy Clyde, Rand Brooks, Ian Wolfe, Dorinda Clifton, Mary Newton, Harry Cording, Earle Hodgins, Dick Bailey. 63 minutes.

61. *Silent Conflict.* United Artists, 1948, George Archainbaud.
William Boyd, Andy Clyde, Rand Brooks, Virginia Belmont, Earle Hodgins, James Harrison, Forbes Murray, John Butler, Herbert Rawlinson, Richard Alexander, Don Haggerty. 61 minutes.

62. *The Dead Don't Dream.* United Artists, 1948, George Archainbaud.
William Boyd, Andy Clyde, Rand Brooks, John Parrish, Leonard Penn, Mary Tucker, Francis McDonald, Richard Alexander, Bob Gabriel, Stanley Andrews, Forbes Murray, Don Haggerty. 62 minutes.

63. *Sinister Journey.* United Artists, 1948, George Archainbaud.
William Boyd, Andy Clyde, Rand Brooks, Elaine Riley, John Kellogg, Don Haggerty, Stanley Andrews, Harry Strang, John Butler, Herbert Rawlinson, Will Orleans, Wayne C. Treadway. 72 minutes.

64. *Borrowed Trouble.* United Artists, 1948, George Archainbaud.
William Boyd, Andy Clyde, Rand Brooks, Elaine Riley, John Kellogg, Helen Chapman, John Parrish, Cliff Clark, Anne O'Neal, Earle Hodgins, Herbert Rawlinson, Don Haggerty, James Harrison. 58 minutes.

65. *False Paradise.* United Artists, 1948, George Archainbaud.
William Boyd, Andy Clyde, Rand Brooks, Joel Friedkin, Elaine Riley, Kenneth MacDonald, Don Haggerty, Cliff Clark, George Eldredge, Richard Alexander, Zon Murray. 59 minutes.

66. *Strange Gamble.* United Artists, 1948, George Archainbaud.
William Boyd, Andy Clyde, Rand Brooks, Elaine Riley, William Leicester, Joan Barton, James Craven, Joel Friedkin, Herbert Rawlinson, Robert B. Williams, Alberto Morin, Lee Tung Foo. 61 minutes.

Taking aim are the Three Mesquiteers, range-riders who popularized the so-called Trio Western. From left, Max Terhune, Robert Livingston, and Ray Corrigan. They teamed up in eight pictures during 1936 and 1937.

THE THREE MESQUITEERS

Hit the Saddle

(1937)

Screenplay by Oliver Drake. Original story by Drake and Maurice Geraghty. Based on characters created by William Colt MacDonald. Music also used in *Robinson Crusoe of Clipper Island* (1936) and *The Lone Ranger* (1938). Song "Winding the Trail" by Sammy Stept and Oliver Drake sung by Robert Livingstone and Rita Cansino (Hayworth). Miss Cansino dances to "La Cucaracha." Produced by Nat Levine. Directed by Mack V. Wright. Released by Republic Pictures. 57 minutes.

Stony Brooke	ROBERT LIVINGSTON
Tucson Smith	RAY CORRIGAN
Lullaby Joslin	MAX TERHUNE
Rita	RITA CANSINO (HAYWORTH)
Rance McGowan	J. P. MCGOWAN
Buck	YAKIMA CANUTT
Sheriff Miller	EDWARD CASSIDY
Tim Miller	SAMMY MCKIM
Joe Harvey	HARRY TENBROOK
Hank	ROBERT SMITH

Pete	ED BOLAND
Henchman	GEORGE PLUES
Rancher	JACK KIRK
Stallion	VOLCANO
Rancher	RUSS POWELL
Rancher	BOB BURNS
Judge	ALLAN CAVAN
Patron	GEORGE MORRELL
Drunk	BUDD BUSTER
Bartender	KERNAN CRIPPS

The scene—a saloon. Cowboy Max Terhune steps up to a crowded bar with his dummy, Elmer.

> BARTENDER: What are you going to have?
> TERHUNE: Spring whiskey.
> ELMER *(Interrupting):* You mean milk.
> TERHUNE: Listen, Elmer. This is Stony's wedding. One drink won't do no harm.
> ELMER: I said milk. And milk it is. I'm getting sick and tired of acting like a nursemaid to you. Unless you stay on the wagon, I'm leaving. *(Pointing to a nearby barfly)* Look at that bum alongside of you. That's what you'll look like if you don't watch your step.
> BARFLY: You keep that dummy quiet or I'll wrap this bottle around your head.
> ELMER: *(Irritated)* I'd rather be a dummy than a drunk any day. I'll bet while you're in here squandering your money, your wife and kids are going hungry. Friend, there's no greater evil in this world today than the curse of drink. *(Turning to all at the bar and raising his voice)* Every one of you gents has an old gray-haired mother waitin' for you to come home. Would they be proud of you at this minute? No. Every time you take a drink, you're one step farther from salvation. *(To barfly)* Boy, it isn't too late. Reform while you still have a spark of manhood.
> BARFLY: Get out of here, will you?
> ELMER: *(Turning to Terhune and chuckling softly)* Say, that was a pretty good speech, wasn't it? I'm kind of dry now. Make me a double whiskey with a gin chaser.

The temperance sequence from *Hit the Saddle* is typical of the humor of the B-western—simple, direct, mildly amusing. Cowboy sidekicks didn't always succeed in bringing down the house. But they did serve a necessary function. Their job was to change the pace and bridge the action scenes and song sequences. Over the years, they became familiar and endearing figures to the Saturday matinee crowd. If their dry, homespun jokes weren't always knee-slappers, well then, a well-directed punch that flattened a villain later in a fight sequence usually atoned for it.

John Wayne, right, temporarily replaced Livingston in 1938 and played in eight films with Terhune and Corrigan. The triumvirate's name was a takeoff on the mesquite plant that flourishes on ranchlands.

Raymond Hatton, left, and Duncan Renaldo, right, joined Livingston in 1939 as still another trio. Renaldo later became one of the four actors who played the Cisco Kid.

The saddle pals are, from left, Tom Tyler, Rufe Davis and Bob Steele who appeared as the Mesquiteers in seven pictures from 1941 and 1942. Davis went on to become Floyd, the conductor in TV's "Petticoat Junction."

The last Mesquiteer bunch was Jimmy Dodd, Tyler and Steele. Dodd later became a "Mouseketeer" on TV. In all, the *Mesquiteers* series totaled 52 B-westerns from 1935 to 1943.

The comedy sidekicks flourished in a format called Trio Westerns, a genre that began in the mid-1930s. Instead of a lone hero galloping across the purple sage in search of adventure, these pictures featured a three-man cowboy team. The idea came from William Colt MacDonald's popular western books about a trio of devil-may-care cowpokes. MacDonald dubbed them the Three Mesquiteers, a take-off on Alexandre Dumas' *Three Musketeers.* (Some also think the name relates to the mesquite plant, a spiny shrub that grows abundantly on ranchlands in the southwest.) Republic Studios felt three cowboy adventurers would make an ideal unit for a fast-paced picture. And so it launched what many western buffs came to rate as the best of all the western series.*

Over the Mesquiteers' eight-year production lifetime—1935 to 1943—twelve actors played the one-for-all and all-for-one leather-slingers. They included such stalwarts of the saddle as John Wayne, Bob Steele, Tom Tyler, Rufe Davis, Raymond Hatton, Duncan Renaldo and Jimmy Dodd (later chief of the TV "Mouseketeers"). Even Ralph Byrd, who played Dick Tracy, was a Mesquiteer in one film.**

The most famous trio was Bob Livingston, Ray (Crash) Corrigan and Max Terhune. The threesome, who teamed in 14 movies, all had strong personalities. Livingston portrayed the brash, young, trouble-prone Stony Brooke. Corrigan was the rough, two-fisted but more level-headed Tucson Smith. Terhune was the likeable, easy-going Lullaby Joslin, whose humor sometimes developed in scenes with his dummy. A natural, fun-loving by-play developed between the three co-stars. It proved infectious and quickly won the loyalty of the popcorn brigade.

Why was the series so popular? Terhune thought it was because it offered something for everybody. "For the girls, it had a running gag of rivalry between Stony and Tucson for the girl in each story," Terhune said in a letter to the author. "It had plenty of action and fights, and the boys liked that. I like to believe the kids liked Elmer, too. And the adults, I think, liked the variety of plots and the scenery and beautiful horses."

Terhune, who was 81 in 1972 and living in Cottonwood, Arizona, added that a lot of credit must go to the famous stuntman, Yakima Canutt. "He directed the action and fights. And he not only directed but performed in horse falls, wagon turnovers, climbing and water stunts."

And so it was not surprising that a rash of cowboy Trio Westerns broke out.

---

*Hopalong Cassidy actually started the Trio Westerns in 1935. But sometimes he appeared with only one sidekick. And he was a dominant personality who always called the shots. The Three Mesquiteers were more nearly partners. And they are generally credited with bringing the Trio Western series to the height of its popularity.

**The series also was a training ground for aspiring leading ladies. Rita Hayworth, Carole Landis, Gale Storm, Phyllis Isley (later Jennifer Jones), Lorna Gray (Adrian Booth), and Jacqueline Wells (Julie Bishop) all played in Mesquiteer pictures. Lois Collier's seven appearances gave her the record for most appearances in the heroine's role.

There were the Rough Riders (Buck Jones, Tim McCoy and Raymond Hatton), the Range Busters (Terhune, Corrigan and John King in most of these), the Trail Blazers (Ken Maynard, Hoot Gibson and Bob Steele, among others), and the Texas Rangers (Dave O'Brien, James Newill and Guy Wilkerson in the majority of them). But the Mesquiteers had the best production values and western fans turned out in largest numbers for their films.

Ironically, none of the three members of the Mesquiteers' best-known trio began his career with the idea of going into movies. Or even becoming an actor.

Livingston, son of a Quincy, Illinois, newspaper editor, started as a reporter for the *Los Angeles Daily News*. But one day he did a story on the Pasadena Playhouse and the acting bug bit him. He started with small parts at Fox and Universal in the late 1920s, then moved up to romantic roles with Metro-Goldwyn-Mayer. But his progress was slow and he left to join Republic. There, he scored a rousing success in 1936 as the masked hero in the serial *The Vigilantes Are Coming*.

Cowboy parts followed, and he was offered one of the leading roles in *The Mesquiteers*. He became a fixture in the series—his 29 appearances are the most anyone made—although he occasionally left it to do other westerns and serials. In 1936, he played Zorro in *The Bold Caballero* and in 1939, he starred in *The Lone Ranger Rides Again*, sequel to the famous original serial. In the 1940s,

Terhune and his dummy sidekick, Elmer Sneezeweed. A versatile vaudevillian before his movie days, Terhune was a magician, juggler, whistler and pitchman, besides being a capable ventriloquist.

Livingston appeared with Al St. John in the *Lone Rider* series, and in western features with Smiley Burnette. He ended his film career in character roles in Columbia's Gene Autry series.

Born in Milwaukee, Corrigan was an outstanding athlete and physical culture devotee. He got started in Hollywood by taking a job teaching movie stars how to stay in condition. He made his film debut in 1932 and began winning attention with action roles in *The Leathernecks Have Landed* (1936) and *Undersea Kingdom* (1936). Corrigan, whose daring stunts and strong physique earned him the nickname "Crash," went on to achieve B-western stardom in the 24 pictures he made with the Mesquiteers. Later, he appeared in 20 of the 24 *Range Busters* series pictures, finally playing heavies and monsters—in such films as *The White Gorilla* (1945), *Killer Ape* (1953) and *It, the Terror from Outer Space* (1958)—before his retirement.

After his film career, he managed a variety of lucrative business interests including Corriganville, an authentic western town and ranch often used as a location site for movies and TV.

Terhune, a native of Franklin, Indiana, was an accomplished vaudevillian before he came to Hollywood. He was a juggler, magician, whistler, card shark, pitchman and impressionist. He once did voice imitations for a Disney cartoon. But his forte was ventriloquism and he became famous on the Orpheum Circuit with his dummy Skully Null (whose name became Elmer Sneezeweed in the movies).

In 1932, Terhune appeared with Gene Autry on the "National Barn Dance" radio program. Four years later, Autry persuaded him to go to Hollywood. He debuted in *Ride Ranger Ride* (1936), and went on to replace Syd Saylor as the comic in the Mesquiteers. It was in this role, which he played in 21 films, that Terhune reached the peak of his screen career. Then, after doing 24 *Range Buster* series pictures, Terhune appeared with Ken Maynard in *White Stallion* (1947), Maynard's last starring film, and co-starred with Johnny Mack Brown in eight movies. In all, he played in 70 pictures, including such big-budget productions as *Rawhide* (1951), with Tyrone Power and Susan Hayward, and *Jim Thorpe—All-American* (1951), with Burt Lancaster. His last major picture was in 1956, when he played a doctor in *Giant* with Elizabeth Taylor.

After his screen career, he had his own television show and appeared on "I Love Lucy," "Ramar of the Jungle" and other programs. Today, his son Bob is a Hollywood stuntman and actor.

What was Terhune's favorite *Mesquiteer* picture? "I guess it's ego, but I liked them all," he said. However, he singled out a trio—*Ghost Town Gold* (1936), his first ("because it showed how I won Elmer in a three-card monte game"), *Riders of the Whistling Skull* (1937) and *Hit the Saddle* (1937).

Hit the Saddle is certainly one of the most interesting on at least three counts.

It centers around the unusual theme of wild horses. Today, less than 20,000 of them remain in ten western states. But at the turn of the century, more than 2 million roamed freely. As cowboys and ranchers captured and sold them for premium prices, their numbers dwindled sharply. To try to save the species, Congress and the states set aside preserves, or protected areas, where they could live free from harassment. *Hit the Saddle* is the story of rustlers who try to circumvent the law.

The picture is also resplendent with authentic scenery. Taken in the Red Rock Canyon of the Mojave Desert, its background is filled with strangely carved rock walls that tower high in the air, petrified trees and stumps, and smoothly carved stumps of old lava flows.

Finally, the film is a kind of curiosity because of the performance of Rita Hayworth. She plays a Spanish cabaret girl.

As the movie opens, Sheriff Miller (Edward Cassidy) and the Three Mesquiteers catch five wild-horse hunters running a herd out of a protected area. The sheriff and the Mesquiteers bring the men into town and haul them before their boss, Rance McGowan (J. P. McGowan). McGowan, who runs a real estate office as a front for his illegal business of selling wild horses, insists his men were only hunting lost strays. The sheriff decides to be lenient. He lets McGowan off with a warning not to let it happen again.

As soon as the sheriff and the Mesquiteers leave, McGowan tells his riders he has just gotten a lucrative order for 1,000 horses. He means to fill it. "There are four men standing between me and a fortune in horses," McGowan says. "The sheriff and the Three Mesquiteers. I want them out of the way. How you do it is your business."

In a saloon, the horse thieves—Buck (Yakima Canutt) and Joe Harvey (Harry Tenbrook)—start a brawl. Tucson, seeing their game, upsets a beer keg to distract their attention and gets the draw on them. To add to their embarrassment, Lullaby makes them apologize to an old swayback horse for mistreating the animal's "uncles and aunts."

But the rustlers are far from through. Harvey has a stallion, Volcano, which he has trained to kill when he hears a shrill whistle. He paints Volcano to look like a pinto who leads the wild horse herd. One day, when the sheriff is inspecting the wild herd, Harvey lets Volcano loose. At his whistle, the killer horse rushes the sheriff and tramples him. The area's ranchers, angered by the lawman's death, insist that the wild pinto be destroyed. Stony says there is no proof the horse is a killer. But the ranchers persist and McGowan wins the right to capture him.

Meanwhile, Stony meets an eye-catching fandango dancer, Rita (Rita Hayworth) in the town cabaret. He takes a shine to her and they sing "Winding the Trail." The budding attraction threatens to break up the trio and Lullaby and Tucson don't think much of Rita. So they decide to tease their pal. Tucking his

Terhune steps between Corrigan, left, and Livingston as tempers flare over Rita Hayworth (in background between Corrigan and Terhune). Rita appeared then under her real name, Rita Cansino. Scene is from *Hit the Saddle* (1937).

Corrigan joshes with little Sammy McKim as Livingston, Terhune and Miss Hayworth look on in *Hit the Saddle*.

tongue firmly in his cheek, Lullaby tells Stony it was a grand duet. "I ain't heerd the likes since the night my grandpappy Zoobey was hung." Tucson joins in the ribbing. "Don't you see she's not your type girl," Tucson says.

"That's enough," Stony replies, his pride wounded. "You can save your Mother Goose rhymes for Lullaby."

When Rita goes backstage, one of the cabaret girls warns her she's going to have a hard time winning Stony. "Those boys are closer than Siamese twins," the girl says.

"Oh yeah," the cocky Rita replies. "Take a look at the baby who's going to perform the operation."

Stony, of course, is too naive to realize he's dealing with a tough cookie. "Rita," he says like a schoolboy, "you don't belong here. I'd like to see you get out of all this." Before he knows it, Rita has set a wedding date and is elatedly doing a fandango to "La Cucaracha."

And so it's up to Lullaby to see that the Mesquiteers aren't broken up. He goes to Rita's dressing room ostensibly to wish her well. She will be popular with the ranch cowhands, he tells her—all 16 of them. They've been looking forward to having a woman do their domestic chores for a long time. Lullaby's words have precisely the desired effect.

"If you think I'm going to the ranch to wash and cook and sew for a bunch of filthy cowboys, you're crazy," Rita explodes. "I'm an actress, not a washer-woman." She says she and Stony are going to New York.

"Hope you've found enough money for the trip," Lullaby says. "Stony's got no money." When Lullaby sees Rita's eyebrows rise, he offers her a one-way ticket east plus $1,500 gettin' around money. Suddenly Rita sees things in a new perspective. She accepts. Within hours, she's riding the rails out of town.

At least one movie writer noticed the early performance of this soon-to-be sex goddess. But he wasn't exactly overwhelmed. "The girl is highly deficient in terps and as an actress," *Variety*'s reviewer said, "but it is of no great consequence." (He was apparently comparing her acting ability with that of the rest of the cast.)

With Rita out of the way, the Mesquiteers go out and trap the pinto. To test him, Stony walks unprotected into his corral—without provoking an attack. When the ranchers meet again, Stony argues that the sheriff's body showed horseshoe marks. But the pinto has never been shod. Nevertheless, at the insistence of McGowan and the ranchers, Tucson, who has now become sheriff, orders the horse shot.

That night, Stony steals the pinto and tries to flee. But McGowan's men ambush him and spirit him and the pinto away to their hideout in the distant hills. There, after Stony discovers the painted Volcano, McGowan binds the Mesquiteer to a stake and lets loose the killer horse. "One more killing blamed on the pinto stallion and the state ban on wild horses will be lifted pronto," McGowan says.

However, he has forgotten about the pinto. And that proves his undoing. The wild pinto, loyal to his new master, Stony, breaks loose and fights Volcano off until Tucson and Lullaby ride up and start a shootout with the renegades. When Buck and McGowan jump on Volcano to try to escape, Stony lets loose a whistle signal. Volcano bucks the two rustlers off and tramples them to death.

And so the moral is clear. Those who live by the hoof die by the hoof.

THE THREE MESQUITEERS SERIES

1. *Powdersmoke Range.* RKO Radio, 1935, Wallace Fox.
   Harry Carey (as Stony Brooke), Hoot Gibson (as Tucson Smith), Bob Steele, Tom Tyler, Guinn Williams (as Lullaby Joslin), "Boots" Mallory, Ray Mayer, Sam Hardy, Adrian Morris, Buzz Barton, Wally Wales (later Hal Taliaferro), Art Mix, Buffalo Bill, Jr., Buddy Roosevelt, Franklyn Farnum, William Desmond, William Farnum, Ethan Laidlaw, Frank Rice, Eddie Dunn, Irving Bacon, Barney Furey, Henry Roquemore. 71 minutes.

2. *The Three Mesquiteers.* Republic, 1936, Ray Taylor.
   Ray Corrigan (as Tucson), Bob Livingston (as Stony), Syd Saylor (as Lullaby), Kay Hughes, J. P. McGowan, Al Bridge, Frank Yaconelli, John Merton, Jean Marvey, Milburn Stone, Duke York, Nina Quartero, Allen Connor. 61 minutes.

3. *Ghost Town Gold.* Republic, 1936, Joseph Kane.
   Bob Livingston, Ray Corrigan, Max Terhune (as Lullaby), Kay Hughes, LeRoy Mason, Burr Carruth, Bob Kortman, Milburn Morante, Frank Hagney, Don Roberts, F. Herrick Herrick, Robert C. Thomas, Yakima Canutt. 55 minutes.

4. *Roarin' Lead.* Republic, 1936, Mack V. Wright and Sam Newfield.
   Robert Livingston, Ray Corrigan, Max Terhune, Christine Maple, Hooper Atchley, Yakima Canutt, George Chesebro, Tommy Bupp, Mary Russell, Tamara, Lynn Kauffman, Beverly Luff, Theodore Frye, Katherine Frye, The Meglin Kiddies. 53 minutes.

5. *Riders of the Whistling Skull.* Republic, 1937, Mack V. Wright.
   Robert Livingston, Ray Corrigan, Max Terhune, Mary Russell, Roger Williams, Fern Emmett, C. Montague Shaw, Yakima Canutt, John Ward, George Godfrey, Earle Ross, Frank Ellis, John Van Pelt. 58 minutes.

6. *Hit the Saddle.* Republic, 1937, Mack V. Wright.
   Bob Livingston, Ray Corrigan, Max Terhune, Rita Cansino (Hayworth), J. P. McGowan, Harry Tenbrook, Yakima Canutt, Edward Cassidy, Sammy McKim, Robert Smith, Ed Boland, George Plues, Jack Kirk. 57 minutes.

7. *Gunsmoke Ranch.* Republic, 1937, Joseph Kane.
   Robert Livingston, Ray Corrigan, Max Terhune, Kenneth Harlan, Julia Thayer, Sammy McKim, Burr Caruth, Allen Connor, Yakima Canutt, Horace Carpenter, Jane Keckley, Bob Walker. 59 minutes.

8. *Come on Cowboys.* Republic, 1937, Joseph Kane.
Robert Livingston, Ray Corrigan, Max Terhune, Maxine Doyle, Willie Fung, Edward Piel, Sr., Horace Murphy, Anne Bennett, Edward Cassidy, Fern Emmett, Roger Williams, Yakima Canutt, George Burton, Merrill McCormick, Loren Riebe, Victor Allen, George Plues. 58 minutes.

9. *Range Defenders.* Republic, 1937, Mack V. Wright.
Robert Livingston, Ray Corrigan, Max Terhune, Eleanor Stewart, Harry Woods, Earle Hodgins, Thomas Carr, Yakima Canutt, John Merton, Harrison Greene, Horace Carpenter, Frank Ellis, Snowflake. 56 minutes.

10. *Heart of the Rockies.* Republic, 1937, Joseph Kane.
Bob Livingston, Ray Corrigan, Max Terhune, Lynne Roberts, J. P. McGowan, Sammy McKim, Yakima Canutt, Hal Taliaferro, Georgia Simmons. 56 minutes.

11. *The Trigger Trio.* Republic, 1937, William Witney.
Ray Corrigan, Max Terhune, Ralph Byrd (as Larry Smith, Tucson's brother), Sandra Corday, Robert Warwick, Cornelius Keefe, Sammy McKim, Hal Taliaferro, Willie Fung. 60 minutes.

12. *Wild Horse Rodeo.* Republic, 1937, George Sherman.
Bob Livingston, Ray Corrigan, Max Terhune, June Martel, Walter Miller, Edmund Cobb, William Gould, Jack Ingram, Snowflake, Dick Weston (Roy Rogers). 55 minutes.

13. *The Purple Vigilantes.* Republic, 1938, George Sherman.
Bob Livingston, Ray Corrigan, Max Terhune, Joan Barclay, Earl Dwire, Earle Hodgins, Francis Sayles, George Chesebro, Robert Fiske, Jack Perrin, Ernie Adams, William Gould, Harry Strang, Edward Cassidy, Frank O'Connor. 58 minutes.

14. *Call the Mesquiteers.* Republic, 1938, John English.
Bob Livingston, Ray Corrigan, Max Terhune, Lynn Roberts, Sammy McKim, Earle Hodgins, Eddy Waller, Maston Williams, Eddie Hart, Pat Gleason, Roger Williams, Warren Jackson, Hal Price, Flash. 55 minutes.

15. *Outlaws of Sonora.* Republic, 1938, George Sherman.
Bob Livingston, Max Terhune, Ray Corrigan, Jack Mulhall, Otis Harlan, Jean Joyce, Sterlita Peluffo, Tom London, Gloria Rich, Edwin Mordant, Ralph Peters, George Chesebro, Frank LaRue, Jack Ingram, Merrill McCormick. 55 minutes.

16. *Riders of the Black Hills.* Republic, 1938, George Sherman.
Bob Livingston, Ray Corrigan, Max Terhune, Ann Evers, Roscoe Ates, Maude

Eburne, Frank Melton, Johnny Fitzgerald, Jack Ingram, Edward Earle, Monte Montague, Ben Hall, Frank O'Connor, Tom London. 55 minutes.

17. *Heroes of the Hills.* Republic, 1938, George Sherman.
Robert Livingston, Ray Corrigan, Max Terhune, Priscilla Lawson, LeRoy Mason, James Eagles, Roy Barcroft, Barry Hays, Carleton Young, Forrest Taylor, John Wade, Maston Williams, John Beach, Jerry Frank, Roger Williams, Kit Guard. 56 minutes.

18. *Pals of the Saddle.* Republic, 1938, George Sherman.
John Wayne (as Stony), Ray Corrigan, Max Terhune, Doreen McKay, Josef Forte, George Douglas, Frank Milan, Ted Adams, Harry Depp, Dave Weber, Don Orlando, Charles Knight, Jack Kirk. 60 minutes.

19. *Overland Stage Raiders.* Republic, 1938, George Sherman.
John Wayne, Ray Corrigan, Max Terhune, Louise Brooks, Anthony Marsh, Ralph Bowman (John Archer), Gordon Hart, Roy James, Olin Francis, Fern Emmett, Henry Ottho, George Sherwood, Archie Hall, Frank LaRue. 55 minutes.

20. *Santa Fe Stampede.* Republic, 1938, George Sherman.
John Wayne, Ray Corrigan, Max Terhune, June Martel, William Farnum, LeRoy Mason, Martin Spellman, Genee Hall, Walter Wills, Ferris Taylor, Tom London, Dick Rush, James F. Cassidy. 55 minutes.

21. *Red River Range.* Republic, 1938, George Sherman.
John Wayne, Ray Corrigan, Max Terhune, Polly Moran, Lorna Gray (Adrian Booth), Kirby Grant, Sammy McKim, William Royle, Perry Ivins, Lenore Bushman, Roger Williams, Olin Francis, Burr Carruth. 56 minutes.

22. *The Night Riders.* Republic, 1939, George Sherman.
John Wayne, Ray Corrigan, Max Terhune, Doreen McKay, Ruth Rogers, George Douglas, Tom Tyler, Kermit Maynard, Sammy McKim, Walter Wills, Ethan Laidlaw, Edward Piel, Sr., Tom London, Jack Ingram, William Nestell. 58 minutes.

23. *Three Texas Steers.* Republic, 1939, George Sherman.
John Wayne, Ray Corrigan, Max Terhune, Carole Landis, Ralph Graves, Roscoe Ates, Collette Lyons, Billy Curtis, Ted Adams, Stanley Blystone, David Sharpe, Ethan Laidlaw, Lew Kelly. 59 minutes.

24. *Wyoming Outlaw.* Republic, 1939, George Sherman.
John Wayne, Ray Corrigan, Raymond Hatton (as Rusty Joslin), Adele Pearce (Pamela Blake), Donald Barry, LeRoy Mason, Yakima Canutt, Charles Middleton, Elmo Lincoln, David Sharpe. 56 minutes.

25. *New Frontier.* Republic, 1939, George Sherman.
John Wayne, Ray Corrigan, Raymond Hatton, Phyllis Isley (Jennifer Jones), Eddy Waller, Sammy McKim, LeRoy Mason, Harrison Greene, Dave O'Brien, Jack Ingram, Bud Osborne. 56 minutes.

26. *The Kansas Terrors.* Republic, 1939, George Sherman.
Robert Livingston (as Stony), Raymond Hatton, Duncan Renaldo (as Rico), Jacqueline Wells (Julie Bishop), Howard Hickman, George Douglas, Frank Lackteen, Myra Marsh, Yakima Canutt. 57 minutes.

27. *Cowboys from Texas.* Republic, 1939, George Sherman.
Robert Livingston, Raymond Hatton, Duncan Renaldo, Carole Landis, Ivan Miller, Charles Middleton, Betty Compson, Ethan Laidlaw, Yakima Canutt, Walter Wills, Edward Cassidy. 57 minutes.

28. *Heroes of the Saddle.* Republic, 1940, William Witney.
Robert Livingston, Raymond Hatton, Duncan Renaldo, Loretta Weaver, Patsy Lee Parsons, Byron Foulger, William Royle, Vince Barnett, Jack Roper, Reed Howes, Ethel May Halls, Al Taylor, Patsy Carmichael. 56 minutes.

29. *Pioneers of the West.* Republic, 1940, Lester Orlebeck.
Robert Livingston, Raymond Hatton, Duncan Renaldo, Noah Beery, Lane Chandler, Beatrice Roberts, George Cleveland, Hal Taliaferro, Yakima Canutt, John Dilson, Joe McGuinn, Earl Askam. 56 minutes.

30. *Covered Wagon Days.* Republic, 1940, George Sherman.
Robert Livingston, Raymond Hatton, Duncan Renaldo, Kay Griffith, George Douglas, Ruth Robinson, Paul Marion, John Merton, Tom Chatterton, Guy D'Ennery, Tom London, Reed Howes. 56 minutes.

31. *Rocky Mountain Rangers.* Republic, 1940, George Sherman.
Robert Livingston, Raymond Hatton, Duncan Renaldo, Rosella Towne, Sammy McKim, LeRoy Mason, Pat O'Malley, Dennis Moore, John St. Polis, Robert Blair, Burr Carruth, Jack Kirk. 58 minutes.

32. *Oklahoma Renegades.* Republic, 1940, Nate Watt.
Bob Livingston, Raymond Hatton, Duncan Renaldo, Lee White, Florine McKinney, William Ruhl, Al Herman, James Seay, Eddie Dean, Harold Daniels, Jack Lescoulie,* Frosty Royce. 57 minutes.

33. *Under Texas Skies.* Republic, 1940, George Sherman.
Robert Livingston, Bob Steele (as Tucson), Rufe Davis (as Lullaby), Lois Ranson,

---

*This is the same Jack Lescoulie who was on the TV program "Today."

Henry Brandon, Wade Boteler, Rex Lease, Jack Ingram, Walter Tetley, Yakima Canutt, Earle Hodgins, Curley Dresden. 57 minutes.

34. *The Trail Blazers*. Republic, 1940, George Sherman.
Robert Livingston, Bob Steele, Rufe Davis, Pauline Moore, Weldon Heyburn, Carroll Nye, Tom Chatterton, Si Jenks, Mary Field, John Merton, Rex Lease, Robert Blair. 58 minutes.

35. *Lone Star Raiders*. Republic, 1940, George Sherman.
Robert Livingston, Bob Steele, Rufe Davis, June Johnson, George Douglas, Sarah Padden, John Elliott, John Merton, Rex Lease, Bud Osborne, Jack Kirk, Tom London, Hal Price. 57 minutes.

36. *Prairie Pioneers*. Republic, 1941, Lester Orlebeck.
Bob Livingston, Bob Steele, Rufe Davis, Esther Estrella, Robert Kellard, Guy D'Ennery, Davison Clark, Jack Ingram, Ken MacDonald, Lee Shumway, Mary MacLaren, Yakima Canutt, Jack Kirk. 58 minutes.

37. *Pals of the Pecos*. Republic, 1941, Lester Orlebeck.
Bob Livingston, Bob Steele, Rufe Davis, June Johnson, Robert Winkler, Pat O'Malley, Dennis Moore, Robert Frazer, Roy Barcroft, John Holland, Tom London. 56 minutes.

38. *Saddlemates*. Republic, 1941, Lester Orlebeck.
Bob Livingston, Bob Steele, Rufe Davis, Gale Storm, Forbes Murray, Cornelius Keefe, Peter George Lynn, Marin Sais, Marty Faust, Glenn Strange, Ellen Lowe, Iron Eyes Cody. 56 minutes.

39. *Gangs of Sonora*. Republic, 1941, John English.
Bob Livingston, Bob Steele, Rufe Davis, Ward McTaggart, Helen MacKellar, Robert Frazer, William Farnum, Budd Buster, Hal Price. 56 minutes.

40. *Outlaws of the Cherokee Trail*. Republic, 1941, Les Orlebeck.
Bob Steele, Tom Tyler (as Stony), Rufe Davis, Lois Collier, Tom Chatterton, Joel Friedkin, Roy Barcroft, Philip Trent, Rex Lease, Peggy Lynn. 56 minutes.

41. *Gauchos of El Dorado*. Republic, 1941, Lester Orlebeck.
Bob Steele, Tom Tyler, Rufe Davis, Lois Collier, Duncan Renaldo, Rosina Galli, Norman Willis, William Ruhl, Tony Roux, Raphael (Ray) Bennett, Yakima Canutt. 56 minutes.

42. *West of Cimarron*. Republic, 1941, Les Orlebeck.
Bob Steele, Tom Tyler, Rufe Davis, Lois Collier, James Bush, Guy Usher, Hugh

Prosser, Cordell Hickman, Roy Barcroft, Budd Buster, Mickey Rentschler, Cactus Mack. 56 minutes.

43. *Code of the Outlaw.* Republic, 1942, John English.
Bob Steele, Tom Tyler, Rufe Davis, Weldon Heyburn, Bennie Bartlett, Melinda Leighton, Donald Curtis, John Ince, Kenne Duncan, Phil Dunham, Max Waizmann, Chuck Morrison, Carleton Young. 57 minutes.

44. *Raiders of the Range.* Republic, 1942, John English.
Bob Steele, Tom Tyler, Rufe Davis, Lois Collier, Frank Jacquet, Tom Chatterton, Charles Miller, Dennis Moore, Fred Kohler, Jr., Max Waizmann, Hal Price. 54 minutes.

45. *Westward, Ho.* Republic, 1942, John English.
Bob Steele, Tom Tyler, Rufe Davis, Evelyn Brent, Donald Curtis, John James, Lois Collier, Emmett Lynn, Tom Seidel, Jack Kirk, Budd Buster, Kenne Duncan, Edmund Cobb, Jayne Hazard. 56 minutes.

46. *The Phantom Plainsmen.* Republic, 1942, John English.
Bob Steele, Tom Tyler, Rufe Davis, Robert O. Davis, Lois Collier, Charles Miller, Alex Callam, Monte Montague, Henry Rowland, Richard Crane, Jack Kirk. 56 minutes.

47. *Shadows on the Sage.* Republic, 1942, John English.
Bob Steele, Tom Tyler, Jimmie Dodd (as Lullaby), Cheryl Walker, Harry Holman, Bryant Washburn, Griff Barnett, Freddie Mercer, Tom London, Yakima Canutt. 57 minutes.

48. *Valley of Hunted Men.* Republic, 1942, John English.
Bob Steele, Tom Tyler, Jimmie Dodd, Edward Van Sloan, Roland Varno, Anna Marie Stewart, Edythe Elliott, Arno Frey, Richard French, Robert Stevenson, George Neise. 60 minutes.

49. *Thundering Trails.* Republic, 1943, John English.
Bob Steele, Tom Tyler, Jimmie Dodd, Nell O'Day, Sam Flint, Karl Hackett, Charles Miller, John James, Forrest Taylor, Edward Cassidy, Forbes Murray, Reed Howes, Bud Geary. 56 minutes.

50. *The Blocked Trail.* Republic, 1943, Elmer Clifton.
Bob Steele, Tom Tyler, Jimmie Dodd, Helen Deverell, George Lewis, Walter Soderling, Charles F. Miller, Kermit Maynard, Pierce Lyden, Carl Mathews, Hal Price, Budd Buster. 55 minutes.

51.   *Santa Fe Scouts.* Republic, 1943, Howard Bretherton.
Bob Steele, Tom Tyler, Jimmie Dodd, Lois Collier, John James, Elizabeth Valentine, Tom Chatterton, Tom London, Budd Buster, Jack Ingram, Kermit Maynard. 55 minutes.

52.   *Riders of the Rio Grande.* Republic, 1943, Albert De Mond.
Bob Steele, Tom Tyler, Jimmie Dodd, Lorraine Miller, Edward Van Sloan, Rick Vallin, Harry Worth, Roy Barcroft, Charles King, Jack Ingram. 55 minutes.

Basil Rathbone as Sherlock Holmes. The British actor played Holmes in 14 pictures from 1939 to 1946.

SHERLOCK HOLMES

Sherlock Holmes and the Secret Weapon

(1942)

Screenplay by Edward T. Lowe, W. Scott Darling and Edmund L. Hartman. Based in part on Sir Arthur Conan Doyle's short story, "The Adventure of the Dancing Men." Adapted by Darling and Lowe. Camera, Lee White. Music, Charles Previn. Directed by Roy Neill. Universal release of Howard Benedict's production. 68 minutes.

Sherlock Holmes	BASIL RATHBONE
Dr. Watson	NIGEL BRUCE
Professor Moriarty	LIONEL ATWILL
Charlotte Eberli	KAAREN VERNE
Dr. Franz Tobel	WILLIAM POST, JR.
Inspector Lestrade	DENNIS HOEY
Sir Reginald	HOLMES HERBERT
Mrs. Hudson	MARY GORDON
Mueller	PAUL FIX
Braun	ROBERT O. DAVIS
Brady	HARRY CORDING
Kurt	PHILLIP VAN ZANDT

Gottfried	GEORGE BURR MCANNAN
Frederick Hoffner	HENRY VICTOR
Peg Leg	HAROLD DE BECKER
Aviatrix	VICKI CAMPBELL

Dr. Franz Tobel, inventor of a secret bombsight, staggers into Sherlock Holmes' flat at 221-B Baker Street. Thugs have assaulted him on the fog-bound London streets. His head is bandaged. His clothes are disheveled.

"Dr. Tobel," Holmes says after a quick glance at the scientist, "do you suspect a woman of arranging the trap?"

"Woman?" asks Dr. John H. Watson, Holmes' companion and chronicler. "What woman?"

"She's blonde, five-foot-six, full-lipped and very affectionate," Holmes says, clicking off these pronouncements like a computer. He turns to Tobel, "You've known her for a long time. You were attacked after leaving her apartment."

"Holmes," says Tobel, puzzled, "how do you know this?"

"The face powder on your coat tells me of her height and her affection for you," Holmes offers dryly. "You—ah—held her close before departing. It's all there for the trained eye to see."

"But look here," Watson asks. "Why couldn't he be attacked on his way *to* the woman's apartment?"

"The mark of a blow has erased some of the powder. Obviously, if the attack came first, the powder would have remained undisturbed."

"And the full lips? That was a guess."

"I never guess, Watson. You [Tobel] have rubbed the lipstick from your face with the handkerchief you now hold in your hand. And that amount of lipstick never came from a pair of thin lips."

"And the blonde hair?" Watson asks, insisting that everything be accounted for.

Holmes carefully lifts a nearly invisible strand of blonde hair from Tobel's lapel.

"Gracious me," Watson sputters.

"Mr. Holmes," says the astonished man of science. "I'm glad you're on my side."

Sherlock Holmes—ascetic, gimlet-eyed, hawk-nosed. The sleuths of a later era would pride themselves on their two-fisted prowess. Holmes would not shirk from a physical encounter. But first and foremost he relies on intellect. He puts his trust in pure reason and his uncanny use of deductive reasoning. In fact, so obsessed is he with logic, that he plays the game of cops and robbers not to bring a criminal to justice but for the stimulation of the intellectual challenge of a case.

However, he is more than just a misplaced egghead. In every aspect of his personality, he marches to a different drummer. He is really a kind of nineteenth-century hippie. He is essentially a man of peace. He takes drugs (cocaine). He lives the life of a nonconformist, scraping on his violin and sending great clouds of smoke through his book-lined bachelor quarters.

Filling the famous flat are Victorian bric-a-brac, a littered chemistry bench, files, unanswered mail pinned to the mantel by a jackknife, and his tobacco kept in the toe of a Persian slipper. His uniqueness and brilliance fascinate people. So popular were Holmes' literary exploits, that he jumped from the pages of literature to become the screen's favorite fictional character. Since his movie debut in 1903, more than 100 films have featured his adventures.* They are, of course, based on Sir Arthur Conan Doyle's celebrated works, detective stories that never seem to grow old. In Great Britain and America and other parts of the world, societies like the Baker Street Irregulars still devote themselves to studying and savoring the minutest details of Holmes' tingling cases. The Irregulars even publish a journal in which debates rage over such weighty matters as the location of the fictional building on Baker Street that housed Holmes, Watson and their landlady, Mrs. Hudson.

So vivid, in fact, were the Doyle stories that many thought Holmes was a real person. The dead-letter office of London's central post office regularly received hundreds of letters addressed to the master detective. Many offered congratulations for work well done. Some sought expert advice. Others attempted to retain Holmes to solve mysteries.**

Ironically, the creation of Holmes stemmed from Doyle's slow start in his chosen profession of medicine. Irish by descent, Scottish by birth, English by adoption, Doyle won his medical degree at the University of Edinburgh in 1885. The young doctor failed to attract much of a following. And so, to pass the time, he began writing detective stories, modeling his hero after Dr. Joseph Bell, one of his instructors. Bell had an amazing diagnostic ability.

"He would sit in his receiving room with a face like a red Indian," said Doyle, "and diagnose the patients as they came through the door—sometimes before

---

*The exact number is a matter of dispute. In his *Annotated Sherlock Holmes,* Baring-Gould says there are more than 120 Holmes films. Another Holmesian buff counts 118. Still another expert says he has documented more than 180. What is certain is that the first known Holmes film was *Sherlock Holmes Baffled,* a silent film made in 1903. It was produced by the American Mutoscope and Biograph Company. Holmes has also been the subject of over 30 plays; countless radio and TV dramatizations; a musical comedy, "Baker Street" (1965), starring Fritz Weaver; even a ballet, "The Great Detective" (1953), presented in London's Sadler's Wells Ballet Theatre.

**Michael E. Pointer, British writer and expert on the subject of Holmes dramatizations, said in a letter to the author: "To this day, letters addressed to Holmes are still being received—mostly by the Abbey Building Society in Baker Street, who generously gave over part of their premises for the Sherlock Holmes Exhibition in 1951. They forward such letters to the Sherlock Holmes Society of London (membership nearly 500) who deal with them as kindly as possible."

Another version of the master-sleuth. Peter Cushing as Holmes in *The Hound of the Baskervilles* (1959), a British-made film.

Robert Stephens as Holmes in Billy Wilder's *The Private Life of Sherlock Holmes* (1970). The confirmed bachelor is seen in this uncharacteristic pose, his arms about the waist of German spy Ilsa von Hoffmanstader (Genevieve Page), posing as a lady in distress. Dr. Watson (Colin Blakely) looks on askance. Actually, Holmes is merely holding the young lady after she jumped from a window.

George C. Scott appears as a wealthy judge whose nervous breakdown has left him with the delusion he is Holmes. With him in *They Might Be Giants* (1971) is Joanne Woodward, playing Dr. Watson, his spinster psychiatrist.

they had opened their mouths. He would tell them their symptoms and even give them details of their past life. And very seldom was he in error."

Doyle first conjured up "Sherrinford" as Holmes' first name. Then he experimented with "Sherrinford Hope." But he finally settled on Sherlock Holmes. That first novel was *A Study in Scarlet*. There were many rejections before it was published in *Beeton's Christmas Annual* in 1887 for the flat fee of about $60. He never got another cent for the work, and, in fact, later repurchased the rights for about $12,000—two thousand times what he was paid for it. It is not clear how most critics received that first opus—of two reviews that have been discovered, one is lukewarm and one is favorable—but *Beeton's* was a sellout. Editors in both Britain and America asked for more.

However, it was not until four years later, when Doyle started turning out short stories, that he began to achieve the full measure of his popularity. The first of these stories, "A Scandal in Bohemia," was so widely acclaimed, that he then devoted full time to writing. And so began a career that would lead to wealth and knighthood.

Predictably, Doyle grew to tire of Holmes. He even tried to kill him off in one of his tales. Actually, the Holmesian stories were uneven. With some, Doyle took great pains. Others he merely turned out as potboilers when he needed cash. Down deep, Doyle felt Holmes' popular appeal obscured his own more serious efforts at historical novels, plays, essays and spiritualism (to which he turned later in life). He thought his writing in these areas would overshadow Holmes in literary value and endurance. They didn't. When Doyle died in 1930, he had produced 56 Holmesian stories and four novels—on which his immortality firmly rests.

Perhaps one reason Doyle underestimated Holmes' longevity is that he could not have imagined the unending line of actors who would portray his indomitable detective team. Those who donned the two-way peaked deerstalker hat, Inverness cape and curved-stem pipe to play Holmes include Charles Brookfield,* John Webb, William Gillette,** Holger Madsen, Harry Benham, Eille Norwood, John Barrymore, Carlyle Blackwell, Clive Brook, Arthur Wontner, Raymond Massey, Robert Rendell, Reginald Owen, Alwin Neuss, Hans Albers, Richard Gordon, Basil Rathbone, John Longden, Peter Cushing, Christopher Lee, John Neville, Ronald Howard (on TV), Robert Stephens, George C. Scott (if you count *They Might Be Giants)* and Stewart Granger (if you count TV movies).

---

*Believed to be the first to play Holmes—in 1893 in a sketch in the English revue entitled "Under the Clock."

**With Doyle's permission, Gillette wrote and starred in a highly successful four-act drama called "Sherlock Holmes." The play, first performed in 1899, was considered the best-realized stage version of Doyle's character. Gillette made a career of playing Holmes, appearing as the sleuth in a silent film and in many revivals of his own play—even as late as 1932 when he was 78. He died in 1937.

Dr. Watson has been played by Hubert Willis, Roland Young, Ian Hunter, Athole Steward, Frederick Lloyd, Reginald Owen (the only actor to play both Holmes and Watson in different films), Heinz Ruhmann, Nigel Bruce, Campbell Singer, Andre Morell, Thorley Walters, Donald Houston and Colin Blakely.

Of course, to the generation who grew up in the 1930s and 1940s, the most familiar of them all is Rathbone. It is difficult to conceive of another actor who could step so easily into the role of Holmes.

Doyle describes Holmes in his first novel. "His [Holmes] very person and appearance were such as to strike the attention of the most casual observer," Doyle wrote. "In height, he was rather over six feet, and so excessively lean that he seemed to be considerably taller. His eyes were sharp and piercing, save during those intervals of torpor to which I have alluded; and his thin, hawk-like nose gave his whole presence an air of alertness and decision."

Doyle never felt it was important to fill in this rough outline. He left the rest to the imagination. But those broad strokes fit Rathbone to a "T." He was made to order in height (six-foot, one-inch), build (sparse), features (aquiline) and eyes (penetrating). And his crisp, confident, modulated voice rounded out the character perfectly.

Rathbone, whose real name was Philip St. John Basil Rathbone, was born in South Africa in 1892. He had English parents and was educated in Britain. From the age of 7, he never wavered in his ambition to be an actor. By 19, he was a member of a touring Shakespearean company. When World War I broke out, he enlisted in the British army and was awarded the Military Cross. With self-effacing modesty, he later spoke of the feat as if it were nothing. "All I did, old man," he told an interviewer," was disguise myself as a tree—that's correct, a tree —and cross no man's land to gather a bit of information from the German lines. I have not since been called upon to play a tree."

After the war, Rathbone returned to the stage playing Romeo, his favorite role, for the first time. He repeated the performance on Broadway in 1933 opposite Katharine Cornell. During his 55-year stage career, Rathbone played 52 parts in 23 Shakespearean plays. Among his many other stage credits were the title role in "Peter Ibbetson," Morell in Shaw's "Candida" opposite Miss Cornell and Dr. Austin Sloper in "The Heiress." He appeared with the great stage actresses, among them Laurette Taylor. Of them all, he considered her the greatest.

Rathbone's first movie was *The Fruitful Vine* (1921). By the 1930s, he was averaging three or four pictures a year. They ranged from *The Last Days of Pompeii* (1935) to *Dawn Patrol* (1938) and *Son of Frankenstein* (1939). Many of his best realized roles were as villains. He was the cruel Mr. Murdstone, David's stepfather in *David Copperfield* (1935), the wicked husband in *Anna Karenina* (1935) opposite Garbo, and the evil Marquis St. Evremonde in *A Tale of Two Cities* (1935). Most memorable were his swashbuckling dueling scenes. He crossed

The game's afoot and Holmes and Watson (Nigel Bruce) exchange remarks over a skeleton in *Sherlock Holmes and the Spider Woman* (1944). Gale Sondergaard plays the diabolical villain.

Holmes and Watson question a waiter in *Pursuit to Algiers* (1946) while trying to run down a lead. Though Rathbone's portrayal of Holmes won him more fame than any of his many other roles, he grew tired of the part. When his contract came up for renewal, he refused.

swords atop a bluff with Errol Flynn in *Captain Blood* (1935) and along a winding castle stairway in *The Adventures of Robin Hood* (1938). When Ronald Colman ran him through in *If I Were King* (1938) and Tyrone Power skewered him in *The Mark of Zorro* (1940), movie audiences cheered.

But of the more than 100 films Rathbone made, it was the 14 he did as Holmes that really won him motion picture fame. With 20th Century-Fox's *The Hound of the Baskervilles* (1939), he began his long association with Nigel Bruce, the son of a Scottish baronet and a veteran of stage and screen.* *The Hound,* an instant success, led the same year to the sequel, *The Adventures of Sherlock Holmes.* But Fox did not continue the series. Instead, Universal Pictures purchased the screen rights in 1942. It brought Holmes up to date in modern dress and timely scenarios that had him battling the Nazis, and launching a new series.

Rathbone eventually tired of the role. Like Doyle, he felt it eclipsed other parts of his career that he thought more important. When it came time to renew his long-term contract in 1946, he steadfastedly refused.

"I played Holmes for seven years and nobody thought I could do anything else," he said. "When I would come onto a set or into a radio station,** it was never 'Hello, Rathbone.' It was always 'Hello, Holmes.' I simply threw away the pipe and hat and came back to Broadway. It was a simple question of survival —Holmes or Rathbone."

In his autobiography, *In and Out of Character,* Rathbone said he would have been quite content with playing Holmes once—in *The Hound of the Baskervilles.* "The continuous repetition of story after story after story left me virtually repeating myself each time in a character I had already conceived and developed," he wrote. "My first picture was, as it were, a negative from which I merely continued to produce endless positives of the same photograph."

His reaction to Holmes after these endless repetitions left him, understandably, somewhat less than sympathetic to the master. "There was nothing lovable about Holmes," Rathbone wrote:

It would be impossible for such a man to know loneliness or love or sorrow because he was completely sufficient unto himself. His perpetual seeming assumption of infallibility; his interminable success (could he not fail just once and prove himself a human being like the rest of us!);*** his ego that seemed at times to verge on the

*In the Doyle stories, Watson, a pensioned British army surgeon wounded in India, is more of a straightforward assistant to Holmes and does not appear anything like the dull-witted blunderer he is shown as on the screen.

**Rathbone and Bruce also did a radio series. (Others who portrayed Holmes on the air include such eminent actors as Sir Cedric Hardwicke and Sir John Gielgud.)

***In fact, Holmes did fail. He arrives too late to apprehend the criminal in a number of Conan Doyle stories. Once, he was outwitted by a woman, Irene Adler. In "Scandal in Bohemia," she got away and Holmes failed to secure the embarrassing papers and photos for his client. But, although he did not catch the crook every time, he always was master of the situation intellectually. Invariably,

superman complex, while his "Elementary, my dear Watson"* with its seeming condescension for the pupil by the master must have been a very trying experience at times for even so devoted a friend as Dr. Watson.

Nevertheless, Rathbone's name will always evoke the image of Holmes. And a fine example of him at his Holmesian best is in *Sherlock Holmes and the Secret Weapon*. It is based in part on the story, "The Adventure of the Dancing Men," which pits Holmes against his arch foe Professor Moriarty, the distinguished mathematician and resourceful criminal whom Holmes once called "the Napoleon of crime."

The game's afoot with Holmes in Switzerland. His assignment is to spirit away to England the renowned physicist and bombsight inventor, Franz Tobel (William Post, Jr.). The Nazis have the same idea. So, disguised as an elderly book peddler, Holmes goes to a cafe where two agents are drinking. Holmes pretends to be a courier passing on secret directives from the German High Command.

"We move tonight," Holmes whispers. "Orders from Berlin. Dr. Tobel must be across the border by dawn."

"But we have orders not to break into his house and he hides there," one agent protests. "He hasn't been outside in weeks."

"When the Führer needs something as badly as he needs the Tobel bombsight, there is always a way," Holmes says. He tells the agents he will get into Tobel's house, lure Tobel out and raise the blinds just before the scientist leaves.

Sure enough, the signal comes at the appointed hour. Out walks Tobel with the old book peddler. Or out comes what seems to be the scientist and the peddler. Actually it is Tobel's servants dressed as their master and the peddler. When the Nazis go after them, Holmes and Tobel steal the agents' car. They race to a secret landing field, rendezvous with an RAF plane and fly to England.

Once in London, Tobel stubbornly refuses to put his invention in the hands of the British War Ministry. Instead, he has his own ideas about its safekeeping. He divides the bombsight into four units, each useless without the other, and gives them to four scientists. Their job is to mass-produce each of the units. None of them knows who the others are.

Then, Tobel goes to the apartment of his fiancée, Charlotte Eberli (Kaaren

---

he solved the mystery. Even so, it seems somewhat paradoxical for Rathbone, having said all this, to then go on and do a Holmes stage play. The work, written by his wife, Ouida, closed after three performances in 1953. It was called "Sherlock Holmes."

*The famous line appears in screen and other media versions of Holmes' exploits but not in Doyle's works. The same flavor, however, is there. For example, a typical exchange goes:
    "Wonderful!" [Watson] ejaculated.
    "Commonplace," said Holmes.
The closest, from "The Crooked Man," is:
    "Excellent," I cried.
    "Elementary," said he.

Verne), and takes the precaution of writing out his plan in code in case the Nazis capture him. In fact, Nazi spies in England have made Tobel their prime target. They first attack, then kidnap him, hoping to torture him into disclosing the bombsight's whereabouts.

When she learns of Tobel's capture, Miss Eberli gives Holmes the envelope in which Tobel has left his coded message. But someone else has been there first. On opening it, Holmes finds only the words, "We meet again, Mr. Holmes."

"Why that's not the same message," says Tobel's fiancee. "It isn't even the same paper. I saw Dr. Tobel draw little sets of figures . . . little dancing men."

"Dancing men," Watson exclaims. "That's curious."

No one has been in the apartment since Tobel encoded his plan, Miss Eberli says, except for a workman who came to fix the switch when the lights went out. Holmes smells a red herring. The light switch has not been touched, he says. The paint still covers the screw heads. "He [the workman] simply threw the main switch in the basement," Holmes explains, "pretended to work on this one. And after a few moments, an accomplice threw the main switch back on."

"Now I realize," says Miss Eberli, "He kept his face averted."

". . . But he was a large man." Holmes declares.

"Yes, very large."

"His eyes, heavily lidded. A thin film over the pupils."

"Yes. I remember now. His eyes. They were like a snake's."

"Miss Eberli," Holmes announces, "Dr. Tobel is being held by one of the most brilliant men in the history of crime."

That man, of course, is Professor Moriarty (Lionel Atwill). He has joined forces with the Nazis not for political motives but for the lucrative fee they offer and the challenge of outwitting Holmes.

Disguised as a dock worker, Holmes hangs out around the waterfront, where he suspects Moriarty has his headquarters. Fooled by Holmes' getup, Moriarty's men obligingly accept Holmes' bribe to take him to their leader. But Moriarty has not been caught off guard.

"Welcome, Holmes," the professor says, warmly greeting Holmes in his hideout. ". . . Just like old times, eh? A battle of wits, of superior intellects . . . Valuable as your doctor and his code are to my business, I think my main interest in this affair is the chance it gives me to battle with you again."

Appealing to Moriarty's patriotism, Holmes warns him that the loss of the bombsight would be a terrible blow to his own country. But the professor says he will make more money from this affair than from all the rest of his "adventures" combined. And he plans to insure his success by liquidating Holmes, the only man who might be clever enough to stand in his way. Moriarty and his henchmen intend to stuff Holmes in the false bottom of a sea chest. A sailor is going to sea that very night and is to push it overboard.

"Perhaps your good friend Dr. Watson can entitle this adventure 'The End of Sherlock Holmes,' " Moriarty laughs.

"He will be disappointed," Holmes says. "He intended to call it 'The End of Professor Moriarty.' "

As his men lug out the sea chest, heavily weighted with Holmes in the bottom, Moriarty shakes his head. The professor says with regret, "Brilliant man, Sherlock Holmes. Too bad he was honest."

But Moriarty's diabolical plan has failed to reckon on the pursuit of Watson and Scotland Yard Inspector Lestrade (Dennis Hoey). Prowling the piers in search of Holmes, they spot the two seamen struggling with the weight of their sea chest. Suspicious, they force them to open the chest. Out steps Holmes, disheveled but none the worse for wear. Pausing only to straighten his hair, he sets right off to Miss Eberli's flat. He wants to have another go at locating Tobel's coded message.

This time, with the aid of some ingenious detective work, he succeeds. Holmes finds the writing pad on which Tobel scrawled his message. He immerses the top sheet—the one directly under the page Tobel wrote on—in a solution of fluorescent salts. Then, he photographs it by ultraviolet light. The fibers broken by the writing absorb less of the solution than other parts of the paper and appear darker. They become visible as stick figures drawn in all different positions—dancing men.

"Splendid, Holmes," says Watson. "Now I recognize that code . . . alphabet substitution."

The good doctor goes on to explain that the code is based on the repetition of the figures. "*E* is the letter most used in the British language," Watson says. "Therefore, the figure most used probably is *E. T, A, O, I* and *N* follow in order of frequency."

But when Watson decodes the message, he can't make any sense out of it. It reads like gibberish.

"Dr. Tobel is a brilliant scientist," Holmes points out. ". . . He wouldn't send us a message so simple to decipher." Holmes calls attention to three dancing men drawn above all the rest. "Neither would he have fixed these [three] top figures without a meaning. You see, the one, two, three figures means we skip letters in that order. In other words, observe, Watson, the first letter, which is *I*, skips one, becomes *J*. The second letter, *Y*, skips two and becomes *A*. And the third skips three and becomes *C*.

"*J-A-C.*"

"*J-A-C-O-B-D-U-R-R-E-R* . . ."

"Jacob Durrer," Miss Eberli exclaims. "A Swiss scientist and friend of Dr. Tobel." "*P-A-L-A-C-E-C-R-E-S* . . ."

"Palace Crescent," Watson declares. "I say, Holmes, this man Durrer must be important."

"Obviously," Holmes says, "He must have some connection with the bombsight or Tobel wouldn't have taken so much trouble to see that I got his name."

The rest of the message spells out the names and addresses of the other scientists who have the bombsight parts. However, the name of the last scientist is in a different code. It proves too difficult to crack. Holmes abandons the task for the moment, rushing off to recover the bombsight parts from the first three men. But Moriarty has also deciphered the code, and has beaten Holmes to the scientists. Moriarty and his men have killed three of the scientists and stolen their bombsight parts. Now the race is on to see who will reach the key fourth man and recover the all-important last part of the bombsight. So far, Tobel has refused to yield to torture. He won't reveal his whereabouts.

Meanwhile, Holmes, Watson and Lestrade have worked far into the night on the second code. They are getting nowhere until Watson, exhausted, shrugs his shoulders. "I'm all in," he says. "Can't think anymore. All those letters and figures whirling through my brain. All twisted round."

"Twisted round," cried Holmes, inspired. "That's it." All the figures of the fourth man's name are written backward. They read—instead of left to right—from right to left.

"Why would Dr. Tobel want to reverse the figures of number four?" Lestrade asks.

"An added precaution, Lestrade," Holmes says. "In case the cipher falls into the wrong hands."

But as Holmes rushes to the home of the last scientist—Frederick Hofner—the clever Moriarty also breaks the code. The professor and his gang dash to the scientist's house and force him to accompany them back to the hideout. There, Moriarty triumphantly opens the box supposedly containing the fourth bombsight part. He finds only a note saying, "We meet again, Professor." Moriarty has kidnaped Holmes masquerading as the scientist. The real Hofner and the fourth bombsight part are in the hands of Scotland Yard.

"So you think you've beaten me, Holmes," Moriarty says, refusing to acknowledge defeat. "I still have Tobel. Now I shall sell Germany the inventor instead of the invention."

"You learned nothing from him in spite of all your torture," Holmes scoffs. "Otherwise you wouldn't be trying so desperately to collect the four sections of the bombsight."

"A keen observation, Holmes," Moriarty says. "But observe further that you are now in my hands. And I profited by my last mistake of allowing underlings to attend to you."

Playing for time, Holmes derides the unimaginative way Moriarty considers getting rid of him. "Gas, poison, bullets. I assure you, Professor, were our positions reversed, I should have something more colorful."

". . . And what, my good Mr. Holmes, could you have conceived?"

"Well, even offhand, I can improve on your suggestions . . . You know that a man dies if he loses five pints of blood. I should have you placed on an operating table, inject a needle in your veins and slowly draw off your life blood."

"The needle to the last, eh Holmes?"

"Slowly, drop by drop. The blood would be drawn from your body," Holmes continues. "You would be aware of every exquisite second to the very end. You would be watching yourself die scientifically, noting every reaction. And in full possession of your faculties."

Intrigued by Holmes' gruesome idea, Moriarty straps Holmes to a table, thrusts a needle into his arm and begins draining his blood in the very way Holmes has outlined.

"It was obvious that I should win in the end," says Moriarty, proudly. "Closer to the end, Holmes. Closer and closer. Each second a few more drops leave your desiccated body. You can feel them, can't you? You're perfectly conscious, aren't you, Holmes?"

"I shall be conscious long after you're dead, Moriarty," Holmes groans feebly.

"Still the same old swaggering, conceited Sherlock Holmes."

What the professor does not know is that Holmes had the real Hoffner attach a special device to Moriarty's car. He planted it when the professor and his men were inside the scientist's house abducting the disguised Holmes. The device drips luminous paint. Watson, Lestrade and Scotland Yard officers are even now following the trail.

Moriarty's men have put Tobel in a motor boat. They are about to leave to meet a Nazi submarine. Losing patience with the bloodletting, Moriarty raises his pistol to end Holmes' life.

"I can't wait any longer, Holmes," the professor says. "You'll have to forgive the crudity, my friend, which is only the *coup de grace.*"

As he is about to squeeze the trigger, there is a report from another gun. A bullet smashes into his arm, jarring loose his gun. Lestrade and Watson bolt into the room and pull the needle from Holmes' arm. Taking advantage of their diverted attention, the wounded Moriarty slips out through a secret passageway. But in a few seconds, a frightened scream pierces the silence. He has fallen 60 feet to the sewers below through a trapdoor left open. "Poor Moriarty," Holmes mutters, lamenting the lost stimulation of a cunning adversary.

As was the custom in the Holmes series during World War II years, the picture ends on a patriotic note. "Germany wanted the Tobel bombsight," a British general says, watching a successful test of the device at the fadeout. "We'll send her thousands of them in RAF planes."

"Things are looking up, Holmes," says Watson. "This little island is still on the map."

"Yes," says the master. Then paraphrasing Shakespeare, Holmes extols his native land. "This fortress built by nature for herself. This blessed plot. This earth. This realm. This England."*

*Some Holmesian movie buffs rate the closing lines from *Voice of Terror* as the most stirring of all: "There's an east wind, Watson . . . Such a wind as never blew on England yet. It will be cold and bitter, Watson. And a good many of us may wither before its blast. But it's God's own wind, nonetheless. And a greener, better, stronger land will lie in the sunshine when the storm has cleared."
The lines are, in fact, a direct quote from Doyle—the final passage of the story, "His Last Bow."

SHERLOCK HOLMES SERIES

1. *Return of Sherlock Holmes.* Paramount, 1929, Basil Dean.
   Clive Brook (as Sherlock Holmes), H. Reeves Smith (as Dr. Watson), Harry T. Morey (as Professor Moriarty), Betty Lawford, Phillips Holmes, Donald Crisp, Arthur Mack, Hubert Druce, Charles Hay. 71 minutes.

2. *The Sleeping Cardinal* (British). (U.S. release as *Sherlock Holmes' Fatal Hour.*) First Division, 1930, Leslie S. Hiscott.
   Arthur Wontner (as Holmes), Ian Fleming (as Dr. Watson), Norman McKinnell (as Moriarty), Minnie Raynor, Phillip Newland (as Inspector Lestrade), Leslie Perrins, Jane Walsh, William Frazer, Sidney King, Gordon Begg, Louis Goodrich, Harry Terry, Charles Paton. 75 minutes.

3. *The Speckled Band.* First Division, 1931, Jack Raymond.
   Raymond Massey (as Holmes), Athole Steward (as Dr. Watson), Lyn Harding, Angela Baddeley, Nancy Price. 66 minutes.

4. *Sign of the Four.* World-Wide, 1932, Graham Cutts.
   Arthur Wontner (as Holmes), Ian Hunter (as Dr. Watson), Isla Bevan, Gilbert Davis, Graham Soutten, Edgar Norfolk, Herbert Lomas, Clair Greet, Miles Malleson, Roy Emerton, Kynaston Reeves. 74 minutes.

5. *Miss Rembrandt.* First Division, 1932, Leslie S. Hiscott
   Arthur Wontner (as Holmes), Ian Fleming (as Dr. Watson), Miles Mander, Francis L. Sullivan, Dino Galvani, Jane Welsh, Phillip Newland, Anthony Holles, Herbert Lomas, Ben Welden. 78 minutes.

6. *Hound of the Baskervilles.* First Division, 1932, V. Gareth Gundrey.
   Robert Rendel (as Holmes), Fred Lloyd (as Dr. Watson), Heather Angel, John Stuart, Reginald Bach, Wilfred Shine, Sybil Jane, Henry Hallett, Elizabeth Vaughan. 72 minutes.

7. *Sherlock Holmes.* Fox, 1932, William K. Howard.
   Clive Brook (as Holmes), Reginald Owen (as Dr. Watson), Ernest Torrence (as Moriarty), Miriam Jordan, Howard Leeds, Alan Mowbray, Herbert Mundin, Montague Shaw, Arnold Lucy, Lucien Prival, Roy D'Arcy, Stanley Fields, Eddie Dillon, Robert Graves, Jr., Brandon Hurst, Claude King. 65 minutes.

8. *A Study in Scarlet.* World-Wide, 1933, Edwin L. Marin.
   Reginald Owen (as Holmes), Warburton Gamble (as Dr. Watson), Alan Mowbray (as Lestrade), Tempe Pigott, Anna May Wong, June Clyde, Alan Dinehart,

J. M. Kerrigan, Doris Lloyd, Billy Bevan, Halliwell Hobbes, Tetsu Komai, John Warburton, Leila Bennett, Cecil Reynolds, Wyndham Standing. 70 minutes.

9. *The Triumph of Sherlock Holmes.* Olympic, 1935, Leslie S. Hiscott.
Arthur Wontner (as Holmes), Ian Fleming (as Dr. Watson), Lyn Harding (as Moriarty), Leslie Perrins, Jane Carr, Charles Mortimer, Minnie Raynor, Michael Shepley, Ben Welden, Roy Emerton, Conway Dixon, Wilfred Caithness, Edmund D'Alby, Ernest Lynds. 75 minutes.

10. *Silver Blaze* (Twinkenham, 1936.) (U.S. release as *Murder at the Baskervilles.*) Astor, 1941, Thomas Bentley.
Arthur Wontner (as Holmes), Ian Fleming (as Dr. Watson), Lyn Harding (as Moriarty), John Turnball (as Lestrade), Robert Horton, Lawrence Grossmith, Judy Gunn, Arthur Macrae, Arthur Goullet, Martin Walker, Eve Grey. 66 minutes.

11. *The Hound of the Baskervilles.* Hammer Films / Columbia, 1959, Terence Fisher.
Peter Cushing (as Holmes), Andre Morell (as Dr. Watson), Christopher Lee, Miles Malleson, Marla Landi, David Oxley, Francis De Wolff, Ewen Solon, John Le Mesurier, Sam Kydd, Judi Moyens, Helen Goss, Dave Birks, Michael Hawkins, Ian Hewitson, Elizabeth Dott, Michael Mulcaster. 84 minutes.

12. *A Study in Terror.* Columbia, 1966, James Hill.
John Neville (as Sherlock Holmes), Donald Houston (as Dr. Watson), John Fraser, Anthony Quayle, Robert Morley, Barbara Windsor, Adrienne Corri, Frank Finlay, Judi Dench, Cecil Parker, Georgia Brown, Barry Jones, Kay Walsh, Terry Downes. 94 minutes.

13. *The Private Life of Sherlock Holmes.* United Artists, 1970, Billy Wilder.
Robert Stephens (as Holmes), Colin Blakely (as Dr. Watson). Irene Handl, Stanley Holloway, Christopher Lee, Genevieve Page, Clive Revill, Tamara Toumanova, George Benson (as Lestrade), Catherine Lacey, Mollie Maureen, Peter Madden, Robert Cawdron, Michael Elwyn, Michael Balfour, Frank Thornton, James Copeland, Alex McCrindle, Kenneth Benda, Graham Armitage, Eric Francis, John Garrie, Godfrey James. 125 minutes.

14. *They Might Be Giants.* Universal, 1971, Anthony Harvey.
George C. Scott (as Justin, who believes that he is Sherlock Holmes), Joanne Woodward (as Dr. Mildred Watson), Jack Gilford, Lester Rawlins, Al Lewis, Rue McClanahan, Ron Weyland, Olive Clark, Theresa Merritt, Jenny Egan. 88 minutes.

(*The Hound of the Baskervilles,* a movie made for television, premiered on the American Broadcasting System channels on Feb. 12, 1972. Stewart Granger played Holmes.)

RATHBONE-BRUCE SERIES

1. *The Hound of the Baskervilles.* Twentieth, 1939, Sidney Lanfield.
    Richard Greene, Basil Rathbone (as Sherlock Holmes), Wendy Barrie, Nigel Bruce (as Dr. Watson), Lionel Atwill, John Carradine, Barlowe Borland, Beryl Mercer, Morton Lowry, Ralph Forbes, E. E. Clive, Eily Malyon, Harry Cording, Mary Gordon (as Mrs. Hudson), Peter Willes, Ivan Simpson, John Burton, Dennis Green, Evan Thomas. 80 minutes.

2. *The Adventures of Sherlock Holmes.* Twentieth, 1939, Alfred L. Werker.
    Basil Rathbone, Nigel Bruce, Ida Lupino, Alan Marshal, Terry Kilburn, George Zucco (as Professor Moriarty), Henry Stephenson, E. E. Clive, Arthur Hohl, May Beatty, Peter Willes, Mary Gordon, Holmes Herbert, George Regas, Leonard Mudie, Mary Forbes, Ivan Simpson, Frank Dawson, Eric Wilton, William Austin, Brandon Hurst, Keith Kenneth, Herbert Evans, Anthony Kemble Cooper, Montague Shaw, Harry Cording. 85 minutes.

3. *Sherlock Holmes and the Voice of Terror.* Universal, 1942, John Rawlins.
    Basil Rathbone, Nigel Bruce, Evelyn Ankers, Reginald Denny, Henry Daniell, Montagu Love, Thomas Gomez, Hillary Brooke, Mary Gordon, Arthur Blake, Leyland Hodgson, Olaf Hytten. 65 minutes.

4. *Sherlock Holmes and the Secret Weapon.* Universal, 1942, Roy William Neill.
    Basil Rathbone, Nigel Bruce, Kaaren Verne, Lionel Atwill (as Professor Moriarty), Dennis Hoey (as Inspector Lestrade), Harold De Becker, William Post, Jr., Mary Gordon, Paul Fix, Robert O. Davis, Holmes Herbert, Harry Cording, Phillip Van Zandt. 68 minutes.

5. *Sherlock Holmes in Washington.* Universal, 1943, Roy William Neill.
    Basil Rathbone, Nigel Bruce, Marjorie Lord, Henry Daniell, George Zucco, John Archer, Gavin Muir, Edmund MacDonald, Don Terry, Bradley Page, Holmes Herbert, Thurston Hall. 71 minutes.

6. *Sherlock Holmes Faces Death.* Universal, 1943, Roy William Neill.
    Basil Rathbone, Nigel Bruce, Hillary Brooke, Milburn Stone, Arthur Margetson, Halliwell Hobbes, Dennis Hoey, Gavin Muir, Frederic Worlock, Olaf Hytten, Gerald Hamer, Vernon Downing, Minna Phillips, Mary Gordon. 68 minutes.

7. *Sherlock Holmes and the Spider Woman.* Universal, 1944, Roy William Neill.
    Basil Rathbone, Nigel Bruce, Gale Sondergaard (as the Spider Woman), Dennis Hoey, Vernon Downing, Alec Craig, Mary Gordon, Arthur Hohl, Teddy Infuhr. 62 minutes.

8.   *The Scarlet Claw.* Universal, 1944, Roy William Neill.
     Basil Rathbone, Nigel Bruce, Gerald Hamer, Paul Cavanagh, Arthur Hohl, Miles
     Mander, Kay Harding, David Clyde, Ian Wolfe, Victoria Horne. 74 minutes.

9.   *The Pearl of Death.* Universal, 1944, Roy William Neill.
     Basil Rathbone, Nigel Bruce, Dennis Hoey, Evelyn Ankers, Miles Mander, Ian
     Wolfe, Charles Francis, Holmes Herbert, Richard Nugent, Mary Gordon, Rondo
     Hatton (as the Creeper). 67 minutes.

10. *House of Fear.* Universal, 1945, Roy William Neill.
     Basil Rathbone, Nigel Bruce, Aubrey Mather, Dennis Hoey, Paul Cavanagh,
     Holmes Herbert, Harry Cording, Sally Shepherd, Gavin Muir, Florette Hillier,
     David Clyde. 68 minutes.

11. *The Woman in Green.* Universal, 1945, Roy William Neill.
     Basil Rathbone, Nigel Bruce, Hillary Brooke, Henry Daniell (as Professor Mori-
     arty), Paul Cavanagh, Matthew Boulton, Eve Amber, Frederic Worlock, Tom
     Bryson, Sally Shepherd, Mary Gordon. 68 minutes.

12. *Pursuit to Algiers.* Universal, 1946, Roy William Neill.
     Basil Rathbone, Nigel Bruce, Marjorie Riordan, Rosalind Ivan, Martin Kosleck,
     John Abbott, Frederic Worlock, Morton Lowry, Leslie Vincent, Gerald Hamer.
     65 minutes.

13. *Terror by Night.* Universal, 1946, Roy William Neill.
     Basil Rathbone, Nigel Bruce, Alan Mowbray, Dennis Hoey, Renee Godfrey,
     Mary Forbes, Billy Bevan, Frederic Worlock, Leyland Hodgson, Geoffrey Steele,
     Boyd Davis, Janet Murdock, Skelton Knaggs. 60 minutes.

14. *Dressed to Kill.* Universal, 1946, Roy William Neill.
     Basil Rathbone, Nigel Bruce, Patricia Morison, Edmond Breon, Frederic Wor-
     lock, Carl Harbord, Patricia Cameron, Tom P. Dillon, Harry Cording, Topsy
     Glyn, Mary Gordon. 72 minutes.

Simon Templar (George Sanders), better known as the Saint, looks down the barrel of two automatics as thugs (John F. Hamilton and Elliott Sullivan) get the drop on him in *The Saint's Double Trouble* (1940).

THE SAINT

The Saint's Double Trouble
(1940)

Screenplay by Ben Holmes from a story by Leslie Charteris. Musical director, Roy Webb. Photography, J. Roy Hunt. Art Director, Van Nest Polglase. Editor, Theron Warth. Directed by Jack Hively. Produced by Cliff Reid for RKO Radio Pictures. 68 minutes.

The Saint	GEORGE SANDERS
The Dutchman (Helm Van Roon)	
Anne Bitts	HELENE WHITNEY
Inspector Fernack	JONATHAN HALE
Partner	BELA LUGOSI
Inspector Bohlen	DONALD MACBRIDE
Limpy	JOHN F. HAMILTON
Professor Bitts	THOMAS W. ROSS
Monk	ELLIOTT SULLIVAN
Express Man	PAT O'MALLEY
Bartender	WALTER MILLER
Ephraim Byrd	BYRON FOULGER

"Simon Templar," says the beautiful Valerie Travers (Wendy Barrie). "I have often wondered why someone, in the course of your brazen existence, hasn't killed you."

"They have often tried, my dear," says Templar (George Sanders), stifling a yawn. "But somehow, they have never yet succeeded."

Templar, of course, is the Saint—dashing, dapper, debonair scourge of the underworld. He gets his nickname from his calling card, which shows a stick figure with a halo. But what makes him truly unique is his working relationship with the cops. The world's police—particularly Scotland Yard—are both his friends and his enemies. They know he can get the man they can't track down.

An outlaw himself, the Saint thumbs his nose at the authorities. He will help them when necessary. But he will often take a direct route against crime. Instead of hauling thugs into court, he will fight murder with murder—if this is the only way he can get justice. And yet, he is always the polished English gentleman, a trait he sometimes shares with his quarry.

Once, when he spots his man—a foreign agent dealing in military secrets—he greets the agent like a long-lost school chum. "Ah, if it isn't my old friend, Rudolph," says Templar. Rudolph responds in kind. After shooting it out until he runs out of bullets, Rudolph gives up gracefully. "You know, Templa-ah, you're becoming rather a nuisance."

If the Saint is a nuisance to crooks, he is just as annoyingly persistent in his pursuit of the ladies. But sex is more a game to him; his real passion is running down bad guys. On one caper, he passes on inside information to Valerie. Valerie, on whom the Saint has designs, immediately suspects an ulterior motive. She insists on knowing why Templar has taken her into his confidence.

"Because," he says, "I love you." But Templar's smile quickly fades. In the next breath, it becomes clear he is only putting her on. "But don't let's get sticky about it," he says. ". . . I also love fireflies, mockingbirds and pink sunsets. I think, however, we could find each other more diverting than a pink sunset."

"I dislike you intensely," says Valerie, not amused.

"Oh, no you don't. You're really very fond of me," he says impertinently.

"Why should I be fond of you?"

"Tell me and you'll answer the riddle of the world. My dear Val, that's what made history, literature and even chemistry. A man and a woman."

This velvet charmer is the creation of Leslie Charteris, an Englishman who has produced over 50 fast-paced mysteries which have sold more than 100 million copies. The Saint's derring-do also appeared in *The Saint* magazine, which Charteris himself edited for a while, as well as on radio, television and in a syndicated comic strip.

A facile writer, Charteris once turned out a book in 10 days. Although he usually spent more time than this on his novels, he rarely took over six months

The Saint with his heart-throb of the moment, Ruth (Wendy Barrie), in *The Saint Takes Over* (1940).

Louis Hayward, who played Templar in the first and last *Saint* pictures, comes upon a corpse in *The Saint's Girl Friday* (1954). Man with the bowler is Charles Victor. The movie closed out the nine-film series.

to do a thriller. Born in China, Charteris was brought up and educated in England and France.

A precocious child, he started a personal typewritten magazine at age 10, which he peddled to his parents, relatives and, as he once put it, "anyone else who could be badgered or blackmailed into forking out for it." Later, Charteris made three round-the-world trips and a walking tour of the European continent. He put his cosmopolitan expertise to good use in his Saint books, which had the world's great cities for their locale.

How did he conceive his famous character?

"Partly from his initials and partly from his saintly way of doing and saying the most unsaintly things," explained Charteris. The first Saint book, *Meet the Tiger*, came out in 1929, when Charteris was only 20. "Nicknames, especially incongruous ones, were very much 'in' at that time," Charteris continued. "Or anyway I had that impression. But whether I picked the names or the nicknames first, I honestly can't recall."

But why Simon?

"I never knew anyone of that name," Charteris said. "But it was uncommon enough to be interesting. I know that I couldn't have a romantic hero being called anything like 'Bill' or 'Jim.' "

Why Templar?

"Ah, there came a truly romantic fetish. My first, even preadolescent, idols were the giants of the legends of chivalry, the Knights of the Round Table—the Chevalier Bayard, Roland and Olivier, D'Artagnan interpreted by Douglas Fairbanks. The age of the Glorified Goon had not yet dawned, thank Heavens, at least in time to influence me. My paladin had to have a symbolic name, something with a hint of swords and plumes and trumpets in it. Templar, to me, was such a name . . ."

The calling card. How did that originate?

"This hero, of course, must have his trademark to leave behind as a signature to his exploits," Charteris said, "his personal snook cocked at the Law and the Ungodly." For that, Charteris went back to a comic strip he had authored in his magazine. "Since drawing came harder to me than writing, I cheated by doing it entirely in matchstick figures which I differentiated from each other with such elementary features as mustaches, beards, balloon bellies, special hats, and so forth. To make one into a saint, all it took was a halo."*

The *Saint* books attracted a wide following. By the mid-1930s, Charteris was writing to an international audience. RKO bought the screen rights and Louis Hayward played the first movie Saint in 1938. But George Sanders took over for

*The Saint caricature could also have been inspired, Charteris said, by the stick figures used in the Sherlock Holmes adventure, "The Dancing Men."

the next five films. And although Hugh Sinclair became the third Saint in two British movies, and Hayward returned to the part in the last *Saint* picture in 1954, it is Sanders who became most identified with the film role.*

Born in St. Petersburg (now Leningrad) in 1906, Sanders was the son of the British consul.** But his stay in Russia was short-lived. At the outset of the Russian Revolution, Sanders' family fled the country through snow-clad forests and frozen rivers, and he completed his education in England.

After starting out in the textile business, the 215-pound, six-foot three-inch Sanders began his theatrical career as a singer, appearing in a London revue called "Ballyhoo." He went on to play minor roles in British movies before coming to the United States, where he launched his movie career as a heavy in 1936. With a dry, supercilious, sometimes arrogant demeanor, he played a succession of cads,*** crooks and cynics. He appeared in such pictures as *Confessions of a Nazi Spy* (1939), *Rebecca* (1940) and *The Picture of Dorian Gray* (1945).

One of his most memorable roles was in *All About Eve,* in which he played that "venomous fish-wife"—as Bette Davis called him—Addison de Witt. For his portrayal of the flippant, acerbic critic who refers to Marilyn Monroe as "a graduate of the Copacabana School of Dramatic Art," he won an Oscar for 1950's best supporting performance.

Off screen, Sanders became known for his marital affairs. His five wives included two of the three Gabor sisters—Zsa Zsa (wife number two) and Magda (number five)—and the late Benita Hume (number three), widow of Ronald Colman. Zsa Zsa rated Sanders as the best of her five husbands. "I thought he hated women and that was a marvelous challenge," she said. "When I met him, I said, 'Mr. Sanders, I'm madly in love with you.' And he said, 'Mrs. Hilton, how well I understand that.'" When they were divorced after five years of marriage, someone asked Sanders how he felt. "Like a squeezed lemon," he replied.

But as witty as he often was, he could also be cantankerous. In a 1969 interview with Rex Reed, he sounded cynical and depressed.

"Do you have fond memories of the pictures you've made?" Reed asked.

"No," Sanders said.

---

*However, it remained for television to give the Saint his widest audience. The series began in England in the 1960s with Roger Moore in the title role. To add romantic spice, Moore appeared opposite such glamorous stars as Julie Christie, Samantha Eggar, Barbara Bates, Honor Blackman and Shirley Eaton. The series soon spread overseas and at its peak was syndicated to 86 countries. Moore won TV popularity awards in Spain and West Germany, among other countries. But perhaps the most unusual tribute came in Australia, where a 20-foot high painting of the Saint, all in white and complete with a halo, appeared overnight on the face of a cliff in Townsville. Nobody ever figured out who did it. Despite all the fanfare, Charteris thought Moore was, at best, only a "synthetic product." "The Saint's TV counterpart," said Charteris, "bears no more relation to the Saint that I wrote . . . than Winnie the Pooh to Captain Blood."

**Sanders' birth was registered with the British Embassy, which made him a British subject.

***His autobiography, written in 1960, is called *Memoirs of a Professional Cad.*

The Falcon (Conway) and a taxi-driver cohort (Veda Ann Borg) poke through dummies in a studio dress factory in *The Falcon in Hollywood* (1944).

Roger Moore, television's Saint, and Julie Christie, who won an Oscar for her performance in *Darling,* toast each other in a TV version of the long-playing series.

"Not even *All About Eve?*"

"No. Why should I?"

"Well, it's the only film you ever won an Academy Award for and it certainly holds fond memories for most movie-goers."

"Well, you may have fond memories of it. But it was just another picture for me.

"I understand you were a great fan of Tyrone Power," Reed continued.

"Who told you that? He died on the set of *Solomon and Sheba.* But he was just someone I knew. One knew lots of people. Every film is like an ocean voyage, a transatlantic crossing. You swear you will meet each other again. But you never do. I have no friends. No relatives. No family. Everyone is dead. Now I am going to die, too."

This was Sanders at 63. Grumpy, bitter and in failing health. His words were to prove prophetic. He died three years later of an overdose of sleeping pills.

Yet, in his salad days, Sanders projected a buoyant, sophisticated personality and it was this quality that made him ideal for the role of the Saint. Unfortunately, the series had a brief, four-year life. It ended in 1941 after only six pictures.

The trouble stemmed from a dispute between RKO and Charteris. The plots were only remotely related to Charteris' stories and he reportedly was not happy with the Saint's screen exploits.* So RKO simply dropped the series and created a new hero called the Falcon, who was nearly a mirror-image of his predecessor. Actually, he had the same girlfriend—Wendy Barrie—through his early films.

A real buff would have seen that the Falcon, which was based on a story called "Gay Falcon" by Michael Arlen, was not as tough an hombre. But a casual movie-goer, walking in late on a double feature, would have had trouble figuring out if he was seeing the Saint or the Falcon. To Charteris, RKO was serving up a "cheap imitation which actually had thousands of dim-witted customers thinking they were still getting the Saint." In fact, Charteris said, he sued RKO for unfair competition and won an out-of-court settlement.

Sanders played in the first four *Falcon* films. But he soon tired of the series. And in an unusual bit of casting, RKO replaced him with his brother, Tom Conway. Sanders and Conway co-starred in *The Falcon's Brother* (1942). When Nazi agents succeeded in assassinating the Falcon (Sanders), he passed the torch to Tom Lawrence (Conway).**

Years later, Maurice Geraghty, who produced half the 16 Falcon movies, disclosed that RKO really wrote in Conway's part as a way of getting Sanders to do one more film. "They gave George a glowing picture of how it would make

*Charteris expressed another view in a 1971 letter to the author. He said: "RKO switched to The Falcon, a flagrant carbon copy of their version of the Saint, in my opinion with the simple mercenary motive of saving the payments they had to make to me for the film rights . . ."

**In one of their posters, Charteris said, RKO billed Conway as "the Saint's brother."

a star out of his brother," Geraghty said. "But actually, they had no such plans or hopes . . . So it was astonishing to them when Tom Conway caught on right away and carried the series on—even outgrossing the pictures George had made."

The elegantly groomed Conway, who was almost as suave as his brother, starred in nine of the 16 *Falcon* pictures. But unlike Sanders, he never broke away from his stereotyped detective roles. During the *Falcon* series, he played Sherlock Holmes and the Saint on the radio.* When *The Falcon* ended, he went on to play Bulldog Drummond at 20th Century-Fox. Later, he appeared as Inspector Mark Sabre in television's early years.

But his life had a sad ending. He grew older, and his parts became fewer and far between. As his career faded, he drank heavily and ran through what was left of an estimated $1 million he amassed in 29 years as an actor. In 1965, Conway was found destitute and ailing in a $2 hotel room in Venice, California. He told reporters his brother was not aware of his plight. "We don't communicate," Conway said. ". . . We had a little set-to quite a while ago. I think we're both happier."

News of his condition brought offers of help from the entertainment community. Two years later, in 1967, Conway died of a liver ailment.

Movie-goers and critics are at odds on which of the series was the better—the Saint or the Falcon. But my choice is the Saint. He gets the nod because of his sinister underworld background and Simon Templar's utterly cool appearance, which Sanders' sangfroid personality and British accent made ring true. One of his more interesting capers—although one the critics felt was flawed—was *The Saint's Double Trouble* (1940), in which Sanders played two parts.

The picture opens as Professor Bitts (Thomas W. Ross), an archeologist at Philadelphia University, receives the mummy of King Aminuk III from his old friend, Simon Templar. A little while later, the Saint arrives unexpectedly as the professor is leaving for a faculty meeting. The Saint asks to see the mummy and the professor gives him the key to the vault. While he is down there, Anne (Helen Whitney), the professor's daughter, walks in and is instantly suspicious. But everything seems in order.

When the Saint leaves, a man's body is found in the garden, with the Saint's calling card in his pocket.** Inspector Bohlen (Donald MacBride) and Inspector

---

*Neither Conway nor Sanders played the Falcon in any other medium. But like the Saint, the Falcon became a popular radio hero in the 1940s. His real name was Mike Waring and he was played by no less than five actors at various times—Les Tremayne, Les Damon, James Meighan, Berry Kroeger and George Petrie. Charles McGraw later starred in a Falcon television series. However, this Falcon was an undercover agent and bore little resemblance to his screen counterpart. Besides Conway, other radio "Saints" were Barry Sullivan, Vincent Price and Brian Aherne. Charteris said he felt Aherne, even though he only appeared on radio, came closest to the character he had in mind when he created the Saint.

**Another characteristic of the Saint was a tune he whistled while walking on the street. It was usually heard when the titles went on and during the introduction to the Saint's radio adventures.

He may look like the Saint, but he's not. It's really the Dutchman, a criminal lookalike seen here disposing of Professor Bitts (Thomas W. Ross). Sanders played both roles in *The Saint's Double Trouble*.

Real-life brothers Tom Conway and Sanders exchanged roles in the *Falcon* series. Sanders got bumped off in *The Falcon's Brother* (1942) and Conway stepped into the lead.

Fernack (Jonathan Hale) take the case, but they have no way of knowing the Saint is an impostor. He is really Helm Van Roon, also known as the Dutchman, an international jewel thief who looks just like the Saint. The Dutchman has used the mummy to smuggle uncut gems out of Egypt. The man he killed was a double-crossing accomplice.

The next day, Templar arrives in Philadelphia and sizes up the situation quickly. From a fence, he learns the Dutchman's waterfront hideout and Templar goes there posing as the ringleader. He fools the Dutchman's henchmen—Monk (Elliott Sullivan), Limpy (John F. Hamilton) and Partner (Bela Lugosi). But the Dutchman shows up, catches him in the act, and promptly locks him in the backroom.

Then, discovering he has left half the diamonds behind, the Dutchman returns to the scene of the crime. This time, the professor discovers him unsheathing the mummy. When he tries to call the police, the Dutchman shoots him.

Meanwhile, back at the gang's den, the Saint has managed to slip out and escape through a manhole. When he learns of the professor's death, he sends word to Fernack to meet him in front of the Dutchman's hideout. The Saint also calls Anne. But when she shows up, the Dutchman is there, too. He orders Monk to put her in her car and drive her into the river.

Just as it is plunging into the black waters, the Saint rushes in and rescues Anne. But then he foolishly returns to the gang's den and walks into a trap. The Boss's henchmen tie him up and toss him into a rowboat. However, the Saint tips it over. As the Dutchman's men open fire, he fights free of his bonds, and swims safely away underwater.

Just then, Fernack arrives and the police haul the gang off to jail, including the Dutchman, whom Fernack mistakes for the Saint. The next day, the Saint gets a message to Fernack telling him that the Saint will escape that night dressed as an old woman.

Thus disguised, the Saint goes to the Dutchman's cell, lets him knock him out, don his disguise and escape. The waiting Fernack promptly cuts him down. When Fernack goes to the cell, he finds the real Saint, who explains the mystery. When the gems are returned, Fernack turns his back as the Saint escapes.

There are a couple of ironic postscripts. RKO's makeup department went to elaborate ends to create Sanders' double identity. When he played the Dutchman, makeup technicians accentuated Sanders' nose, chin and hairline to give him a tougher appearance. But this escaped the notice of many moviegoers, who learned, instead, to depend on the clothes Sanders wore to keep his two personalities apart. The Saint wore a dark suit while the Dutchman had on pinstripes. Sometimes even that didn't help. "He looks so much like himself in the role of the Boss [the Dutchman]," said Archer Winsten of the *New York Post,* "that you can't blame the other characters for not knowing the two apart."

But the unkindest cut of all came from, of all things, a parent-teachers group. The Schools Motion Picture Committee, which reviewed movies for children, took exception to the movie's billing with Walt Disney's *Pinocchio.* The committee said the Disney production could not be recommended because it was coupled with a grade-B melodrama featuring a gem smuggler, a waterfront den, a hail of police bullets and three murders. RKO declined to change the program.

THE SAINT SERIES

1. *The Saint in New York.* RKO, 1938, Ben Holmes.
   Louis Hayward (as Simon Templar, "the Saint"), Kay Sutton, Sig Rumann, Jonathan Hale (as Inspector Fernack), Jack Carson, Paul Guilfoyle, Frederick Burton, Ben Welden, Charles Halton, Cliff Bragdon. 72 minutes.

2. *The Saint Strikes Back.* RKO, 1939, John Farrow.
   George Sanders (as Simon Templar, "the Saint"), Wendy Barrie, Jonathan Hale, Jerome Cowan, Neil Hamilton, Barry Fitzgerald, Robert Elliott, Russell Hopton, Edward Gargan, Robert Strange, Gilbert Emery, James Burke, Nella Walker. 67 minutes.

3. *The Saint in London.* RKO, 1939, John Paddy Carstairs.
   George Sanders, Sally Gray, David Burns, Gordon McLeod (as Inspector Teal), Henry Oscar, Ralph Truman, Carl Jaffee, Norah Howard, Ballard Berkeley. 72 minutes.

4. *The Saint's Double Trouble.* RKO, 1940, Jack Hively.
   George Sanders, Helene Whitney, Jonathan Hale, Bela Lugosi, Donald Mac-Bride, John F. Hamilton, Thomas W. Ross, Elliott Sullivan, Pat O'Malley, Donald Kerr. 68 minutes.

5. *The Saint Takes Over.* RKO, 1940, Jack Hively.
   George Sanders, Wendy Barrie, Jonathan Hale, Paul Guilfoyle (as Pearly Gates), Morgan Conway, Robert Emmett Keane, Cyrus W. Kendall, James Burke, Robert Middlemass, Roland Drew, Nella Walker, Pierre Watkin. 69 minutes.

6. *The Saint in Palm Springs.* RKO, 1941, Jack Hively.
   George Sanders, Wendy Barrie, Paul Guilfoyle, Jonathan Hale, Linda Hayes, Ferris Taylor, Harry Shannon, Eddie Dunn, Richard Crane. 65 minutes.

7. *The Saint's Vacation.* RKO, 1941, Leslie Fenton.
   Hugh Sinclair (as Simon Templar, "the Saint"), Sally Gray, Arthur Macrae, Cecil Parker, Leueen McGrath, Gordon McLeod, John Warwick, Ivor Barnard, Manning Whiley, Felix Aylmer. 61 minutes.

8. *The Saint Meets the Tiger.* Republic, 1943, Paul Stein.
   Hugh Sinclair, Jean Gillie, Gordon McLeod, Clifford Evans, Wylie Watson, Dennis Arundell, Charles Victor, Louise Hampton, John Salew, Arthur Ham-

bling, Amy Veness, Claude Bailey, Noel Dainton, Eric Clavering, Ben Williams, John Slater, Tony Quinn, Alf Goddard. 70 minutes.

9.   *The Saint's Girl Friday.* RKO, 1954, Seymour Friedman.
      Louis Hayward (as Simon Templar "the Saint"), Naomi Chance, Sidney Tafler, Charles Victor (as Inspector Teal), Harold Lang, Jane Carr, Russell Enoch, Diana Dors, Fred Johnson, Thomas Gallagher. 70 minutes.

THE FALCON SERIES

1. *The Gay Falcon.* RKO, 1941, Irving Reis.
   George Sanders (as the Falcon), Wendy Barrie, Allen Jenkins (as Goldy), Anne Hunter, Gladys Cooper, Edward S. Brophy (as Bates), Arthur Shields, Damian O'Flynn, Turhan Bey, Eddie Dunn, Lucile Gleason, Willie Fung, Hans Conreid, Virginia Vale. 67 minutes.

2. *A Date with the Falcon.* RKO, 1941, Irving Reis.
   George Sanders, Wendy Barrie, James Gleason (as Mike O'Hara), Allen Jenkins, Mona Maris, Victor Kilian, Frank Moran, Russ Clark, Ed Gargan (as Bates), Alec Craig, Frank Martinelli, Hans Conreid, Elizabeth Russell. 63 minutes.

*3. *The Falcon Takes Over.* RKO, 1942, Irving Reis.
   George Sanders, Lynn Bari, James Gleason, Allen Jenkins, Helen Gilbert, Ward Bond, Edward Gargan, Anne Revere, George Cleveland, Harry Shannon, Hans Conreid, Mickey Simpson, Selmer Jackson, Turhan Bey. 63 minutes.

4. *The Falcon's Brother,* RKO, 1942, Stanley Logan.
   George Sanders, Tom Conway, Jane Randolph, Don Barclay (as Goldy), Amanda Varela, George Lewis, Gwili Andre, Cliff Clark, Edward Gargan, James Newill, Charlotte Wynters, Andre Charlot, Eddie Dunn, Mary Halsey, Richard Martin, Kay Aldridge. 63 minutes.

5. *The Falcon Strikes Back,* RKO, 1943, Edward Dmytryk.
   Tom Conway (as the Falcon), Harriet Hilliard, Jane Randolph, Edgar Kennedy, Cliff Edwards (as Goldy), Rita Corday, Erford Gage, Wynne Gibson, Richard Loo, Andre Charlot, Cliff Clark (Inspector Timothy Donovan), Ed Gargan, Byron Foulger, Joan Barclay, Frank Faylen, Jack Norton. 66 minutes.

6. *The Falcon and the Co-Eds,* RKO, 1943, William Clemens.
   Tom Conway, Jean Brooks, Rita Corday, Amelita Ward, Isabel Jewell, George Givot, Cliff Clark, Ed Gargan, Barbara Brown, Juanita Alvarez, Ruth Alvarez, Nancy McCullum, Patti Brill, Dorothy Malone(y). 68 minutes.

7. *The Falcon in Danger.* RKO, 1943, William Clemens.
   Tom Conway, Jean Brooks, Elaine Shepard, Amelita Ward, Cliff Clark, Ed Gargan, Clarence Kolb, Felix Basch, Richard Davies, Richard Martin, Erford

---

*This movie, based on Raymond Chandler's novel *Farewell, My Lovely,* was remade two years later as *Murder, My Sweet* with Dick Powell. This was the picture that changed Powell's image from a boyish crooner to a hard-boiled detective.

Gage, Eddie Dunn, Russell Wade, Bruce Edwards, Joan Barclay, Jack Mulhall. 69 minutes.

8. *The Falcon in Hollywood.* RKO, 1944, Gordon Douglas.
    Tom Conway, Barbara Hale, Veda Ann Borg, John Abbott, Sheldon Leonard, Konstantin Shayne, Emory Parnell, Frank Jenks, Jean Brooks, Rita Corday, Walter Soderling, Usaf Ali, Robert Clarke. 67 minutes.

9. *The Falcon in Mexico.* RKO, 1944, William Berke.
    Tom Conway, Mona Maris, Martha MacVicar (Vickers), Nestor Paiva, Mary Currier, Cecilia Callejo, Emory Parnell, Joseph Vitale, Pedro de Cordoba, Fernando Alvarado, Bryant Washburn, George Lewis, Julian Rivero, Juanita and Ruth Alvarez. 70 minutes.

10. *The Falcon Out West.* RKO, 1944, William Clemens.
    Tom Conway, Carole Gallagher, Barbara Hale, Joan Barclay, Cliff Clark, Ed Gargan, Minor Watson, Don Douglas, Lyle Talbot, Lee Trent, Lawrence Tierney. 64 minutes.

11. *The Falcon in San Francisco.* RKO, 1945, Joseph H. Lewis.
    Tom Conway, Rita Corday, Edward S. Brophy (Goldy), Sharyn Moffett, Fay Helm, Robert Armstrong, Carl Kent, George Holmes, John Mylong, Edmund Cobb, Myrna Dell, Esther Howard. 65 minutes.

12. *The Falcon's Alibi.* RKO, 1946, Ray McCarey.
    Tom Conway, Rita Corday, Vince Barnett (Goldy), Jane Greer, Elisha Cook, Jr., Emory Parnell, Al Bridge, Esther Howard, Jean Brooks, Edmund Cobb, Myrna Dell. 62 minutes.

13. *The Falcon's Adventure.* RKO, 1946, William Berke.
    Tom Conway, Madge Meredith, Edward S. Brophy (Goldy), Robert Warwick, Myrna Dell, Steve Brodie, Ian Wolfe, Carol Forman, Joseph Crehan, Phil Warren, Tony Barrett, Harry Harvey, Jason Robards, Dave Sharpe. 61 minutes.

14. *The Devil's Cargo.* Film Classics, 1948, John F. Link.
    John Calvert (as the Falcon), Rochelle Hudson, Roscoe Karns, Lyle Talbot, Tom Kennedy, Paul Regan, Theodore Von Eltz, Paul Marion. 61 minutes.

15. *Appointment with Murder.* Film Classics, 1948, Jack Bernhard.
    John Calvert, Catherine Craig, Jack Reitzen, Lyle Talbot, Robert Conte, Peter Brocco, Ben Welden, Carlos Schipa, Ann Demitri, Pat Lane, Eric Wilton, Robert Nadell, Michael Mark, Carole Donne, Gene Garrick, Frank Richards, Carl Sklover, Jay Griffith, Jack Chefe. 67 minutes.

16. *Search for Danger.* Film Classics, 1949, Don Martin.
John Calvert, Albert Dekker, Myrna Dell, Ben Welden, Douglas Fowley, Michael Mark, Anne Cornell, James Griffith, Mauritz Hugo, Peter Brocco, Peter Michael, Jack Daly, Billy Nelson. 62 minutes.

The screen's symbol of married love, Myrna Loy and William Powell as Nick and Nora Charles. With them is their wire-hair terrier, Asta.

THE THIN MAN

The Thin Man

(1934)

Screenplay by Albert Hackett and Frances Goodrich based on Dashiell Hammett's novel. Film editor, Robert J. Kern. Photographer, James Wong Howe. Recording engineer, Douglas Shearer. Assistant director, Les Selander. Art director, Cedric Gibbons. Musical numbers, Dr. William Axt. Produced by Hunt Stromberg. Directed by W. S. Van Dyke and presented by Metro-Goldwyn-Mayer. 93 minutes.

Nick Charles	WILLIAM POWELL
Nora Charles	MYRNA LOY
Dorothy Wynant	MAUREEN O'SULLIVAN
Guild	NAT PENDLETON
Mimi Wynant	MINNA GOMBELL
MacCaulay	PORTER HALL
Tommy	HENRY WADSWORTH
Gilbert Wynant	WILLIAM HENRY
Nunheim	HAROLD HUBER
Chris Jorgensen	CESAR ROMERO

Julia Wolf	NATALIE MOORHEAD
Morelli	EDWARD BROPHY
Clyde Wynant	EDWARD ELLIS
Tanner	CYRIL THORNTON

SHE: Is that my drink over there?
HE: What are you drinking?
SHE: Rye.
HE: *(Picks up the glass, guzzles down its contents, then smacks his lips)* Yes. Yes. It's yours.

SHE: What are you going to give me for Christmas? *(Pauses; then, before he answers, she speaks again)* I hope I don't like it.
HE: Well, you'll have to keep them anyway. There's a man at the Aquarium who said he wouldn't take them back.

SHE: *(Commenting on a woman she has seen her husband with)* Pretty girl.
HE: *(Agreeing)* Very nice type.
SHE: You got types?
HE: Only you, darling. Lanky brunettes with wicked jaws.

These crisp flashes of repartee come from Nick and Nora Charles. Remember that debonair husband and wife detective team? In between dry martinis, they quipped their way through six *Thin Man* films from 1934 to 1947.* They were urbane, engaging, witty. But they did more than add sophisticated dialogue to detective movies. They changed the course of screen love.

Before William Powell and Myrna Loy made the first *Thin Man* film, celluloid heroes and heroines were nearly always single. Producers felt sex and marriage were like oil and water—they didn't mix. If heroines married, they usually took the plunge in the last scene. If they had any life after marriage, Hollywood gingerly skirted the romance angle.

In 1934. Director W. S. Van Dyke decided to try to change all that. He made Nick Charles, a retired detective, and his wife as affectionate and gay in matrimony as they had been before wedding bells pealed.

Even when they bickered, there was a fresh appeal and delicious charm to their thrusts and parries:

*There was also a radio series with Lester Damon (and later Les Tremayne, Joseph Curtin, David Gothard and Bill Smith) and Claudia Morgan, and a television series with Peter Lawford and Phyllis Kirk. Though neither Powell nor Miss Loy appeared on these shows, they did recreate their original roles on "The Lux Radio Theatre" version of *The Thin Man* in June, 1936. Four years later, they made a return appearance and did *After The Thin Man*.

It's nighty night for the Charleses. When *The Thin Man* was made, couples always slept in twin beds—in the movies, anyway.

Lieutenant Abrams (Sam Levene) questions Selma Landis (Elissa Landi) as the Charleses and David Graham (Jimmy Stewart) look on. Scene is from *After the Thin Man.*

SHE: *(Pouting because Nick is not taking her on a dangerous assignment)* I think it's a dirty trick to bring me all the way to New York just to make a widow out of me.

HE: You wouldn't be a widow long.

SHE: You bet I wouldn't.

HE: Not with all your money.

HE: How'd you like Grant's Tomb?

SHE: It's lovely. I'm having a coffin made for you.

To be sure, the idea of fun and games after marriage took a little getting used to. Gilbert Seldes, writing in *Photoplay,* wondered what on earth Nick hoped to gain by making love to his own wife. He puzzled over what Nick's wife was after —"wasting her time being in love with her own husband." But Seldes had to admit he enjoyed the movie. More important, movie-goers did, too. They were, in fact, delighted with the idea that wedded life could be fun. And so the Charleses became the screen's first symbol of married love.

And what a team they were. They liked acting opposite each other and their styles, which produced a happy chemistry of spontaneous joy, complemented each other beautifully. They became Metro-Goldwyn-Mayer's keystone romance team. "Everyone in America thought we were married," Miss Loy recalled. Years later, fans would come away shaking their heads after going up for an autograph and finding that Miss Loy's husband was really somebody else.

Despite their popularity, the climb up the acting ladder was a long one for both.

Before she became the perfect wife, Miss Loy played Oriental roles. Rudolph Valentino saw her picture as a slant-eyed dancer in Grauman's Chinese Theatre. She tested for the lead in *Cobra* (1925), but didn't get the part. However, she got some bit roles and eventually began playing Oriental sirens. "I had these slinky eyes," she said.

She was born Myrna (after a railroad whistle stop sign her Dad saw) Williams at Helena, Montana. When her family moved to California, she studied dancing. Before she was 16, she was giving lessons in the Los Angeles suburb of Culver City. When she got into movies, the studio changed her name to Loy because it sounded Oriental. For nearly a decade, she played Chinese, Japanese, Javanese, Malayan, Hindu and Mexican sirens. She was the sadistic daughter of Boris Karloff in *The Mask of Fu Manchu* (1932).

"I finally got fired because they ran out of hussies for me to play," she said. But MGM began giving her some smart roles. She more than proved she could play them. Her early romantic pictures include *Love Me Tonight* (1932), *Men in White* (1934) and *Manhattan Melodrama* (1934)—the latter film the one Dillinger saw just before the FBI gunned him down.

Despite her smashing comedy success with Powell, she was just as popular in her roles opposite Clark Gable. They were dubbed "the king and queen of the movies."

"I still have the crown they gave me somewhere," she said in a recent interview. "We all had nicknames on the set. Clark called me 'Queenie,' Spencer Tracy was the 'Iron Duke,' and Victor Fleming, who directed all three of us in *Test Pilot* (1938), was 'the monk.' "

Married and divorced four times—her husbands were producer Arthur Hornblow, Jr., John Hertz, Jr., writer Gene Markey and Howland Sargeant—she made over 100 movies. Asked if she liked being remembered chiefly for her roles in the *Thin Man* mysteries, Miss Loy said she doubted it was true. She noted she also starred in the 1946 classic, *The Best Years of Our Lives.*

Powell's ascent to stardom came after a long career as a silent screen villain. When talkies evolved, Paramount liked the way his mature, mellow voice recorded and cast him as S. S. Van Dine's sleuth Philo Vance in *The Canary Murder Case* (1929).

The son of a Pittsburgh accountant, Powell studied drama in New York and began his acting career in the theatre. His first Broadway success, "Spanish Love" (1920), led to a film offer to play the villain in John Barrymore's *Sherlock Holmes* (1922). Among his many silent "heavy" roles was that of the Italian thief in *Beau Geste* (1926), starring Ronald Colman. After sound came and he switched to good guy parts, he played in the *Philo Vance* detective films (1929–33), then appeared opposite Clark Gable and Miss Loy in *Manhattan Melodrama* (1934). That led to *The Thin Man,* a low-budget movie from Dashiell Hammett's famed detective novel. He went on to do his most memorable movies. They include *My Man Godfrey* (1936) with Carole Lombard, his second wife,* *The Great Ziegfeld* (1936), *Libeled Lady* (1936), *Life with Father* (1947), *How to Marry a Millionaire* (1953) with Marilyn Monroe, and *Mister Roberts,* (1955), his last picture. But the role of Nick Charles remains his most famous characterization.

Ironically, according to one report, Louis B. Mayer, MGM's production head, did not want to cast either Powell or Miss Loy in the picture. He thought of them as heavies. He doubted they would jell as a droll comedy team. But director Van Dyke appealed to Mayer to give them a chance, insisting they could do the job. Mayer finally relented with the stipulation that Van Dyke make the picture quickly and cheaply. "I shot it in 16 days, retakes and all," Van Dyke recalled. "And that sweet smell of success was in every frame."**

Unquestionably, Powell and Loy's effortless, slightly mad diversions give the

---

*His first was actress Eileen Wilson. After his second marriage, he was engaged to Jean Harlow, but her untimely death in 1937 cut short their romance. However, his third marriage to Diana Lewis, an MGM starlet, lasted. That was in 1940 when he was 47 and she was 21. They were still husband and wife in 1972.

**Both Powell and *The Thin Man* got Academy Award nominations. In fact, the film was one of the pre-balloting favorites. But *It Happened One Night* scored an upset. It walked off with all the major Oscars and Clark Gable won the acting award.

It's Christmas Day after a well-celebrated Christmas Eve in *The Thin Man.* Nick aims his popgun, a present from his wife, at balloons on their Christmas tree.

Dorothy Wynant (Maureen O'Sullivan) implores Nick to take her case and help find her missing father, an eccentric inventor known as the "thin man." It is he—not Charles—who inspired the series' title.

picture such sparkle that nobody seems to care if they can't keep up with the fast and furious plot turns. Nevertheless, that original *Thin Man* movie—despite its rousing reviews and big box office—has so many suspects poking in and out, they seem as memorable as last week's laundry list.

In that film, the Nick Charleses have come to New York from California for the Christmas holidays. They're making the most of their trip by imbibing the local liquor in all the posh speakeasies in town. "The important thing is the rhythm," Nick says to his favorite bartender. "The dry martini you always shake to waltz time."

A former detective, Nick is now retired and devoting himself to managing the private affairs of his heiress wife. He is not, as popularly believed, the "thin man" of the title. That is Clyde Wynant (Edward Ellis), a reed-tall, eccentric inventor whose disappearance becomes the prelude to a series of slayings.

At the film's outset, Wynant is going into seclusion to work on a new invention. He won't even disclose his intended whereabouts to his daughter, Dorothy (Maureen O'Sullivan). However, he promises to return for her Christmas wedding. Wynant, divorced because of a liaison with his pretty secretary Julia Wolf (Natalie Moorhead), puts his lawyer, MacCaulay (Porter Hall), in charge of his affairs.

Just before Wynant departs, the inventor discovers $50,000 in government bonds missing from his safe. He was going to give them to his daughter as a wedding present. Enraged, he storms into his secretary's apartment. Wynant gets her to confess she took the money and then divided it with an accomplice. She won't disclose his name. But Wynant intercepts a telephone call and tells her he has a pretty good idea who he is.

That's the last anyone sees of the thin man. Months later, after he has failed to show up for his daughter Dorothy's wedding, she asks Nick Charles to find him. He's reluctant to interrupt his vacation.

Now, if you're still with us, the situation suddenly becomes more serious. Wynant's money-hungry ex-wife, Mimi (Minna Gombell), finds Wynant's secretary, Julia, shot to death. Mimi takes from her hand Wynant's watch chain. That clue immediately prompts an unimaginative police detective (Nat Pendleton) to suspect Wynant.

While Charles is still undecided about taking the case, a thug bursts into his hotel suite in the middle of the night. The crook says he thinks he may be arrested for the murder and asks Charles' help. But he gets flustered when police bang on the door, and draws his gun. Thinking fast, Nick kayoes Nora to get her out of the line of fire. He tosses a pillow in the gunman's face and escapes with a flesh wound when the thug pulls the trigger. Next morning, Nora, peeved at missing the show, gives Nick a popgun for his Christmas present. He promptly uses it to pick off balloons from their Christmas tree.

When he opens the morning papers, Nick sees the shooting on the front page.

"I'm a hero," Nick says, "I was shot twice in the *Tribune.*"

"I read you were shot five times in the tabloids," Nora says.

"It's not true. He didn't come anywhere near my tabloids."

Later, Nick gets a telegram, ostensibly from Wynant, asking Nick to clear the inventor. The mystery deepens when a stool pigeon named Nunheim (Harold Huber) is also killed. Nunheim had claimed to have seen Julia's murder. The same gun that killed Julia has been used on Nunheim.

Still, Nick has a hunch Wynant isn't the killer. Goaded by Nora, he decides to do some sleuthing.

With his dog, Asta,* Nick searches Wynant's shop for clues. Put on the trail by the pooch's sharp nose, Nick finds a body buried in the basement. The body is beyond recognition and the coroner is unable to identify the victim. But while examining the body, Nick notices an old shrapnel wound in the corpse's leg.

Still convinced Wynant is innocent, Nick invites all the suspects to a dinner. "The murderer is right in this room," Nick tells his startled guests. Then, step

The Charleses combine merriment with a murder case in *The Thin Man* (1934). Standing at left with thumb in vest is Charlie Williams. At right, with glasses, are Ben Taggart and Harry Tenbrook. Huey White is at the piano.

---

*Miss Loy says even today people still ask about Asta. "He was a wire-hair terrier and they were not popular at all at the time," she said, in a 1970 interview. "His name was really Skippy and he was highly trained to do all of his tricks for a little squeaky mouse and a biscuit. He'd do anything for that reward. But the minute his scenes were over, it was definitely verboten to hug him or have any further contact with him off the set."

by step, he analyzes the crimes, winding up by disclosing that Wynant himself was the third victim. Nick knows this because Wynant had a war wound in his shin. Julia, says Nick, was killed by the man she conspired with to steal Wynant's bonds. The killer shot her because he was afraid she would betray him. Then he killed Nunheim because he knew too much. Wynant was killed and his body hidden to cast suspicion on him.

That's as far as we can go without giving away this mystery. We'll leave you to the late show to let you match wits with Nick Charles.

THE THIN MAN SERIES

1. *The Thin Man.* MGM, 1934, W. S. Van Dyke.
William Powell (as Nick Charles), Myrna Loy (as Nora Charles), Maureen O'Sullivan, Nat Pendleton (as Guild), Minna Gombell, Porter Hall, Henry Wadsworth, William Henry, Harold Huber, Cesar Romero, Natalie Moorhead, Edward Brophy, Edward Ellis (as Wynant, the "Thin Man"), Cyril Thornton. 93 minutes.

2. *After the Thin Man.* MGM, 1936, W. S. Van Dyke.
William Powell, Myrna Loy, James Stewart, Elissa Landi, Joseph Calleia, Jessie Ralph, Alan Marshal, Teddy Hart, Sam Levene, Dorothy McNulty (Penny Singleton), William Law, George Zucco, Paul Fix. 107 minutes.

3. *Another Thin Man.* MGM, 1939, W. S. Van Dyke.
William Powell, Myrna Loy, Virginia Grey, Otto Kruger, C. Aubrey Smith, Ruth Hussey, Nat Pendleton, Patric Knowles, Tom Neal, Phyllis Gordon, Sheldon Leonard, Don Costello, Harry Bellaver, William A. Poulsen, Muriel Hutchison, Abner Biberman, Marjorie Main, Renee and Stella. 101 minutes.

4. *Shadow of the Thin Man.* MGM, 1941, W. S. Van Dyke.
William Powell, Myrna Loy, Barry Nelson, Donna Reed, Sam Levene, Alan Baxter, Henry O'Neill, Dickie Hall, Loring Smith, Joseph Anthony, Stella Adler, Lou Lubin, Louise Beavers. 97 minutes.

5. *The Thin Man Goes Home.* MGM, 1944, Richard Thorpe.
William Powell, Myrna Loy, Lucile Watson (as Mrs. Charles), Gloria DeHaven, Anne Revere, Helen Vinson, Harry Davenport (as Dr. Bertram Charles), Leon Ames, Donald Meek, Edward Brophy, Lloyd Corrigan, Anita Bolster, Ralph Brooke, Donald MacBride. 100 minutes.

6. *Song of the Thin Man.* MGM, 1947, Edward Buzzell.
William Powell, Myrna Loy, Keenan Wynn, Dean Stockwell, Phillip Reed, Patricia Morison, Leon Ames, Gloria Grahame, Jayne Meadows, Ralph Morgan, Bess Flowers, Don Taylor, Warner Anderson, Bruce Cowling, Connie Gilchrist, Henry Nemo, William Bishop, Marie Windsor. 86 minutes.

The Crime Doctor (Warner Baxter) reassures a troubled patient (Ellen Drew) who has sought his help in a case involving a twin sister. Scene is from *Crime Doctor's Man Hunt* (1946), sixth of the ten-film series.

CRIME DOCTOR

Shadows in the Night

(1944)

Based on the radio program "Crime Doctor" by Max Marcin. Story and screenplay by Eric Taylor. Art director, John Datu. Set director, Sidney Clifford. Editor, Dwight Caldwell. Director, Eugene J. Forde. Assistant director, Richard Monroe. Produced by Rudolph C. Flothow. Released by Columbia Pictures. 67 minutes.

Dr. Robert Ordway	WARNER BAXTER
Lois Garland	NINA FOCH
Frank Swift	GEORGE ZUCCO
Frederick Gordon	MINOR WATSON
Stanley Carter	LESTER MATHEWS
Nick Kallus	BEN WELDEN
Jess Hilton	EDWARD NORRIS
Sheriff	CHARLES C. WILSON
Doc Stacey	CHARLES HALTON
Adele Carter	JEANNE BATES
Riggs	ARTHUR HOHL

A car speeds along a deserted country road late at night. Suddenly, one of its doors swings open and a man falls out.

He lies on the shoulder of the road, still and unmoving until passersby see him and take him to a hospital. There, doctors find the man is badly wounded but alive. However, when he at last regains consciousness, he finds he has lost his memory. Not a clue can be found among his personal effects.

As weeks pass and he regains his health, nurses begin calling the dark, handsome patient "Ordway"—after the name of their medical center—and the nickname sticks. Ordway, who proves to have a sharp intelligence, makes friends with one of the staff psychiatrists, Dr. Carey (Ray Collins). And the doctor helps him build a new life, studying medicine.

Ten years go by. Ordway has become a successful psychiatrist. He is particularly skillful rehabilitating criminals. He rises to become a respected criminologist. Eventually, he is appointed chairman of the state parole board.

Then, one day, a woman prisoner comes before him. When Ordway denies her parole, she turns on him in a fury and discloses that he himself is a criminal. She says it was Ordway who masterminded a $200,000 payroll robbery 15 years before. The woman, who says she was one of the gang, tells Ordway the others entrusted him with the loot. But at a meeting that night, he showed up empty-handed. That was the reason his pals had taken him for a ride and left him for dead.

And so begins the saga of Dr. Robert Ordway, a criminologist who comes out of a mental fog to discover his own lurid past.* From 1943 to 1949, Columbia Pictures turned out 10 *Crime Doctor* movies that attracted a loyal following. But even before it reached the screen, the series already had a built-in audience. As a half-hour drama on the Columbia Broadcasting System's network (8:30 P.M. EDT, Tuesday), it played to 11 million listeners each week. Remember that familiar announcement: "Dr. Ordway will be back in exactly fifty-one seconds with the solution to tonight's mystery?" Written by former newspaperman Max Marcin for Philip Morris Cigarettes, the popular program revolved around Ordway's treatment of people with psychiatric problems related to crime. Ray Collins created the role in 1940. Later, House Jameson, Everett Sloane and John McIntire played the part. But the actor most identified with the character was, of course, Warner Baxter, who portrayed Dr. Ordway in the movies.

Baxter came through as a somewhat stiff and conservative hero. Although he was a bachelor, he was by then too old for romance. So after his first picture— in which he romances Margaret Lindsay—he was all business. However, his saving grace was his reliability and his compassion for his clients. He appeared

---

*It takes another rap on the head for Ordway's memory to return. Later, a jury exonerates him for his past acts. And he is free to continue his career as a psychiatrist.

nattily dressed in the latest style of the 1940s—wide-brim fedora, double-breasted suit with vest and padded shoulders, and a handkerchief in his breast pocket. True to his character as a doctor of medicine, he rarely resorted to violence. In the time-honored tradition of the intellectual sleuth, he solved murders on the basis of evidence, clues and deductive reasoning. The trouble was the audience rarely was made privy to the same information.

It was the second series for Baxter, a veteran performer who had been one of the screen's leading men during the early days of sound. In fact, Baxter won the movies' second Oscar for his performance as the happy-go-lucky Cisco Kid in *In Old Arizona*. The 1929 picture was the first outdoor talking film. He went on to play Cisco in two more movies in the 1930s. But his career had as many ups and downs as a roller coaster.

"I was a failure and a success three times in Hollywood," Baxter once said. "I have even had troubles paying my rent . . . My three depressions were suddenly ended by three pictures, each of which boosted me higher than I had ever been. *In Old Arizona* ended a two-year slump. *The Cisco Kid* [1931] brought me back into popular favor after a series of bad stories. And *42nd Street* [1933] revived me after the *Cisco Kid* had worn off. Like most actors, I wanted to cling to juvenility to the bitter end. But after I had repeated *42nd Street* several times, it occurred to me that actors, drugged by pride, can make first-class asses of themselves."

Born in Columbus, Ohio, in 1892, Baxter showed an early disposition for show business. "I discovered a boy a block away who would eat worms and swallow flies for a penny," Baxter said. "For one-third of the profits, I exhibited him in a tent." His mother closed the show very early in its run.

When he was nine, Baxter's widowed mother moved the family to San Francisco, only to be wiped out by the famous earthquake. The disaster made an indelible impression on Baxter. "For two weeks, we lived in a tent, in mortal terror of the fire," he said. "I can remember a young woman, almost naked, hysterically rubbing her head into the ground. And the countless thousands frantically searching for their kin."

He started in vaudeville in 1910 and stayed in show business thereafter, except for brief periods as a salesman. His career included acting in touring stage companies, Broadway plays and finally films. His curly hair and dark good looks made him a matinee idol in silent movies. However, his big break came in the sound era in the Cisco Kid role. And it came as a result of an accident.

Raoul Walsh, the famous actor-director, had been chosen for the part. But he was blinded in his right eye when a frightened jackrabbit crashed through his windshield while he was driving home at night after location work near Cedar City, Utah. Fox tested a dozen actors. Baxter got the role. He went on to play in *Squaw Man* (1931) with Lupe Velez, *Penthouse* (1933) with Myrna Loy and *Broadway Bill* (1934), again with Miss Loy. Some feel his best film was *The*

Frank Sully gets set to send a candle-holder crashing down on Crime Doctor's head while an accomplice (Bernard Nedell) moves in during *Crime Doctor's Man Hunt*. The series, filmed from 1943 to 1949, was the second for Baxter, who was the original Cisco Kid of sound movies.

A police laboratory expert (Robert Emmett Keane) analyzes a clue for Inspector Manning (Cliff Clark) and Dr. Ordway in *Crime Doctor's Diary* (1949), last of the series.

Prisoner of Shark Island (1936), in which he played the doctor who unwittingly treated Lincoln's assassin and went to prison for it. That year, his $284,000 earnings put him tops in the industry.

At the height of his career, he got as much fan mail as Gable or Taylor. In fact, with pencil mustache and resonant voice, he vaguely resembled Gable. "Women liked him because he was dark and mature," David Shipman wrote in *The Great Movie Stars.* "He was a good work-horse of an actor, often at the mercy of his material. When it was good, he gave positive, likeable performances."

But even in that peak year of 1936, Baxter was 44. And he knew his days as a leading man were fading. He began to accept character roles and B-pictures assignments. In 1943, seven years after his triumph in *Shark Island,* he became Dr. Robert Ordway. It was the tail end of a long career and he took the part in stiff-upper-lip tradition.

"Most actors object to typing," Baxter said. "I don't. In the first place, it is the public who types an actor, not the studio. If an actor is so good in a certain character, he can afford to submerge his urge to portray many parts in favor of a neat financial return." He cited a number of instances where typing did actors plenty of good. "Mickey Rooney was made a star because of *Andy Hardy,* " he said. "Bill Boyd was about ready to give up the screen for ranching when *Hopalong Cassidy* came along. *Frankenstein* did wonders for Boris Karloff. American audiences love to make their own heroes. Then, when they've made them, they can't see them in any other character until the series has run its course of popularity."

Which was just fine as far as Baxter was concerned. "Yes, sir, give me a character that American audiences want to see me in and the typing won't worry me."

Despite Baxter's obviously artificial put-on enthusiasm for typing, the series turned out to be a blessing in disguise. He had suffered a nervous breakdown in the early 1940s. And the relatively easy demands the series made on him—the pictures were shot on studio sets in one month and he did only two a year—enabled him to work without taxing himself physically. The series came to an end two years before his death in 1951 from pneumonia. His illness followed a lobotomy performed to try to relieve him of arthritic pains.

No one has ever recorded Baxter's favorite of his ten *Crime Doctor* movies. But one that showed him to advantage was *Shadows in the Night* (1944), third in the series, a better-than-average mystery that put him opposite a rising but as yet unknown Nina Foch.

At three o'clock in the morning in the midst of a rainstorm, a terrified young woman pounds on Dr. Ordway's door. She apologizes for the intrusion, but begs him to see her. "I know I should have called for an appointment," she says. "But I was afraid I wouldn't live until morning."

The girl is Lois Garland (Nina Foch), a textile designer and heiress. Ordway invites her into his study and then startles her with a question that would have done Holmes himself proud.

"Was tonight the first time you had an impulse to kill yourself?"

"What makes you think that's what I'm afraid of?" the incredulous woman asks.

"You're not afraid of dying from a physical illness," Ordway explains, "or you would have gone to a physician. If you feared an attack on your life, you would have gone to the police. But when you come to a psychiatrist in the middle of the night with an explanation that to wait until morning would be fatal, then self-destruction is the obvious conclusion."

Ordway is, of course, right. Miss Garland tells him that she has been having nightmares in her house, Ravencliff, which overlooks craggy ocean breakers. "I dream a woman comes to my window dripping wet," Miss Garland says. "She looks as if she just walked out of the sea. She looks like a woman from another time. She seems to be part of the fog that drifts through the window. She crosses to the door. And as she leaves, she turns and beckons me to follow . . . When the dream kept coming back night after night, I began to get the feeling that I was going to follow her into the ocean. Tonight, in my sleep, I must have gone down on the beach. Look." She shows him her shoes, filled with sand.

Warner Baxter, playing Robert Ordway, the Crime Doctor, comforts sleep-walking Lois Garland (Nina Foch) in *Shadows in the Night* (1944). She has been having nightmares about a woman coming dripping wet into her room, luring her to the sea outside.

Ordway agrees to take the case. The next night, when he arrives at the Garland home, he takes Lois' place in her bedroom. After he falls asleep, a foglike mist clouds the room. Then, just as she said, a hooded sepulchral figure appears. In a daze, Ordway follows it to surf-battered rocks below the house. Luckily, a fall revives him in the nick of time. However, that's just his first surprise. When he returns to the house, he stumbles across a man's body in the hall. He rushes to wake Lois. But when they return to the hall, the body is gone.

The next morning, Ordway meets Lois' houseguests—a weird collection of potential villains. Among them are:

• Frank Swift (George Zucco)—Lois' eccentric uncle, a chemist who is working in a lab on the grounds. He is searching for a formula to produce a new synthetic fabric. It will later be brought out that 15 people died as a result of a mistake he made as a chemist working for a drug company. He later had a nervous breakdown.

• Jess Hilton (Edward Norris)—junior partner in the textile firm that employs Lois. He is in love with Lois but seems to be getting nowhere because she is totally devoted to her boss, Raymond Shields.

• Nick Kallus (Ben Welden)—a tough bird who works as Lois' cook. He did a prison stretch after killing a customer in an argument in his diner. But he has reformed. And Lois, feeling sorry for him, has taken him in until he can find a permanent job. Nick is in no hurry to leave.

• Adele and Stanley Carter (Jeanne Bates and Lester Mathews)—Lois' sister and unemployed actor brother-in-law. All seems sweetness and light here. But we later learn that Stanley is a gigolo. He has previously married and divorced a steel baron's daughter. Now he is suing to try to win custody of their child—offering to drop the suit for a cash settlement.

• Frederick Gordon (Minor Watson)—the family lawyer. Ordway has found the dead body outside his door. But Gordon maintains he heard nothing because he's a sound sleeper.

• Riggs (Arthur Hohl)—the gardener. Think of him as the butler. Just a red herring.

After breakfast, Ordway goes for a stroll. On the beach, he finds the corpse about to be swept out to sea with the tide. The body, its head badly crushed, is that of Raymond Shields, Lois' employer. Nobody believes Ordway had first seen Shields in the hall. And attorney Gordon advises him not to tell this to the police because, he says, Shields obviously died from a fall. Ordway's incredible story would only subject the family to an investigation, Gordon says.

Ordway decides to do some investigating of his own. In Shields' laboratory, he finds chemicals capable of producing a mistlike vapor. Next, the crime doctor discovers a laundry chute in a bathroom near the hall area where he had first seen Shields' body. The chute leads to the basement, which, in turn, opens onto the beach. In the basement, Ordway finds a brass candlestick, heavy enough to have fractured a man's skull.

That night, when Ordway goes to bed, he hides the candlestick, which he believes is the murder weapon. Again, the mysterious cloud appears, drugging Ordway. A figure wearing a gas mask slips into his room, and locates the candlestick. As he is about to leave, the figure hears a sudden noise. Riggs, the gardener, comes into Ordway's room and the figure in the gas mask clobbers him with the candlestick, making Riggs murder victim number two. When Ordway comes to, he wakes all the guests. One fails to show up. Mrs. Carter, Lois' sister, lies drugged in her bed.

The next night, Ordway climbs to the dusty attic and locates an air vent leading to Lois' room. Next to it, he finds gas powder and acid. He knows now that the nightmares were produced by hypnotic gas. He has figured out, too, that both Riggs and Shields were killed with the candlestick. Riggs, because he was about to give Crime Doctor some information. Shields, because he ran into whomever was manipulating his nightmare. His body disappeared down the laundry chute.

As Ordway is puzzling this out, he comes across actor Carter bound and gagged, locked in a room leading to the attic. Then, Ordway learns an intriguing bit of information about Carter. The actor has filed his child custody lawsuit without telling Lois. She has warned him that she will testify against him. She knows he stole $4,000 while he was on a charity drive committee and she has made the money good for him.

Things have gone far enough and Crime Doctor assembles all the guests in the living room. The police are on the scene, too. Lights go out and a ghostly figure of a woman creeps into the room. When the lights go on, it turns out to be a police official disguised as a woman. He is wearing a mask and wig. His body is hidden under a full cloak. This was the "nightmare" that haunted Lois and Ordway.

"Now do you see how it was worked?" Ordway asks. "You see, a moving figure attracts anyone under the influence of a gas."

Next, Ordway asks Nick to show everyone the "rope trick." Taking the same rope that had bound Carter, Nick demonstrates how he can tie himself.

"What are you all looking at me for?" Carter asks. "That only proves it's possible for a man to tie himself up. It doesn't prove anything against me."

"You're right, Carter," Ordway says. "But I found the key inside the closet underneath some linen. That's why I had Nick get these slacks from your bedroom. You'll notice that the knees are stained with pitch—just like mine are. You see, it's practically impossible to reach the air conditioning outlet from Lois' bedroom without kneeling in pitch."

"But what could I have possibly gained by putting on that cloak and mask and scaring Lois?"

"The repetition of those nightmares would have induced a mental disorder that would have caused Lois to be called legally incompetent to have testified against you in court."

And so the jig is up for Carter. He makes a bold dash for freedom. But police cut him down with a bullet in the leg.

Crime Doctor Robert Ordway's perceptive mind has solved yet another mystery.*

---

*Movie critics rarely had favorable things to say about series movies—if they wrote anything at all. And *Crime Doctor* was no exception. One of the nicer reviews on *Shadows in the Night* appeared in *Variety,* which found it "better than average." *New York Daily News* writer Dorothy Masters complained, with tongue in cheek, that it was a snide trick to put bogeyman George Zucco in the cast without letting him be responsible for either murder. Still, she conceded, the picture was "satisfactorily suspenseful." But a more typical review appeared in the now defunct newspaper *PM* over the initials J. T. M. *"Shadows in the Night* is probably the most ado about nothing that anybody ever bothered to concoct," said the irate reviewer. "It has more villains to the square foot than Wall Street and not even a butler to hang the thing on at the end. I left when I thought I had figured out who put the hypnotic gas in the air-cooling system. But there were still two murders unaccounted for. This is another Crime Doctor case with Warner Baxter as the medico-meddler. I suggest eating an apple instead." There are times when B-pictures rate such a zinger. This wasn't one of them.

CRIME DOCTOR SERIES

1. *Crime Doctor*. Columbia, 1943, Michael Gordon.
   Warner Baxter (as Dr. Robert Ordway, the Crime Doctor), Margaret Lindsay, John Litel, Ray Collins, Harold Huber, Don Costello, Leon Ames, Constance Worth, Dorothy Tree, Vi Athens. 66 minutes.

2. *Crime Doctor's Strangest Case*. Columbia, 1943, Eugene J. Forde.
   Warner Baxter, Lynn Merrick, Lloyd Bridges, Rose Hobart, Barton MacLane, Virginia Brissac, Gloria Dickson, Reginald Denny, Sam Flint, Jerome Cowan, Constance Worth, Thomas Jackson, George Lynn. 68 minutes.

3. *Shadows in the Night*. Columbia, 1944, Eugene J. Forde.
   Warner Baxter, Nina Foch, George Zucco, Minor Watson, Lester Matthews, Ben Welden, Edward Norris, Charles Wilson, Charles Halton, Jeanne Bates. 67 minutes.

4. *Crime Doctor's Courage*. Columbia, 1945, George Sherman.
   Warner Baxter, Hillary Brooke, Jerome Cowan, Robert Scott, Lloyd Corrigan, Emory Parnell, Stephen Crane, Charles Arnt, Anthony Caruso, Lupita Tovar, Dennis Moore, King Kong Kashay, Jack Carrington. 70 minutes.

5. *Crime Doctor's Warning*. Columbia, 1945, William Castle.
   Warner Baxter, John Litel, Dusty Anderson, Coulter Irwin, Miles Mander, John Abbott, Eduardo Ciannelli, Alma Kruger, J. M. Kerrigan, Franco Corsaro. 69 minutes.

6. *Crime Doctor's Man Hunt*. Columbia, 1946, William Castle.
   Warner Baxter, Ellen Drew, William Frawley, Frank Sully, Claire Carleton, Bernard Nedell, Jack Lee, Francis Pierlot, Myron Healey, Olin Howlin, Ivan Triesault, Paul E. Burns, Mary Newton, Leon Lenoir. 61 minutes.

7. *Just Before Dawn*. Columbia, 1946, William Castle.
   Warner Baxter, Adelle Roberts, Martin Kosleck, Mona Barrie, Marvin Miller, Charles D. Brown, Craig Reynolds, Robert Barrat, Wilton Graff, Charles Lane, Charles Arnt, Ted Hecht, Peggy Converse, Irene Tedrow, Thomas Jackson. 65 minutes.

8. *The Millerson Case*. Columbia, 1947, George Archainbaud.
   Warner Baxter, Nancy Saunders, Clem Bevans, Griff Barnett, Paul Guilfoyle, James Bell, Addison Richards, Mark Dennis, Robert Stevens, Eddie Parker, Vic

Potel, Eddy Waller, Russell Simpson, Sarah Padden, Barbara Pepper, Frances Morris. 72 minutes.

9.   *Crime Doctor's Gamble.* Columbia, 1947, William Castle.
     Warner Baxter, Micheline Cheirel, Roger Dann, Steven Geray, Marcel Journet, Eduardo Ciannelli, Maurice Marsac, Henri Letondal, Jean Del Val, Leon Lenoir, Wheaton Chambers, Emory Parnell, George Davis. 66 minutes.

10. *Crime Doctor's Diary.* Columbia, 1949, Seymour Friedman.
     Warner Baxter, Stephen Dunne, Lois Maxwell, Adele Jergens, Robert Armstrong, Don Beddoe, Whit Bissell, Cliff Clark, Lois Fields, George Meeker, Crane Whitley, Claire Carleton, Selmer Jackson, Sid Tomack, Robert Emmett Keane. 61 minutes.

"Ah, chemicals leave no doubt Lady Warford's drink poisoned," Warner Oland seems to say as he holds a test tube in *Charlie Chan's Secret* (1935). Herbert Mundin's eyes betray his surprise.

CHARLIE CHAN

Charlie Chan at the Wax Museum
(1940)

Screenplay by John Larkin based on the character created by Earl Derr Biggers. Camera, Virgil Miller. Editor, James B. Clark. Music, Emil Newman. Assistant directors, Richard Day and Louis Creber. Directed by Lynn Shores. A 20th Century-Fox release of Walter M. Morosco and Ralph Dietrich's production. 63 minutes.

Charlie Chan	SIDNEY TOLER
Jimmy Chan	VICTOR SEN YUNG
Dr. Cream	C. HENRY GORDON
Steve McBirney	MARC LAWRENCE
Lily Latimer	JOAN VALERIE
Mary Bolton	MARGUERITE CHAPMAN
Tom Agnew	TED OSBORN
Dr. Otto von Brom	MICHAEL VISAROFF
Mrs. Rocke	HILDA VAUGHN
Willie Fern	CHARLES WAGENHEIM
Carter Lane	ARCHIE TWITCHELL

That's Jon Hall wielding a gun in *Charlie Chan in Shanghai* (1935). He acted then under his real name, Charles Locher. Among many other members of the Chan Alumni Association are Rita Hayworth, Ray Milland and Boris Karloff. The smartly tailored girl next to Hall is Irene Hervey.

A dapper Cesar Romero plays a magician who joins forces with Toler to expose a crooked medium in *Charlie Chan at Treasure Island* (1939). Many fans rate it the best in the series. The young lady with the picture hat is Sally Blane, Loretta Young's sister.

Grenock	EDWARD MARR
Inspector Matthews	JOE KING
Edwards	HAROLD GOODWIN

Let's start with some "wasn'ts" about Charlie Chan.

• He wasn't played on the screen by a Chinese. The six actors who portrayed him were Japanese (George Kuwa and Kamiyama Sojin), English (E. L. Park), Swedish (Warner Oland) and American (Sidney Toler and Roland Winters).

• He wasn't always brilliant or profound when spouting his famous aphorisms. But more often than not, they had a sparkle of humor and a glimmer of wisdom. "Bad alibi like dead fish," said Charlie in one typical observation. "Can't stand test of time."

• And, of course, he wasn't the movies' only Oriental sleuth. There were Mr. Moto and Mr. Wong.

But let's look at some Chan "was-es."

• The *Chan* series was a training ground for some of Hollywood's brightest stars. They included Rita Hayworth (who played under her real name, Rita Cansino), Jon Hall (also billed under his real name, Charles Locher), Ray Milland, George Brent and Robert Young. Others who appeared in the films included Cesar Romero, Mary Beth Hughes, Stepin Fetchit, Lynn Bari, Slim Summerville and bogeymen Boris Karloff, Bela Lugosi and Lon Chaney, Jr.

• Charlie was the only fictional detective to have a major museum film festival held in his honor. That was in 1968 at the prestigious Museum of Modern Art in New York City.

• And he was the screen's most prolific investigator. From 1926 to 1949, Hollywood made 46 *Chan* films and one serial.

But no compendium of facts and figures holds the key to his popularity. Chan became an enduring movie hero because he brought a gentle spoofing quality to a favorite genre. "Perhaps the most endearing feature of the *Chan* films is the humor," said Gary Carey of the Modern Museum's film study center. "[It] rises from the plot machinations of a foreign intellect [Chan] penetrating native culpability."

Chan won audiences with such pithy observations as: "Two lovers in moonlight cast only one shadow. One shadow now—many shadows later." Or, on strategy: "When player cannot see man who deal cards, much wiser to stay out of game." Or, on personality: "Confidence—like courage of small boy at dentist—most evident after tooth extracted." Or, on friends: "Man without enemies like dog without fleas."

Yet, the chunky, round-faced policeman from Honolulu was more than a low-key comedian. He brought a scholarly, courteous manner to the detective story. Instead of brawn, he relied strictly on brains. And his meticulous methods stood him in good stead. Everyone else invariably picked the most obvious suspect as the criminal. Not Charlie. He refused to jump to conclusions. He went his own way, puttering around, turning up clues. His phlegmatic meanderings sometimes allowed for another murder or two. But it kept the tension mounting.

Then, at the climax, Charlie would set a trap, using himself as the bait. Or he would gather his suspects together and re-enact the crime. He would gamble that the culprit would give himself away. It always worked. Sometimes a slip of the tongue undid the felon. He would mention a detail only the guilty party could know. Then, panicking, the frightened criminal would break down and confess. Or, in an act of desperation, he might douse the lights and try to kill Chan. Occasionally, this added still another corpse to the caper—a fact that made at least one writer complain that Chan's slow-motion tactics kept the scales of justice from balancing. "Chan usually gets his murderer," said Frank S. Nugent, a *New York Times* movie reviewer. "But the incidental carnage is never short of terrific."

None of this bothered the true Chan devotee. He was so dedicated that he cheerfully overlooked the familiar formula plots. He grew fond of the pattern, became comfortable with the ritual. And so, he never failed to delight in the great exposé at the grand finale—give or take the extra cadaver or two.

The idea for Chan's creation goes back to 1919. Writer Earl Derr Biggers, on vacation in Honolulu, read about a local Chinese police official named Chang Apana. The notion of an Oriental detective operating in a western culture intrigued him. Six years later, he wrote a *Saturday Evening Post* serial called "House Without a Key." Chan was the hero and the mystery was an instant success. Five more *Post* serials followed.*

In 1926, Pathé Studios bought the screen rights to Biggers' first story as a vehicle for its serial team Allene Ray and Walter Miller. Since they were the primary box office draw, the Chan role was relegated to a minor part. Kuwa, the veteran Japanese stage and screen actor who played Chan, was billed twelfth in the cast listing. In 1928, Chan became a major figure in the second film and Sojin, Chan number two, got good notices. But Universal, which produced the movie, decided against making any other *Chan* movies. Fox brought out the third *Chan* picture one year later. But, as in the first movie, Charlie was again little more than a walk-on character. Englishman Park was billed last in the cast.

Then, in 1931, Oland stepped into the part. He did not appear until halfway through the film, *Charlie Chan Carries On*. But so engaging and so distinctive was his interpretation that he stole the picture. It was Oland, then, who really created Chan's screen character. Audiences responded enthusiastically, and he

---

*All were also published as books. Nevertheless, Chan was fundamentally a movie character. Five *Chan* films are based on the Biggers novels. The remaining 42 are original screenplays.

Douglass Dumbrille (eye patch) is an eccentric millionaire and student of medieval history in *Castle in the Desert* (1942). With him are Toler and Sen Yung.

A squinting Roland Winters was the third and last movie Charlie Chan. He played the part despite a prominent nose (most shots were taken head-on), blonde hair (he wore a black wig), and unslanting eyes ("I just squinted"). Winters is seen here with Sen Yung in *The Chinese Ring* (1947).

made 16 more pictures—about two per year, for $50,000 each, for the next seven years.

Almost overnight, the series became popular in dozens of countries, including the Far East. But the ensuing notoriety extended not so much to Oland but to the fictional character he played so imaginatively. When Princess Alexandra Klashkin, a member of the Shanghai Russian colony, visited the United States in 1936, she said China's favorite movie stars were "Shirley Temple and Charlie Chan." In fact, Oland became so convincing in the role that he was even taken for a native when he made a trip to China. "Everywhere I went," Oland said, "people addressed me in Chinese. I was always introduced as 'Mr. Chan.' "

Ironically, many of his fans did not know that he had been a serious stage actor. Born in Stockholm, he played in a Shakespearean company after coming to this country as a youth. He also appeared with a Sarah Bernhardt troupe and went on to put on his own plays. But his producing venture failed and he went to Hollywood where he broke into movies in four Theda Bara silents.

Subsequently, he became an outstanding character actor. He played Al Jolson's father, a cantor, in *The Jazz Singer* (1927), the first talking picture. One of his favorite parts was that of a Chinese villain. He was the Orient's cunning and sinister crime lord in *The Mysterious Dr. Fu Manchu* (1929). And he played a Chinese warlord in *Shanghai Express* (1932). But it was the Chan role that brought him international fame, and no other actor played the role until his death in 1938.

Both Leo Carrillo and Noah Beery tested to be Oland's successor. However, the man taking the torch was Sidney Toler. A six-foot, Missouri-born actor of Scotch descent, Toler had been a David Belasco star on Broadway and a playwright. Although Toler had made 50 pictures before succeeding Oland, he had never before appeared as a Chinese. But he fitted into the Chan role with a minimum of makeup. All he did was paste on a mustache and a wisp of beard, darken his graying hair and comb it straight back. His eyes, he said, had a natural slant.

Some fans asked him not to vary from Oland's conception of the role. But he decided against imitating his predecessor. Instead, he read all the Biggers novels and modeled his style on the fictional Chan. He was so successful, he went on to play Charlie 25 times—more than any other actor—from 1938 until he died in 1947.

Roland Winters, a character actor who during World War II had broadcast in German as America's voice in reply to Lord Haw Haw, was the sixth and last screen Chan. His blonde hair and prominent nose made him an unlikely Oriental. But he won the part by using a little ingenuity.

"They had never seen me when I was invited to go out to Hollywood for a screen test," Winters said. "I'd sent them a picture, of course. But it didn't bear

J. Edward Bromberg hands a roll of bills to Oland in *Charlie Chan on Broadway* (1937). Eyes glued to the money are Keye Luke (second from left) and Harold Huber.

Something sinister lurking in the shadows seems to have everyone under its spell in *Charlie Chan at the Wax Museum* (1940). From left, Michael Visaroff, Victor Sen Yung, Marc Lawrence (face in bandages), Toler and C. Henry Gordon.

the slightest resemblance to me. I wore a hat and a mustache in it and squinted my eyes because, you see, I knew they were looking for someone to play Charlie Chan. And I assumed this made me look inscrutable.

"When I walked in and they really got a look at me for the first time, they were appalled. But for some reason, I was hired."

Some adjustments had to be made for the nose. "I always looked straight into the camera," Winters said. "And when I was talking to someone at the side, I just moved my eyes. I never saw half the people I was supposed to be talking to. But at least, my nose didn't give me away."

Winters, who later played in the TV series "Meet Millie," made up for the Chan role by simply wearing a black hairpiece and squinting. "They tried makeup on my eyes. But it wouldn't work," he said. "They fiddled around with wax for the eyes, putty and stuff. But it didn't work either. So I did it myself. I just squinted. Before every shot, the director would say, 'Remember the eyes.' "

The last half-dozen *Chans*, shot by Monogram, were low, low budget affairs. The studio turned them out in two weeks or less. "It wasn't amazing," Winters said. "It was horrible."*

Almost as famous as the actors playing Chan, of course, was Keye Luke, who appeared as Charlie's number-one son 11 times. Born in Canton, China, he went to the University of Southern California. But he had to go back to college to learn Mandarin for the Marines in World War II. Not so well known but a more prolific performer was Victor Sen Yung, who played Charlie's number-two son in 18 pictures. He later appeared in the "Bonanza" television series. Other Chan offspring were portrayed by Benson Fong (six times), Layne Tom, Jr. (twice), and Edwin Luke (once). In addition, Marianne Quon and Frances Chan each made one appearance as Charlie's daughters. Several actresses were seen briefly as Charlie's wife but none ever got screen credit. In all, the Chan brood numbered thirteen. His sons all stalked criminals with zest and gusto, but unfortunately they usually ended up spinning their wheels. None inherited their father's shrewd investigative ability.

What was the best of the *Chan* films?

Many fans single out *Charlie Chan on Treasure Island* (1939). Others cast their vote for *Charlie Chan at the Opera* (1936). There are those who favor *Charlie Chan in Panama* (1940), *Charlie Chan on Broadway* (1937) or *Charlie Chan at Monte Carlo* (1937). I like them all. But their complicated plots make it difficult to do justice to them in print. So my choice for this chapter is a simple mystery, usually not named in popularity polls—*Charlie Chan at the Wax Museum* (1940). It gets our ballot because of its suspense and eerie setting and a storyline that

*J. Carrol Naish played the Oriental sleuth in an unsuccessful TV series. Others who appeared as the benign Chinese investigator were William Harrigan on the stage and Walter Connolly, Ed Begley and Santos Ortega on radio.

keeps you guessing as to who is dead, who is alive and who is a dummy.

As the movie opens, gangster-killer Steve McBirney (Marc Lawrence), convicted by evidence gathered by Chan (Toler), escapes while being taken to prison. He hides in a wax museum of crime run by Professor Cream (C. Henry Gordon), a plastic surgeon who gives new faces to old crooks in an operating theatre in the museum basement. "I want the best face you ever made," McBirney says. "So I can walk up to Chan and say, 'Hiya Charlie,' before I let him have it."

McBirney undergoes surgery. Then, he and Professor Cream plot to kill Chan. They have the perfect setup. The Crime League's weekly broadcast on controversial murder cases is done at the museum. The doctor invites Chan as a panelist. When he accepts, McBirney wires the chair in which Chan will sit so McBirney can electrocute him.

On the night of the broadcast, seated around the microphone in the museum's main hall are Chan, criminologist Dr. Otto von Brom (Michael Visaroff), reporter Mary Bolton (Marguerite Chapman), program director Tom Agnew (Ted Osborn) and Cream. McBirney is lurking in the shadows. So is Mrs. Joe Rocke (Hilda Vaughn), widow of a criminal who has gone to the chair professing his innocence. The Rocke case is the subject of the broadcast.

When they go on the air, Chan supports the theory that Rocke was unjustly executed. He thinks the crime was really committed by the notorious gangster Butcher Dagan. Von Brom, whose scientific evidence sent Rocke to his death, is in the chair that had been intended for Chan.

Suddenly the lights go out. When they come on, Von Brom rises, then slumps over the table, dead. Chan quickly discovers Von Brom has not been electrocuted. "Observe small puncture on back of neck," says Charlie. A poisoned dart has killed the criminologist. Broadcaster Agnew cuts the program off the air.

Prowling through the museum's spooky corridors, Chan discovers Cream's operating room. Butcher Dagan has gotten a new face, Chan speculates, and killed Von Brom because the criminologist has found out his new identity.

Then, McBirney, the man who planned to murder Chan, is found dead, killed by another poisoned dart. Mrs. Rocke is discovered nearby. But she swears she wasn't involved. She says she only wanted to confront Von Brom and get him to reconsider her husband's case.

Police are about to take her away. But Chan calls together all the people who were at the broadcast and starts to demonstrate how Von Brom was killed. He shoots a dart at one of the wax dummies.

The dummy springs to life. It's the broadcaster Tom Agnew (alias Butcher Dagan). "Give me that antidote," he pleads. "Quick."

"You killed Von Brom," Chan says, calmly.

"Yes."

"Also Steve McBirney."

"Yes, I had to."

"You framed Joe Rocke, innocent man."

"Yes," Agnew admits. "But hurry. Give me that stuff."

"Dart only broken match stick," Chan discloses. "Original needle of death still in pocket."

As police lead off Agnew, reporter Mary Bolton scratches her head and says she should have guessed Agnew was the killer. "Any other radio man would have stayed on the air to broadcast Von Brom's murder," she says.

Chan agrees. "Small nose for news in radio man," he remarks, "brings aroma of suspicion."

CHARLIE CHAN SERIES

1. *The House Without a Key.* Pathé, 1926, George B. Seitz.
   Allene Ray, Walter Miller, George Kuwa (as Charlie Chan).

2. *Chinese Parrot.* Universal, 1928, Paul Leni.
   Marian Nixon, Florence Turner, Hobart Bosworth, Edmund Burns, Capt. Albert
   Conti, Kamiyama Sojin (as Charlie Chan).

3. *Behind That Curtain.* Fox, 1929, Irving Cummings.
   Warner Baxter, Lois Moran, Gilbert Emery, Claude King, Philip Strange, Boris
   Karloff, Jamiel Hasson, Peter Gawthorne, John Rogers, Montague Shaw, Finch
   Smiles, Mercedes De Valasco, E. L. Park (as Charlie Chan).

4. *Charlie Chan Carries On.* Fox, 1931, Hamilton MacFadden.
   Warner Oland (as Charlie Chan), John Garrick, Marguerite Churchill, Warren
   Hymer, Marjorie White, C. Henry Gordon, William Holden, George Brent, Peter
   Gawthorne, John T. Murray, John Swor, Goodee Montgomery, Jason Robards,
   Lumsden Hare, Zeffie Tilbury, Betty Francisco, Harry Beresford, John Rogers,
   J. G. Davis. 69 minutes.

5. *The Black Camel.* Fox, 1931, Hamilton MacFadden.
   Warner Oland, Sally Eilers, Bela Lugosi, Dorothy Revier, Victor Varconi, Robert
   Young, Marjorie White, Richard Tucker, J. M. Kerrigan, Mary Gordon, C.
   Henry Gordon, Violet Dunn, William Post, Dwight Frye, Murray Kinnell, Otto
   Yamaoka, Rita Roselle. 71 minutes.

6. *Charlie Chan's Chance.* Fox, 1932, John Blystone.
   Warner Oland, Linda Watkins, H. B. Warner, Alexander Kirkland, Marian
   Nixon, Ralph Morgan, James Kirkwood, James Todd, Charles McNaughton,
   Herbert Bunston, Edward Peil, Sr., Jimmy Wang. 73 minutes.

7. *Charlie Chan's Greatest Case.* Fox, 1933, Hamilton MacFadden.
   Warner Oland, Heather Angel, Roger Imhof, John Warburton, Walter Byron,
   Ivan Simpson, Virginia Cherrill, Francis Ford, Robert Warwick, Frank
   McGlynn, Clara Blandick, Claude King, William Stack, Gloria Roy, Cornelius
   Keefe. 71 minutes.

8. *Charlie Chan's Courage.* Fox, 1934, George Hadden.
   Warner Oland, Donald Woods, Drue Leyton, Paul Harvey, Murray Kinnell,
   Harvey Clark. 72 minutes.

9. *Charlie Chan in London.* Fox, 1934, Eugene Forde.
Warner Oland, Drue Leyton, Raymond Milland, Mona Barrie, Alan Mowbray, Murray Kinnell, Douglas Walton, Walter Johnson, E. E. Clive, George Barraud, Madge Bellamy, David Torrence, John Rogers, Paul England, Elsa Buchanan, Perry Ivins. 79 minutes.

10. *Charlie Chan in Paris.* Fox, 1935, Lewis Seiler.
Warner Oland, Mary Brian, Thomas Beck, Erik Rhodes, John Miljan, Murray Kinnell, Minor Watson, John Qualen, Keye Luke (as Lee Chan), Henry Kolker, Dorothy Appleby. 70 minutes.

11. *Charlie Chan in Egypt.* Fox, 1935, Louis King.
Warner Oland, "Pat" Paterson, Thomas Beck, Rita Cansino (later Rita Hayworth), Stepin Fetchit, Jameson Thomas, Frank Conroy, Nigel de Brulier, James Eagles, Paul Porcasi, Arthur Stone. 72 minutes.

12. *Charlie Chan in Shanghai.* 20th Century-Fox, 1935, James Tinling.
Warner Oland, Irene Hervey, Charles Locher (Jon Hall), Russell Hicks, Keye Luke, Halliwell Hobbes, Frederick Vogeding, Neil Fitzgerald, Max Wagner. 70 minutes.

13. *Charlie Chan's Secret.* 20th Century-Fox, 1936, Gordon Wiles.
Warner Oland, Rosina Lawrence, Charles Quigley, Henrietta Crosman, Edward Trevor, Astrid Allwyn, Herbert Mundin, Jonathan Hale, Egon Brecher, Gloria Roy, Ivan Miller, Arthur Edmund Carew, William Norton Bailey. 72 minutes.

14. *Charlie Chan at the Circus.* 20th Century-Fox, 1936, Harry Lachman.
Warner Oland, Keye Luke, George and Olive Brasno, Francis Ford, Maxine Reiner, John McGuire, Shirley Deane, Paul Stanton, J. Carroll Naish, Boothe Howard, Drue Leyton, Wade Boteler, Shia Jung. 72 minutes.

15. *Charlie Chan at the Race Track.* 20th Century-Fox, 1936, H. Bruce Humberstone.
Warner Oland, Keye Luke, Helen Wood, Thomas Beck, Alan Dinehart, Gavin Muir, Gloria Roy, Jonathan Hale, G. P. Huntley, Jr., George Irving, Frank Coghlan, Jr., Frankie Darro, John Rogers, John H. Allen, Harry Jans. 70 minutes.

16. *Charlie Chan at the Opera.* 20th Century-Fox, 1936, H. Bruce Humberstone.
Warner Oland, Boris Karloff, Keye Luke, Charlotte Henry, Thomas Beck, Margaret Irving, Gregory Gaye, Nedda Harrigan, Frank Conroy, Guy Usher, William Demarest, Maurice Cass, Tom McGuire. 66 minutes.

17. *Charlie Chan at the Olympics.* 20th Century-Fox, 1937, H. Bruce Humberstone.
Warner Oland, Katherine DeMille, Pauline Moore, Allan Lane, Keye Luke, C. Henry Gordon, John Eldredge, Layne Tom, Jr., Jonathan Hale, Morgan Wallace, Frederick Vogeding, Andrew Tombes, Howard Hickman. 71 minutes.

18. *Charlie Chan on Broadway.* 20th Century-Fox, 1937, Eugene Forde.
Warner Oland, Keye Luke, Joan Marsh, J. Edward Bromberg, Douglas Fowley, Harold Huber, Donald Woods, Louise Henry, Joan Woodbury, Leon Ames, Marc Lawrence, Toshia Mori, Charles Williams, Eugene Borden, Lon Chaney, Jr. 68 minutes.

19. *Charlie Chan at Monte Carlo.* 20th Century-Fox, 1937, Eugene Forde.
Warner Oland, Keye Luke, Virginia Field, Sidney Blackmer, Harold Huber, Kay Linaker, Robert Kent, Edward Raquello, George Lynn, Louis Mercier, George Davis, John Bleifer, Georges Renavent. 71 minutes.

20. *Charlie Chan in Honolulu.* 20th Century-Fox, 1938, H. Bruce Humberstone.
Sidney Toler (as Charlie Chan), Phyllis Brooks, Sen Yung (as Jimmy Chan), Eddie Collins, John King, Claire Dodd, George Zucco, Robert Barrat, Marc Lawrence, Richard Lane, Layne Tom, Jr., Phillip Ahn, Paul Harvey. 67 minutes.

21. *Charlie Chan in Reno.* 20th Century-Fox, 1939, Norman Foster.
Sidney Toler, Ricardo Cortez, Phyllis Brooks, Slim Summerville, Kane Richmond, Sen Yung, Pauline Moore, Eddie Collins, Kay Linaker, Louise Henry, Robert Lowery, Charles D. Brown, Iris Wong, Morgan Conway, Hamilton Mac-Fadden. 70 minutes.

22. *Charlie Chan at Treasure Island.* 20th Century-Fox, 1939, Norman Foster.
Sidney Toler, Cesar Romero, Pauline Moore, Sen Yung, Douglas Fowley, June Gale, Douglass Dumbrille, Sally Blane, Billie Seward, Wally Vernon, Donald MacBride, Charles Halton, Trevor Bardette, Louis Jean Heydt. 72 minutes.

23. *Charlie Chan in City in Darkness.* 20th Century-Fox, 1939, Herbert I. Leeds.
Sidney Toler, Lynn Bari, Richard Clarke, Harold Huber, Pedro de Cordoba, Dorothy Tree, C. Henry Gordon, Douglass Dumbrille, Noel Madison, Leo Carroll, Lon Chaney, Jr., Louis Mercier, George Davis, Barbara Leonard, Adrienne d'Ambricourt, Fredrik Vogeding. 69 minutes.

24. *Charlie Chan in Panama.* 20th Century-Fox, 1940, Norman Foster.
Sidney Toler, Jean Rogers, Lionel Atwill, Mary Nash, Sen Yung, Kane Richmond, Chris-Pin Martin, Lionel Royce, Helen Ericson, Jack La Rue, Edwin Stanley, Don Douglas, Frank Puglia, Addison Richards, Edward Keane. 67 minutes.

25. *Charlie Chan's Murder Cruise.* 20th Century-Fox, 1940, Eugene Forde.
Sidney Toler, Marjorie Weaver, Lionel Atwill, Sen Yung, Robert Lowery, Don Beddoe, Leo Carroll, Cora Witherspoon, Kay Linaker, Harlan Briggs, Charles Middleton, Claire Du Brey, Leonard Mudie, James Burke, Richard Keene, Layne Tom, Jr., Montague Shaw. 70 minutes.

26. *Charlie Chan at the Wax Museum.* 20th Century-Fox, 1940, Lynn Shores.
Sidney Toler, Sen Yung, C. Henry Gordon, Marc Lawrence, Joan Valerie,
Marguerite Chapman, Ted Osborn, Michael Visaroff, Hilda Vaughn, Charles
Wagenheim, Archie Twitchell, Edward Marr, Joe King, Harold Goodwin. 63
minutes.

27. *Murder over New York.* 20th Century-Fox, 1940, Harry Lachman.
Sidney Toler, Marjorie Weaver, Robert Lowery, Ricardo Cortez, Donald Mac-
Bride, Melville Cooper, Joan Valerie, Kane Richmond, Sen Yung, John Sutton,
Leyland Hodgson, Clarence Muse, Frederick Worlock, Lal Chand Mehra. 65
minutes.

28. *Dead Men Tell.* 20th Century-Fox, 1941, Harry Lachman.
Sidney Toler, Sheila Ryan, Robert Weldon, Sen Yung, Don Douglas, Katherine
Aldridge, Paul McGrath, George Reeves, Truman Bradley, Ethel Griffies, Lenita
Lane, Milton Parsons. 61 minutes.

29. *Charlie Chan in Rio.* 20th Century-Fox, 1941, Harry Lachman.
Sidney Toler, Mary Beth Hughes, Cobina Wright, Jr., Ted (Michael) North,
Victor Jory, Harold Huber, Sen Yung, Richard Derr, Jacqueline Dalya, Kay
Linaker, Truman Bradley, Hamilton MacFadden, Leslie Denison, Iris Wong,
Eugene Borden, Ann Codee. 60 minutes.

30. *Castle in the Desert.* 20th Century-Fox, 1942, Harry Lachman.
Sidney Toler, Arleen Whelan, Richard Derr, Douglass Dumbrille, Henry Daniell,
Edmund MacDonald, Sen Yung, Lenita Lane, Ethel Griffies, Milton Parsons,
Steve Geray, Lucien Littlefield. 61 minutes.

31. *Charlie Chan in the Secret Service.* Monogram, 1944, Phil Rosen.
Sidney Toler, Gwen Kenyon, Mantan Moreland (as Birmingham), Marianne
Quon, Arthur Loft, Lelah Tyler, Benson Fong (as Tommy Chan), Gene Stuten-
roth, Eddy Chandler, George Lessey, George Lewis, Muni Seroff. 65 minutes.

32. *The Chinese Cat.* Monogram, 1944, Phil Rosen.
Sidney Toler, Benson Fong, Mantan Moreland, Weldon Heyburn, Joan Wood-
bury, Ian Keith, Sam Flint, Cy Kendall, Anthony Warde, Dewey Robinson, John
Davidson, Betty Blythe. 64 minutes.

33. *Black Magic.* Monogram, 1944, Phil Rosen.
Sidney Toler, Mantan Moreland, Frances Chan, Joe Crehan, Jacqueline deWit,
Ralph Peters, Helen Beverley, Frank Jaquet, Dick Gordon, Charles Jordan,
Claudia Dell, Geraldine Wall, Harry Depp, Edward Earle. 67 minutes.

34. *Jade Mask.* Monogram, 1945, Phil Rosen.
Sidney Toler, Mantan Moreland, Edwin Luke (as Tommy Chan), Janet Warren,

Edith Evanson, Hardie Albright, Frank Reicher, Cyril Delevanti, Alan Bridge, Dorothy Granger, Joe Whitehead. 66 minutes.

35. *The Scarlet Clue.* Monogram, 1945, Phil Rosen.
Sidney Toler, Benson Fong (as Tommy Chan), Mantan Moreland, Helen Devereaux, Robert Homans, Virginia Brissac, Stanford Jolley, Reid Kilpatrick, Jack Norton, Charles Sherlock, Janet Shaw, Milt Kibbee. 65 minutes.

36. *The Shanghai Cobra.* Monogram, 1945, Phil Karlson.
Sidney Toler, Benson Fong, Mantan Moreland, Joan Barclay, James Flavin, Addison Richards, Walter Fenner, James Cardwell, Arthur Loft, Gene Stutenroth, Janet Warren, Joe Devlin, Roy Gordon. 64 minutes.

37. *The Red Dragon.* Monogram, 1945, Phil Rosen.
Sidney Toler, Fortunio Bonanova, Benson Fong, Robert Emmett Keane, Willie Best, Carol Hughes, Marjorie Hoshelle, Barton Yarborough, George Meeker, Don Costello, Charles Trowbridge, Mildred Boyd, Jean Wong, Donald Dexter Taylor. 64 minutes.

38. *Dark Alibi.* Monogram, 1946, Phil Karlson.
Sidney Toler, Mantan Moreland, Ben Carter, Benson Fong, Teala Loring, George Holmes, Joyce Compton, John Eldredge, Russell Hicks, Edward Earle. 61 minutes.

39. *Shadows over Chinatown.* Monogram, 1946, Terry Morse.
Sidney Toler, Mantan Moreland, Victor Sen Yung (as Jimmy Chan), Tanis Chandler, John Gallaudet, Paul Bryar, Bruce Kellogg, Alan Bridge, Mary Gordon, Dorothy Granger, Jack Norton. 64 minutes.

40. *Dangerous Money.* Monogram, 1946, Terry Morse.
Sidney Toler, Gloria Warren, Victor Sen Yung, Rick Vallin, Joseph Crehan, Willie Best, John Harmon, Bruce Edwards, Dick Elliott, Joe Allen, Jr., Amira Moustafa, Tristam Coffin, Alan Douglas, Selmer Jackson, Dudley Dickerson, Rito Punay, Elaine Lange, Emmett Vogan, Leslie Denison. 66 minutes.

41. *The Trap.* Monogram, 1947, Howard Bretherton.
Sidney Toler, Mantan Moreland, Victor Sen Yung, Tanis Chandler, Larry Blake, Kirk Alyn, Rita Quigley, Anne Nagel. 68 minutes.

42. *Chinese Ring.* Monogram, 1947, William Beaudine.
Roland Winters (as Charlie Chan), Warren Douglas, Victor Sen Yung, Mantan Moreland, Philip Ahn, Louise Currie, Byron Fougler, Thayer Roberts, Jean Wong, Chabing, George L. Spaulding, Paul Bryar, Charmienne Harker, Thornton Edwards, Lee Tung Foo, Richard Wang, Spencer Chan, Kenneth Chuck. 67 minutes.

43. *Docks of New Orleans.* Monogram, 1948, Derwin Abrahams.
    Roland Winters, Victor Sen Yung, Mantan Moreland, John Gallaudet, Virginia
    Dale, Boyd Irwin, Carol Forman, Howard Negley, Douglas Fowley, Emmett
    Vogan, Harry Hayden, Rory Mallinson, Stanley Andrews, George J. Lewis, Dian
    Fauntelle, Ferris Taylor, Haywood Jones, Eric Wilton, Forrest Matthews, Wally
    Walker, Larry Steers, Paul Conrad, Frank Stephens, Fred Miller, 67 minutes.

44. *Shanghai Chest.* Monogram, 1948, William Beaudine.
    Roland Winters, Mantan Moreland, Deannie Best, John Alvin, Victor Sen Yung,
    Tim Ryan, Pierre Watkin, Russell Hicks, Philip Van Zandt, George Eldredge,
    Willie Best, Tristram Coffin, Milton Parsons, Edward Coke, Olaf Hytten, Erville
    Alderson, Charlie Sullivan, Paul Scardon, William Ruhl, Lois Austin, Chabing,
    John Shay. 65 minutes.

45. *The Golden Eye.* Monogram, 1948, William Beaudine.
    Roland Winters, Mantan Moreland, Victor Sen Yung, Tim Ryan, Bruce Kellogg,
    Wanda McKay, Ralph Dunn, Forrest Taylor, Evelyn Brent, Lois Austin. 69
    minutes.

46. *The Feathered Serpent.* Monogram, 1948, William Beaudine.
    Roland Winters, Keye Luke, Victor Sen Yung, Mantan Moreland, Robert Living-
    ston, Beverly Jons, Nils Asther, Carol Forman. Leslie Denison, George Lewis,
    Martin Garralaga, Erville Alderson, Charles Stevens, Milton Ross, Fred Cordova,
    Jay Silverheels, Frank Leyva. 61 minutes.

47. *Sky Dragon.* Monogram, 1949, Lesley Selander.
    Roland Winters, Keye Luke, Mantan Moreland, Tim Ryan, Milburn Stone, Joel
    Marston, Noel Neill, Elena Verdugo, Iris Adrian, Lyle Talbot, Paul Maxey, John
    Eldredge, Eddie Parks, Lyle Latell, Gaylord (Steve) Pendleton, Emmett Vogan,
    Edna Holland, Joe Whitehead, Lee Phelps, Frank Cady, Charlie Jordan, Louise
    Franklin, Suzette Harbin, George Eldredge, Bob Curtis. 64 minutes.

Peter Lorre was Mr. Moto, the quiet, unobtrusive but brilliant Japanese detective, in eight pictures from 1937 to 1939. Series was based on John Marquand's *Saturday Evening Post* stories.

MR. MOTO

The Mysterious Mr. Moto
(1938)

Original screenplay by Philip MacDonald and Norman Foster. Based on John P. Marquand's "Mr. Moto" character. Music director, Samuel Kaylin. Film editor, Norman Colbert. Photography, Virgil Miller. Directed by Norman Foster. Produced by Sol M. Wurtzel for 20th Century-Fox. 62 minutes.

*Kentaro Moto**	PETER LORRE
Anton Darvak	HENRY WILCOXON
Ann Richman	MARY MAGUIRE
David Scott-Frensham	ERIK RHODES
Ernst Litmar	HAROLD HUBER
Paul Brissac	LEON AMES
George Higgins	FORRESTER HARVEY
Gottfried Brujo	FREDRIK VOGEDING
Sir Charles Murchison	LESTER MATTHEWS
Sniffy	JOHN ROGERS
Lotus Liu	KAREN SORRELL

*In the Marquand books, his name was "I. A. Moto."

Norman Foster (center) director of *Thank You, Mr. Moto* (1937), second in the series, strolls arm in arm with his cast. From left, Lorre, Philip Ahn, Foster, Pauline Frederick and Thomas Beck.

Film beauty Rochelle Hudson made her one appearance in the series as an aviatrix and spy in *Mr. Moto Takes a Chance* (1938). Robert Kent doesn't seem too happy watching Lorre fiddle with his camera.

Nola	MITCHELL LEWIS
Captain	ADIA KUZNETZOFF
Customs Inspector	BILLY BEVAN
Lord Gifford	MAJOR SAM HARRIS
Constable	HERBERT EVANS
Bouncer	FRANK HAGNEY
News Peddler	JIMMY AUBREY
Gallery Assistant	LEONARD MUDIE

The time—midnight.

The scene—an archeological dig in Indochina.

An assassin, knife in hand, lurks outside the hut of an Oriental archeologist. The shadowy figure climbs through the window. Slowly, he approaches the bespectacled scientist, who stands with back turned and is so absorbed in polishing his glasses that the assassin seems confident his victim is unaware of his presence.

The assassin stalks closer. But we can see that the archeologist has spotted his killer's reflection in his lens. With the coolness and control of a highly trained athlete, the scientist is waiting for just the precise instant. When it comes, he moves with the suddenness and fury of an uncoiling cobra. Even as the knife flashes, the scientist whirls. In one movement, he seizes his assailant's arm and tosses the surprised, off-balance thug over his shoulder. As his assailant crashes to the floor, still holding the knife, he shrieks the horrid shriek of a dying man. The gleaming blade has plunged deep into his own heart.

The archeologist is, of course, not really an archeologist. He is Mr. Moto, renowned Japanese detective, expert at jiujitsu, master of disguise, intrepid foe of criminals the world over.

Like his inscrutable countrymen, Mr. Moto is courteous, apologetic, diffident, polite to the point of self-effacement. But Moto is also nimble-witted and alert to the slightest clue. For example, in *Mr. Moto Takes a Vacation* (1939), he catches a master criminal by spotting a minute variation in his rain-soaked footprints. The crook has posed as a lame philanthropist. But his telltale prints show up as regular footsteps, disclosing that he was really a healthy man assuming a limp only when people were around.

However, unlike his Chinese colleague Charlie Chan, Moto does not rely entirely on intellect to overcome his adversaries. He is equally a man of action. He is mild mannered in appearance, and his build is puny. But he is fearless, cool in the most harrowing of situations, utterly unflappable, resourceful to the point of disbelief.

In fact, some of his admirers have wondered if he is just too perfect even to be a fictional hero. "Mr. Moto is bullet proof," wrote Bosley Crowther of the

New York Times, ". . . unsusceptible to ambush, espionage, riot, tornado or falling aircraft and invincible when the issue descends to anything so vulgar as physical violence . . . Providence, or its equivalent in Shinto or the Shogunate, has enabled him to be everywhere at once."

The Oriental super-sleuth is the creation of Pulitzer Prize-winning novelist J. P. Marquand.* The New England writer, noted for his smoothly written books satirizing proper Bostonians and their rigid family traditions, wrote his first Moto stories as *Saturday Evening Post* serials. They were a by-product of a more serious assignment to the Far East. "I was sent to China in 1934 by the *Saturday Evening Post* with instructions to do a series of stories with an authentic Oriental background," Marquand said. "Naturally, I did a great deal of poking around in Chinese cities and eventually wandered to Japan. There I was constantly shadowed by a polite little Japanese detective. Suddenly, it dawned on me that he was just the protagonist I was looking for—and while my shadow did his duty very conscientiously, 'Mr. Moto,' the shrewd, the polite, the efficient sleuth was born."

Marquand wrote five *Moto* novels beginning with *Thank You, Mr. Moto* in 1936. Then came *Think Fast, Mr. Moto* (1937), *Last Laugh, Mr. Moto* (1939) and *Mr. Moto's Three Aces* (1942). Japanese heroes were not saleable during World War II and its aftermath, and so the next and last book, *Stopover Tokyo,* was not written until 1957, three years before Marquand's death.**

But despite the popularity of the Marquand novels, most people remember Mr. Moto from the movies. In an inspired bit of casting, 20th Century-Fox gave the role to Peter Lorre, who played him in all eight series pictures from 1937 to 1939. Physically, he seemed perfect and, in fact, he did the part with a minimum of makeup. He relied chiefly on plastered down hair, steel rimmed glasses and false buck teeth.

The series never matched the best of the *Chan* pictures in plot or production values. But as it turned out for Lorre, it was a springboard to his great character roles at Warner Brothers.***

Who will forget Lorre's whiny, mournful voice, his twisted, sneer-smile, his startled, poached-egg eyes as he played the prissy, scented Joel Cairo in *The Maltese Falcon* (1941). "I am not a violent man, Mr. Spade," the little con man quietly advised Humphrey Bogart. "But if you do not give me the black bird,

*For *The Late George Apley* in 1938.
**20th Century-Fox bought *Stopover Tokyo,* but it deleted Moto from the script—a maneuver that did not really require major surgery. Unlike other mystery writers, who created dominant heroes, Marquand usually preferred to focus, instead, on an array of colorful and bizarre secondary characters. He played them off against each other. Meanwhile, the self-effacing Moto slipped in and out of the story like a shadow. His role was that of a catalyst. And so, studio writers had no trouble eliminating him. (Instead, Solly Nakamura played Mr. Nobika, a thinly disguised Moto who was killed off in the film.)
***In a 1970 poll, members of the Nostalgia Book Club voted Lorre second only to Walter Brennan as their all-time favorite supporting actor.

Sig Rumann peers curiously over the shoulder of Lotus Long in *Think Fast, Mr. Moto*. At Lorre's right is Murray Kinnell.

Keye Luke, Charley Chan's number-one son, steps out of character to become aide to Lorre in *Mr. Moto's Gamble* (1938). Actually, the picture was intended as a *Chan* film. But Warner Oland died during the shooting. So the studio rewrote the picture into the *Moto* series.

Some top talent appeared in the *Moto* series, including George Sanders, here with monocle and pith helmet in *Mr. Moto's Last Warning* (1939). With him are Lorre and Margaret Irving.

Warren Hymer (in straw hat) has a "Who me?" expression as he looks skeptically at Richard Lane in *Mr. Moto in Danger Island* (1939). Hymer played Moto's assistant.

I shall be compelled to murder you without mercy." Later, when Sydney Greenstreet cuts into the supposedly jewel-stuffed porcelain falcon and finds it's a fake, Lorre is beside himself with rage. "You imbecile," he squeals. "You bloated idiot. You stupid fathead."

In *Casablanca* (1942), Lorre plays Ugarte, a little weasel who makes a profitable living forging exit visas for Nazi refugees. "You despise me, don't you?" Lorre asks Bogart, playing Rick, the cynical yet idealistic cafe owner.

"Oh, if I gave you any thought, I probably would," says Bogie, in one of moviedom's great put-downs.

Born Lazlo Loewenstein in 1904 in a remote part of Hungary's Carpathian Mountains,* Lorre was the son of a well-to-do tradesman. His parents moved to Vienna, where Lorre was educated. But he quarreled with his family over his acting ambitions and ran away from home at 15. For years, he scratched out a meager existence, sleeping on benches in the famous Prater amusement park. However, he eventually got parts in a stock company, where Fritz Lang saw him and offered him a role in a German picture, *M*. It was to be Lorre's most famous part. He played a psychopathic child-murderer and the chilling film became a classic of its genre. When the movie played in this country, Hollywood offered Lorre a contract. Josef von Sternberg gave him the starring role in Dostoevsky's *Crime and Punishment* (1935) and Lorre went on to play villains in over 50 films until he died at the age of 60 in 1965.

With his breathless voice, toadlike features and sly, menacing looks he always managed to instill the parts with an element of comedy because, as he put it, "that's what makes the character human."

The first *Moto* picture was only Lorre's seventh in America. Yet, some film buffs rate them in quality near the top of the series pictures of the 1930s and 1940s, a golden era for B-films.** But Lorre hated their maddeningly involved plots and cliché-ridden, paper-thin characters. He said later that he did them only for the money and acting credits. And indeed, he seemed to walk through them, giving only a one-dimensional performance that fell far short of his later efforts.

Nevertheless, the scripts were well-laced with action and they retained an element of suspense that held up until the murderer was flushed out in the last sequence. One of the best is *The Mysterious Mr. Moto,* in which the Japanese detective takes a long-shot gamble to win the confidence of an international crook.

Out to find the leader of a gang called the "League of Assassins," Moto has himself committed to the dreaded French penal colony at Devil's Island. There, he becomes friendly with Paul Brissac (Leon Ames), one of the ringleaders, and

---

*The setting for *Dracula* and other vampire stories.
**In 1965, an attempt was made to revive the series with Henry Silva in *The Return of Mr. Moto.* But it was a shoddy effort and Moto was buried even before he was resurrected.

escapes with him. Brissac, convinced Moto is a Japanese house-servant serving time for murder, gratefully makes him his houseboy when they get to England.

"You can trust him," Brissac tells his cronies. "He had a room next to me in that French hotel." Brissac's first visitors—gangsters Ernst Litmar (Harold Huber) and George Higgins (Forrester Harvey)—have come to map new plans. Their latest scheme is to force Prague steel baron Anton Darvak (Henry Wilcoxon) into surrendering his priceless formula for a revolutionary steel process. Darvak is now in London.

Hours later, Darvak's pretty secretary (Mary Maguire) gets an anonymous phone call. If Darvak doesn't part with the formula, the caller warns, his life will be snuffed out at 3:00 P.M. the next day. Darvak's old school chum, art fancier David Scott Frensham (Erik Rhodes), urges him to contact Scotland Yard. But Darvak thinks the call came from a crank.

Neither Darvak nor the gang suspect that at this very moment, Moto is at Scotland Yard. He has gone there to see the renowned Sir Charles Murchison (Lester Matthews), the Yard's chief inspector and Moto's old friend. "If you think you're going to see anyone in there," an old cockney woman advises the unassuming Moto as he sits outside Sir Charles' imposing office, "you're very much mistaken." When a sergeant ushers him in instantly, she does a double take.

"In accordance with regulations, I'm reporting my presence in London," says Moto, a member of the International Police.

"Really," says Sir Charles. "On what case?"

"Oh, in connection with an organization which some newspapers so picturesquely named the League of Assassins," Moto says casually.

"What assistance can we give you?"

"None at the moment. But when the time arrives, I shall be grateful for your help."

"You're a strange person, Moto," Sir Charles muses. "Always playing the lone hand."

The underplaying of this dialogue is more evident if one thinks of the league as the Cosa Nostra. Sir Charles has been restraining himself to give Moto a free hand. That is, until Moto discloses he has infiltrated the league. That's going too far. Sir Charles insists that *Moto* let the Yard arrest its members. But Moto urges him to wait until he learns the big boss' identity.

"Look here Moto," Sir Charles roars, his patience strained. "You can't come to Scotland Yard and tell us there's a nest of murderers in London and then not tell us where to find them."

"Your own motto, Sir Charles," says Moto, pointing to a slogan carved in wood on Sir Charles' massive desk. It says, "Softly, softly—Catchee monkey."

Nevertheless, Sir Charles assigns two plainclothes detectives to follow Moto. Moto easily shakes them with the oldest of ruses. He gets into a taxi and steps out the other side as it pulls away.

Moto then contacts his assistant, Lotus Liu (Karen Sorrell), who has traced the league's headquarters to a Limehouse pub. She tells Moto she has overheard one thug make a call to a Mr. Darvak. This link to the Czech steel czar makes it clear to Moto why the league has concentrated in London.

While Moto goes to see Darvak, Lotus gets gangster Higgins drunk. He starts telling her about the league's plan to bump off Darvak. But he is seen and the gang kills him. The signal for his execution—and the gang's other crimes—is the spritely tune "Madrid" played by musicians acting as lookouts.

Next, the gang runs over a friend of Darvak's to show the steel magnate they mean business. Then, they corner Moto on a fogbound street and try to take him for a ride. But the gang has met its match. Moto is alerted to the impending kidnaping when he hears the death tune. Before the crooks can force him into their car, he rushes the driver, pushes him out and speeds off, leaving his assailants empty-handed.

Undismayed, the league sets the stage for Darvak's assassination. An accomplice has gotten Darvak interested in attending an art exhibition on the very afternoon his death is plotted. Darvak thinks the threat is a false alarm and won't be dissuaded from going. The league's plan is to have its own boss of bosses greet Darvak on his arrival and engage him in conversation under a huge center chandelier. At that moment, the chieftain will say, "Help me, Mr. Darvak." That will be a signal for the orchestra to play "Madrid." The melody is the signal for a thug in the attic to cut down the chandelier.

But Lotus has learned the gang's plan. She tells Moto and together with Scotland Yard, he makes his own counterplan. Meanwhile, Darvak's playboy friend Scott-Frensham has gotten two "protectors" from Scotland Yard to shadow Darvak. When they spot Moto, they say they have orders to take Moto in. Moto bumps one of them hard, shaking loose the man's gun, then flees. Moto's suspicions are aroused because he knows Scotland Yard police carry no weapons.

Just before the fatal hour at the exhibition, Moto arrives disguised as a seedy German painter. Darvak has not yet shown up so Moto mixes with the crowd and engages one of Darvak's friends in an art discussion. As they drift around the gallery, Moto and the man walk under the chandelier. For a moment they pause on the very spot marked for the victim. Suddenly speaking loudly, Moto insists that the man buy one of his pictures. When he begs off, Moto shouts, "I know you're a patron of the arts, Mr. Darvak." Heads turn. Eyebrows raise among the crowd.

"You're mistaking me for someone else," the man says in a quavering voice. "Leave me alone, will you?"

"But I'm a good painter, Mr. Darvak," Moto persists. "Please help me."

"Get away from me."

"But Mr. Darvak. You must not go away. Please help me, Mr. Darvak."

The orchestra strikes up the death tune. In the attic, a henchman cuts the chandelier cord and the massive ornament crashes to the floor, crushing the league's top man. He is, of course, the last person you would suspect.

But the league's assailant is still loose in the attic. From a gaping hole in the ceiling, Brissac, the man who escaped from Devil's Island, opens fire. As Scotland Yard's men scatter, Moto streaks for the attic, dives at Brissac and knocks his gun loose. Two roundhouse blows to the jaw send Moto sprawling. But the quick-moving Moto recovers, flips Brissac with a jiujitsu twist and sends him hurtling headlong into the wall. The battle royal rages on, sending great chips of plaster to the floor of the art gallery floor below. Then, all is quiet.

A concerned Sir Charles looks up at the ceiling hole. Mr. Moto's serene but bruised face peeks out. "Yessir," he tells Sir Charles with an apologetic smile. "Catchee monkey. But not so softly."

MR. MOTO SERIES

1. *Think Fast, Mr. Moto.* 20th Century-Fox, 1937, Norman Foster.
Peter Lorre (as Mr. Moto), Virginia Field, Thomas Beck, Sig Rumann, Murray Kinnell, John Rogers, Lotus Long, George Cooper, J. Carrol Naish, Fredrik Vogeding. 66 minutes.

2. *Thank You, Mr. Moto.* 20th Century-Fox, 1938, Norman Foster.
Peter Lorre, Thomas Beck, Pauline Frederick, Jayne Regan, Sidney Blackmer, Sig Rumann, John Carradine, William von Brincken, Nedda Harrigan, Philip Ahn, John Bleifer. 68 minutes.

*3. *Mr. Moto's Gamble.* 20th Century-Fox, 1938, James Tinling.
Peter Lorre, Keye Luke, Dick Baldwin, Lynn Bari, Douglas Fowley, Jayne Regan, Harold Huber, Maxie Rosenbloom, John Hamilton, George E. Stone, Bernard Nedell, Charles Williams, Ward Bond, Cliff Clark, Edward Marr, Lon Chaney, Jr. Russ Clark, Pierre Watkin, Charles D. Brown, Paul Fix, Fred Kelsey, George Chandler, Irving Bacon. 71 minutes.

4. *Mr. Moto Takes a Chance.* 20th Century-Fox, 1938, Norman Foster.
Peter Lorre, Rochelle Hudson, Robert Kent, J. Edward Bromberg, Chick Chandler, George Regas, Fredrik Vogeding. Al Kikume, Gloria Roy, Tetsu Komai. 63 minutes.

5. *The Mysterious Mr. Moto.* 20th Century-Fox, 1938, Norman Foster.
Peter Lorre, Mary Maguire, Henry Wilcoxon, Erik Rhodes, Harold Huber, Leon Ames, Forrester Harvey, Fredrik Vogeding, Lester Matthews, John Rogers, Karen Sorrell, Mitchell Lewis. 62 minutes.

6. *Mr. Moto's Last Warning.* 20th Century-Fox, 1939, Norman Foster.
Peter Lorre, Ricardo Cortez, Virginia Field, John Carradine, George Sanders, Joan Carol, Robert Coote, Margaret Irving, Leyland Hodgson, John Davidson, Teru Shimada (fake Mr. Moto), Georges Renavent, E. E. Clive, Holmes Herbert, C. Montague Shaw, George Humbert, Jimmy Aubrey, Bert Roach. 71 minutes.

7. *Mr. Moto in Danger Island.* 20th Century-Fox, 1939, Herbert I. Leeds.
Peter Lorre, Jean Hersholt, Amanda Duff, Warren Hymer, Richard Lane, Leon Ames, Douglass Dumbrille, Charles D. Brown, Paul Harvey, Robert Lowery,

*This picture took over from a Charlie Chan movie after Warner Oland died suddenly while it was in production. The studio simply reshot some footage and made Charlie's number-one son, Keye Luke, an aide to Moto.

Eddie Marr, Harry Woods, Neely Edwards, Harry Strang, Grace Hayle, Don Douglas, Renie Riano, Willie Best, Ray Walker, Gloria Roy, Ward Bond. 70 minutes.

8. *Mr. Moto Takes a Vacation.* 20th Century-Fox, 1939, Norman Foster.
Peter Lorre, Joseph Schildkraut, Lionel Atwill, Virginia Field, John King, Iva Stewart, George P. Huntley, Jr., Victor Varconi, John Bleifer, Honorable Wu, Morgan Wallace, Anthony Warde, Harry Strang, John Davidson, Willie Best, George Chandler, William Gould, Stanley Blystone, Jadine Wong. 61 minutes.

9. *The Return of Mr. Moto.* 20th Century-Fox, 1965, Ernest Morris.
Henry Silva (as Mr. Moto), Terence Longdon, Suzanne Lloyd, Marne Maitland, Martin Wyldeck, Brian Coburn, Stanley Morgan, Peter Zander, Harold Kasket, Anthony Booth, Gordon Tanner. Henry Gilbert, Richard Evans, Dennis Holmes, Ian Fleming, Tracy Connell, Alister Williamson, Sonyia Benjamin. 71 minutes.

Seated on his ornate throne, Boris Karloff as the insidious Fu Manchu raises his long-nailed hand to signal one of his dacoits to approach.

FU MANCHU

The Mask of Fu Manchu
(1932)

Screenplay by Irene Kuhn, Edgar Allan Woolf and John Willard. Based on the novel by Sax Rohmer, serialized in *Collier's,* May 7–July 23, 1932, published in book form by Doubleday, Doran, October, 1932. Camera, Tony Gaudio. Editor, Ben Lewis. Art director, Cedric Gibbons. Directed by Charles Vidor and Charles Brabin. Released by Metro-Goldwyn-Mayer. 72 minutes.

Dr. Fu Manchu	BORIS KARLOFF
Sir Dennis Nayland Smith	LEWIS STONE
Sheila Barton	KAREN MORLEY
Terrence Granville	CHARLES STARRETT
Fah Lo Suee	MYRNA LOY
Professor Von Berg	JEAN HERSHOLT
Sir Lionel Barton	LAWRENCE GRANT
McLeod	DAVID TORRENCE
Gay Lo Sung	E. ALYN WARREN

An English newspaperman is walking through dark, fogbound streets. For weeks, he has been searching the Limehouse district, London's Chinatown, for a shadowy figure believed to be operating an international drug ring among British society.

So far, his wanderings have brought no leads. But on this night, a blade of light splits the darkness. The newsman quickly slips into an alleyway. Thirty feet away, a black limousine pulls up. A chauffeur jumps out, crosses to the street side and opens the door. Out steps a tall, imposing man.

"He was Chinese, but different from any Chinese I had ever met," the journalist later wrote. "He wore a long, black topcoat and a queer astrakhan cap. He strode into the house followed by an Arab girl. Or she may have been an Egyptian . . . The chauffeur closed the car door, jumped to his seat and backed out the way he had come. The headlights faded in the mist . . ."

Sax Rohmer, the reporter, never found out if the exotic Oriental he had seen was, in fact, the head of a dope syndicate. But the sense of power, authority and malevolence the mysterious stranger transmitted was unforgettable. Rohmer found himself compelled to recreate the character on paper. And so Dr. Fu Manchu was born.

Over the years, Dr. Fu began to take an almost human form in Rohmer's mind. "Little by little that night, and on many more nights, I built up Dr. Fu Manchu until I could both hear him and see him . . . ," Rohmer said. "I seemed to hear a sibilant voice saying, 'It is your belief that you have made me. It is mine that I shall live when you are smoke.' "

As he took shape in print, Dr. Fu became a sinister, power-mad crime lord whose singular obsession was to crush the white race with his yellow hordes and win world domination. Physically, he seemed the very embodiment of evil.

Rohmer wrote: "Imagine a person tall, lean and feline, high-shouldered with a brow like Shakespeare and a face like Satan, a close-shaven skull, and long, magnetic eyes of the true cat-green. Invest him with all the cruel cunning of an entire Eastern race accumulated in one giant intellect with all the resources of science past and present. Imagine that awful being and you will have a mental picture of Fu Manchu."

Though this writing style lacked polish, Rohmer's stories bristled with excitement, mystery and, best of all, fascinating characters. There were Fu's rivals—stalwart Sir Dennis Nayland Smith of Scotland Yard and his trusted companion, Dr. Petrie. They bore a vague resemblance to Holmes and Watson—like Watson, Petrie narrated the stories—as did Fu to Professor Moriarty. But why not? The Conan Doyle detective stories were the hottest magazine fiction going in those days.

There was Fu's sloe-eyed temptress daughter, Fah Lo Suee (played in the movies by Anna May Wong, and, believe it or not, by Myrna Loy), and assorted Asian badmen. The most fearful of them, Fu's "dacoits" (pronounced dah-koits) —fierce, bald henchmen with scarred foreheads. The jagged scar represented an

Sax Rohmer, garbed in flowing Oriental gown, smokes his pipe in his study, where he created the diabolical supervillain, Dr. Fu Manchu. Rohmer, a British journalist whose real name was Arthur Sarsfield Ward, got $30,000 for each Fu piece he wrote for *Collier's*.

Warner Oland as the mysterious mandarin, hands together, leers at Evelyn Hall as Tetsu Komai stuffs a gag in her mouth. Scene is from *The Return of Fu Manchu* (1930).

incision where Fu had cut into the brain of each one and removed his frontal lobe. The operation deprived them of will power and made them Fu's slaves. In one episode, Fu proposes to operate on Smith to change him into a dacoit. But Smith's pals rescue him in the nick of time.

However, what undoubtedly fascinated the public was Fu's exquisitely conceived tortures, especially as they came to life in the movies.

• In the serial *Drums of Fu Manchu* (1940), the master criminal (played superbly by Henry Brandon) drops the hero through a trap door into a pool where a hungry octopus waits to squeeze him to death. Shades of James Bond!

• In *The Mask of Fu Manchu* (1932), Fu (Boris Karloff) locks Jean Hersholt in a room with walls covered with daggers. Suddenly, the walls start closing in.

• In the same movie, Fu ties another victim (Lawrence Grant) to a table underneath a huge bell which starts ringing. Its peal begins driving him mad slowly.

But to give Dr. Fu his due, he was, despite his diabolical torture schemes, a cultured man. While his actions were ruthless, he was rarely crude or boorish in his personal relations with his adversaries. Unlike other brash czars of crime, he seldom shouted or raged or lost his temper. He addressed his victims with the deference, courtesy and decorum of a true gentleman of the East. All of this accentuated the cold-bloodedness of his plots, making them seem even more fiendish and loathsome.

Finally, in his own way, he was a man of principle. When Mary Randolph (Luana Walters) double-crosses him during a kidnap exchange in *Drums of Fu Manchu,* he is insulted. She has put his life in jeopardy. But he is even more irritated by her breach of faith in their bargain. "I must remind you," Fu tells her icily, "that among my people, honor is a sacred thing. Those who defile it can expect no mercy."

Fu, one of modern fiction's most popular villains, first appeared in print in a short story in 1911. Rohmer followed this in 1913 with the first Fu novel, *The Mystery of Fu Manchu.* (The work in its American edition is titled *The Insidious Dr. Fu Manchu.)* Over the next four decades, Fu's diabolical deeds were celebrated in 13 more novels—the last one, *Re-Enter Dr. Fu Manchu,* in 1957, two years before Rohmer's death.

Rohmer, whose real name was Arthur Sarsfield Ward—he took the pen name Sax Rohmer simply because he liked the sound of it—was born in London of Irish parents in 1883. He went to London University. After a brief but unsuccessful career as a bank clerk and as an artist, he became a Fleet Street journalist. He soon branched off into fiction and began collecting a pile of rejection slips until he sold an adventure story called "The Leopard Couch" to *Chambers' Journal* and another entitled "The Mysterious Mummy" to *Pearson's Magazine.* His schoolboy interest had focused on ancient Egypt, and he used his knowledge of

Henry Brandon, who gave one of the most convincing portrayals of Fu in the 1940 serial, *Drums of Fu Manchu*. With him is John Merton as Fu's chief dacoit, a slave whose willpower has been removed by a brain operation.

Christopher Lee, the veteran British actor who played Fu in three films in the 1960s.

Egyptian lore, hieroglyphics and the occult as background for these pieces.

But his success really began when he switched to the Far East and started writing about Fu Manchu. Most of the Fu novels were serialized in *Collier's* magazine, which paid him about $30,000 each. There seems to be no accurate figure of the sales of his books, which were translated into dozens of languages, including Urdu. But estimates are that they totaled more than 20 million copies.

Rohmer twice tried to kill off Fu—once at the urging of the Chinese government—but the wily and profitable Oriental always managed to be revived. Rohmer, whose sharp features, pipe and serious expression reminded people of a latter-day Sherlock Holmes, lived well and traveled extensively on the money he made from his fiction. Many of his stories were written in the United States, where he had a home in suburban White Plains outside New York City.

Eventually Rohmer tired of Fu. He wrote scores of other short stories and novels. He once collaborated on the book of a London musical called "Round in Fifty" and he composed a number of songs. But despite his own preference, the public's main interest focused on Fu Manchu.

Fu was featured in a series of silent British two-reelers in the 1920s. Then, in the later 1920s and early 1930s, Fu became the subject of a radio program in the United States and a number of Hollywood movies. Warner Oland was the first to play him in talking pictures in the 1929 film, *The Mysterious Dr. Fu Manchu.* Oland repeated his role in *The Return of Dr. Fu Manchu* (1930) and *Daughter of the Dragon* (1931). But he was a benevolent-looking, overweight Fu—the result, no doubt, of too many egg rolls—and his movies tended to be stodgy and slow-paced.

Karloff, who succeeded him in *The Mask of Fu Manchu* (1932), was a more cold and ruthless villain, as was Brandon in the excellent Republic serial, *Drums of Fu Manchu.* (The serial, by the way, got its name from distant drums that rolled menacingly just before Fu claimed a victim.) Republic planned a sequel serial called *Fu Manchu Strikes Again.* But it dropped the project in 1942 after the Chinese government reportedly informed the State Department of its objections to the picture.

After another lull of 25 years, the versatile British actor Christopher Lee portrayed Fu in *Face of Fu Manchu* (1965), *Brides of Fu Manchu* (1966), *The Vengeance of Fu Manchu* (1968) and *Kiss and Kill* (1969) (also known as *The Blood of Fu Manchu*). The latter productions were an attempt to cash in on the James Bond wave of blood and guts. But Lee played the clever old doctor in uninspired, lifeless fashion, and the pictures themselves, although they were in color, were flat and disappointing.

Most Fu buffs rate the Karloff movie as the best of the feature-length series. It is true that its action scenes seem hokey and its dialogue florid. But the movie is all so overdone that it is impossible to take it seriously. Actually, audiences were receptive to its wild and wooly sequences, reminiscent of silent serials. And the picture seemed to fit neatly into the pattern of the era. Escapist movies flourished in the Depression years and Fu's battles with Nayland Smith were in the full-blooded tradition of exotic high adventure.

The movie tells of the plans of British Museum archeologists to mount an expedition to the great Gobi Desert in northern China. The scientists are searching for the tomb of Genghis Khan, the Asiatic ruler who nearly conquered Europe in the thirteenth century.

They don't know it, but Fu Manchu is also looking for the tomb. He wants the sword, golden mask and scroll that lie buried with the dead leader. With these symbols of Genghis Khan's power, Fu plans to present himself to the yellow race as a reincarnation of the mighty warrior. In this Messiahlike guise, he plans to lead a united Asiatic uprising in a global war to destroy the white race.

Nayland Smith (Lewis Stone) learns of Fu's plot and warns the expedition. But too late. As they are about to leave England, Fu's henchmen kidnap Sir Lionel Barton (Lawrence Grant), chief of the party, and smuggle him to Shanghai.

There, we find Fu, resplendent in silken gowns, in his spectacular palace. At the outset, we see his cultured and intellectual side. In one sequence, he makes reference to his doctorate degrees in philosophy, law and medicine. In another, he tells an adversary to put down his gun "so we can talk like gentlemen."

But there is the dark side, too, and it, of course, prevails. Barton refuses to divulge the tomb's location. At first, Fu is gentle. He tempts him with bribes—including the charms of his lovely daughter Fah Lo Suee (Loy).

Barton is unyielding. "Fu Manchu," he says, "I'm not for sale!" Unfazed, Fu chains him to a table to subject him to the insidious torture of the bell. "It never stops," Fu warns, smiling. "Hour after hour. Day after day . . . You can't move. You can't sleep . . . Here you will lie until you tell."

However, Barton is a stiff-upper-lip Briton of the old school. Even when Fu pours salt water down his parched throat, Barton won't crack. Unhappily, his courage will lead to his death.

Meanwhile, Smith, Barton's daughter Sheila (Karen Morley), and her fiancé Terrence Granville (Charles Starrett) rush to China, hoping to find the sacred objects and rescue Barton. They reach the tomb and unearth the relics. But when they start searching for Barton, Fu's men capture them.

Then, Fu begins a series of uncanny tortures. He ties up Smith and lowers him head first into a pit of bellowing crocodiles. He straps Von Berg (Hersholt), a German member of the party, between converging walls of spikes. Fu affectionately called this torture his "room of slim silver fingers." He prepares Sheila for a human sacrifice. Finally, he straps Terrence to a surgical table and injects him with a serum composed of snake and gila monster poison. The serum is supposed to make him obey all orders.

Dr. Fu smiles leeringly behind a skull in his
laboratory. A cultured man of the East, he held
doctorates in law, medicine and philosophy.

Fu's daughter, Fah Lo Suee (Myrna Loy), clutches Terence Granville
(Charles Starrett) as Fu shows them the ancient sword of Genghis Khan.
With it and other symbols of the thirteenth-century conqueror, Fu plans to
lead an Asiatic uprising to crush the white race.

At this point, we come to a cinematic crossroad. There apparently were two endings. One appeared in the original script and also showed up in the studio pressbook prepared for newspapers and theatres. The other was the one that was actually filmed.

In major productions, it was not unusual for a script to undergo half a dozen revisions even after shooting started. In this case, there was an added concern that might have contributed to last-minute tinkering. Metro-Goldwyn-Mayer was not used to doing horror-type productions. (Universal, of course, became the specialist in this genre.) And studio executives, sensitive to the fact that a bad production might adversely affect the reception of other big productions, may have wielded an unusually heavy hand in reshaping the script.

The film did, in fact, go through a stormy shooting schedule. "Director number one [Charles Vidor] was fired to be replaced by Director number two [Charles Brabin]," said film historian William K. Everson. "And many scenes were reshot for the flimsiest of reasons. For example, at one point, it was Lewis Stone who was trapped in the spiked torture device until somebody thought it would be more menacing and potentially more gory to have fat and perspiring Jean Hersholt quivering before those spikes."

So we have two denouements. The first, the one that appears in the studio pressbook, gives more emphasis to Myrna Loy's role. In this version, the vulnerability of Fu's daughter leads to his downfall. Fah Lo Suee becomes infatuated with Terrence.* She nurses him until the serum wears off. Then, she releases Smith from the spike torture and leads the two Occidentals through the palace catacombs to Fu's laboratory. There, she reveals her father's great secret—how with a super electrical ray he controls a huge, all-powerful robot. He counts on this automaton to help lead his world rebellion.

Quickly, Smith crosses the wires in the ray machine and hides as Fu enters the lab. Sheila, desperate, has surrendered the Genghis Khan relics in an attempt to save her father and Terrence.

But Fu can't be assuaged. He starts the electric ray that will turn the robot on them. However, instead of working the automaton, the ray backfires and radiates Fu with an apparently lethal dose.

In the filmed version, we get none of this hanky-panky between Fah Lo Suee and Terrence. Instead, when the serum wears off of itself, Terrence overcomes

---

*Apparently, some of this treatment showing Fah Lo Suee's amorous side was filmed—although it was cut from the version I saw. But Kenneth G. Lawrence, cinema buff who runs the Movie Memorabilia Shop in Hollywood, recalls seeing a version showing Fah Lo Suee asking for Terrence after her father is through torturing him. Karloff, looking at him strapped on the table, tells his daughter there won't be much left of any use to her. "Loy then proceeds to the strapped down Starrett," Lawrence says, "looks longingly at him, rubs his chest and caresses one of his nipples (he's barechested)." To Lawrence, Loy was depicted as "a nymphomaniac." He added: "Her scenes hold up best."

his guards. Smith, too, loosens his bonds and escapes from the pit of crocodiles, using their flat heads as a bridge to safety. Then, the two join forces, rescue Von Berg and race to Fu's lab.

Through a window they can see a vast temple below. Fu has put Sheila on a sacrificial table. Holding the sword of Genghis Khan, he stands over her white-gowned, seductive body. Hundreds of his followers look on. "Would you all like to have a mate like this?" Fu asks. "The treasures of the world are yours." He turns to the white goddess and raises the ancient saber. "In the blood of Sheila Barton, I baptize this sword."

But Terrence and Smith have found Fu's electric ray. They open the window, train it on Fu and switch it on. The ray hits the sword and it falls from Fu's hand. Terry runs to the altar, picks it up and brings its cutting edge across Fu's neck. Then, Smith turns the lethal ray on Fu's multitudes, sending scores to their death.

And so ends the harrowing tale. But have we seen the last of this master crime lord? It seems most unlikely. Even as China has finally taken its seat in the United Nations, we know that somehow Fu will return. Is there not now somewhere, an opulent mansion where silken curtains line the wall? Where the sweet smell of incense fills the air and a gong is sounding? And inside is there not a tall, gaunt, green-eyed man quietly muttering, "The world shall hear from me again."

DR. FU MANCHU SERIES

1. *The Mysterious Dr. Fu Manchu.* Paramount, 1929, Rowland V. Lee.
   Warner Oland (as Dr. Fu Manchu), Neil Hamilton (as Dr. Jack Petrie), Jean
   Arthur (as Lia Eltham), O. P. Heggie (as Nayland Smith), William Austin,
   Claude King, Charles Stevenson, Noble Johnson, Lawford Davidson, Evelyn
   Selbie, Laska Winter, Chapel Dossett, Charles Stevens, Donald Mackenzie,
   Charles Giblyn. 78 minutes.

2. *The Return of Dr. Fu Manchu.* Paramount, 1930, Rowland V. Lee.
   Warner Oland, Neil Hamilton, Jean Arthur, O. P. Heggie, William Austin, Eve-
   lyn Hall, Margaret Fealy, Evelyn Selbie, Shayle Gardner, David Dunbar, Tetsu
   Komai, Toyo Fujita, Ambrose Barker. 71 minutes.

3. *Daughter of the Dragon.* Paramount, 1931, Lloyd Corrigan.
   Anna May Wong (as Ling Moy), Warner Oland, Sessue Hayakawa (as Ah Kee),
   Bramwell Fletcher, Frances Dade, Holmes Herbert (as Sir John Petrie), Nella
   Walker, Nicholas Soussanin, Lawrence Grant, Harold Minjir, E. Alyn Warren,
   Harrington Reynolds, Tetsu Komai, Oie Chan, Olaf Hytten. 70 minutes.

4. *The Mask of Fu Manchu.* MGM, 1932, Charles Vidor and Charles Brabin.
   Boris Karloff (as Fu Manchu), Lewis Stone (as Sir Nayland Smith), Karen Mor-
   ley, Myrna Loy (as Fah Lo Suee), Charles Starrett, Jean Hersholt, Lawrence
   Grant, David Torrence. 72 minutes.

5. *Drums of Fu Manchu.* Republic, 1940, William Witney and John English.
   Henry Brandon (as Fu Manchu), William Royle (as Sir Nayland Smith), Robert
   Kellard, Gloria Franklin (as Fah Lo Suee), Olaf Hytten (as Dr. Jack Petrie), Tom
   Chatterton, Luana Walters, Lal Chand Mehra, George Cleveland, John Dilson,
   John Merton, Dwight Frye, Wheaton Chambers. (*Drums of Fu Manchu* was
   originally released in 1940 as a 15-episode serial. The first episode was 30 minutes
   and all others 20 minutes. In 1943, the serial was released as a feature-length film
   under the same title. The running time was 68 minutes.)

6. *The Face of Fu Manchu.* Warner Brothers-Seven Arts, Ltd., 1965, Don Sharp.
   Christopher Lee (as Fu Manchu), Nigel Green (as Sir Nayland Smith), James
   Robertson Justice, Howard Marion Crawford (as Dr. Walter Petrie), Tsai Chin
   (as Lin Tang), Joachim Fuschsberger, Karin Dor, Walter Rilla, Harry Brogan,
   Poulet Tu, Peter Mossbacher. 96 minutes.

7. *The Brides of Fu Manchu.* Warner Brothers-Seven Arts, Ltd., 1966, Don Sharp. Christopher Lee, Douglas Wilmer (as Sir Nayland Smith), Marie Versini, Tsai Chin, Henrich Wilhelm Drache, Howard Marion Crawford, Harald Leipnitz, Rupert Davies. 94 minutes.

8. *The Vengeance of Fu Manchu.* Warner Brothers-Seven Arts, Ltd. 1968, Jeremy Summers.
Christopher Lee, Tony Ferrer, Tsai Chin, Douglas Wilmer, Wolfgang Kieling, Susanne Roquette, Howard Marion Crawford. 91 minutes.

9. *Kiss and Kill* (also known as *The Blood of Fu Manchu*). Commonwealth United, 1969, Jess Franco.
Christopher Lee, Richard Greene (as Nayland Smith), Howard Marion Crawford (as Dr. Petrie), Shirley Eaton, Goetz George, Tsai Chin, Maria Rohm, Richard Palacios, Frances Kahn, Loni von Friedl, Isaura De Oliveira. 91 minutes.

James Bond (Sean Connery), indestructible British agent 007, levels his gun in *Diamonds Are Forever* (1971).

JAMES BOND

You Only Live Twice
(1967)

Screenplay by Roald Dahl based on a novel by Ian Fleming. Music by John Barry. Title song lyrics by Leslie Bricusse. Director of photography, Freddie Young. Editor, Thelma Connell. Production designed by Ken Adams. Special effects, John Stears. Action sequences by Bob Simmons. Produced by Albert R. Broccoli and Harry Saltzman. Directed by Lewis Gilbert. A United Artists release in Panavision and Technicolor. 117 minutes.

James Bond	SEAN CONNERY
Aki	AKIKO WAKABAYASHI
Tiger Tanaka	TETSURO TAMBA
Kissy Suzuki	MIE HAMA
Osato	TERU SHIMADA
Helga Brandt	KARIN DOR
Miss Moneypenny	LOIS MAXWELL
"Q"	DESMOND LLEWELYN
Henderson	CHARLES GRAY
Chinese Girl	TSAI CHIN
"M"	BERNARD LEE
Blofeld	DONALD PLEASENCE

A tall, athletic-looking man approaches a heavily veiled woman after a funeral. She is dressed in black. With the utmost sensitivity and grace, the man expresses his condolences. Suddenly, in the midst of a sentence, he smashes a shattering blow to the point of her chin, jarring loose hat, veil, and an expensively coiffed wig. Beneath the trappings is a man.

"Careful how you get out of cars next time," says James Bond to a downed but not out enemy spy.

From a prone position, the spy whips out a knife. He hurls it at Bond, missing but pinioning Bond's jacket and arm to a huge bookcase. The spy rushes in for the kill. But Bond, with a herculean effort, pulls the entire bookcase crashing down on his assailant's head.

Three armed thugs race into the room—too late. Bond is already out the door, through a window, across a roof span. Within seconds, he has donned a Buck Rogers-type jet-pack, attached it to his back and rocketed off out of range of their blazing guns.

There may be suaver heroes, operatives with sharper intellects, men who have shown more bravery. But no one has ever put together all these elements as well as James Bond, indestructible British Agent 007. The rare double-oh prefix, of course, licenses him to kill when on active duty.

Bond, the ultimate parody of the superhero, has strong masculine features, iron nerves and a difficult-to-define quality that comes close to what Ernest Hemingway once called "grace under pressure."

But he is more than just tough and cool. He moves easily in the world of posh casinos, exclusive Caribbean resorts and elegant continental hotels. He appreciates good food and wine and his precise, knowledgeable orders draw compliments from the most seasoned of maitre d's. They are all quite familiar with his favorite mixed drink—vodka martini, very dry, shaken, not stirred.*

Then, there is Bond's ugly side. He is a crack shot with a .25-caliber Beretta automatic (carried in his left arm holster) and a superb fighter who knows both judo and karate. He is, in short, a professional killer who never sentimentalizes over death.

Some have said he is totally lacking in morality. But death is an inevitable part of his job—as it is of a surgeon's. He doesn't like killing. But if it happens, it happens. The next time, it could be him.

There is Bond the expert driver, too. His hobby is fast cars. Among his favorite is his $45,000 Aston Martin DB 5 sportscar specially equipped with an ejector seat for unwanted passengers. Its extras include revolving license plates, retractable bullet-proof window shields, a radar screen, a fog thrower and twin Browning machine guns mounted behind the parking lights.

---

*In 1971, a British liquor survey reported that when Bond was at the height of his popularity, England's consumption of vodka martinis rose steadily. When 007 began to fade, vodka sales fell off.

However, 007 is perhaps most famous for Bondsmanship, his ability to get beautiful women to jump into bed with him. Some of these desirable females are counterspies—that is, until they meet Bond and defect right into his rugged arms. His choices in women equal his gourmet taste in food. They are young, fresh and seducible. The list includes:

• Tiffany Case (Jill St. John), sultry member of an international smuggling ring in *Diamonds Are Forever* (1971). The sleek redhead abandons her illegal activities after she has an amorous encounter with Bond on a plastic water-bed filled with fish.

• Pussy Galore (Honor Blackman), the man-hating aviatrix of *Goldfinger* (1964). A judo expert, she delights in slamming 007 to the ground—until Bond makes her forget judo. She ends up tossing with him in a barn and becomes his ally.

• Honey Ryder (Ursula Andress), the bronze nature girl he meets on Dr. No's mysterious island near Jamaica. Her magnificent torso rises mermaidlike from the sea.

• Kissy Suzuki (Mie Hama), a Japanese beauty whom Bond married in *You Only Live Twice* (1967) to lend credibility to his disguise as a Japanese fisherman.

• Tatiana Romanova (Daniela Bianchi), the beautiful but vulnerable Soviet cypher clerk assigned to lure Bond into a trap in *From Russia with Love* (1963). Instead, she ends up falling for him.

• Jill Masterson (Shirley Eaton), the series' most opulent corpse. Goldfinger's henchmen brush her nude body with gold paint, closing her pores and suffocating her.* All because the gilded beauty told Bond Goldfinger's card-cheating tricks. (While Goldfinger played gin at poolside, she spotted his opponents' cards through a telescope from her balcony suite and relayed the information to Goldfinger via a radio transmitter. Goldfinger used a hearing aid as his receiver.)

• Fiona (Luciana Paluzzi), the titian-hair Spectre agent who rides a motorbike equipped with a flame-thrower in *Thunderball* (1965). She meets an untimely end when Bond uses her as a shield—while they are dancing—to escape the bullets of her cutthroat colleagues. Then, he casually deposits her body at a ringside table. "Do you mind if my friend sits down?" Bond says. "She's just dead."

• Tracy (Diana Rigg), an international gangster's daughter in *On Her Majesty's Secret Service* (1969). She marries Bond—for love—and then is murdered.

• Miss Moneypenny (Lois Maxwell), the devoted private secretary to Bond's boss, M. She has had a crush on 007 that never seems to get very far. He's seldom around headquarters long enough to have a decent affair.

Except for Miss Moneypenny, none of these voluptuous gals stay on the scene

---

*Using a camel's hair brush, it took makeup artist Paul Rabafer about 25 minutes to slap on each of four coats of special paint. He spent about two hours removing it. Said Miss Eaton: "He was as impersonal about gilding me as if he was painting a barn." Maybe, but you can't stop a guy from dreaming.

VILLAINS

Some of the super-villains who try—unsuccessfully—to make mincemeat of 007.

The diabolical Dr. No (Joseph Wiseman).

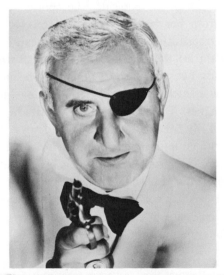

SPECTRE agent Emilio Largo (Adolfo Celi).

Shaven-head, sabre-scarred SPECTRE chief Ernst Stavro Blofeld (Donald Pleasence).

Auric Goldfinger (Gert Frobe), solid gold menace.

Oddjob (Harold Sakata), Goldfinger's right-hand man.

Alley Oop. Pussy Galore (Honor Blackman)
uses a judo twist in *Goldfinger* to send Bond
flying head over heels.

Bond plants a solid right-cross on the chin of a lovely lady in black. Only it
turns out to be a SPECTRE agent (stunt coordinator Bob Simmons) masquerading as a woman. Scene is from *Thunderball.*

very long. Bond hews to the lone wolf's motto—love 'em and leave 'em. And so no leading lady has ever appeared twice with Sean Connery, the foremost screen Bond.

Equally fascinating, in a rather perverse way, are the arch-villains who do battle with Bond. There are:

• Dr. No (Joseph Wiseman), mad Chinese scientist and designer of a secret weapon capable of destroying Cape Kennedy. He operates from a subterranean base on a private Caribbean island defended by his fanatically loyal workers.

• Ernst Stavro Blofeld (Donald Pleasence, Telly Savalas and Charles Gray), the shaven-head, saber-scarred chief of the international criminal organization Spectre (Special Executive for Counterintelligence, Terrorism, Revenge and Extortion). A hard taskmaster, he punishes failure with instant death, while stroking his white Persian cat.

• Emilio Largo (Adolfo Celi), Spectre agent and A-bomb hijacker who has a pool full of tiger sharks and a 95 mile-per-hour giant hydrofoil cocooned in a yacht.

• Auric Goldfinger (Gert Frobe), "the man with the Midas touch." A greedy millionaire, he is obsessed by gold and a yen to turn Fort Knox's gold radioactive and unusable, so his own gold would increase in value tremendously.

• Oddjob (Harold Sakata), Goldfinger's mute chauffeur-bodyguard. The squat, rocklike killer can crush a man's neck with one karate chop, decapitate a foe by flinging his razor-brimmed bowler hat.

• Russian Colonel Rosa Klebb (Lotte Lenya), a toad of a woman. The torture queen of Spectre nearly does Bond in with a swift kick from one of the poison-tipped blades that flick out from her shoes.

This sadistic cast all come from the pen of Ian Fleming, whose 13 books on Bond sold more than 30 million copies and brought him $3 million in royalties. It was often said that Fleming, who died in 1964 at the age of 56, created Bond in his own image. Son of a Conservative member of Parliament, Fleming was, in fact, a sports car enthusiast, gambler, firearms expert and connoisseur of good food. Like Bond, he was once a Royal Navy commander and had an aristocratic school background. He went to Eton, Britain's most exclusive prep school, and Sandhurst, the military academy. But Fleming felt he really had little in common with 007. "I do rather envy him his blondes and his efficiency," he once said. "But I can't say I like the chap."

Critics differed widely on the merits of his work. Some accused Fleming of being a British Mickey Spillane, pandering to the public's insatiable lust for flesh and brutality.* The Vatican newspaper, L'Osservatore romano, called Bond a man of "violence, vulgarity, sadism and sex."

*In the movies, Bond's unique ways of disposing of villains included suffocating one victim under a mountainous pile of bird dung (Dr. No), and luring another into the churning blades of a snow blower (On Her Majesty's Secret Service).

BEAUTIES

A few of the luscious and sometimes lethal beauties who furnish Bond with both amatory and predatory moments in his movie adventures.

Jill St. John in *Diamonds Are Forever.*

Akiko Wakabayashi in *You Only Live Twice.*

Mona Chang in *On Her Majesty's Secret Service.*

Trina Parks and Donna Garrattin in *Diamonds Are Forever*.

Shirley Eaton in *Goldfinger*.

Karin Dor in *You Only Live Twice*.

On the beach with Domino (Claudine Auger) in *Thunderball* (1965).

Bond has a run of luck at the dice tables in Las Vegas, where he is befriended by Plenty O'Toole (Lana Wood) in *Diamonds Are Forever*. Miss Wood, younger sister of Natalie Wood, plays a Las Vegas casino chip follower.

Others considered Fleming a craftsman, a master of suspense and the spy thriller genre. His books, they also pointed out, had a spoofing tongue-in-cheek quality running through them, which the films developed more fully.

Despite the disagreement, Fleming had a following that reached into the highest political circles. President Kennedy and Allen Dulles, while he headed the Central Intelligence Agency, were Bond fans. And so was Britain's Prince Philip.

But it was the movies that turned Bond into a household name—mainly because of the inspired casting of Sean Connery. Son of a Scottish truck driver, Connery (his real first name is Tommy), grew up in Edinburgh. He quit school at 15, joined the navy at 16, but hated it and was medically discharged at 19 with ulcers. He was considered 20 percent disabled and given a pension of nine shillings ($1.08) a week. Two tattoos, reminders of this part of his life, are indelibly carved on his right wrist. They say "Scotland Forever" and "Mum and Dad."

A succession of odd jobs followed his brief navy life. He was a plasterer's helper, bricklayer, coffin polisher, milkman, lifeguard, printer's devil. Then, one day, he read that a touring production of "South Pacific" needed chorus boys. He took a cram course in dancing, went to London and landed a part. "I couldn't think of any job but show business again," he said. "I was hooked."

The virile, 200-pound, six-foot-two-inch Connery went into stock, repertory, Shakespeare, and television. After small roles in four pictures in 1957, he played in a first-rate BBC production of *Requiem for a Heavyweight.* That led to a movie part in London opposite Lana Turner, who was then in her late thirties. Connery thought the film, called *Another Time, Another Place (1958),* would be his big break. It wasn't. It was a disaster. In addition, Connery's relations with Miss Turner, which were warm at first, cooled after he had a run-in with Johnny Stompanato, her gangster friend.* Connery went back to stock, but there were those who remembered him from his television days.

Harry Saltzman and Albert R. (Cubby) Broccoli, two American producers, had bought movie rights to all the *Bond* novels except *Casino Royale* and *Thunderball.*** They were going into production with *Dr. No.* and eagerly searching for a leading man. Fleming's choice was said to be an actor resembling David Niven, Richard Burton or James Mason. Broccoli, too, favored someone very smooth, an old-school establishment type. But Saltzman, convinced a polished veneer could always be assumed, wanted fire and toughness. Despite the different

*During an argument with Miss Turner, Stompanato was later fatally stabbed by her teen-aged daughter, Cheryl.

**Saltzman and Broccoli reached an agreement with writer-producer Kevin McClory, who claimed ownership of *Thunderball.* It was released with McClory credited as producer and co-author—along with Fleming and Jack Whittingham—of an original story upon which the film was based. But Saltzman and Broccoli never got rights to *Casino Royale.* This Fleming book, produced by Charles K. Feldman (who owned its movie rights) and released by Columbia, appeared on the screen as an uneven, overdone 007 spoof starring David Niven.

Bond sends Emilio Largo (Adolfo Celi) reeling aboard a hydrofoil in *Thunderball.*

George Lazenby as 007 in *On Her Majesty's Secret Service* (1970).

A laser beam inches its way toward 007 tied to a laboratory table in *Goldfinger* (1964). At left, the millionaire criminal with an insatiable lust for gold (Gert Frobe) laughs at his cunning use of this new electronic instrument as an instrument of torture.

conceptions, the two producers were both sold on the spot when they auditioned Connery.

"It was the sheer self-confidence he exuded," Broccoli said. "I've never seen a surer guy. Every time he made a point he hit the desk with that great fist of his, or slapped his thigh. It wasn't just an act, either. When he left we watched him through the window as he walked down the street. He walked like the most arrogant son-of-a-gun you've ever seen . . . 'That's our Bond,' I said."

(Years later, Connery was not so gushing in his appraisal of Messrs. Saltzman and Broccoli. "For every good idea Harry had, he's gone on to eight flops," Connery said. He added: "They're [Saltzman and Broccoli] not exactly enamored of each other. Probably because they're both sitting on $50 million and looking across the desk at each other and thinking: 'That bugger's got half of what should be all mine.' ")

The first *Bond* film, *Dr. No,* drew long lines at the box office, and it grossed nearly $6 million on a $1.5 million investment. Connery, who insisted on making one independent picture between Bond films, did five 007 movies from 1963 to 1967. To date, they have grossed over $125 million, with *Thunderball* the leading money earner at $27 million.

Connery became an international folk hero, the ideal of every bachelor. In Italy, they admiringly dubbed him, "Mr. Kisskiss Bangbang."

But in real life Connery is, in many ways, the opposite of Bond. Where Bond is a bachelor, Connery has two children by his wife, actress Diane Cilento. Before they separated, they lived in an unfashionable suburb of West London. He is earthy where Bond is urbane. Where Bond gambles for $50,000 on the turn of a card, Connery plays nickel and dime poker. Where Bond is a fearless skindiver, Connery is deathly afraid of sharks and barracudas. Where Bond has a full head of hair, Connery is fast losing his. (He wears a toupee in Bond films.) "I'm obviously not Bond," Connery has said many times. "And Bond is obviously not really a human being."

In fact, in a candid *Playboy* interview, he betrayed a kind of love-hate attitude toward 007. Said Connery: "Let me straighten you out on this. The problem in interviews of this sort is to get across the fact, without breaking your arse, that one is *not* Bond, that one was functioning reasonably well *before* Bond and that one is going to function reasonably well *after* Bond. There are a lot of things I did before Bond—like playing the classics on stage—that don't seem to get publicized. So you see, this Bond image is a problem in a way and a bit of a bore, but one has just got to live with it."

Yet, at the same time, Connery, who today is the director of a London bank, is well aware that without Bond, he would not be the rich man he is.

Perhaps his closest resemblance to his fictional counterpart is his rugged Scottish individualism and straightforwardness. "There are two sorts of people in the

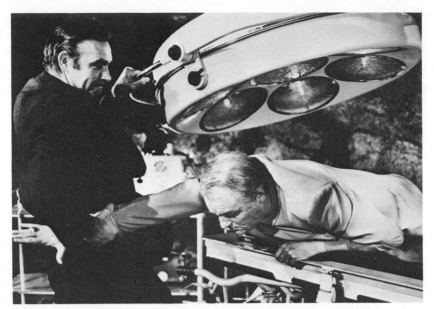

Bond slams a broiler over archfoe Blofeld (Charles Gray) that sizzles him in *Diamonds Are Forever* (1971). But Bond later finds out the cooked villain is Blofeld's double.

Using a chair to keep SPECTRE agent Rosa Klebb (Lotte Lenya) at bay, Bond tries to stay clear of her poisoned steel shoe-tips in *From Russia with Love* (1963).

world," Connery says. "Those who live under a shell and just wait for their pensions. And those who move around and keep their eyes open. I have always moved around and kept my eyes open—and been prepared to raise my middle finger at the world. I always will."

When Connery's contract ran out, he vowed he would never make another *Bond* picture. "They're like comic strips," he said. "The producers constantly have to come up with bigger and better gimmicks. That's all that sustains the pictures."

George Lazenby, an Australian who graduated from a grease monkey's job to TV commercials, succeeded Connery in *On Her Majesty's Secret Service* (1969). It was his first movie and possibly his last. The reviews were unanimously bad. *Variety* reported that the film earned only about $18 million—short of its $21 million break-even point. Previous *Bonds,* with Connery starring, nearly doubled their investment. For a while, it looked as if we might have seen the last of 007. But in 1971, Connery had a change of heart—lured back by a deal that gave him a chance to produce two films of his own. His seventh *Bond* movie, *Diamonds Are Forever,* paid him a handsome $1 million salary plus 12 1/2 percent of the box office.*

A stouter Connery, graying at the temples, played opposite Jill St. John in the first of the series to be shot in the United States. The film drew less enthusiastic notices than some of Connery's earlier efforts. But critics generally liked it. (In the New York City area, the count was six favorable reviews, six mixed, two unfavorable.)

My own impression was that director Guy Hamilton knew exactly what he was doing. He kept the action brisk and the dialogue droll. There were, of course, times when things were a bit overdone. When Bond uses a corpse to smuggle a cache of diamonds into the United States, someone asks where he hid the loot. "Alimentary, my dear Watson," he replies.

"Great, absurd fun," said Vincent Canby of the *New York Times.* Still, Bond seemed oddly anachronistic, out of step with the 1970s, a kind of nostalgic caricature of his old self. "Although Connery is still suave," wrote Paul D. Zimmerman of *Newsweek,* "the whole operation has become faded and formularized . . . James Bond movies belong to the 1960s."

As critics disagree with the impact *Diamonds* had, so do Bond fans debate his all-time best movie. Many choose *Goldfinger.* Others pick *From Russia with Love.* Without trying to settle anything, let's look at *You Only Live Twice*—for no better reason than it is probably the least known of the series, and it's the only film where Bond gets married and killed, though not in that order.

*United Artists said Connery donated that $1 million to a charity he helped organize, the Scottish International Educational Trust Fund. It provides educational opportunities for poor children.

For openers, we have a fantastic space kidnapping. An astronaut is walking in space while tethered to his orbiting Gemini capsule. Suddenly, he spots an unidentified flying object, which starts closing fast. It is another spacecraft, a strange ship that opens its nose cone like a monster lobster claw and swallows the Gemini craft. As the great jaw snaps shut, it severs the astronaut's oxygen line linking him to his ship. He whirls off into the endless reaches of the universe.

The United States angrily accuses Russia of a blatant attempt to get control of space for military purposes. It threatens the Soviets with war if a repetition of the space piracy occurs. A few days later, the same thing happens to a Soviet spacecraft. Russia hurls similar charges. And so with the world on the brink of a third world war, Bond is sent to Japan—over which the missing ship was last tracked—to investigate.

To operate undetected, 007 fakes his own death. The camera cuts to a Hong Kong hotel room, where Bond is in bed kissing a Chinese girl.

"Why do Chinese girls taste differently from all other girls," Bond asks.

"You think we better, yes?"

"No. Just different. Like Peking duck is different from Russian caviar."

"Darling, I give you very best duck."

Suddenly, the girl hops out of bed and presses a button. The bed, with Bond still in it, springs back into a recess in the wall. Men with tommy guns race into the room, spray the closed bed, then rush out. Minutes later, British police inspectors and Chinese police dash in and pull back the bed. Bond lies motionless.

"We're too late."

"Well, he died on the job."

"He'd have wanted it this way."

The next day, there is a burial at sea aboard a British warship. Bond's body, wrapped in a shroud, is sent to the bottom. But only for a few moments. Underwater frogmen scoop him up and carry him to a waiting submarine. There, officials cut open the shroud. Bond lies within a clear plastic inner lining, getting oxygen through a closed-circuit rebreather. (It keeps bubbles from escaping so snoopers will think the burial is real.) Dressed in his commander's uniform, Bond stands erect and executes a snappy salute.

"Request permission to come aboard, sir," Bond says.

Back in London briefly, Bond gets a rundown from M (Bernard Lee), his boss. The Japanese are not geared to launch an interceptor rocket, M says. It is up to Bond to find out who else is, before the United States and Russia get involved in a full-scale war. As Bond dutifully leaves, Miss Moneypenny has one question of her own.

"Oh, by the way," she asks, "how was the girl?"

"Which girl?"

"The Chinese girl we fixed you up with."

"Oh, another five minutes and I'd have found out."

In Tokyo, Bond meets a contact, who is stabbed just as he's disclosing who he thinks is behind the space plot. Bond catches the assassin, knocks him out, switches clothes and runs to a waiting car. He crouches as if wounded, then huddles, moaning in the back. The driver, unaware Bond is in the car, speeds to the expensive, modern headquarters of Osato Chemical and Engineering Co., Ltd. There, he unsuspectingly carries Bond to a huge executive suite and dumps him on a couch.

"Good evening," Bond says. Then he proceeds to knock thug number two unconscious after a gruelling fight.

Using an ultrasonic device, Bond opens the office safe but he triggers an alarm. He dashes out just a few steps ahead of armed security guards. Conveniently waiting for him in a sports car is a beautiful Japanese girl. She races off and eludes Bond's pursuers. When he insists on knowing who she is, the girl skids to a stop and dashes into a deserted subway. Bond chases her. Suddenly, a trap door springs and he slides down a long chute onto a plush couch in the office of Tiger Tanaka (Tetsuro Tamba), head of the Japanese secret service.

"Welcome," Tiger says. "It is a great pleasure to meet you at last."

The next day, Bond returns to the chemical company to see the president, Osata (Teru Shimada) himself. Bond uses the cover name, Mr. Fisher, pretending to be a manufacturing director on a buying trip. In his sumptuous office, Osata sits behind a desk with a fluoroscope X-ray screen that reveals Bond's gun. They discuss Bond's business trip and then he leaves. As Bond steps out of the room, Osata bites off an order to his aide: "Kill him." Gunmen in a black sedan take out after Bond. But Tiger's agents have a reception of their own. A helicopter flies over the gunman's car, lowers a magnet, lifts the auto high into the air and drops it neatly into the ocean.

Every Bond movie has its gimmicks and this one is no exception. It's a tiny but lethal autogyro that comes packed in four suitcases. Bond uses the 250-pound plane, which looks like a castoff from an amusement park, to go on a reconnaissance flight. While he's airborne, four "enemy" helicopters close in and start firing. But they are unaware that Bond's craft is equipped with air-to-air missiles, flame throwers and rockets. They are no match for his modern arsenal and in a wild dogfight, he downs them all.

In between feats of derring-do, Bond makes two more lady friends. He dallies with Helga Brandt (Karin Dor), Osaka's assistant, and Aki (Akiko Wakabayashi), Tiger's secretary. When Helga is dropped into a pool of flesh-eating piranhas and Aki swallows poison meant for Bond, 007 goes on to marry a third beauty —Kissy Suzuki (Mie Hama). The Shinto wedding serves as a cover to get Bond, disguised as a Japanese fisherman, onto an island suspected of harboring the missing spaceships.

The craft have been hidden in a dead volcano, camouflaged by a false roof. It's actually a sliding green fiber glass top simulating a crater lake. Below lies SPECTRE's great secret underground launching base, complete with gantry, control room and monorail (for quick transportation within the complex). The crime syndicate has been behind the space snatches, hired by a third power—never named—to promote hostilities. When the United States and Russia annihilate each other, so the plan goes, the third power will then dominate the world.

Early one morning, Bond and his Japanese wife discover the volcano hideaway. Bond sends Kissy back for help from Tiger's elite corps of Ninjas (commandos). Meanwhile, he steals into the space complex only to be discovered and hauled before SPECTRE's dreaded boss. The film's final 20 minutes take place inside the underground launch site, a gigantic set which, the studio said, was the largest and most expensive ever built. It was 200 feet wide, 120 feet high and had a stainless steel monorail encircling the entire interior. Cost: $1 million.

Another first for the film was the sight of the SPECTRE chief's face. We had previously only seen his body and his hands stroking his furry cat. But now we see the hideous scarred features of the bald crime czar as he confronts the captured Bond.

"Allow me to introduce myself," he says with a slight European accent. "I am Ernst Stavro Blofeld. They told me you were assassinated. You only live twice, Mr. Bond."

As Bond looks on, the crater opens and SPECTRE launches its interceptor rocketship. Its mission is to bring back another U.S. Gemini capsule, a feat it expects will trigger a shooting war. Suddenly, Tiger's raiders slip in through the volcano's great sliding overhead and launch a spectacular invasion. With submarine gunfire crackling all around, Bond works his way into the control room. At the last minute, he throws a destruct switch. It blows up the SPECTRE rocket —only seconds before it would have engulfed the U.S. space capsule.

Blofeld slips away and, in a frenzy, he pushes a button that destroys his base. But Bond and his teammates have escaped through an underwater tunnel. At the fadeout, Bond and Kissy are blissfully embracing in a life raft.* The scene was reportedly done in a single take because Kissy seemed to convey just the right touch of passion. A testimony to Bond's inspiring powers as a lover? "No," says Mie Hama. "Sean was tickling my stomach and making me wriggle."

*Curiously, all the Connery Bond movies end with 007 on, or near, the water with his girl of the moment.

JAMES BOND SERIES

1. *Dr. No.* United Artists, 1962, Terence Young.
    Sean Connery (as James Bond), Ursula Andress (as Honey Ryder), Joseph Wiseman (as Dr. No), Jack Lord, Bernard Lee (as "M"), Anthony Dawson, John Kitzmiller, Zena Marshall, Eunice Gayson, Lois Maxwell (as Miss Moneypenny), Lester Prendergast. III minutes.

2. *From Russia with Love.* United Artists, 1963, Terence Young.
    Sean Connery, Daniela Bianchi (as Tatiana Romanova), Pedro Armendariz, Lotte Lenya (as Rosa Klebb), Robert Shaw, Bernard Lee, Eunice Gayson, Walter Gotell, Francis de Wolff, George Pastell, Nadja Regin, Lois Maxwell. 118 minutes.

3. *Goldfinger.* United Artists, 1964, Guy Hamilton.
    Sean Connery, Gert Frobe (as Auric Goldfinger), Honor Blackman (as Pussy Galore), Shirley Eaton (as Jill Masterson), Tania Mallett, Harold Sakata (as Oddjob), Bernard Lee, Martin Benson, Cec Linder, Lois Maxwell. 108 minutes.

4. *Thunderball.* United Artists, 1965, Terence Young.
    Sean Connery, Claudine Auger (as Domino), Adolfo Celi (as Emilio Largo), Luciana Paluzzi (as Fiona), Rik Van Nutter, Bernard Lee, Martine Beswick, Guy Doleman, Molly Peters, Desmond Llewelyn, Lois Maxwell, Roland Culver. 125 minutes.

5. *You Only Live Twice.* United Artists, 1967, Lewis Gilbert.
    Sean Connery, Akiko Wakabayashi, Tetsuro Tamba, Mie Hama (as Kissy Suzuki), Teru Shimada, Karin Dor, Lois Maxwell, Desmond Llewelyn, Charles Gray, Tsai Chin, Bernard Lee, Donald Pleasence (as Blofeld), Alexander Knox, Robert Hutton. 117 minutes.

6. *Casino Royale.* Columbia, 1967, John Huston, Ken Hughes, Val Guest, Robert Parrish, Joe McGrath.
    Peter Sellers, Ursula Andress, David Niven (as James Bond), Orson Welles, Joanna Pettet, Daliah Lavi, Woody Allen, Deborah Kerr, William Holden, Charles Boyer, John Huston, Kurt Kasznar, George Raft, Jean-Paul Belmondo, Terence Cooper, Barbara Bouchet (as Moneypenny). 131 minutes.

7. *On Her Majesty's Secret Service.* United Artists, 1969, Peter Hunt.
    George Lazenby (as James Bond), Diana Rigg (as Tracy), Telly Savalas (as Blofeld), Ilse Steppat, Gabriele Ferzetti, Bernard Horsfall, George Baker, Bernard Lee, Lois Maxwell, Desmond Llewelyn, Angela Scoular, Brian Worth, Geoffrey

Chesire, Irvin Allen, Les Crawford, George Cooper, Catherina von Schell. 140 minutes.

8. *Diamonds Are Forever*. United Artists, 1971, Guy Hamilton.
Sean Connery, Jill St. John (as Tiffany Case), Charles Gray (as Blofeld), Lana Wood (as Plenty O'Toole), Jimmy Dean, Bruce Cabot, Bruce Glover (as Wint), Putter Smith (as Kidd), Norman Burton, Desmond Llewelyn, Leonard Barr. 119 minutes.

9. *Live and Let Die*. United Artists, scheduled for 1973, Guy Hamilton.
Roger Moore (as James Bond). In production when this book was published.

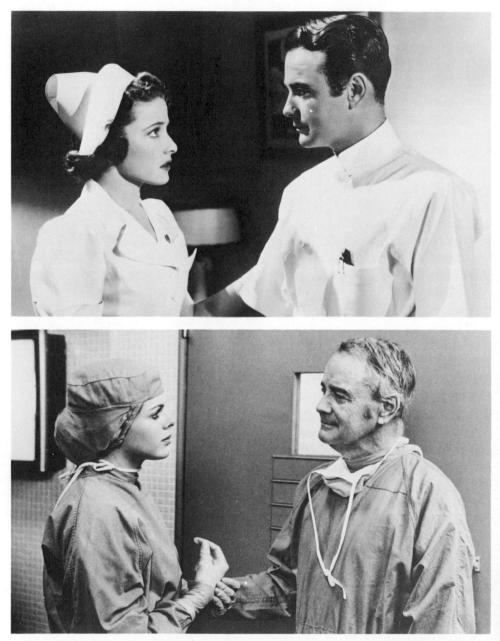

Lew Ayres, top picture, as Dr. James Kildare in the *Kildare* movie series in 1940. With him is Laraine Day, his nurse sweetheart. In bottom photo, 30 years later, Ayres is shown making a guest appearance on the CBS television show "The Interns." He is seen with Sari Price, his operating room nurse.

DR. KILDARE

Dr. Kildare Goes Home
(1940)

Based on an original story by Max Brand and Willis Goldbeck. Screenplay by Harry Ruskin and Goldbeck. Music director, David Snell. Camera, Harold Rosson. Editor, Howard O'Neill. Directed by Harold S. Bucquet. A Metro-Goldwyn-Mayer production and release. 78 minutes.

Dr. James Kildare	LEW AYRES
Dr. Leonard Gillespie	LIONEL BARRYMORE
Mary Lamont	LARAINE DAY
Dr. Stephen Kildare	SAMUEL S. HINDS
George Winslow	GENE LOCKHART
Dr. Davidson	JOHN SHELTON
Joe Wayman	NAT PENDLETON
Mrs. Martha Kildare	EMMA DUNN
Molly Byrd	ALMA KRUGER
Dr. Walter Carew	WALTER KINGSFORD
Nurse Parker	NELL CRAIG
Dr. Jordan	CLIFF DANIELSON
Collins	HENRY WADSWORTH

In *Young Dr. Kildare* (1938), Ayres made his debut as the dedicated, idealistic intern. Here crusty Dr. Leonard Gillespie (Lionel Barrymore), Blair General Hospital's renowned diagnostician, asks Kildare to take his pulse. A group of recently graduated medical students watch, including Don Barry (striped suit behind Ayres).

Dr. Gillespie and his protege exchange sharp remarks as they air their differences in *Young Dr. Kildare*.

Joiner	TOM COLLINS
Mr. Brownlee	DONALD BRIGGS
Mrs. Brownlee	LEONA MARICLE
Bates	ARCHIE TWITCHELL
Sally	MARIE BLAKE
Atkinson	CHARLES TROWBRIDGE
Conover	GEORGE H. REED
Foghorn Murphy	HORACE MCMAHON
Mike Ryan	FRANK ORTH
Interne	ARTHUR O'CONNELL
Boylston	ERVILLE ALDERSON
Dickinson	KEN CHRISTY

The big day has arrived for the Kildare family in the quaint New England town of Dartford. Young Jimmy (Lew Ayres) has finished his internship and come back a full-fledged doctor. His father, Dr. Stephen Kildare (Samuel S. Hinds), proudly puts up his son's shingle next to his own.

But Jimmy's ambitions lie beyond life as a country doctor. He does not have the heart to tell his father. But that night, as he sits on the porch with Alice Raymond (Lynne Carver), who has been in love with him since high school, he gropes for the right words to make his plans clear.

"Alice, there are two ways of being a doctor. One is for the living you can make out of it. Now I could marry you, settle down and count on taking over my father's practice."

"Why don't you?" Alice asks, hoping this is what he will opt for.

"Because being a doctor can be bigger than three meals a day. Ehrlich was that kind of doctor. So was Lister. I'm certainly no Lister. But . . . I know somehow I have to find out where I belong in medicine. And there's no way to do that in Dartford."

This is young Dr. Kildare—idealistic, dedicated, ambitious. In a few days, he will return to Blair General Hospital in the big city to start his career as the protégé of master diagnostician Dr. Leonard Gillespie (Lionel Barrymore). And working in this hospital-based setup, he will set the standards for television's men-in-white in generations to come.*

Yet, despite the generally soap opera-like picture it presented of the medical profession, the series was honest enough to show us that not all young doctors were as altruistic and serious-minded as Kildare. In *Young Dr. Kildare* (1938), an internes' bull session touches reality as they lightheartedly talk about their futures.

*From 1961 to 1966, Richard Chamberlain played Kildare on TV and Raymond Massey was Gillespie. In 1972, Mark Jenkins and Gary Merrill took over.

Just when Dr. Randall Adams (Van Johnson) begins making headway with lovely Ruth Edly (Marilyn Maxwell), he's called out on an emergency by ambulance driver Joe Wayman (Nat Pendleton). Scene is from *Dr. Gillespie's Criminal Case* (1943). Johnson played Gillespie's chief assistant after Ayres became a conscientious objector in World War II.

Joel McCrea was the first Dr. Kildare and Lloyd Nolan played a gangster kingpin in *Internes Can't Take Money* (1937).

"When I take out Park Avenue appendixes at ten grand a slice, you boys will go around bragging you used to room with me," says one aspiring medic.

"I've got the best idea in the world," says another. "A very smart doctor tipped me off. I'm going to be a skin specialist. Your patients never die. And they never get well."

"If you're really being serious," says a third, "I'm going to be an OB [obstetrician] at $5,000 a baby. Terms—COD. And a special check from Grandma."

But Kildare doesn't join in this banter. Medicine is no joke to him. It is the be-all and end-all of his existence. And anyone who would be his wife has to realize this. "Remember, a doctor is a doctor 24 hours a day," Gillespie warns Kildare's fiancée, nurse Mary Lamont (Laraine Day), in *Dr. Kildare's Wedding Day* (1941), "The rest of the time he can be a husband."

Of course, no such lecture is needed for Kildare. He has been aware of his obligations from the very start. In the first *Kildare* film, *Internes Can't Take Money*, Kildare (played by Joel McCrea in his only such appearance) is in a bar when a mob boss (Lloyd Nolan) is shot. The gangster refuses to go to a hospital, so Kildare operates in the bar's backroom. As he wields his scalpel swiftly and surely, the gangster's henchmen watch, fascinated. An awed hoodlum remarks, "The kid's got eyes in his fingers." Later, the grateful gang boss tries to give Kildare $1,000. But such a gift would be violating Kildare's hospital oath. "I'm not allowed to take money," he tells the startled underworld czar. "Internes can't do that while they're serving time at a hospital."

"Did you ever hear of a guy giving back dough before," one incredulous crook whispers.

"Sure," his pal answers, "But he had a .38 sticking in his ribs."

The ten-picture *Kildare* series ran from 1937 to 1942. Then, when Ayres became a conscientious objector and dropped out, it continued—using Gillespie's name, instead, in the titles. Six *Gillespie* movies were made through 1947. But they were no match for the *Kildare* pictures because the crusty, tyrannical Gillespie could never be as appealing a central figure as the handsome and personable Kildare.

One of the *Gillespie* subplots had Keye Luke and Van Johnson as rivals for Kildare's prized job as Gillespie's assistant. Another story-line had Johnson romancing super-stacked blonde nurse Marilyn Maxwell.* The twist here was that Miss Maxwell responded immediately and affirmatively to all his passes. But at the climactic moment, the telephone would ring to call him out on yet another emergency.

In *Dr. Gillespie's Criminal Case* (1943) their sprightly dialogue fantasizes every bachelor's dream of his first encounter with a beautiful girl. It went like this:

---

*Miss Maxwell, a former big-band singer and a film fixture of the 1940s and 1950s, died in Beverly Hills in 1972 of a heart attack. She was 49.

The *Kildare* series was a great testing ground for MGM starlets, including Lana Turner. She is seen here in a publicity still from *Calling Dr. Kildare* (1939).

The Blair General Hospital team—plus patient —in *Dr. Kildare's Wedding Day* (1941). Dr. Gillespie is in front. Standing from left: orderly Vernon Briggs (Red Skelton), nurse Lamont (Miss Day), Kildare (Ayres), and patient Constanzo Labardi (Nils Asther), an orchestra leader who learns that the ringing in his ear comes from—believe it or not—eating spaghetti.

Dr. Gillespie peers into the microscope to try to identify the strange malady affecting Mary Lamont's brother (Robert Young). Laraine Day and Ayres look on. Scene is from *Dr. Kildare's Crisis* (1940).

JOHNSON: *(Catching up to Miss Maxwell in a hospital corridor)* Pardon me, young lady. Are you in love with anybody? And remember it's a felony to lie to a doctor.

MAXWELL: I'm not in love with anybody. But I like doctors. Are you available?

JOHNSON: Holy smoke! What night are we going to get together?

MAxwell: Make it easy for yourself.

JOHNSON: I'm off Friday night.

MAXWELL: I've got a date. But I'll break it.

JOHNSON: I'll buy you a swell dinner.

MAXWELL: Save your money. I'll give you a swell dinner at my place.

JOHNSON: Then, I'll bring a bottle of gin.

MAXWELL: You don't have to. I've got everything you can think of in my apartment.

JOHNSON: What kind of apartment have you got?

MAXWELL: Only five rooms. After all, what does one girl need when she lives alone.

JOHNSON: Would you mind pinching me to see if I'm awake?

MAXWELL: Oh, you're awake all right. I can tell by that look in your eye.

JOHNSON: I'm off at 7. I'll be there at 7:30.

MAXWELL: Make it 8. I want to be beautiful for you . . . I'll leave the door unlatched because it's the maid's night off.

JOHNSON: Holy smoke!

The series gave steady work to a host of familiar character actors. Samuel S. Hinds played Kildare's compassionate father. Emma Dunn was his matronly mother. Nat Pendleton, a former Olympic wrestler, was the dumb but dependable ambulance driver. Alma Kruger and Nell Craig were two nurses constantly bullied by the irascible Gillespie. Walter Kingsford was the harried hospital administrator. Marie Blake was the gossipy switchboard operator. And George H. Reed was the loyal attendant.

The *Kildare* pictures also gave a chance to aspiring young contract players like Lana Turner, Ava Gardner, Red Skelton and Donna Reed. And Laraine Day was Kildare's sweetheart, nurse Mary Lamont, until the wiser heads at MGM thought the time had come for bigger and better roles. In addition, Robert Young, who had already reached star status, made a cameo appearance. He was Kildare's patient, a harbinger of the future when he would himself don a white gown and play Marcus Welby, M.D. Young's medical drama would lead the television ratings in 1970 and 1971 with 40 million viewers.

But undoubtedly the success of the pictures stemmed from the fresh and convincing performance of Ayres. A banjo and guitar player in a big band, Ayres came to Hollywood in 1928. He switched to acting and got his big break almost immediately. After a few bit parts, he was chosen for the lead opposite Greta

Garbo in *The Kiss* (1929). Then he rocketed to international acclaim with a poignant performance as a young soldier in the antiwar film *All Quiet on the Western Front* (1930).

However, after this breathtaking start, his career slowly fizzled. His pictures failed to attract attention. Critics said his performances became lackluster. He made an attempt at directing—*Hearts in Bondage* (1936). But the movie was not successful. His private life was going downhill, too. Marriages to Lola Lane and then to Ginger Rogers ended in divorce.* He slipped into B-movies. But then his career turned a corner. MGM rescued him from oblivion by casting him as the lead in *Young Dr. Kildare* (1938).

At first, Ayres thought the picture was just another bad chapter in his fading career. "When I saw the preview, it made me pretty miserable," Ayres said. "Frankly, I thought it was terrible." However, critics disagreed. They were enthusiastic. And so was the public. In fact, the *Kildare* series became so popular that the expression, "Calling Dr. Kildare," became an everyday expression. Ayres signed a long-term contract and found himself in demand for other top roles as well.

Then, suddenly, his whole life changed. World War II broke out and the Army drafted him. But since his experience in *All Quiet,* killing had become as abhorrent to him in real life as it was on the screen. So, unlike other stars, he refused to fight. He became America's number-one conscientious objector. He did so at the sacrifice of his career. Movie-goers reacted negatively. Theatre-owners boycotted the *Kildare* movies. And his studio, fearing it would inherit some of the backlash, quickly disowned him.

Nicholas Schenk, MGM president, said Ayres' film career was over. "As far as I'm concerned", Schenck sacid, "I am no party of interest one way or the other. Lew Ayres is washed up with us since he's washed himself up with the public."

One of the few who refused to abandon him was Hollywood columnist Hedda Hopper. "I'm not defending Lew Ayres' convictions," she said on her radio program. "But I am defending his right to his own conscience. It's no part of a brave and free people to brand as a coward a man who dares disagree with them."

In 1942, Ayres went to a conscientious objectors' camp in Oregon—one of 25 such sites scattered throughout the country. He joined other war protesters in clearing underbrush, felling trees, cutting firebreaks and doing other work similar to that performed by the Civilian Conservation Corps in the Depression years of the 1930s.

Ayres had maintained he was willing to serve in the military if he didn't have to use weapons. After friends talked with General Lewis B. Hershey, director of

*In 1964, after 24 years of bachelorhood, he married a third time—to Diana Hall. They were still wed in 1972.

Selective Service, Ayres was later inducted as a noncombatant. He served as a chaplain's assistant and Medical Corps sergeant in the Pacific, treating wounded soldiers under fire.

After the war, he resumed his acting career and made some notable films. He appeared opposite Olivia de Havilland in *The Dark Mirror* (1946) and as the sympathetic doctor in *Johnny Belinda* (1948) with Jane Wyman. But Hollywood is slow to forget those who it believes have betrayed their benefactor. The parts were few and far between.

In 1955, he took time out to study the world's religions and produced a book and a five-hour cycle of films called *Altars of the East.* Ayres toured with the films, showing them in theatres throughout the country. Running on three successive nights, they covered Hinduism, Shintoism, Islam, Judaism, Sikhism, Parsism, Jainism, Buddhism, Confucianism, and Taoism.

In the 1960s, Ayres made occasional television appearances. But he appeared in only two pictures—*Advise and Consent* (1962), in which he played the vice president, and *The Carpetbaggers* (1964), in which he played Jason Cord's righteous right-hand man. In 1972, he had supporting roles in *The Man* and *The Biscuit Eater,* his last roles to date.

Unquestionably, his fame will rest on the early years of his life—his moving performance in *All Quiet* and his role as the sincere young doctor in *Kildare.* Of all his series pictures, perhaps the most unusual is *Dr. Kildare Goes Home* (1940), which focuses around an unusual experiment in socialized medicine nearly a decade before the British began their controversial tax-supported National Health Service.

As the picture opens, Kildare is a staff physician at Blair and about to fulfill his cherished ambition of becoming the assistant to Dr. Gillespie. But when his mother telephones to congratulate him, Kildare senses something is wrong at home. And he takes off to investigate.

He finds his father nearly exhausted. The neighboring town of Parkersville is broke. The paper mill that supported it has closed. It's the depth of the Depression. Nobody has money and the town's only doctor has moved away. So, the elder Kildare has tried to care for Parkersville's patients as well as his own. Eventually, the long hours have taken their toll.

The next day, Gillespie arrives to see why Kildare has left so suddenly. When he hears about the doctor shortage, Gillespie is immediately struck by the irony of the situation. With 10,000 doctors sorely in need of practice—some even washing windows or working as janitors—it is a pity they can't serve people who need them.

But why can't they? If people in Parkersville don't have the money to go to a doctor, Kildare suggests, why not try another approach?

In *Dr. Kildare Goes Home* (1940), Kildare returns to his New England hometown of Dartford to help his overworked father, Dr. Stephen Kildare (Samuel S. Hinds).

Just before their long-awaited trip to the altar, Mary (Miss Day) is fatally injured when a truck hits her in *Dr. Kildare's Wedding Day*. Her last words to Kildare are: "This is going to be much easier for me than it is for you."

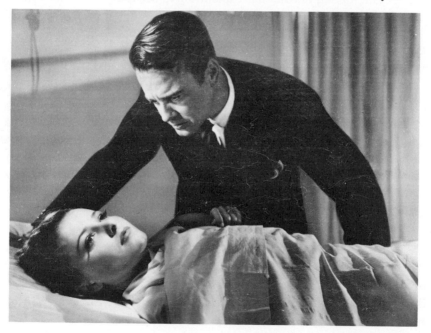

"How about the theory that the community can afford what the individual can't?" says Kildare.

"Oh, so you've been bitten by that bug," says Gillespie.

"If the people of Parkersville would pay, say 10 cents each week, we could give them medical service."

"That's a very clever idea," says Gillespie. "And maybe in 1960 a practical one. But it doesn't work now."

"Well, why not?"

"Because people won't believe that for 10 cents a week you can take care of them properly when they need it."

"Well, we'll have to make them believe it."

"Naw," Gillespie scoffs. "You can't break down prejudice with logic and reason."

Actually, what Kildare is proposing is the revolutionary concept of prepaid group practice—an idea that actually did come to fruition in some areas of the United States after World War II. Its principle is to supplant the traditional single-doctor, fee-for-each-service practice with teams of doctors working together for a set annual payment. Proponents say it makes sense for people to pay for health care when they are well and best able to afford it, rather than when they are sick and least able to pay. They say prepaid group practice enables the same number of doctors to treat twice as many patients. Finally, proponents contend, it puts emphasis on preventive medicine since doctors are paid exactly the same salary if their patients stay well. In real life, unlike the *Kildare* movie, however, it has been the traditionally conservative American Medical Association —not patients—which has opposed the idea.

But getting back to fantasyland, Kildare, despite Gillespie's arguments, decides to organize a clinic for Parkersville. He recruits Dr. Davidson (John Shelton) and Dr. Jordan (Cliff Danielson), two young, unemployed doctors. They set up their offices and then Kildare tries to sell the town on the clinic idea at a mass meeting. But just as Gillespie warned, the going is rough.

The lively town meeting give-and-take goes like this:

KILDARE: Cold figures prove we can make it work.

MAN: Let's hear your cold figures.

KILDARE: Well, suppose we took a 1,000 dimes in cash every week. That's $100. That would meet our clinic's expenses and pay our doctors enough to keep going.

MAN: A hundred dollars a week, eh. Well, why don't a couple of regular doctors settle down here and split the practice?

KILDARE: Because then the $100 a week would have to be met by the comparatively few people who need doctors. And those people haven't got that much.

SECOND MAN: Suppose I pay you boys for four weeks and suddenly I need an appendix operation. Am I going to get it for 40 cents?

FIRST MAN: Now, that's my point. It might work for sore throats or bunions. But you can't give 100 percent service to serious disease.

KILDARE: You're right. Not if there are too many of them. But one of the basic principles of this plan is the prevention of disease.

FIRST MAN: Prevention? So 10 cents includes miracles, too.

KILDARE: Not miracles. But just a few modern scientific precautions . . . First, fill in the stone well. Last year in that section there were four cases of typhoid— four of them fatal . . . Then, I have a list of livestock known to be infected. The town should order them destroyed immediately. Something must be done about the sanitary conditions of the grade schoolhouse. I'm not talking about your children's health—but their very lives. Then, there's Parker's Creek [for swimming]. That's been the breeding place for several deadly menaces in your community. Then, I hate to mention this. But really, gentlemen, Parkersville should stop spitting on the sidewalk.

But the townsfolk are suspicious of the "10-cent doctors" and their newfangled ideas. "My grandfather lived to be 90," one man says, "and he never even heard of them."

Winslow (Gene Lockhart), a prominent merchant, leads the people in protesting against Kildare's efforts to close the well and the ole swimming hole. Even after Kildare makes a special appeal to him, he turns a deaf ear. But Kildare notices Winslow's habit of holding his nose and blowing to clear his ears and suggests he be examined. Of course, Winslow turns the young medic down.

A week passes. Few patients have used the clinic. Its fate seems sealed. Then, Winslow suddenly collapses . . . His spine has become infected with a strain of streptococci. He has contracted the bacteria from swimming in the disease-ridden creek. As Kildare suspected, his habit of holding his nose and blowing was a symptom.

Kildare and his colleagues administer a new drug—sulfapyradine—and, with it, they save Winslow's life. The case, of course, turns the town's attitude around. And when the town council meets, it enthusiastically endorses the clinic.

Oops. Nearly forgot. Two subplots have been working right along in the background. First, Kildare has spotted a cancerous growth on Gillespie. But the stubborn old curmudgeon has insisted on ignoring it. Second, Kildare has agreed to elope with nurse Lamont. At the end, the two themes are tied up in a nice bow when Gillespie tells the couple that he plans to go west to take treatment from a cancer specialist. He suggests that if they put off their elopement, they will be able to take a month off for a honeymoon when he gets back. And they agree.

Those wedding bells were never sounded. Miss Day dropped out of the series to move up to big-budget films. Studio writers extricated her somewhat flamboyantly by having a truck roll over her just before she was to go to the altar in *Dr.*

Kildare's Wedding Day (1941). Before she floated up to cinema heaven where stars are made, she had one last moment before the cameras. "This is going to be much easier for me than it is for you," Miss Day told Ayres. "Poor sweet Jimmy." In more than one way, the words proved to be prophetic.

DR. KILDARE SERIES

1. *Internes Can't Take Money.* Paramount, 1937, Alfred Santell.
    Barbara Stanwyck, Joel McCrea (as Jimmie Kildare), Lloyd Nolan, Stanley
    Ridges, Lee Bowman, Barry Macollum, Irving Bacon, Gaylord (Steve) Pendleton,
    Pierre Watkin, Charles Lane, Priscilla Lawson, James Bush, Nick Lukats, An-
    thony Nace, Fay Holden. 77 minutes.

2. *Young Dr. Kildare.* MGM, 1938, Harold S. Bucquet.
    Lew Ayres (as Dr. James Kildare), Lionel Barrymore (as Dr. Leonard Gillespie),
    Lynne Carver, Nat Pendleton (as Joe Wayman), Jo Ann Sayers, Samuel S. Hinds
    (as Dr. Stephen Kildare), Emma Dunn (as Mrs. Martha Kildare), Walter Kings-
    ford (as Dr. Walter Carew), Truman Bradley, Monty Woolley, Pierre Watkin,
    Nella Walker. 81 minutes.

3. *Calling Dr. Kildare.* MGM, 1939, Harold S. Bucquet.
    Lew Ayres, Lionel Barrymore, Laraine Day (as nurse Molly Lamont), Nat Pen-
    dleton, Lana Turner, Samuel S. Hinds, Lynne Carver, Emma Dunn, Walter
    Kingsford, Alma Kruger (as nurse Molly Byrd), Harlan Briggs, Henry Hunter,
    Marie Blake, Phillip Terry, Johnny Walsh, Reed Hadley, Nell Craig (as nurse
    Parker), Marie Blake (as Sally, the switchboard operator). 86 minutes.

4. *The Secret of Dr. Kildare.* MGM, 1939, Harold S. Bucquet.
    Lew Ayres, Lionel Barrymore, Lionel Atwill, Helen Gilbert, Nat Pendleton,
    Laraine Day, Sara Haden, Samuel S. Hinds, Emma Dunn, Walter Kingsford,
    Grant Mitchell, Alma Kruger, Robert Kent, Marie Blake, Martha O'Driscoll,
    Nell Craig, George H. Reed (as Conover), Frank Orth. 83 minutes.

5. *Dr. Kildare's Strangest Case.* MGM, 1940, Harold S. Bucquet.
    Lew Ayres, Lionel Barrymore, Laraine Day, Shepperd Strudwick, Samuel S.
    Hinds, Emma Dunn, Nat Pendleton, Walter Kingsford, Alma Kruger, John
    Eldredge, Nell Craig, Marie Blake, Charles Waldron, George Lessey, Tom Col-
    lins, George H. Reed, Paul Porcasi, Horace McMahon, Frank Orth, Margaret
    Seddon, Fay Helm. 76 minutes.

6. *Dr. Kildare Goes Home.* MGM, 1940, Harold S. Bucquet.
    Lew Ayres, Lionel Barrymore, Laraine Day, Samuel S. Hinds, Gene Lockhart,
    John Shelton, Nat Pendleton, Emma Dunn, Alma Kruger, Walter Kingsford,
    Nell Craig, Cliff Danielson, Henry Wadsworth, Tom Collins, George H. Reed,
    Donald Briggs, Leona Maricle, Archie Twitchell, Marie Blake, Charles Trow-
    bridge. 78 minutes.

7. *Dr. Kildare's Crisis.* MGM, 1940, Harold S. Bucquet.
   Lew Ayres, Lionel Barrymore, Laraine Day, Robert Young, Nat Pendleton, Walter Kingsford, Alma Kruger, Bobs Watson, Nell Craig, George H. Reed, Frank Orth, Marie Blake, Horace McMahon, Ann Morriss, Frank Sully, Byron Foulger, Gladys Blake. 73 minutes.

8. *The People Vs. Dr. Kildare.* MGM, 1941, Harold S. Bucquet.
   Lew Ayres, Lionel Barrymore, Laraine Day, Bonita Granville, Alma Kruger, Red Skelton, Paul Stanton, Diana Lewis, Walter Kingsford, Nell Craig, Tom Conway, Marie Blake, Eddie Acuff, George H. Reed, Chick Chandler, Frank Orth, Gladys Blake, Grant Withers. 76 minutes.

9. *Dr. Kildare's Wedding Day.* MGM, 1941, Harold S. Bucquet.
   Lew Ayres, Lionel Barrymore, Laraine Day, Red Skelton, Alma Kruger, Samuel S. Hinds, Nils Asther, Walter Kingsford, Emma Dunn, Miles Mander, Nell Craig, Frank Orth, George H. Reed, Marie Blake, Margaret Seddon. 82 minutes.

10. *Dr. Kildare's Victory.* MGM, 1942, W. S. Van Dyke, II.
    Lew Ayres, Lionel Barrymore, Ann Ayars, Robert Sterling, Jean Rogers, Alma Kruger, Walter Kingsford, Nell Craig, Edward Gargan, Marie Blake, Frank Orth, George H. Reed, Barry Nelson, Eddie Acuff, Gus Schilling, Stuart Crawford, William Bakewell, Charlotte Wynters. 92 minutes.

11. *Calling Dr. Gillespie.* MGM, 1942, Harold S. Bucquet.
    Lionel Barrymore, Philip Dorn, Donna Reed, Mary Nash, Walter Kingsford, Philip Brown, Alma Kruger, Nell Craig, Nat Pendleton, Nana Bryant, Jonathan Hale, Charles Dingle. 82 minutes.

12. *Dr. Gillespie's New Assistant.* MGM, 1943, Willis Goldbeck.
    Lionel Barrymore, Van Johnson (as Dr. Randall (Red) Adams), Susan Peters, Richard Quine, Keye Luke (as Dr. Lee Wong Howe), Alma Kruger, Nat Pendleton, Horace (Stephen) McNally, Frank Orth, Walter Kingsford, Nell Craig, Marie Blake, George H. Reed, Ann Richards, Rose Hobart, Eddie Acuff. 86 minutes.

13. *Dr. Gillespie's Criminal Case.* MGM, 1943, Willis Goldbeck.
    Lionel Barrymore, Van Johnson, Donna Reed, Keye Luke, John Craven, Nat Pendleton, Alma Kruger, William Lundigan, Margaret O'Brien, Walter Kingsford, Marilyn Maxwell, Michael Duane, Henry O'Neill, Marie Blake, Frances Rafferty. 88 minutes.

14. *Three Men in White.* MGM, 1944, Willis Goldbeck.
    Lionel Barrymore, Van Johnson, Marilyn Maxwell, Keye Luke, Ava Gardner,

Alma Kruger, "Rags" Ragland, Nell Craig, Walter Kingsford, George H. Reed. 85 minutes.

15. *Between Two Women.* MGM, 1944, Willis Goldbeck.
Van Johnson, Lionel Barrymore, Gloria DeHaven, Keenan Wynn, Marilyn Maxwell, Alma Kruger, Marie Blake, Keye Luke, Nell Craig, Edna Holland, Lorraine Miller, Walter Kingsford, Tom Trout, Shirley Patterson. 83 minutes.

16. *Dark Delusion.* MGM, 1947, Willis Goldbeck.
Lionel Barrymore, James Craig, Lucille Bremer, Jayne Meadows, Warner Anderson, Henry Stephenson, Alma Kruger, Keye Luke, Art Baker, Lester Matthews, Marie Blake, Ben Lessy, Geraldine Wall, Nell Craig, George H. Reed, Mary Currier. 90 minutes.

Jean Hersholt as the folksy, dedicated Dr. Christian, a small-town doctor who cared.

DR. CHRISTIAN

The Courageous Dr. Christian

(1940)

Screenplay by Ring Lardner, Jr. and Ian McLellan Hunter. Film editor, Edward Mann. Camera, John Alton. Musical director, Constantin Bakaleinikoff. Art Director, Bernard Herzbrun. Producer, William Stephens. Associate producer, Monroe Shaff. Director, Bernard Vorhaus. Assistant director, Gordon S. Griffith. An RKO-Radio production. 67 minutes.

Dr. Paul Christian	JEAN HERSHOLT
Judy Price	DOROTHY LOVETT
Roy Davis	ROBERT BALDWIN
Dave Williams	TOM NEAL
Mrs. Hastings	MAUDE EBURNE
Mrs. Norma Stewart	VERA LEWIS
Harry Johnson	GEORGE MEADER
Jack Williams	BOBBY LARSON
Ruth Williams	BABETTE BENTLEY
Sam	REGINALD BARLOW
Martha	JACQUELINE DE RIVER
Tommy Wood	EDMUND GLOVER

Jane Wood	MARY DAVENPORT
Grandpa	EARLE ROSS
Mrs. Sam	SYLVIA ANDREWS
Mrs. Morris	CATHERINE COURTNEY
Sheriff	ALAN BRIDGE
Bailey	JAMES C. MORTON
Wilson	FRED HOLMES
Stanley	FRANK LA RUE
Jones	BUDD BUSTER
Harris	BRODERICK O'FARRELL
Pinball Addict	HEINIE CONKLIN

He was an overworked country doctor who still had time to listen to a doll's heart because he had a generous one of his own. He had a folksy bedside manner and an abiding interest in his patients that went beyond their symptoms. He not only cured their ills but helped them face their personal problems.

Dr. Paul Christian—the warm, kindly, compassionate general practitioner from the mythical town of Rivers End, Minnesota—a physician who cared. As played by the veteran actor Jean Hersholt, he was the embodiment of the American myth of the small-town doctor. "If anything goes wrong," he often reassured a distraught patient, "don't hesitate to call me."

If Dr. Christian's dedication seems ironic today, it is only because the realities of medical care have changed. Where Dr. Christian made house calls even when his patients didn't ask, many contemporary doctors have long since abandoned the practice. Where Dr. Christian was always available, today many patients can only reach an answering service. Where Dr. Christian rarely brought up the subject of fees or readily accepted a cream pie as barter for an unpaid bill, today's doctors are the country's highest paid professionals. They earn an average income of $40,000 a year—after expenses but before taxes.

But these inconsistencies did not exist in pre–World War II America, when *Dr. Christian* movies were in their heyday. The doctor's image then was not controversial. In fact, most of us can probably fondly recall a family doctor who in some way resembled the beloved Dr. Christian of the movies.

Hersholt played the rural sawbones so convincingly that he had a loyal following among the chronically ill and disabled. Even physicians admired him. When country doctors made trips to Hollywood, they often visited the RKO lot to see Hersholt. They liked to tell the folks back home they had shaken hands with Dr. Christian. Others wrote to him asking his advice on their problems. His universal acceptance stemmed from his homespun personality. "If Hersholt continues his gentle propaganda for another ten years," columnist John Crosby wrote, "he may yet succeed in imposing his art upon nature."

Dorothy Lovett, who plays the doctor's nurse, calls his attention to a newspaper article in *Dr. Christian Meets the Women* (1940). The comely brunette, constantly besieged by eligible young men, provided the series' romantic interest.

Lighting his pipe at his rolltop office desk, Dr. Christian leans forward to listen to a troubled patient (Barton Yarborough) in *They Meet Again* (1941), last of the six-picture series.

Hersholt, who in real life was an easy-going, friendly man, not unlike the screen doctor he portrayed, had a simple explanation for his success. "I'm not temperamental," he said. "That's the chief reason I've survived so long."

Born of theatrical parents in Copenhagen in 1886, Hersholt made his movie debut in 1905 in the first film produced in Denmark. In 1913, at the age of 27, he came to the United States and began acting in Hollywood films at a salary of $15 a week. Through a career that would span four decades, he played in nearly 500 movies—working in as many as 90 a year during the early days of the silent era. Originally, he appeared as a leering heavy. He portrayed sleazy characters in *Tess of the Storm Country* (1922) with Mary Pickford, in *Greed* (1924) and in *Stella Dallas* (1925). As a character actor, he ranked alongside Erich von Stroheim and Lon Chaney.

But his career took a new turn in 1936 when he played in *The Country Doctor*, a picture based on the life of Dr. Allan Dafoe, who became famous after he delivered the Dionne quintuplets. Hersholt, with his heavy build, stooped shoulders and tousled hair, used almost no makeup. And with his laconic Danish accent, he seemed perfectly cast as the rural French-Canadian doctor.

The part was a springboard to a succession of medical pictures culminating in the popular "Dr. Christian" radio program. It began as a 15-minute afternoon soap opera in November, 1937. Remember the theme? "Rainbow on the River." In the first episode, he performed an emergency appendectomy on a fisherman's son, with a kitchen knife.

The series quickly won a large following. It soon moved to prime time, an evening half-hour show on Wednesdays (CBS, 8:30 P.M., EST). One of the show's novelties was to invite listeners to send in scripts. The response was overwhelming. Producers claimed that some 8,000 manuscripts poured in during 1945 alone. First of the $2,000 prizes went to John League Oberg, who went on to write for the movies and television. The program, which continued for 16 years through 1953, claimed an audience of 20 million. And so, with that built-in following, it was only a matter of time before Dr. Christian made the transition to the screen.*

As busy as he was, acting consumed only a part of Hersholt's time. He had an abiding interest in the life work of Hans Christian Andersen. Hersholt not only compiled the largest collection of the author's letters, manuscripts and first editions outside the Royal Danish Museum, he translated Andersen's fairy tales and wrote his biography. He was also a leader in his own industry. For four years, he was president of the Academy of Motion Picture Arts and Sciences and he was honored with special Oscars in 1939 and 1941 for his activities on behalf of his

---

*A "Dr. Christian" TV series ran in 1956 with Macdonald Carey playing the doctor's nephew, Mark Christian. But the new Dr. Christian was a modern, sophisticated big city M.D. and the old nostalgia just wasn't there. The half-hour show quickly faded into oblivion.

Dr. Christian visits Mrs. Stewart (Vera Lewis), a wealthy widow who has designs on him in *The Courageous Dr. Christian*. In the end, she breaks her engagement but adopts the two squatter children.

Miss Merrick has suddenly collapsed and the good doctor is at her bedside with his nurse. The young lady's parents—Edgar Kennedy and Lelah Tyler —look on.

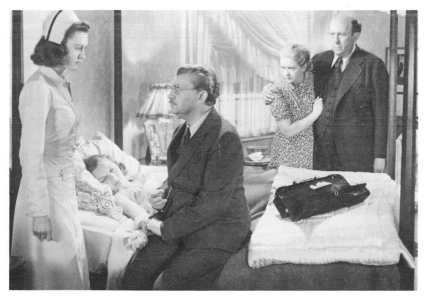

fellow actors. One of his achievements was helping build the Motion Picture Country House and Hospital, a home for old and ailing actors and film workers. In 1946, ten years before his death at the age of 69, Hersholt was knighted by King Christian X of Denmark for his humanitarian achievements.

But to millions of movie-goers, Hersholt will be best remembered as the pipe-smoking, chuckling Dr. Christian, who doled out counsel with medicine. In 1939, *Meet Dr. Christian* began the movie series.* The six pictures were distinctly low-budget fare, but among those in supporting roles were Fay Wray (who appeared as a nurse in one film), Edgar Kennedy, Neil Hamilton and Veda Ann Borg. Continuing characters, holdovers from the radio program, were played by Judy Price (Dorothy Lovett), the doc's pretty nurse; Roy Davis (Robert Baldwin), the local druggist who courted Judy; and Mrs. Hastings (Maude Eburne), Christian's capable housekeeper.

Critics found the pictures, at best, only mildly entertaining. However, families and radio fans enjoyed seeing their big-hearted hero sorting out the problems and the ills of his flock. And they turned out to see the Christian flicks whenever they turned up as second entries on double-feature bills. Of the half-dozen, the one that perhaps tested the good doctor's mettle most severely was *The Courageous Dr. Christian,* second in the series.

The picture opens with Dr. Christian trying to improve the conditions of squatters in a disease-ridden shanty-town on the outskirts of River's End. One of them is Dave Williams (Tom Neal), a youthful drifter scratching out a living while caring for his little brother Jack (Bobby Larson) and sister Ruth (Babette Bentley). When Dave's shack burns down, the doctor takes all three into his sprawling house. That is, until his housekeeper, Mrs. Hastings, finds a home for them with widow Stewart (Vera Lewis), who has a crush on Dr. Christian.

Meanwhile, Dr. Christian appeals to the River's End Council to move the squatters into better quarters. He proposes financing a modern housing project. The city fathers show little interest. "Those people are not like us," one councilman says. But they finally agree to back the plan if Christian can fulfill one stipulation. He must persuade the rich but penny-pinching Mrs. Stewart to donate her vacant lot in the center of town—a feat the council is convinced is impossible.

Undaunted, the doctor approaches Mrs. Stewart, who immediately misinterprets his charity plea as a bashful proposal. Using the two squatter children as messengers, she sends him the deed with a letter saying that if he accepts it, she will know he wants her to marry him. Naturally, the kids lose the letter. So when Christian tells the startled councilmen that the widow has, indeed, agreed to

*The films eventually dropped Christian's name from the title. Studio executives thought the public wouldn't be able to keep track of new films.

donate her land, he has also hooked himself to a ball and chain. In time he learns the whole truth. But after taking another look at the squalid settlement, he doesn't have the heart to leave them to their misery.

While all this serious stuff is going on, David is making a play for the doctor's pert nurse Judy. Pharmacist Roy Davis, fancying himself Judy's steady, doesn't like that one bit. He promptly gets into an argument with Dave and the hot-tempered Dave almost clobbers him. The word quickly spreads that Dr. Christian has brought a hoodlum to town. People are fearful that the housing project will bring in more of the same. Indignant businessmen withdraw their support. Council members follow suit.

But the squatters, who are suddenly close to having decent quarters for the first time, will not be denied now. When the town reneges on its commitment, Dave inspires the squatters to move their shacks to the widow's lot. The next day, the townspeople are outraged over this eyesore in the center of town. The council declares it a health menace. Rifle-bearing police move in to clean them out. Christian, too, is upset over the squatters' disregard for the law.

But suddenly something happens that changes the whole situation. Christian discovers that an epidemic of spinal meningitis has broken out among the squatters. Even as the police are closing in with drawn weapons, he faces them down and makes them back off. Taking personal charge, he quarantines the section and Dave, Judy, Roy, Mrs. Hastings and widow Stewart all pitch in to help him fight the spread of the highly infectious disease.

Christian's quick action pays off. He manages to contain the meningitis to the campsite. The near-tragedy has a sobering effect on the council. It is well aware of the stigma the town could have borne if its poor had died because of the neglect of its citizenry. Such an epidemic, they realize, would not likely occur under the project Christian has proposed. And so at its next meeting, the council members unanimously approve the housing units.

With victory in hand, Dave fades out of the picture, deserting little Ruth and Jack, who by now have captured the widow Stewart's tender heart. She decides she just wants to be a "mother" to the orphans and breaks her engagement to Dr. Christian, who now goes off on his never-ending round of house calls with a sprightlier step.

DR. CHRISTIAN SERIES

1. *Meet Dr. Christian.* RKO, 1939, Bernard Vorhaus
    Jean Hersholt (as Dr. Christian), Dorothy Lovett (as nurse Judy Price), Robert
    Baldwin (as pharmacist Roy Davis), Enid Bennett, Paul Harvey, Marcia Mae
    Jones, Jackie Moran, Maude Eburne (as Mrs. Hastings, the doctor's housekeeper),
    Frank Coghan, Jr., Patsy Lee Parsons, Sarah Edwards, John Kelly, Eddie Acuff.
    68 minutes.

2. *The Courageous Dr. Christian.* RKO, 1940, Bernard Vorhaus.
    Jean Hersholt, Dorothy Lovett, Robert Baldwin, Tom Neal, Maude Eburne, Vera
    Lewis, George Meader, Bobby Larson, Babette Bentley, Reginald Barlow, Jacque-
    line de River, Edmund Glover, Mary Davenport, Earle Ross, Catherine Court-
    ney, Alan Bridge, James C. Morton, Fred Holmes, Frank La Rue, Budd Buster,
    Broderick O'Farrell, Heinie Conklin. 67 minutes.

3. *Dr. Christian Meets The Women.* RKO, 1940, William McGann.
    Jean Hersholt, Dorothy Lovett, Edgar Kennedy (as grocer George Browning),
    Rod LaRocque, Frank Albertson, Marilyn (Lynn) Merrick, Maude Eburne, Veda
    Ann Borg, Lelah Tyler, William Gould, Heinie Conklin, Phyllis Kennedy, Bertha
    Priestley, Diedra Vale. 68 minutes.

4. *Remedy for Riches.* RKO, 1940, Erle C. Kenton.
    Jean Hersholt, Dorothy Lovett, Edgar Kennedy, Jed Prouty, Walter Catlett,
    Robert Baldwin, Warren Hull, Maude Eburne, Margaret McWade, Hallene Hill,
    Renie Riano, Barry Macollum, Lester Scharff (Sharpe), Prudence Penny, Stanley
    Blystone, Tom Herbert, Junior Coghlan, Maynard Holmes, Dick Rush, Edward
    Hearn. 60 minutes.

5. *Melody for Three.* RKO, 1941, Erle C. Kenton.
    Jean Hersholt, Fay Wray, Walter Woolf King, Schuyler Standish, Patsy Lee
    Parsons, Maude Eburne, Astrid Allwyn, Irene Ryan, Donnie Allen, Leon Tyler,
    Andrew Tombes, Irene Shirley, Alexander Leftwich. 67 minutes.

6. *They Meet Again* RKO, 1941, Erle C. Kenton.
    Jean Hersholt, Dorothy Lovett, Robert Baldwin, Maude Eburne, Neil Hamilton,
    Anne Bennett, Frank Melton, Barton Yarborough, Leon Tyler. 69 minutes.

Simon Sparrow (Dirk Bogarde) is taken in tow at St. Swithan's Hospital by perennial med student Richard Grimsdyke (Kenneth More). Grimsdyke isn't short on brains. He never wants to graduate because his grandmother has left him a thousand pounds a year—but only as long as he is a student. Scene is from *Doctor in the House* (1954).

DOCTOR ...

Doctor in the House
(1954)

Screenplay by Nicholas Phipps based on the novel by Richard Gordon. Directed by Ralph Thomas. Produced by Betty E. Box. A Republic release of the J. Arthur Rank presentation in Technicolor. 92 minutes.

Simon Sparrow	DIRK BOGARDE
Richard Grimsdyke	KENNETH MORE
Tony Benskin	DONALD SINDEN
Taffy Evans	DONALD HOUSTON
Joy	MURIEL PAVLOW
Isobel	KAY KENDALL
Sir Lancelot Spratt	JAMES ROBERTSON JUSTICE
Stella	SUZANNE CLOUTIER
Dean	GEOFFREY KEEN
Briggs	GEORGE COULOURIS
Sister Virtue	JEAN TAYLOR-SMITH
Jessup	HARRY LOCKE
May	ANN GUDRUN
Rigor Mortis	JOAN SIMS

Mrs. Cooper	MAUREEN PRYOR
Milly Groaker	SHIRLEY EATON
Magistrate	NICHOLAS PHIPPS
Jane	LISA GASTONI
Barbara	SHIRLEY BURNISTON

Sir Lancelot Spratt, the big, blustering, bearded professor of surgery, is beginning grand rounds at St. Swithan's Hospital. Grand rounds is the time-honored practice of teaching medicine by having students follow their professor as he checks his patients in a ward.

"Now, you just hold still, old fellow," Sir Lancelot says to an apprehensive bedridden man. "I'm just going to discuss your case with these—uh—young doctors here. You! Examine his abdomen."

A frightened student begins probing his stomach tentatively.

"Whoooop!" Sir Lancelot roars. "Take that grubby fist away. The first rule of diagnosis, gentlemen—eyes first and most. Hands, next and least. And tongue not at all. Look! Have you looked?"

"Yes sir."

"See anything?"

"No sir."

"Very good, carry on," Sir Lancelot says.

The student begins kneading the patient's stomach.

"Gently, man, gently," Sir Lancelot explodes. "You're not making bread. To be a successful surgeon, you need the eye of a hawk, the heart of a lion, and the hands of a lady . . . found it?"

"Yes sir."

"Well, what is it?"

"A lump."

"Well, what do you make of it? Is it kidney? Is it liver? Is it spleen? Is it dangerous?"

The patient's eyes are popping. His lips are quivering. Beads of perspiration dot his forehead.

"Don't worry, my good man," Sir Lancelot says. "You won't understand our medical talk."

"You," Sir Lancelot darts a glance at another student. In a voice slightly lower than a foghorn, he asks, "What are we going to do about it?"

"Ummm."

"Cut it out, man! Cut it out! Where shall we make the incision?"

The student puts his finger on the spot and indicates a two-inch incision.

"Nothing like large enough," Sir Lancelot grumps. "Keyhole surgery. Damnable. Couldn't see anything." He draws an imaginary incision stretching across the man's full abdomen. "Like this," he bellows.

The patient's color now seems to blend with the bedsheets.

"Now don't worry. This is nothing whatever to do with you," Sir Lancelot says to the man. "You," turning to another cowed student. "When we've got through the skin, what's the first substance we shall find?"

"Subcutaneous matter."

"Quite right. And then we come across the surgeon's worst enemy, which is what?"

Silence.

"Speak up man."

Total silence.

"Blood, you numbskull!" Sir Lancelot roars. "You cut a patient, he bleeds until the processes of nature form a clot and stop it. This interval is known scientifically as the bleeding time."

Sir Lancelot spots a student who seems to have his thoughts elsewhere.

"You!" Sir Lancelot darts a question. "What's the bleeding time?"

"Ten past ten, sir," the student responds.

This is Britain's version of the medical profession as seen in the hilarious and highly successful *Doctor* series. The broad satire is poles apart from the U.S. way of portraying doctors. Where American movies, until recently,* have taken a staid, serious, respectful approach toward physicians, the English have treated the profession with tongue firmly in cheek.

The reason goes to the heart of their vastly contrasting concept of health care. America's doctors have traditionally relied on a private practice, fee-for-service system, resisting all attempts at government control. To the British, who began socialized medicine in 1948, a doctor is a public servant. Because he is a salaried government employee, he usually makes no more than comparable civil service officials. And so he is far from a sacred cow.

Richard Gordon, the pen name of the London physician who wrote the *Doctor* books upon which the film series was based, feels there is another transatlantic difference—an historical one:

In the formative years of U.S. society—say after the Civil War—the doctor in America was already becoming a respected figure. But England has for some long time known the local apothecary, or doctor, who was never regarded as great shakes (rightly, by his results). Even in early Victorian times, he was expected to enter the better houses via the tradesmen's entrance.

*As in *M*A*S*H, The Hospital* and *Such Good Friends.*

Dr. Sparrow and Dr. Bingham (Michael Medwin) are intrigued by the most interesting nose to turn up in casualty (the emergency room). Nurse Nan (Shirley Eaton) is fascinated by its color. Scene is from *Doctor at Large* (1957).

One consolation for a tired doctor is a pretty nurse. Here Simon helps Nurse Nan (Miss Eaton, later of *Goldfinger* fame), break an egg in *Doctor at Large*.

I've given much thought to this [the American attitude], and decided the answer is very complicated or very simple. I fancy that the U.S., being a science-dominated sort of society, gives much more respect to the scientist than in the United Kingdom. We have a cheerful skepticism toward doctors and suchlike, as, for a vague example, the American has toward [royal] titles.

The whole idea of a doctor as a fictional hero seems to be a recent development. In a January 16, 1972 *New York Times Magazine* article, Dr. Michael J. Halberstam points out that the doctor as a romantic hero did not exist in nineteenth-century pop fiction:

> Decent as he might have been, there wasn't anything magical about his work. Patients lived or died regardless of his intervention.
>
> It was not until the successive scientific triumphs of the 20th century were added to those of the 19th—anesthesia, asepsis, immunization, surgery—that the public saw in the physician a figure to rival the priest and alchemist of medieval literature —someone with the power of life and death. Doctor-heroes are both a cause and effect of society's increased secularism. We tend to worry more about our mortal bodies than our immortal souls, and the physician is the guardian of that body.

Whatever the reason, it is certain that two distinct concepts exist. Where America's Dr. Kildare is portrayed as brilliant, dedicated and idealistic, his British counterpart is often seen as bumbling, bored, even mercenary. If this overdraws the point, it is nonetheless irreverently funny and in the end makes the English M.D. emerge the more human for his foibles. Dirk Bogarde, who starred in all but one of the five-picture *Doctor* series, thought the movies actually turned out to be a public relations boost for the medical profession. "The *Doctor* films made people less frightened to go to the hospitals," he said.

The series was based on the best-selling novel *Doctor in the House*, which tickled the British funnybone with an account of the escapades of four internes at a London hospital. Gordon, who keeps his real name secret to avoid criticism from his peers, wrote the book the summer after he graduated from medical school. Short of cash and in need of a vacation, he took a job as a doctor aboard a cargo ship bound from Britain to Australia. He did his writing during his many free hours on the voyage. The resultant novel—it was to be followed by a series of *Doctor* books that would be translated into 19 languages—provided the basis for a film that broke all box office records in English theatres.

That first *Doctor* film, which played to smaller but equally appreciative audiences in America, inspired four other lighthearted medical tales—well-sprinkled with amply proportioned actresses. A lithe, bosomy Brigitte Bardot added spice to *Doctor at Sea* (1956) and Shirley Eaton, who was to become Goldfinger's gilded girl, was the sexpot in *Doctor at Large* (1957). *Doctor in Love* (1962), the fourth offering, told of young physician Simon Sparrow's remarkable affinity for romantic attachments. And in *Doctor in Distress* (1964), Sir Lancelot pursues a svelte physiotherapist.*

Bogarde played earnest, fumbling Simon Sparrow in all but one picture and the series catapulted him to the height of popularity. In 1953, before the *Doctor* series began, Bogarde had already climbed to a position among the top-ten favorites at the British box office. But by 1958, after he had made three *Doctor* movies, he was named Britain's number-one star in an audience poll.

Thereafter, his roles steadily increased in importance and his film image changed from lightweight to serious actor. He scored personal triumphs in *Victim* (1961), *The Servant* (1963), *Darling* (1965) and most recently *Death In Venice* (1971). His characterizations in *The Servant* and *Darling* won him British Academy Awards.

But the actor whose career was most affected by the series was robust, bearlike James Robertson Justice, who played the fearful chief of surgery. The 250-pound, six-foot-four-inch Scotsman had held 64 different jobs—none of which required acting ability. A graduate of England's Marlboro College and Germany's Bonn University (Ph.D.), he began traveling around the world during the Depression. He was a gold miner, foreign correspondent, coal-barge mate, truck driver, lumberjack, naturalist and ice-rink manager, among others.

His acting career began by chance when a man in a London bar suggested he go into the movies. "Since I was out of work at the time," he said, "I agreed to give it a try. Next morning, I showed up at one of Mr. [J. Arthur] Rank's studios, was introduced to a director who turned out to be an old friend . . . And here I am."

His movie career, which began with *Fiddlers Three* in 1944, includes *Captain Horatio Hornblower* (1951), Disney's *Sword and The Rose* (1953) and *Rob Roy* (1953). But he was so perfectly cast as Sir Lancelot that he became the mainstay of the *Doctor* series. To many Britons, he represented the epitome of the gruff but hearty hospital head-surgeon.

Like most series, the *Doctor* pictures ran a downhill course. The humor got progressively frailer and more familiar. In the end, they aptly named their last effort *Doctor in Distress*. Quipped *Time:* "Anyone for euthanasia?"

But *Doctor in the House,* the first and funniest, was a bright, intelligently scripted gem. If it did nothing else, it showed that medicine was not a sacrosanct profession and the halls of a hospital were not always grim. They could become a setting for a comedy that would have audiences laughing on both sides of the

*The movies evolved into a half-hour television comedy, "Doctor in the House," which told about the exploits and misadventures of high-spirited medical students and young doctors. The series, produced in England, starred Barry Evans. It came to the United States in 1971 after running in Britain and Australia.

The fetching young thing smiling at Dr. Sparrow is—believe it or not—Brigitte Bardot. They were together in *Doctor at Sea* (1956), second of the British series that dispensed medicine with mirth.

James Robertson Justice, who played a tyrannical surgeon in most of the series, appears here as a gruff sea captain in *Doctor at Sea*.

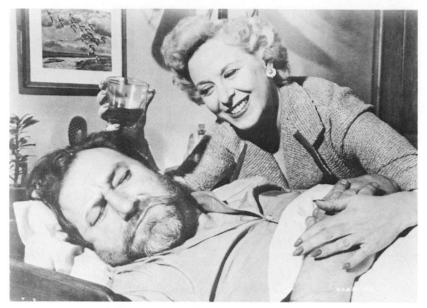

Justice can dish it out, but can he take it? Brenda de Banzie plays nurse in
Doctor at Sea.

Mylene Demongeot is a shapely physiotherapist pursued by Justice in *Doctor
in Distress* (1964), last in the series. Bogarde is at right.

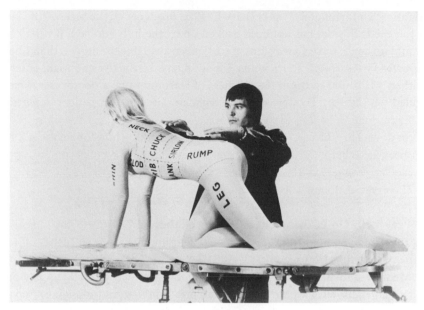

Barry Evans' surgical experiences have given him nightmares—making him dream he's become a butcher.

Here's the rowdy, irreverent group of residents who make up the TV version of the *Doctor in the House* series. First row: Barry Evans. Second row: Jonathan Lynn (left) and George Layton (right). Third row: (left to right) Simon Cuff, Robin Nedwell and Geoffrey Davies.

Atlantic. "Unfortunately," said Betty E. Box, producer of the series, "the laughter [on the U.S. side] has not been backed up by the lolly [dollar]. If it had been, I would no doubt have a great deal more finance available for movies than I have."

Doctor in the House starts when Simon, a shy, serious young man, enters St. Swithan's Hospital to begin the business of learning to be a doctor. His first day is filled with terror. To start with, he wanders into the out-patient department.

"Excuse me."

"Sit down here, please," snaps a busy nurse, mistaking him for a patient. "Have you been here before?"

"No."

"Have you a doctor's letter?"

"No."

"Very well. Go in there and take your clothes off."

After Simon escapes from the super-efficient nursing staff, he rushes off to the dean's welcoming lecture.

"Medical students were described by the novelist Charles Dickens as a parcel of lazy, idle fellows who are always smoking, drinking and lounging," says the proper, ultra-conservative dean (Geoffrey Keen). "That is unfortunately still true."

Of course, Simon is immediately taken in tow by three champion malingerers. The lecherous Tony Benskin (Donald Sinden) thinks the nursing staff is there for the students' comfort rather than the patients'. Taffy Evans (Donald Houston) devotes more time and energy to rugby football than to surgery. And Richard Grimsdyke (Kenneth More) dedicates himself to failing exams. His grandmother has willed him 1,000 pounds a year as long as he is in school—and not a farthing thereafter.

Grimsdyke has been a student so long he practically knows the dean's welcoming talk by heart. "Three minutes shorter than usual," he tells Simon. After the lecture, he introduces Simon to the local pub, run by a man the students call "Padre." Explains Grimsdyke: "In the hospital, patients might get a bit upset if the doctor goes to the pub for a quick one. On the other hand, if he says he's going to chapel for half an hour, they're quite surprised."

Simon soon finds the problems of a would-be doctor are not limited to medical school. When he moves into a boarding house, Milly Groaker (Shirley Eaton), the landlady's winsome daughter, soon gets romantic notions. "I always think it's nice to have a doctor in the house," she says. "I saw a lovely film about a doctor once. He operated on a beautiful girl and married her." A few moments later, Milly knocks at Simon's door complaining of a sore foot. She starts hiking up her dress and pulling off her stockings. Simon shoos her out.

The next day, Simon goes for his books, medical supplies and his first stethoscope. "I think that's a little old for you, sir," the clerk tells him as Simon mulls over the portentous purchase. "What about this one? Perhaps you'd care to try it for size? Oh, yes, That's very much more *you,* sir. Comfy? Comfy?"

But Simon almost wishes he had never gotten a chance to use it when he runs into a fiery head-nurse (Jean Taylor-Smith) at the beginning of his clinical training. "You will replace the bed clothes neatly," she barks. "You will not walk upon any part of the floor that has been recently polished. And you will not talk to nurses on any but strictly professional matters."

As Simon's training begins, the story becomes more a series of comic episodes than a coherent narrative. And the jokes come thick and fast:

• Simon's first patient is a knowledgeable hypochondriac. As Simon starts to take his pulse, the man tells him it's 76. "I just took it," he says. When Simon examines his chest, the patient advises him it's his stomach that's troubling him. But it is when Simon asks his symptoms that he feels most helpless. "I have," the patient says, matter of factly, "hydroephrosis, nephrolyphrosis and attacks of renal cholic."

• "Don't forget," says Sir Lancelot, "if you feel faint, fall backwards, not across the patient." Just before he makes the first incision, Sir Lancelot says, "Hang on to your swabs, gentlemen. You can cut the patient's throat while he is under an anesthetic and nobody will mind. But if you leave anything inside, you will be in the Sunday papers in no time."

• After a football match with a rival medical school, Simon and his chums get hauled before the courts and school authorities. They have "borrowed" an ambulance to retrieve their stolen school mascot—a stuffed gorilla. But Sir Lancelot, who years ago donated the mascot when he was a student, comes to their rescue by secretly paying their stiff fine. He saves the day, too, when Simon falls through a skylight, sneaking a nurse back after hours, and crashes into bed with the head-nurse. The dean wants to expel Simon. But Sir Lancelot reminds the dean that "another student" once introduced a carthorse into the nurses' home and induced a nurse to play Lady Godiva. "Who was the student?" a member of the hospital board asks. Says Sir Lancelot: "I expect I'm the only person who hasn't forgotten." The dean suddenly changes his mind about Simon and gives him a light fine.

In final exams, Simon is called on to diagnose a hospitalized patient. By a coincidence, he gets his old hypochondriac friend, who promptly outlines all his newest ailments before the examiner comes in. When Simon ticks off his rare symptoms one by one, the examiner is amazed. "Splendid," he exclaims.

And so end the zany trials and tribulations of Simon's adventures on the trail of his coveted M.D. degree. As for Simon's pals, Grimsdyke and Taffy Evans run true to form, fail and resign themselves to another year at school. But Tony, the ladies' man, fools everyone by winning his diploma. And he gets a choice assignment to boot—assistant medical officer in a women's prison.

1. *Doctor in the House.* Republic, J. Arthur Rank, 1954, Ralph Thomas.
   Dirk Bogarde (as Simon Sparrow), Muriel Pavlow (as Joy), Kenneth More, Donald Sinden, Kay Kendall, James Robertson Justice (as Sir Lancelot Spratt), Donald Houston, Suzanne Cloutier, Geoffrey Keen, George Coulouris, Jean Taylor-Smith, Harry Locke, Ann Gudrun, Joan Sims, Maureen Pryor, Shirley Eaton, Geoffrey Sumner, Nicholas Phipps. 92 minutes.

2. *Doctor at Sea.* Republic, J. Arthur Rank, 1956, Ralph Thomas.
   Dirk Bogarde, Brigitte Bardot, Brenda de Banzie, James Robertson Justice, Maurice Denham, Michael Medwin, Hubert Gregg, James Kenney, Raymond Huntley, Geoffrey Keen, George Coulouris, Noel Purcell, Jill Adams, Joan Sims. 93 minutes.

3. *Doctor at Large.* Universal, J. Arthur Rank, 1957, Ralph Thomas.
   Dirk Bogarde, Muriel Pavlow, Donald Sinden, James Robertson Justice, Shirley Eaton, Derek Farr, Michael Medwin, Freda Bamford, Abe Barker, Martin Benson, Cyril Chamberlain, John Chandos, Edward Chapman, Peggy Ann Clifford, Campbell Cotts, George Coulouris, Judith Furse, Junia Crawford, Gladys Henson, Anne Heywood, Ernest Jay, Lionel Jeffries, Mervyn Johns, Geoffrey Keen, Dilys Laye, Harry Locke, Terence Longdon, A. E. Matthews, Guy Middleton. 104 minutes.

4. *Doctor in Love.* Governor, J. Arthur Rank, 1962, Ralph Thomas.
   Michael Craig, Virginia Maskell, Leslie Phillips, James Robertson Justice, Carole Lesley, Reginald Beckwith, Nicholas Phipps, Liz Fraser, Joan Sims, Ambrosine Philpotts, Irene Handl, Nicholas Parsons, Moira Redmond, Ronnie Stevens, Fenella Fielding. 97 minutes.

5. *Doctor in Distress.* Governor, J. Arthur Rank, 1964, Ralph Thomas.
   Dirk Bogarde, Samantha Eggar, James Robertson Justice, Mylene Demongeot, Donald Houston, Barbara Murray, Dennis Price, Jill Adams, Timothy Bateson, Jessie Evans, Fenella Fielding, Frank Finlay, Michael Flanders, Derek Fowlds, Pauline Jameson, Bill Kerr, Ann Lynn, Joe Robinson, Madge Ryan, David Weston, Paul Whitsun-Jones. 102 minutes.

Betsy Booth (Judy Garland) and Andy are down at the corner drugstore for a chocolate soda. It's all innocent fun because they're just good pals. But Lana Turner, Andy's current flame, thinks otherwise. The picture, *Love Finds Andy Hardy* (1938), was the first of three series movies to pair Judy and Mickey.

ANDY HARDY

Love Finds Andy Hardy
(1938)

Screenplay by William Ludwig. Based on the stories by Vivian R. Brotherton, taken from the characters created by Aurania Rouverol. Songs: "Meet the Beat of My Heart" and "It Never Rains but It Pours" by Mack Gordon and Harry Revel; and "In Between" by Roger Edens. Camera, Lester White. Film Editor, Ben Lewis. Directed by George B. Seitz and presented by Metro-Goldwyn-Mayer. 90 minutes.

Judge James Hardy	LEWIS STONE
Andrew Hardy	MICKEY ROONEY
Betsy Booth	JUDY GARLAND
Marian Hardy	CECILIA PARKER
Mrs. Hardy	FAY HOLDEN
Polly Benedict	ANN RUTHERFORD
Aunt Milly	BETSY ROSS CLARKE
Cynthia Potter	LANA TURNER
Augusta	MARIE BLAKE
Dennis Hunt	DON CASTLE
Jimmy MacMahon	GENE REYNOLDS

Lionel Barrymore, who played Judge Hardy in *A Family Affair* (1937), the first *Hardy* movie, talks with son Andy (Mickey Rooney) and daughter Marian (Cecilia Parker) in his study. Lewis Stone later took over the elder Hardy's role.

Judge Hardy extends a firm handclasp to Eric Linden in another scene from *A Family Affair*. Other Hardy family members looking on are Joan Hardy (Julie Haydon), Marian, Aunt Milly (Sara Haden), and Mrs. Hardy (Spring Byington, later replaced by Fay Holden).

Mrs. Tompkins	MARY HOWARD
"Beezy"	GEORGE BREAKSTON
Peter Dugan	RAYMOND HATTON
Bill collector	FRANK DARIEN
Judge	RAND BROOKS
Court attendant	ERVILLE ALDERSON

He was everybody's kid brother—cocky, wisecracking, always getting into trouble but happy-go-lucky and full of life. He was crazy about cars and just beginning to get crazy about girls. He was a judge's son. But he was no judge of money or of manners or modesty, for that matter. Still, he had his dad's virtue of openness and honesty. And somehow, that made up for it all.

He was, of course, Andy Hardy, the teen-ager who sums up small-town America of the 1930s—at least, as it was romantically depicted by Metro-Goldwyn-Mayer.

In those halcyon days, houses had porches, cars had running boards and children walked to school. Kids thought "pot" was what Mom cooked in. A "joint" was a rundown establishment. And a "demonstration" was when an auto salesman took you for a ride in a new model.

No one in Andy's hometown of Carvel (population: 25,000) then dreamed there would one day be freedom rides, sit-ins, flag-burnings, hippies or women's lib. It was a time of normalcy. And Andy and his family are a reminder of that lost world, that mainstream U.S.A. that has faded into oblivion.

But these middle-class qualities struck a responsive chord even in their own era. After the illusion-shattering Depression years, MGM production chief Louis B. Mayer figured movie-goers would want to see pictures that showed how "nice" American life was. And, he thought, they would particularly like wholesome stories close to their own everyday lives and simple tastes. So in 1937, MGM made *A Family Affair,* a low-budget comedy about a typical small-town family. When the movie met with modest success, the studio filmed two more pictures around the same domestic theme— *You're Only Young Once* (1937) and *Judge Hardy's Children* (1938). More sophisticated reviewers found them maudlin and trite. But they made money.

Then came *Love Finds Andy Hardy* (1938), which tripled the box office of its predecessors. From then on, MGM launched the series in earnest. Through 1946, the studio made 14 *Hardy* films. They grossed more than $73 million, drew more fan mail than that received by the industry's five top stars and made Mickey Rooney the nation's number-one box office attraction.*

*In 1958, an unsuccessful attempt was made to revive the series. Rooney played Andy as a successful lawyer returning to Carvel in *Andy Hardy Comes Home.* His own boy, Teddy, 8, played his screen son. But America had entered the space age. To a more discerning audience reared on a decade of television, the old formula seemed dated.

But Mayer—who took a personal interest in the pictures to the extent that he even rewrote some scenes—was careful to see that they never outgrew their homey, mediocre format. When someone suggested that a first-rate director be brought in, Mayer quickly vetoed the idea. "If you had a stronger director," he said, "the films wouldn't be as good." He was, of course, right.

If the Hardy pictures hit the popularity jackpot, then success brought some headaches, too. Because of the widespread public interest, the studio had to go to great pains to see that the films were as authentic as possible in every detail. For example, screen writers gave close attention to such trivial items as the amount of money the Hardys paid for a car, wallpaper for the sitting room, new clothes for an out-of-town trip.

They even figured out Judge Hardy's salary so the family budget could be planned accordingly. Based on the average earnings for men of his age and circumstances, it was put at $70 a week, or about $3,500 a year. (If that seems low, remember this was during the Depression years of the 1930s.)

An ironclad test of every story conference was—could this happen to the average family? Other ground rules were: (1) the Hardys could never go into debt; (2) the judge and his wife never disagreed in front of the children; (3) the Hardy children got free voice in any family discussion but they never interrupted their parents.

Who were the Hardys?

At the head of the family, there was Judge James Hardy, white-haired and strict but kindly and understanding, too. Lionel Barrymore played him in the first film. When he became ill, Lewis Stone replaced him and then continued in the role for the rest of the series.

The judge was a solid citizen, an establishment man, a pillar of the community. He was also old-fashioned, square, a bit on the fuddy-duddy side. "You can say that again," Andy tells him, agreeing with him in *The Courtship of Andy Hardy* (1942). "Why should I say it again," the judge asks. "Didn't you understand me the first time?"

Still, he was a born psychologist. And he had a way with people—particularly in court.

In *Andy Hardy's Private Secretary* (1941), police haul a confused runaway into court. The six-foot stringbean says he left home because he towers over his eighth-grade classmates. He can't stand their razzing. "I know a man who was six feet tall at your age who split rails to earn a meager education," the judge says. "His name was Abraham Lincoln." The boy's eyes brighten. Somehow, you know he's going to make it now.

Stone, a veteran character actor who was considered the Clark Gable of 1915, was soon typecast in the role. When MGM had him play a drunken ambulance-chaser in *The Chaser* (1938), so many movie-goers complained about the fine old judge degrading himself that the studio had to yank the film from general distribution. It cost $150,000. In *Stolen Heaven* (1938), Stone played a drunken old pianist whose memory is failing. "As soon as the old musician appeared," Stone said, "the audience all said, 'Ho, ho, ho. There's Judge Hardy. It spoiled the show.' " Thereafter the studio cast him only in *Hardy* films. He never complained. He got a whopping salary and only had to work 12 weeks each year to make two movies.

Mrs. Hardy has an important place, too. As played by Fay Holden,* she was the typical American mom—warm, sympathetic, cheerful, lovable and, of course, a marvelous cook. One virtue she shared with the judge—and perhaps it was the Hardys' single most important character trait—was out-and-out integrity.

In *The Hardys Ride High* (1939), they are about to inherit a fortune when the judge and his wife learn their ancestor was only an *adopted* son. The will stipulates that they must be blood relatives or they get nothing. But they can easily burn the evidence, an old book, which traces the family record, and a yellowed photograph.

"You and I are the only two people in the world who know," Judge Hardy tells his wife. ". . . It's two million dollars. If I put this book and that picture in the fire, the money is ours."

"But James," Mrs. Hardy says. "Wouldn't that be dishonest?"

"You want me to tell them we won't take the money?"

"Well, that's what you've already decided to do, isn't it?" she replies, giving her husband full credit for what clearly is her initiative. ". . . We'd never be the Hardy family with two million dollars."

There was a big sister, Marion (Cecilia Parker), just beginning to suffer all the exquisite tortures of young love; Aunt Milly (Sara Haden and Betsy Ross Clarke), a maiden schoolteacher who lives with the family; and Polly Benedict (Ann Rutherford and Margaret Marquis), Andy's often-jilted but always faithful girlfriend. MGM also used the series to give exposure to budding contract actresses.** Esther Williams and Kathryn Grayson debuted in the *Hardy* pictures. And Lana Turner, Susan Peters and Donna Reed made early career appearances.

But unquestionably, it was Rooney who was the key character. His exuberant portrayal of Andy was instrumental in making the series so popular. Curiously, his choice was an afterthought. As Miss Rutherford recalls, a juvenile actor named Frankie Thomas was almost picked for the role. "Then, they decided to find a boy who was smaller than me," she said. "Carey Wilson [the producer] said

*Spring Byington played Judge Hardy's wife in *A Family Affair* (1937). But Miss Holden took the part in all subsequent films.

**"There was, in fact, a standard studio recipe," Rooney wrote in his book, *I. E. An Autobiography.* "Take one young actress, pluck her eyebrows, cap her teeth, shape her hairline, pad as required and throw her into the ring with Andy Hardy. Then wait and see. If the public responded, the starlet became a star."

every boy always had a girl who was taller. And that was always funnier. So they looked around the studio and tested Mickey. He was three inches shorter than me. [Rooney was five-foot, three-inches tall.] So they gave him the part. It wasn't anything of a part. But Mickey stole the picture."

It isn't hard to see why. Rooney was already a veteran actor. He had started his career when he was only 18 months old. Dressed in a miniature tuxedo, he played in his parents' burlesque routine. He trouped as Joe Yule, Jr., his real name. He broke into movies acting in silent shorts, rechristened and playing Mickey McGuire, a cigar-chewing, derby-sporting comic strip character created by Fontaine Fox.

When MGM put him in the *Hardy* series, his dynamic vitality and Huck Finn looks made him seem perfectly cast. His career began a meteorlike rise. Before he was 20, he was reportedly earning $300,000 a year. In 1938, he got a special Academy Award for "bringing to the screen the spirit and personification of youth." He was the leading box office attraction for the next three years, from 1939 to 1941. In 1942, the series itself won an Oscar for its achievement in representing the American way of life.

Bags of mail poured into MGM addressed to "Andy Hardy." Mickey told his fans that Andy never strayed far from his thoughts. "It's funny how a character can grow on a feller," Rooney said. "I depend on Andy all the time. When I'm not sure whether I should do a certain thing, I ask myself, 'Would Andy do it?' And if Andy won't do it, I won't.' "

But there was a comic irony to all this. Actually, the celluloid Rooney and his real-life counterpart were poles apart. While on screen, he was America's teen-age idol; off screen he was betting on horses, cultivating a taste for hard liquor, carousing with Hollywood starlets.

In his autobiography, Rooney called his life a classic case of too much too soon. Deep down, he realized that his immense popularity had to be ephemeral. "All of this time, I knew some day it would have to end," he said, looking back reflectively. ". . . How soon they forget."

His decline began when he outgrew juvenile roles. And the downhill journey went fast. The war ended his Andy Hardy parts. A quarrel with Mayer ended his lucrative association with MGM.

But Rooney's free-wheeling private life was the key to his fall. His extracurricular activities were reported in the press and the stories ruined his image with the public. "He lost his innocence and their respect," said Jon Tuska, executive editor of *Views and Reviews* magazine. "Mayer knew the importance of these ingredients and sought to control Mickey while he was at MGM. That's what they fought about. By the time Mickey realized that Mayer was right, it was too late for his career."

Rooney's ventures in independent productions proved disastrous for the most

Ann Rutherford, playing Andy's loyal but often neglected girl Polly Benedict, hears the latest football news hot off the gridiron. The movie is *The Hardys Ride High* (1939), sixth in the series.

Esther Williams was a 19-year-old MGM starlet in 1942 when she appeared in *Andy Hardy's Double Life,* her first film.

Andy gives a steno pad to winsome Kathryn Grayson, making her movie debut in *Andy Hardy's Private Secretary* (1941).

part. So did his marriages, always the subject of sensational publicity. In 1941 when he married Ava Gardner—she was his first wife—MGM tried to send a press agent on their honeymoon. They were divorced in 16 months. Mickey married six more times. His mates included Betty Jane Rase, Miss Birmingham of 1944, and the late actress Martha Vickers, whom he married in 1949. When he went to the altar for the fifth time, the *New York Daily News* headlined: "Half-Pint Takes a Fifth."

All these years, his drinking and free-spending continued. He once dropped $55,000 in a single night at Las Vegas. Ultimately, there was bankruptcy. He said he made a career total of $12 million. But in 1962, he filed a bankruptcy petition claiming assets of $1,500 and debts of $350,000.

The setback proved to be temporary, however. With his boundless energy, Rooney started a comeback. He took character parts. And by 1965, he was reported to have put his financial affairs in the black. One of his recent ventures was to start an acting school in Fort Lauderdale, Florida. He also starred in "W. C.," a stage musical based on the life of W. C. Fields. But it folded before reaching Broadway.

Only time can tell what the ultimate assessment of his checkered career will be. But one thing is certain. Nothing can efface the screen immortality of his adolescent roles in such classics as *Captains Courageous* (1937), *Boys Town* (1938), *Babes in Arms* (1939), *The Human Comedy* (1943) and *National Velvet* (1944). And, of course, who can forget Mickey in his first picture with Judy Garland—*Love Finds Andy Hardy* (1938)? It sums up the basic appeal of the most popular series of Hollywood's golden era.

As the picture opens, 15-year-old Andy is buying his first car. The price is $20. He puts down $12 and owes a balance of $8, which he must pay before he can drive the jalopy off the lot. He needs the second-hand auto to take his best girl, Polly Benedict (Ann Rutherford), to the big Christmas Eve Dance. But when he sees Polly that day, she has bad news. Her family is going out of town for the holidays. She won't be able to go with Andy.

"And me with a new evening dress that has a low neck and practically no sleeves," Polly sighs.

"Polly," Andy says, still not giving up. "At the Country Club, there are a lot of swell little places where you can sneak out between dances."

"Really," Polly says primly. "I think we're getting much too old for that sort of thing—hugging and kissing."

"I ain't never gonna get too old for huggin' and kissin'," Andy chuckles. "Besides, you didn't act no nine years old last night on the porch yourself."

"Why, Andrew Hardy," Polly exclaims. "You kissed me last night by force."

"Well, it's good that way too."

Even though Polly can't make the dance, Andy wants his car in the worst way. And he starts trying to figure out ways of coming up with $8 to get it. When he sees his Dad walking home from court, Andy sounds out the judge (Lewis Stone).

"When you were young, everybody used to ride horses," Andy says.

"Guess so."

"Did you have your own horse?"

"Yes, indeed, I did."

"That's fine. Now today everybody rides an automobile."

But as sound as Andy's logic is, Judge Hardy doesn't think Andy is old enough. And the elder Hardy doesn't believe in installment buying, either.

"When you can pay cash for a car out of your own money, well, that's something else again," the judge says.

It isn't long before Andy gets a chance to raise the extra cash. His pal "Beezy" (George Breakston) is going away for the holidays. He asks Andy to squire his girl, Cynthia Potter (Lana Turner), so the other guys will keep away. Andy agrees to do it for $8 plus expenses. Beezy promises to mail Andy the money as soon as his mother gives him his Christmas-shopping allowance.

So, without further ado, Andy knocks on Cynthia's door to ask her to the Christmas Dance. Out steps an adolescent version of Lana Turner—17 years old, sweet and innocent-faced. Still, she already has a mature, full-breasted figure (as audiences saw later in a swimming scene), and MGM, grooming her for future roles, has given her the part of a "fast" girl. When Andy pops the question, Lana busses him, calls him "darling," then dashes inside. Beezy, watching all these goings-on from a distance, is incensed. "It didn't mean a thing," Andy says, pooh-poohing it all. "It was just a kiss of gratitude like a dog licking a hand or something . . . She's just eight bucks and expenses to me."

The *Hardy* series usually had three or four plots working at the same time. And this version was no different. In plot two, Marian (Cecilia Parker) bursts into tears when she learns her boyfriend has gone out with another girl. Curiously, director George B. Seitz lets this drop, and that's the sum and substance of this subplot.

In plot three, Mrs. Hardy (Fay Holden) gets a telegram, an experience which MGM thought comparable to getting a transatlantic telephone call. She's so agitated she can hardly open the wire until the judge calms her down. "Mother, when we were young, telegrams were new, exciting and expensive," he tells her. "But today, they're ordinary postal cards." With that reassurance, she opens the telegram. It says her mother is seriously sick in Canada. Even though it's Christmas time, Mrs. Hardy decides to rush to her side.

Meanwhile, Andy makes friends with a 12-year-old girl visiting next door. She's Betsy Booth (16-year-old Judy Garland), whose mother is a musical comedy star. It's the first of Judy's three appearances in the *Hardy* series. And she makes the most of it—displaying a fresh, vibrant voice that will eventually blossom to become her trademark.

Betsy gets a crush on Andy. But he barely gives her a tumble. So in the first

Mickey, a little older and wiser—and sadder, too, in this scene—and an almost grown-up Judy sporting a mink coat, share a solemn moment in *Andy Hardy Meets a Debutante* (1940).

This rare shot shows Rooney with his own 8-year-old son Teddy in the last series picture, *Andy Hardy Comes Home* (1958). The movie was an attempt to revive the series with Mickey returning to Carvel as a successful lawyer and taking his Dad's place in the man-to-man talks. But a more sophisticated America found the movie dated.

It's a moment of truth for Judge Hardy (Lewis Stone) and his wife (Fay Holden). The Hardys stand to inherit $2 million. But they find their claim is really a false one. And so, rather than accept it dishonestly, they renounce the family inheritance. Scene is also from *The Hardys Ride High*. Families found the Hardys' basic integrity reassuring because they upheld traditional virtues that were slowly changing in a society in transition from peace to war.

of her three songs, she laments that she's just an in-between girl—too old for toys, too young for boys.

Andy does break down long enough to treat Betsy to a chocolate ice cream soda at the drug store. But his kindness nearly proves his undoing. Who should be there but Cynthia. When she sees Andy with another girl, she jealously storms out.

Andy catches up, convinces her that Betsy is only a little kid visiting next door, and asks Cynthia for a date. At the indoor swimming pool, Cynthia shows off a well-turned figure. But she turns out to be a spoilsport. She won't go in the water. She doesn't want to wet her hairdo. She doesn't want to play tennis either. It will give her muscles, she says. Finally, she agrees to go for a walk. That gives Andy ideas. "I know just the place," he says, brightening.

The camera cuts to a secluded wooded area. Andy is shown surfacing for air after a long, impassioned clinch. "Wahoo," he shouts. "I finally found something you like to do."

Now, complications arise. Cynthia won't let Andy alone. She has fast become a nuisance. Then, Polly wires, saying she's persuaded her folks to let her come home for the big dance after all. So Andy has two girls on his hands. Finally, Beezy sends a special delivery letter saying he's fallen in love with another girl. He doesn't care whom Cynthia goes out with, so he won't be sending the $8.

Bewildered and downhearted, Andy goes to his father for a heart-to-heart chat. The scene had basic appeal and MGM repeated it in almost all the *Hardy* films.

"Dad, can I talk to you man to man?" Andy asks. They're in the judge's book-lined study. "Can a guy be in love with two girls at once?"

"Both estimable young ladies?"

"Huh? Oh, we just do a little hugging and kissing, Dad. Good clean fun—just like Polly and me."

"Object matrimony?"

"Matrimony?" Andy gulps. "Oh, Dad, you don't have to worry. I'm never gonna get married—ever."

"That's a momentous decision."

"At least, not until middle age—25 or 26."

"That's a sound idea."

"Dad, I just don't understand these modern girls."

"In what way?"

"Well, Polly, for instance. Sometimes she won't let you kiss her at all. But this Cynthia. Oh, she'll let you kiss her whenever you want. She doesn't want to swim. She doesn't want to play tennis . . . All she wants to do is kiss you. I'm a nervous wreck. Do you think there's anything wrong with a guy if he doesn't want a girl kissing him all the time?"

Andy goes on to make a clean breast of his troubles and his understanding Dad bails him out of the car deal. Now Andy has wheels. But he still has one girl too many for the dance. It's Betsy's turn to rescue him. She takes Cynthia for a walk, points out an old junk heap at the car lot and convinces her that Andy plans to use it to take her to the dance. "Of all the nerve," Cynthia snaps. She calls Andy and cancels their date. Meanwhile, Polly learns about Andy's dating Cynthia and also turns a cold shoulder.

So the night of the dance rolls around. And Andy, who had two dates, finds himself without anyone. Hapless and forlorn, he sits on the running board of his car. The headlights are on. Suddenly, Betsy steps into their bright beam. She is wearing an off-the-shoulder gown her mother has sent. Betsy has persuaded her mother to let her wear it just for one night. "Betsy, you're grown up," Andy exclaims. Overjoyed, he asks her to the dance.

"This is going to be a world record," he shouts hysterically. "I'm going to put on my tuxedo and my opera hat." As he sprints into the house, he adds, "Maybe I'll shave."

Betsy turns out to be the hit of the ball. The band leader recognizes her as the daughter of a famous vocalist and invites her to sing with the band. She belts out two winning numbers. To the applause of everyone, she and Andy lead the grand march.

The next day, Mrs. Hardy unexpectedly comes home with good news. Her mother has completely recovered. Meanwhile, Betsy has explained everything to Polly and reconciled her with Andy. Betsy is a little sad at having to leave and give up Andy. But she takes it philosophically. "On account of you, I was grown up for one day," she tells Andy. "Now I know how wonderful life's gonna be when I'm 18."

So with everything tied up in neat, happy bows, Polly asks Andy if he liked kissing Cynthia more. Well, Andy shrugs, he's not sure. It's been a long time since he's kissed Polly. Perturbed, Polly embraces him and kisses him long, hard and soulfully.

It takes more than a few seconds for Andy's speech to return. "Cynthia," he says in a quavering voice, "was just one of the errors of my childhood."*

*Ann Rutherford, still best remembered as Andy's girl, made a nostalgic return to MGM in 1972. After a 22-year absence from the screen, she came out of retirement to play a housewife in the murder mystery, *They Kill Only Their Masters*. The studio said the set for her small town home was Andy's house, complete with porch and railing. Even though two decades had passed, the old MGM showmanship was still there. The day she showed up they flew a banner over the front gate that read, "Welcome Home Polly." But it was clear that it was another era. "The first thing I did was head for the commissary to have a bowl of Louis B. Mayer's famous chicken soup with matzoth balls, Miss Rutherford said. "Well, they had never even heard of it. They even wanted to know who Mr. Mayer was. I was so devastated I couldn't eat my lunch." The movie was to be the last film on the old MGM lot. After its completion, a demolition crew was to tear down the Hardy house, the street, the backlot (including Tarzan's jungle), and Waterloo Bridge. A 38-acre automobile city with 12 new car dealerships is going up in its place.

ANDY HARDY SERIES

1. *A Family Affair.* MGM, 1937, George B. Seitz.
    Lionel Barrymore (as Judge Hardy), Cecilia Parker (as Marian Hardy), Eric Linden, Mickey Rooney (as Andy Hardy), Charles Grapewin, Spring Byington (as Mrs. Hardy), Julie Haydon (as Joan Hardy), Sara Haden (as Aunt Milly), Allen Vincent, Margaret Marquis (as Polly), Selmer Jackson, Harlan Briggs. 67 minutes.

2. *You're Only Young Once.* MGM, 1938, George B. Seitz.
    Lewis Stone (as Judge Hardy), Cecilia Parker, Mickey Rooney, Fay Holden (as Mrs. Hardy), Frank Craven, Ann Rutherford (as Polly), Eleanor Lynn, Ted Pearson, Sara Haden, Charles Judels, Selmer Jackson. 77 minutes.

3. *Judge Hardy's Children.* MGM, 1938, George B. Seitz.
    Lewis Stone, Mickey Rooney, Cecilia Parker, Fay Holden, Betsy Ross Clarke (as Aunt Milly), Ann Rutherford, Robert Whitney, Jacqueline Laurent, Ruth Hussey, Jonathan Hale, Janet Beecher, Leonard Penn. 102 minutes.

4. *Love Finds Andy Hardy.* MGM, 1938, George B. Seitz.
    Lewis Stone, Mickey Rooney, Judy Garland (as Betsy Booth), Cecilia Parker, Fay Holden, Ann Rutherford, Betsy Ross Clarke, Lana Turner, Marie Blake, Don Castle, Gene Reynolds, Mary Howard, George Breakston, Raymond Hatton. 90 minutes.

5. *Out West with the Hardys.* MGM, 1938, George B. Seitz.
    Lewis Stone, Mickey Rooney, Cecilia Parker, Fay Holden, Ann Rutherford, Sara Haden (as Aunt Milly), Don Castle, Virginia Weidler, Gordon Jones, Ralph Morgan, Nana Bryant, Tom Neal, Anthony Allan. 84 minutes.

6. *The Hardys Ride High.* MGM, 1939, George B. Seitz.
    Mickey Rooney, Lewis Stone, Cecilia Parker, Fay Holden, Ann Rutherford, Virginia Grey, Minor Watson, John King, John T. Murray, Halliwell Hobbes, George Irving, Aileen Pringle, Marsha Hunt, Donald Briggs, William Orr, Truman Bradley. 80 minutes.

7. *Andy Hardy Gets Spring Fever.* MGM, 1939, W. S. Van Dyke II
    Lewis Stone, Mickey Rooney, Cecilia Parker, Fay Holden, Ann Rutherford, Sara Haden, Helen Gilbert, Terry Kilburn, John T. Murray, George Breakston, Charles Peck, Sidney Miller, Addison Richards, Olaf Hytten, Erville Alderson, Robert Kent. 85 minutes.

8. *Judge Hardy and Son.* MGM, 1940, George B. Seitz.
Lewis Stone, Mickey Rooney, Cecilia Parker, Fay Holden, Ann Rutherford, Sara Haden, June Preisser, Maria Ouspenskaya, Henry Hull, Martha O'Driscoll, Leona Maricle, Margaret Early, George Breakston, Egon Brecher, Edna Holland, Marie Blake. 88 minutes.

9. *Andy Hardy Meets Debutante.* MGM, 1940, George B. Seitz.
Lewis Stone, Mickey Rooney, Cecilia Parker, Fay Holden, Judy Garland, Ann Rutherford, Diana Lewis, George Breakston, Sara Haden, Harry Tyler, Addison Richards, George Lessey, Gladys Blake, Cy Kendall, Clyde Dillson. 85 minutes.

10. *Andy Hardy's Private Secretary.* MGM, 1941, George B. Seitz.
Lewis Stone, Mickey Rooney, Fay Holden, Ann Rutherford, Sara Haden, Kathryn Grayson, Ian Hunter, Gene Reynolds, George Breakston, Todd Karns, Addison Richards, Margaret Early, Bertha Priestley, Joseph Crehan, Lee Phelps, John Dilson. 97 minutes.

11. *Life Begins for Andy Hardy.* MGM, 1941, George B. Seitz.
Lewis Stone, Mickey Rooney, Judy Garland, Fay Holden, Ann Rutherford, Sara Haden, Patricia Dane, Ray McDonald. 100 minutes.

12. *The Courtship of Andy Hardy.* MGM, 1942, George B. Seitz.
Lewis Stone, Mickey Rooney, Cecilia Parker, Fay Holden, Ann Rutherford, Sara Haden, Donna Reed, William Lundigan, Steve Cornell, Frieda Inescourt, Harvey Stephens. 94 minutes.

13. *Andy Hardy's Double Life.* MGM, 1942, George B. Seitz.
Lewis Stone, Mickey Rooney, Cecilia Parker, Fay Holden, Ann Rutherford, Sara Haden, Esther Williams, William Lundigan, Robert Pittard, Bobby Blake, Susan Peters. 91 minutes.

14. *Andy Hardy's Blonde Trouble.* MGM, 1944, George B. Seitz.
Lewis Stone, Mickey Rooney, Fay Holden, Sara Haden, Herbert Marshall, Bonita Granville, Jean Porter, Keye Luke, Lee Wilde, Lyn Wilde, Marta Linden. 107 minutes.

15. *Love Laughs at Andy Hardy.* MGM, 1946, Willis Goldbeck.
Mickey Rooney, Lewis Stone, Sara Haden, Bonita Granville, Lina Romay, Fay Holden, Dorothy Ford, Hal Hackett, Dick Simmons, Clinton Sundberg, Geraldine Wall, Addison Richards. 93 minutes.

16. *Andy Hardy Comes Home.* MGM, 1958, Howard Koch.
Mickey Rooney, Patricia Breslin, Fay Holden, Cecilia Parker, Sara Haden, Joey Forman, Jerry Colonna, Vaughn Taylor, Frank Ferguson, William Leslie, Tom Duggan, Jeanne Baird, Gina Gillespie, Jimmy Bates, Teddy Rooney, Johnny Weissmuller, Jr., Pat Cawley. 80 minutes.

Uh-oh. Someone Henry (Jimmy Lydon) and Homer (Charles Smith) don't want to see has just shown up at a luncheon in *Henry Aldrich Plays Cupid* (1944). Diana Lynn is the unsuspecting gal.

HENRY ALDRICH

Henry Aldrich for President
(1941)

Screenplay by Val Burton based on Clifford Goldsmith's "Henry Aldrich" stories. Camera, John Mescall. Editor, Thomas Neff. Directed by Hugh Bennett. A Paramount Picture produced by Sol C. Siegel. 73 minutes.

Henry Aldrich	JAMES LYDON
Dizzy Stevens	CHARLES SMITH
Geraldine Adams	JUNE PREISSER
Phyllis Michael	MARY ANDERSON
Mary Aldrich	MARTHA O'DRISCOLL
Mrs. Aldrich	DOROTHY PETERSON
Mr. Aldrich	JOHN LITEL
Ed Calkins	ROD CAMERON
Marvin Bagshaw	FRANK COGHLAN, JR.
Mr. Crosley	LUCIEN LITTLEFIELD
Irwin Barrett	KENNETH HOWELL
Johnny Beal	BUDDY PEPPER
Mr. Bradley	VAUGHAN GLASER
Red MacGowan	DICK PAXTON

Tubby Gibbons	PAUL MATTHEWS
Elmer Pringle	FREDERICK CARPENTER
Students:	
Bob	BOB PITTARD
Bud	(LON) BUD MCCALLISTER
Carmen	CARMEN JOHNSON
Helen	HELEN WESTCOTT
Rosita	ROSITA BUTLER
Georgia	GEORGIA LEE SETTLE
Mr. McCloskey	IRVING BACON
Lucinda	LILLIAN YARBO
Department of Commerce	
Inspector	ARTHUR LOFT
Sidney	SIDNEY MILLER
Miss Patterson	RUTH ROBINSON
Noel, a student	NOEL NEILL
Janitor	CHRISTIAN RUB

Hen–reeee! Hen–ry Ald–rich."

"Coming, Moth-er!"

Remember that squeaky-voiced teen-ager with the two left feet and the habit of doing the wrong thing in the wrong place at the wrong time?

Most of us who grew up in the 1930s and 1940s remember the radio program starring Ezra Stone. The half-hour comedy always opened with Henry's mother calling him and then Henry's unsteady, falsetto reply. But Henry's exploits also became the subject of a movie series. Even though he didn't have the following that Andy Hardy did, he was the subject of 11 pictures from 1939 to 1944. They didn't win any Oscars, but they got lots of laughs from the peanut gallery.

Henry Aldrich. He was pleasant, well-intentioned and certainly willing enough. But he was awkward, inexperienced and somehow always gumming up the works. Yet, it was his very penchant for blundering that made him so appealing. Henry was the anti-hero. He was someone kids could identify with much more easily than they could with an All-American like Jack Armstrong.

If Henry wasn't good enough to make his school football team, neither could most teen-agers. If he got into trouble for forgetting his dad's advice, so did every boy some time or other. And if he came within a hair's-breadth of flunking Latin, didn't this reflect every average student's anxiety?

Some say Henry was a kind of poor kid's Andy Hardy. And, in fact, when you take a close look, it's amazing how much alike they were. They both lived in a small town. They came from respectable middle-class families, had their own

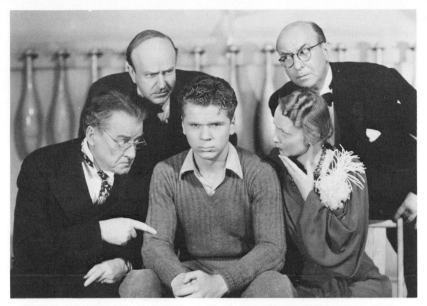

It seems like just about everyone on the Centerville High School faculty has a word of advice for glum-looking Henry Aldrich. Jackie Cooper plays the trouble-prone teen-ager in *What a Life* (1939), first of the series. Others, from left, are Vaughan Glaser (Mr. Bradley, the principal), Lucien Littlefield, Dorothy Stickney and Andrew Tombes.

After only two pictures, Cooper outgrew the role and made way for Jimmy Lydon, who played Henry in the remaining nine series movies. Here Jackie visits Jimmy on the set.

secondhand car, and were just beginning to find out there were other things to do with girls than dip their pigtails in ink wells.

But there the resemblance ends. The *Hardy* pictures reportedly made over $73 million for MGM. The *Aldrich* movies could never match even a fraction of this box office gross. For one thing, Paramount never pumped enough money into them to lift them out of the "B" category. For another, the Aldrich radio series had been an established national hit before the film series started. And the screen Henry Aldrich lacked the comedy material to outshine his airwaves counterpart. Andy Hardy never had that hurdle to overcome.

Nevertheless, if Henry Aldrich remains a nostalgic touchstone for millions, it is due to the fertile imagination of one Clifford Goldsmith. The son of a East Aurora, New York, high school principal, Goldsmith studied drama and then made his living lecturing in high schools throughout the country. While touring, he took note of the colorful characters here and there. In time, they inspired him to write a juvenile comedy about a modern-day Peck's Bad Boy. He called his play "What a Life!," and mailed it to producer George Abbott. To Goldsmith's amazement, Abbott liked it so much he put it on Broadway. It opened in 1938 with 19-year-old Ezra Stone as Henry and Betty Field as his girlfriend. The comedy—the story of Henry's complicated love life—failed to excite the critics. But the dynamic Stone, a director now, saved the day by stumping the high schools in the New York area to drum up an audience.

A child actor, Stone had appeared on radio and in such Broadway hits as "Three Men on a Horse" and "Brother Rat" even before "What a Life!" The Goldsmith play ran for a year and then toured the country. But while it was on the boards in New York, Rudy Vallee saw the show and put it in his program as a seven-minute sketch. The Aldriches were an immediate hit.

Three months later, in October, 1939, Kate Smith took the family on her program. By July, 1940, the Aldriches had their own summer show, replacing the vacationing Jack Benny for Jell-O. Later, when they got their own year-round Thursday night spot, the Aldrich family drew an audience of over 30 million. They eventually became radio's second most popular household, trailing only "One Man's Family." In addition to Stone, the cast included Katherine Raht, an ex-schoolteacher, as Mother; veteran radio actor House Jameson as Father; June Allison as sister Mary; and Jackie Kelk as pal Homer Brown.*

While their radio popularity was still rising, Paramount made the original play into a movie with Jackie Cooper. Betty Field, making her screen debut, was co-starred. But Eddie Bracken, as Henry's sidekick Homer, stole the show.

*Others who appeared on the long-running show were—Henry: Norman Tokar, Raymond Ives, Dickie Jones and Bobby Ellis; Father: Clyde Fillmore; Mother: Lea Penman; Mary: Betty Field, Mary Mason, Charita Bauer, Mary Shipp, Mary Rolfe and Ann Lincoln; Will Brown (Homer's father): Ed Begley and Howard Smith. Remember the name of the theme? It was "This Is It."

Joan Mortimer, playing a scientist's daughter, tries an experiment on a skeptical-looking Henry. From *Henry Aldrich Haunts a House.*

Henry is the lucky target for all these smiles at the class prom. That's Diana Lynn shaking hands with him and Gail Russell to Henry's immediate right. Shirley Mills is at extreme left and Ann Rooney is partly shielding Miss Russell. Scene is from *Henry Aldrich Gets Glamour* (1943).

Cooper's good looks were a handicap. His curly hair and clean-cut regular features opened a yawning credibility gap between Jackie, the actor, and the blundering character he played. On the other hand, Bracken, ungainly, rubber-faced and crack-voiced, seemed perfect for Henry. He did, in fact, play the role in the touring version of the play.

However, Cooper didn't stay in the part long. After the second *Aldrich* film, *Life with Henry* (1941), Cooper outgrew the role. Nevertheless, Paramount decided to make a series and tested Stone for the lead.* But the part went to Jimmy Lydon, a straight-haired, lanky, callow youth who had won first-rate notices in the title role in *Tom Brown's Schooldays* (1940). Lydon had been picked for the coveted Tom Brown role out of 1,500 lads in a national contest for the "typical American boy." He had a brief career on radio and on the stage before his film debut in *Back Door to Heaven* (1939).

Lydon went on to play Henry in nine pictures, beginning in 1941 and extending to 1944. He was a better casting choice than Cooper. But he was the victim of dull, unimaginative, low-budget scripts. And his series movies—although they may have filled the bill for the Saturday matinee crowd—fell far short of their potential.**

Other Aldrich movie series regulars, or almost-regulars, include veteran Broadway actor John Litel as Henry's father, a Princeton graduate and attorney who can't understand why his son won't follow in his confident footsteps; Charles Smith as Basil (Dizzy) Stevens, Henry's chum, whose claim to fame is his ability to wiggle his ears to attract girls; Olive Blakeney (whose real-life daughter married Lydon) as Henry's overbearing mother; and Vaughn Glaser as the sour-tempered principal, Mr. Bradley.

Diana Lynn made occasional featured appearances as Henry's best girl, and Rod Cameron, Gail Russell, Martha O'Driscoll and Vera Vague played bit parts. Hedda Hopper, believe it or not, was Henry's mother in the original film, *What a Life* (1939).

One character who showed promise as being more than a one-dimensional stereotype was Henry's pretty but practical sister, Mary, played by Kay Stewart. She disappeared from later series movies. But in *Life with Henry* (1941) she showed herself to be a fickle little lady who knew the value of a bird in the hand.

---

*Stone played in *Those Were the Days* (1940), a college story, for Paramount. But he never appeared as Henry Aldrich on the screen.

**Lydon later co-starred in *The Town Went Wild* (1944) with Freddie Bartholomew and had top billing in four films, including *When The Lights Go On Again* (1944) and *Strange Illusion* (1945). He also played in *Life with Father* (1947), *Joan of Arc* (1948) and *The Time of Your Life* (1948). Then, in 1951, Lydon created another series character, Skeezix, the comic strip hero of "Gasoline Alley." But it stopped production after only two pictures. The public had lost interest in B-pictures and Hollywood was beginning to feel the pinch. Lydon went on to appear in supporting roles, but he never realized his early promise as an adolescent. More recently, he went behind the cameras as associate producer of a number of television productions.

In one scene, she's shopping at the grocery where Dizzy (Eddie Bracken) has just gotten a part-time job. While he's supposed to be sweeping out the store, he tries for a date. The conversation goes like this:

DIZZY: Are you doing anything tonight?

MARY: Well, I'm not sitting on the porch and being silly—if that's what you mean.

DIZZY: Oh, we don't have to sit on the porch. I'm making money now. We can go to a movie.

MARY: I have a date for the movies.

DIZZY: Including dancing afterward?

MARY: *(Suddenly taking interest)* Where would we dance?

DIZZY: At the Country Club. And it's a dollar a couple.

MARY: *(Goes to the phone)* Elm 443 . . . Dennis, about tonight. I have a headache . . . I can't help it if I have a headache, can I?

GROCER   (George Meader): *(Infuriated to see Dizzy gold-bricking, he marches over and yanks the broom away)*

DIZZY: Well, Mr. Allen, if you're going to sweep, what would you like me to do?

GROCER: Nothing. You can go.

DIZZY: We're closing early?

"But gosh, Dad, it wasn't my fault," Henry seems to be saying in *Henry Aldrich, Boy Scout.* His father, played by John Litel, starts a slow burn while mother, actress Olive Blakeney, holds Henry for reassurance. In real life, Lydon is married to Miss Blakeney's daughter. Minor Watson is at center.

GROCER: *You* are. You're fired.

MARY: *(Still on the phone)* Dennis. My headache's nearly all gone. See you at eight o'clock.

Even though the series left no indelible mark on the comedy scene, it did have its moments. Instead of fast-paced one-liners, the movies managed to cook up some intricate plots that put Henry deeper and deeper in trouble until he seemed hopelessly ensnared in a tangled web. Somehow he always managed to wriggle free, as he did in *Henry Aldrich for President* (1941), Lydon's first effort.

As the film opens, Henry, characteristically late for school, tears through the halls. He knocks down the janitor (Christian Rub), then jolts a flower vase out of the hands of the principal's secretary. In class, he keeps up the bad work. Mr. Crosley (Lucien Littlefield) is lecturing about the theory of centrifugal force. When Crosley asks for an example, Irwin Barrett (Kenneth Howell), who is running for school president, suggests an airplane in a spin.

Henry bolts up and volunteers to tell what causes the phenomenon. "It's auto-rotation," Henry says. At a loss for words, Henry ends up with his arms spread-eagled revolving like a ballet dancer. Despite the class's laughter, Henry insists he knows what flying is all about because he says he has piloted a plane himself. That draws skeptical looks. "Aldrich," says Crosley, "I've never encountered such a fabrication of the truth."

Irwin is running for president in a tight race against Phyllis Michael (Mary Anderson). Aldrich's speech gives Irwin an idea. "There's the guy we've been looking for," Irwin says to his pals. "We need somebody to chisel a few votes from that Michael dame. There's the third candidate—Tailspin."

Irwin's cronies nominate Henry and Irwin gets his girl, Geraldine Adams (June Preisser), the school's sexiest blonde, to persuade Henry to run. If he does, Geraldine promises to be his steady. "It means a great deal to a girl to be seen out with someone important . . . ," she tells Henry, batting her big eyelashes. ". . . The school needs a man with your imagination."

But Henry's candidacy doesn't exactly thrill his family. "I don't want to be known as the sister of the school clown," says sister Mary (Martha O'Driscoll), rather indelicately. Henry's father doesn't offer much comfort either. He tells Henry he's only a political patsy, a "dummy," nominated only to split votes.

"What chance does a guy have," sighs Henry, throwing up his hands, "when his own father and sister don't have faith in him?"

As Henry sulks on the porch, Phyllis drops by. The pretty brunette, who has a crush on Henry, tells him she's dropped out of the race. Now there's nothing left for Henry but to go through with it.

Meanwhile, Irwin, the town's rich boy, goes all out to win. He floods Center-ville with leaflets and buys free ice cream sodas for everybody. However, Phyllis has thrown her support to Henry and that has made the race close.

Henry and his best pal, Homer Brown (Charles Smith), are momentarily distracted by some of the local bobby-soxers. Scene is from *Henry Aldrich for President* (1941), Lydon's first effort.

June Preisser, the school's sexiest blonde, has suddenly become impressed with Henry now that he's running for school president. Henry's girl, Mary Anderson, sends an icy stare June's way in *Henry Aldrich for President*.

As they near Election Day, everything hinges on the speeches Henry and Irwin will make. An hour before the candidates are to address the student body, Dizzy overhears Mr. Crosley coaching Irwin. In fact, Crosley, who dislikes Henry, has even written Irwin's speech. "Satisfied with it?" Crosley asks, as they rehearse in an empty classroom. "It's very good," Irwin replies. "Very good?" Crosley exclaims, "Why, it's excellent. It had me elected president of the student body at State Normal."

Thinking fast, Dizzy steals a copy and gives it to Henry, whose speech is still in the opening "Fellow Students" stage. Dizzy claims to have authored the address for Henry and then arranges for Henry to be the first speaker.

At first, Henry's squeaky voice draws only laughter. But before he's finished, the students are cheering him. "I feel I have the imagination and vision which will lead the student body into undreamed of fields of activity," Henry says. Mr. Crosley and Irwin are flabbergasted. Losing his cool, Irwin storms to the microphone and calls Henry a "lying, thieving cheat." That turns the students off. "Throw him [Irwin] out," they shout. "He's a rotten sport."

Henry is still on thin ice. But Crosley doesn't dare expose him without exposing his own shenanigans. So the big day comes. And Henry goes on to score an upset. In the midst of the celebrating, Irwin congratulates Henry. "It was a good fight," he says, sportingly, but a little too sportingly.

It doesn't take Henry long to find out the reason for Irwin's unaccustomed sweetness. "Do you know how many students came to school today?" principal Bradley (Vaughan Glaser) asks. "There were 1,214. And there were 1,414 votes cast. Two hundred counterfeit ballots were found—all marked in your favor." And so Bradley feels he has no choice but to expel Henry.

His elation cruelly deflated, Henry prepares to move upstate with his relatives. "You know, Henry," his father says lamely, "I've often thought everyone should be thrown out of school at least once." But the world has tumbled down around Henry and nothing can console him. Nothing, that is, except Dizzy and Phyllis. Just when Henry has reached the bottom of despondency, Dizzy and Phyllis rush in. They've discovered it was Irwin who really faked the ballots. The phony ballots and Irwin's campaign leaflets came from the same printer.

Now their job is to find the printer and get him to identify Irwin. They scour the town and find that he's a fellow named McCloskey (Irving Bacon), now with a carnival about 200 miles away.

In desperation, Henry rushes to Ed Calkins (Rod Cameron), a grounded pilot who has secretly taught Henry to fly. Henry breathlessly explains the emergency and persuades Calkins to fly him to the fair. When he gets there, Henry talks the printer into returning to Centerville to bail Henry out of his troubles.

But just as they're taking off, an inspector warns Calkins he'll never fly again if he gets in the plane. Henry, determined to exonerate himself, jumps to the controls. "Don't be concerned," he assures the startled printer as the plane soars wildly into the blue, "I have the plane in perfect control." Whereupon Henry brushes a tree top, skims a barn and flies through a haystack. "I thought you'd feel safer closer to the ground," Henry says, smiling unconvincingly. A mouse, picked up as they buzzed through the haystack, jumps into Henry's trousers. Suddenly, he's off on wild gyrations. One of them flings the printer outside, onto a wing. When he crawls back in, Henry asks the ashen-faced printer to hand him a book. Its title is *How to Land.* By now, all the blood has drained from the printer's face and his eyes look like poached eggs. "There's always a first time for everything," Henry says sappily.

Calkins, fearing a crackup, has telephoned ahead. The whole town is on hand when Henry makes a forced landing on the high school football field, knocking down the goal post.

As Bradley and the students haul Henry out of the plane, the printer identifies Irwin as the student who ordered the ballots. "I think the entire student body, including me, owes an apology to Henry Aldrich," says Bradley.

But it's not like Henry to be out of trouble for long. When the exhausted printer starts to pass out, Henry runs for a bucket of water. As he's about to throw it, the printer faints. The water goes straight into Bradley's face. And we hear Bradley's exasperated voice intoning those familiar words, "Hen–reee. Hen–ry Aldrich."

HENRY ALDRICH SERIES

1. *What a Life.* Paramount, 1939, Ted Reed.
   Jackie Cooper (as Henry Aldrich), Betty Field, John Howard, Janice Logan, Vaughan Glaser, Lionel Stander, Hedda Hopper, James Corner, Dorothy Stickney, Kathleen Lockhart, Lucien Littlefield, Sidney Miller, Andrew Tombes, George Guhl, Arthur Aylesworth, Wilda Bennett, Bennie Bartlett, Kay Stewart, Leonard Sues, Eddie Brian, Janet Waldo, Betty McLaughlin, Douglas Fahy, Roberta Smith, Nora Cecil. 75 minutes.

2. *Life with Henry.* Paramount, 1941, Ted Reed.
   Jackie Cooper, Lila Ernst, Eddie Bracken (as Dizzy), Fred Niblo, Hedda Hopper, Kay Stewart, Moroni Olsen, Rod Cameron, Pierre Watkin, Lucien Littlefield, Frank M. Thomas, Etta McDaniel, Hanley Stafford, Edith Evanson, Rand Brooks, Doris Lloyd, Frances Carson, Charlotte Treadway, Josephine Whitell, Thurston Hall, Winifred Harris, Theodore von Eltz, Mary Currier, Wanda McKay. 80 minutes.

3. *Henry Aldrich for President.* Paramount, 1941, Hugh Bennett.
   James Lydon (as Henry Aldrich), Charles Smith (as Dizzy Stevens), June Preisser, Mary Anderson, Martha O'Driscoll (as Mary Aldrich), Dorothy Peterson, John Litel (as Mr. Aldrich), Rod Cameron, Frank Coghlan, Jr., Lucien Littlefield, Kenneth Howell, Buddy Pepper, Vaughan Glaser, Dick Paxton, Paul Matthews, Bob Pittard, Bud McCallister, Carmen Johnson, Helen Westcott, Rosita Butler, Georgia Lee Settle. 73 minutes.

4. *Henry and Dizzy.* Paramount, 1942, Hugh Bennett.
   Jimmy Lydon, Mary Anderson, Charles Smith, John Litel, Olive Blakeney (as Mrs. Aldrich), Maude Eburne, Vaughan Glaser, Shirley Coates, Olin Howland, Minerva Urecal, Trevor Bardette, Carl "Alfalfa" Switzer, Warren Hymer, Noel Neill, Jane Cowan. 71 minutes.

5. *Henry Aldrich, Editor.* Paramount, 1942, Hugh Bennett.
   Jimmy Lydon, Charles Smith, John Litel, Olive Blakeney, Rita Quigley, Vaughan Glaser, Charles Halton, Francis Pierlot, Cliff Clark, Bennie Bartlett, Fern Emmett, Maude Eburne. 71 minutes.

6. *Henry Aldrich Gets Glamour.* Paramount, 1943, Hugh Bennett.
   Jimmy Lydon, Charles Smith, John Litel, Olive Blakeney, Diana Lynn, Frances Gifford, Gail Russell, Vaughan Glaser, Ann Rooney, William Blees, Janet Beecher, Bill Goodwin. 75 minutes.

7. *Henry Aldrich Swings It.* Paramount, 1943, Hugh Bennett.
Jimmy Lydon, Charles Smith, John Litel, Olive Blakeney, Mimi Chandler, Vaughan Glaser, Marion Hall, Beverly Hudson, Fritz Feld, Charles Arnt, Steve Geray, Matt McHugh. 64 minutes.

8. *Henry Aldrich Haunts a House.* Paramount, 1943, Hugh Bennett.
Jimmy Lydon, Charles Smith, John Litel, Olive Blakeney, Joan Mortimer, Vaughan Glaser, Jackie Moran, Lucien Littlefield, George Anderson, Mike Mazurki, Edgar Dearing, Charles Cane, Kernan Cripps, Jack Gardner, William Inman, Ferris Taylor, Anita Bolster, George M. Carleton, Dick Rush, Ray Walker, George Sherwood, Paul McVey, Paul Phillips. 73 minutes.

9. *Henry Aldrich, Boy Scout.* Paramount, 1944, Hugh Bennett.
Jimmy Lydon, Charles Smith, John Litel, Olive Blakeney, Joan Mortimer, Minor Watson, Darryl Hickman, David Holt, Richard Hayden. 66 minutes.

10. *Henry Aldrich Plays Cupid.* Paramount, 1944, Hugh Bennett.
Jimmy Lydon, Charles Smith, John Litel, Olive Blakeney, Diana Lynn, Vaughan Glaser, Vera Vague, Paul Harvey, Harry Bradley, Betty Farrington, Gladden James, Shirley Coates. 65 minutes.

11. *Henry Aldrich's Little Secret.* Paramount, 1944, Hugh Bennett.
Jimmy Lydon, Charles Smith, Joan Mortimer, John Litel, Olive Blakeney, Ann Doran, John David Robb, Tina Thayer, Sarah Edwards, Harry Bradley, Lucille Ward, Almira Sessions, Tom Fadden, George Carleton, Byron Foulger, Fern Emmett, Dorothy Vaughn, Eddie Dunn, Hal K. Dawson, Noel Neill. 75 minutes.

The Bumstead family: Dagwood (Arthur Lake), Blondie (Penny Singleton) and Baby Dumpling (Larry Simms). In front are Daisy and Cookie (Marjorie Kent). They tickled America's funnybone in 28 pictures from 1938 to 1950.

BLONDIE

Blondie Meets the Boss
(1939)

Screenplay by Richard Flournoy from a story by Kay Van Riper. Based on the comic strip by Chic Young. Camera, Henry Freulich. Editor, Gene Havlick. Directed by Frank R. Strayer. A Columbia Picture. 58 minutes.

Blondie	PENNY SINGLETON
Dagwood	ARTHUR LAKE
Baby Dumpling	LARRY SIMMS
Daisy	HIMSELF
Dot Miller	DOROTHY MOORE
J. C. Dithers	JONATHAN HALE
Marvin Williams	DON BEDDOE
Francine Rogers	LINDA WINTERS (DOROTHY COMINGORE)
Alvin Fuddle	DANNY MUMMERT
Ollie Shaw	STANLEY BROWN
Freddie Turner	JOEL DEAN
Nelson	RICHARD FISKE
Betty Lou Wood (Singer)	INEZ COURTNEY

Mailmen	IRVING BACON AND WALTER SANDE
Henry Philpot	WALLIS CLARK
Men	JAMES CRAIG AND ROBERT STER-LING
Marvin's wife	SALLY PAYNE
Laundryman	GEORGE CHANDLER
Peddler	EDDIE ACUFF
Bouncer	ED GARGAN
Morgan	WALTER SODERLING
McGuire	EDGAR DEARING
Kirk	DICK DURRELL
Sanders	DAVID NEWELL

AND

Skinnay Ennis and His Band

"Blond–dee. Oh, Blond—eee—eee."

That's Dagwood Bumstead calling. Remember the fellow with the spit-curl forelocks, the squeaky voice and the addiction to nine-decker sandwiches? Dagwood's really a well-meaning, good-natured hubby. But he's also a bumbler, a blunderer and a boob. And try as he may, he can't change his ineffectual personality.

"You weigh 163 pounds," a penny-fortune scale tells him in the original *Blondie* film (1938). "You are a very stupid fellow and not likely to succeed." Dagwood, miffed, puts in another penny. A second card comes out. "You weigh 163 pounds," the scale repeats. "You are a very stupid fellow and not likely to succeed." Infuriated, Dagwood drops in a third coin. "Save your money, sucker," the machine says. "I've told you twice already."

Of course, we all remember Blondie. She's the All-American housewife. Five-feet, four-inches tall, 116 pounds. Pert, understanding and patient. She may sometimes seem scatterbrained and slightly irresponsible. But her feet are planted more firmly than Dagwood's. In fact, Blondie really wears the pants in the Bumstead family—although she does her best to hide the fact.

When Dagwood stumbles into a lucrative $200,000 construction deal in *Blondie,* it's Blondie who has to stand eyeball to eyeball with hard-nosed boss J. C. Dithers to win a raise and bonus.

"Dagwood can take this contract and go into business for himself," Blondie serves warning.

"All right," Dithers grumps, giving in weakly. Then, to retain a modicum of self-respect, he tells Dagwood, "But don't be late [to the office] tomorrow."

"What!" Blondie exclaims.

"I mean," Dithers says, flinching like a beaten man. "Send him over at a reasonable hour."

"Dagwood," Blondie coos. "You were wonderful."

Because *Blondie* was aimed at family audiences, Columbia Pictures had ground rules for the series. Dagwood didn't drink, rarely flirted and seldom talked harshly to Blondie. Except for being a dunderhead, his major vice was pipe smoking. Blondie abstained from liquor and tobacco and wore no plunging necklines.

The heart of the couple's movie appeal was their believability as down-to-earth, plain, everyday young folks. Unlike the Hardys—Andy Hardy's father was a judge—who are members of the establishment in their small town, the Bumsteads are just struggling suburbanites. They have a six-room cottage, not much in the bank, and a heavy mortgage. Like millions of workingmen of the 1930s and 1940s, Dagwood had no car. He took a bus to work—ads puffing *Blondie* read, "As Human as Missing the 8:15"—and carried his lunch in a brown paper bag.

Many young families in a nation emerging from the Depression easily identified with the Bumsteads. And they understood their shortcomings, too. If Dagwood was harried, over-domesticated and frozen to inaction in a crisis, so were the husbands laughing at him—if the truth were told. But it was less traumatic and much more fun to watch Dagwood become the butt of all jokes.

If Blondie was temperamental and dizzy at times, so were the women who chuckled at her eccentricities. But there was satisfaction in knowing that it was Blondie—not Dagwood—who steered the straight course when life got stormy. "Sometimes, I think it's harder to raise a husband than a baby," Blondie says.

Chic Young created "Blondie" as a comic strip in 1930. He had started his career with strips called "The Affairs of Jane," "Beautiful Babs" and then "Dumb Dora." However, the public became more interested in his fourth creation, "Blondie Boopadoop," a flapper-golddigger type. Her boyfriend, Dagwood, was the son of a millionaire railroad magnate, J. Bolling Bumstead. When Young got them married in 1933, Dagwood's snobbish parents disowned them. But a couple starting out broke was much more palatable to the common man. And "Blondie" quickly attracted one of the biggest followings of any comic strip.

Before the decade was over, King Features was syndicating "Blondie" to over 250 newspapers with an estimated readership of 50 million. (In 1970, the strip ran in 1,600 papers,—500 more than its nearest rival—was translated into 17 languages and read by more than 100 million people.) Capitalizing on this built-in popularity, Columbia bought the motion picture rights and began a series of what first was projected to be only three *Blondie* films.

The studio cast in the title roles Arthur Lake, a character actor who had gained some success in comedy films, and Penny Singleton, a singer and dancer who had appeared chiefly in supporting roles. Her hair was then chestnut brown.

"The role [Blondie] came so naturally," Miss Singleton said, "it seemed all I did was play myself." Born Mariana Dorothy Agnes Letitia McNulty in 1909, she was the daughter of Irish Philadelphia newspaperman Bernard McNulty. He was related to James J. Farley, the campaign manager for President Franklin D. Roosevelt and later U.S. Postmaster-General.

Miss Singleton's career began about the time she started school. She sang at an amateur contest in a Philadelphia movie house. "I wanted to buy my mother a birthday present," she recalled. Penny got her wish. She won the $5 first prize. Later, she sang illustrated songs at a silent movie theater. It convinced her that she wanted to go on the stage. She went on the road after the sixth grade to join a touring vaudeville act called "The Kiddie Kabaret." Shortening her billing to "Dorothy McNulty," she appeared as a singer and dancer along with such youngsters as Milton Berle and Raymond Guion (later Gene Raymond). She went on to get her first speaking part on Broadway in a show called "Great Temptations" with Jack Benny. Eventually, she went to Hollywood, where she coined her stage name after marrying dentist Lawrence Singleton in 1937.* Her first name came from her habit of saving pennies until she amassed a huge pile and then bestowing them on someone.

Early movies included a succession of comedy and shady lady roles, as in *After the Thin Man* (1936) with William Powell (in which she played a tough nightclub dancer) and *Swing Your Lady* (1938) with Humphrey Bogart,**in which she danced and sang as well as acted. Ironically, she stopped appearing as floozies to avoid being identified as a one-part actress.

"I was the economical Claire Trevor," she told the author in an interview in New York City. "I just didn't want to be typed. It goes to show you how you can eat your words. I became probably the most typed actress in the world. But, at least, it [Blondie] had some dignity.

"I'm proud and grateful I was Blondie . . . She was dumb and shrewish sometimes. But she was real and sympathetic and warm, a real woman, a human being. And that's how I tried to play her."

Ironically, Miss Singleton was an afterthought for the role. Shirley Deane, who had played the eldest daughter in the *Jones Family* series, was originally signed for the part. However, she became sick. So the studio called Penny and she made her test without even a blonde wig. But when she won the role, she bleached her hair. It has stayed that way ever since.

Before Arthur Lake became identified as Dagwood, he was Arthur Silverlake from Corbin, Kentucky, the son of circus acrobats. Born in 1905, young Arthur

---

*They were divorced in 1939 after having one child, Dorothy. In 1941, Miss Singleton married Robert Sparks, producer of most of the *Blondie* films and later a TV-film producer. He died in 1963. They had one child, Robin Susan.
**Bogie called the picture, a kind of hillbilly farce, the worst movie he ever made.

The fur-clad brunette on Dagwood's arm is none other than Rita Hayworth, a fact that neither Blondie nor Baby Dumpling nor Daisy appreciate. Scene is from *Blondie on a Budget* (1940).

A baby-faced Glenn Ford tries to comfort the Bumsteads, who have found the going a bit sloppy in *Blondie Plays Cupid* (1940). That's Luana Walters on extreme right.

Dagwood's after-dinner conversation raises his boss' eyebrows (Jerome Cowan) in *Blondie's Big Moment* (1947). Others listening skeptically are Anita Louise, second from right, and Blondie. In foreground are Larry Simms and Marjorie Kent, the Bumstead children.

was cradled in a dressing-room trunk. Later, he became part of his parents' act after they switched to vaudeville and when they toured California, he landed a job in the movies. There, the elder Carl Laemmle, who founded Universal Pictures, took the "silver" out of his name.

Even from the start, when he played youthful roles in the silent films of the 1920s, Lake got parts as characters deficient in brain cells. He was a fixture in a comedy short subject series called *Sweet Sixteen*. His flair for light comedy led to the title role as the comic strip character Harold Teen (1928) and—with time out for roles in such films as *On with the Show* (1929), *Topper* (1937) and *Everybody's Doing It* (1938)—to his long career as Dagwood.*

Both Miss Singleton and Lake bore reasonable resemblances to their comic strip counterparts as did Larry Simms, who played their son Baby Dumpling in all 28 films. Simms had attracted Columbia's attention when the *Saturday Evening Post* used his picture for a color cover. Over the 13-year life of the movie series, he was the one who matured most discernably, appearing first at age four. In the eleventh *Blondie* movie, he dropped his "Baby" nickname and became "Alexander." Later, following the strip's story line, he got a sister, Cookie (Norma Jean Wayne and later Marjorie Kent). Another series regular was Daisy, the family's clever little tail-wagging mutt, who knew how to steal a scene with a well-timed bit of mugging. He was a regular canine Franklin Pangborn, complete with double takes and ears that elevated—as if to say "Is this for real?"— whenever Dagwood stumbled into hot water.

Stars or character actors who made brief appearances include Rita Hayworth, Glenn Ford, Janet Blair, Larry Parks, Anita Louise, Stuart Erwin and Shemp Howard of the Three Stooges.

With the exception of 1938, when the series started, Columbia made at least two and sometimes three *Blondie* movies a year until 1950, when the last picture, *Beware of Blondie,* was made. Judging by the series' longevity, the public enjoyed the antics of the screen Bumsteads almost as much as they did the comic strip characters. One of the best in the series was *Blondie Meets the Boss* (1939), in which Dagwood suffers the ultimate humiliation of the henpecked husband.

The Bumsteads are having breakfast as the movie opens, eagerly talking about their long-awaited vacation. Suddenly, Dagwood jumps up. As usual, he's late for his bus. The household streaks to its battle stations. Blondie and Baby Dumpling

---

*Miss Singleton and Lake also appeared on a half-hour (7:30–8:00 P.M., EDT) "Blondie" radio series beginning in 1939 over the Columbia Broadcasting System. The program began with announcer Bill Goodwin saying, "Uh-uh-uh. Don't touch that dial. It's time for . . ." And then Lake would respond with his familiar cry: "Blond–dee." By the time it ended in 1950, the show had moved to the two other networks—the American Broadcasting Company and the National Broadcasting Company. Brunette Ann Rutherford filled in for the last year, becoming a blonde even though the show was on radio. Also doing a stint in the title role were Alice White and Patricia Van Cleve, Lake's real-life wife. They have two children, Arthur and Marion.

hold the door open as Dagwood dashes out, running down the postman (Irving Bacon).

At the J. C. Dithers Construction Company, Mr. Dithers (Jonathan Hale) announces he's got to go to Washington on a big real estate deal. Dagwood will have to work over the weekend. But Dagwood unexpectedly shows gumption and stands up to his boss. It's Dagwood's first vacation in two years, he says. He'll have it—or else.

"Or else what?" Dithers demands, smoldering.

"Or else," Dagwood sputters, his back to the wall, "I'll resign."

"Make out Bumstead's check," Dithers roars to his cashier. "He's just re-signed."

At home, Blondie offers little solace. She calls Dithers and asks him to give Dagwood another chance. Dithers, who has always thought Blondie had un-tapped executive ability, gets an idea. He agrees, but only if Blondie takes over the office while he flies to Washington. He's going there to find out which parcel of land the aviation board will pick for its new airport. Then, he wants Blondie to buy it right away before the owner realizes its new value.

Though this is three decades before women's lib, it's a challenge Blondie can't turn down. She strings her apron around Dagwood and hands him a broom.

"Whenever I'm miserable," she tells her out-of-work husband, as she dons her hat and coat, "I just sweep and sweep. You'll be surprised how quickly your troubles will disappear. And have a good cry, too. It'll make you feel better."

Dagwood's protests are all in vain. As Blondie marches out the front door, a salesman rings the back doorbell. "Pardon me, Madam," the salesman says to Dagwood, still wearing a frilly apron. "Is your husband home?" Dagwood slugs him.

Seething and bored with housework, Dagwood goes fishing with his pal Marvin (Don Beddoe). He leaves Baby Dumpling with Blondie's younger sister, Dot (Dorothy Moore), and her beau, who have come to town to dance in a jitterbug contest at the popular Garden Cafe.

At the lake, Dagwood and Marvin meet a couple of Marvin's girlfriends who work at the cafe. And Marvin invites them to join the fishing party. When one of the girls, Francine (Linda Winters),* loses her balance getting into the boat, Dagwood catches her. Just at that moment, the other girl snaps a picture.

But Dagwood is too domesticated to have fun. He's up tight all day and ends by running home that night when the overfriendly Francine busses him. By

*This was then the stage name of Dorothy Comingore, who, under her real name, would turn in the extraordinary portrayal of Susan Alexander in *Citizen Kane* (1941). Yet, after this triumph, she made only three more movies. Her unpopular actors' union activities and her refusal to tell the House Un-American Activities Committee if she had ever been a Communist Party member helped bring an untimely end to her promising career. Miss Comingore died in 1971 at the age of 53.

A salesman (Eddie Acuff) catches Dagwood in Blondie's apron in *Blondie Meets the Boss*. When the salesman calls him "Madam," Dagwood socks him.

Dagwood strains to chomp into one of his midnight, king-sized sandwiches.

Miss Singleton was a singer and dancer in pre-*Blondie* days. And she got her chance to strut her stuff in *Blondie Goes Latin* (1941). Tito Guizar strums guitar.

mistake, he brings home the camera. And the next day, Blondie—without suspecting anything—takes the film to work to get it developed. She sprints out in the same frantic rush as Dagwood, bowling over the postman. "I like it better this way," he smiles, getting up with lipstick on his forehead.

That night, Blondie has to wait at the office for Dithers' phone call from Washington. But when the pictures come back developed, she sees the incriminating photo of a woman in Dagwood's arms and forgets all about the real estate deal. She calls home and there's no answer. Blondie doesn't know that Dagwood, in a rare burst of independence, is playing pool with the boys. So, frantic with worry, she calls the police.

In a brilliantly comic scene, a cop walks into a crowded poolhall. "Say, some guy's wife has been squawking to the chief all evening," he announces. "Says her husband should have been home by six o'clock. Now I don't want to embarrass anyone by naming names. But whoever it is . . ." Every man in the hall makes a mad dash for the door. In two seconds, the place is empty.

Meanwhile, the jitterbug finals are on. Since nobody's around to take care of Baby Dumpling, Dot and her boyfriend take him to the Garden Cafe. The scene shifts to Blondie getting a telegram from Dithers. It says the aviation board has picked the Garden Cafe property for its proposed airport. She takes off with a check. The camera cuts to Dagwood in breathless pursuit of Baby Dumpling. He, too, is dashing to the cafe.

At the cafe, Dagwood bumps into Francine, who turns out to be a featured swing band singer. When Blondie rushes in, she recognizes Francine as the girl in Dagwood's arms in the snapshot. Whammo, Blondie clobbers him with her purse. Out falls the telegram—unnoticed. Of course, of all people, cafe-owner Henry Philpot (Wallis Clark) picks it up and learns what Dithers had hoped would stay a secret until the deal was closed.

Meanwhile, Dot's beau, fuming because they have had to drag around Baby Dumpling, has walked out on her. She grabs Dagwood, still reeling from Blondie's clout, and yanks him into the jitterbug finals. His dizzy antics à la Jerry Lewis captivate the audience and—you guessed it—they win first prize.

Back home, Blondie is packing to leave. But Baby Dumpling tells her that he has overheard a lady telling Daddy that her girlfriend took a picture when she accidentally slipped into Daddy's arms. Blondie, realizing that Dagwood has been a victim of circumstance, quickly unpacks. When Dagwood comes home they kiss and make up, then streak back to the cafe to try to close the property deal. But the wary owner wants twice what they can offer. And the deal falls through.

Moments later, Dithers rushes in. "Doggone it. I had the rottenest luck," he fumes to Blondie. "When I left Washington, I got a telegram saying some lobbying politician had stuck his nose into the deal. And everything was off. There I was 8,000 feet in the air and you down here. Ten thousand dollars. Probably cost you that much, didn't it?"

"No sir," says Blondie. "We didn't buy it."

"You see," says Dagwood, "It was all my fault."

"Nobody in the world could mess up a deal the right way but you," Dithers shrieks, slapping Dagwood on the back. "I always said he's a man in a million. Why, I couldn't run my business without him."

So Dithers goes off jumping for joy. Dagwood has his job back. And off the Bumsteads go on that vacation after all.

Despite the remarkable hold they had over Blondie and Dagwood's identity in the public mind, it's questionable whether Miss Singleton and Lake *really* did justice to the roles. Though they at times seemed ideally cast, they fell short of the potential the parts offer. Part of the problem may have been the scripts, which, as the series went along, failed to show innovation and settled for weak, stock situations. But even in their best films, the two never matched the brilliant humor cartoonist Young instilled in his comic strip characters. Lake played Dagwood as an outright simpleton—which the comic strip Dagwood is not—and as a result Dagwood's long-suffering qualities seem less funny because they seem less human. Miss Singleton, for all her energy, never played Blondie with enough variety to make her more than a one-dimensional character. Bosley Crowther of the *New York Times* once said, "Miss Singleton interprets Blondie less as a woman than as a composite statistic." Nevertheless, so totally did she and Lake become Dagwood and Blondie that no other performers ever took the parts in the movies —a rare distinction for any series.

Lake never made another film after the *Blondie* movie series. In fact, so typed was he as Dagwood that he found very little acting work. He took his family to Guatemala for a while, where they did a travelogue, and he took actors on tours, entertaining soldiers. He built one of his routines around himself as Dagwood in a mad chase with a mailman and a dog. In 1957, Lake, a somewhat mature Dagwood at 52, appeared in a "Blondie" television series. Pamela Britton was Blondie. But it didn't catch on and was shown only briefly. Television attempted another "Blondie" revival in 1968. Patricia Harty and Will Hutchins played the Bumstead couple. This "Blondie," too, came a cropper and was not renewed after its 13-week contract ran out.

After the *Blondie* series, Miss Singleton made the nightclub circuit with a song and dance act, toured in road shows of "Call Me Madam," "Never Too Late" and "Gentlemen Prefer Blondes," and made one more movie, *The Best Man* (1964). Her biggest post-*Blondie* role came in the summer of 1971, when she did a two-week vacation stint for Ruby Keeler in the nostalgic Broadway musical "No, No Nanette."

But Miss Singleton became best known in later years as a hard-fighting union executive—a real-life role far removed from her Blondie image. However, close friends were not surprised. Down deep, they say, she is a "tough cookie." In addition, the labor movement had roots in her family. "My father was a trade unionist," she said. "And my grandfather was a close friend of Samuel Gompers [founder of the American Federation of Labor]."

In 1958, she became interim president of the American Guild of Variety Artists, which represents entertainers ranging from nightclub and vaudeville performers to circus clowns and chorus girls. She lost the election for president to Joey Adams in 1961, then accused the union of failing to enforce so-called "sweetheart" contracts with nightclub owners, who, she said, were victimizing entertainers.

When she crusaded for union reform, she was sued for slander* and suspended. In 1962, when Senator John McClellan (Democrat-Arkansas) probed conditions in the entertainment field, she testified at his subcommittee hearings in Washington. Wearing a picture hat and reading glasses that sat midway down her nose, she testified that racketeer-dominated clubs forced strippers and exotic dancers to double as B-girls (bar girls), mix with customers and solicit drinks. Other performers supported her testimony, adding that some girls really worked as prostitutes.

Some in the entertainment field were critical of her. They felt she had hurt both the union and the industry. But that didn't faze her. The scrappy Penny bounced back to become AGVA's second vice president and, as such, led the Rockettes, the famous chorines of the Radio City Music Hall in New York City, in a 1967 strike for better pay and working conditions. She won the high-kickers a first-year minimum jump from $99 a week to $175 a week. She went on to negotiate better contracts for Las Vegas showgirls and Disneyland employees, among other union members.

Later, AGVA increased its strength by joining the massive, 39-union AFL-CIO Maritime Trades Department,** the seafaring union. And Miss Singleton became the only woman on its powerful executive board. In 1972, she held the position of AGVA's executive secretary, highest-ranking full-time post in the 10,000-member union.

However, she is the first to concede that it will be the *Blondie* movies for which both she and Lake will be best remembered. They were a screwball American couple trying to make ends meet in a simpler era. They brought to the screen a wholesome, if topsy-turvy, picture of domestic life, a human comedy that plain, everyday people came back again and again to see and laugh at.

---

*She said it cost her over $80,000 of her own money in legal fees to successfully contest the suits, which totaled several million dollars.

**AGVA qualifies for this ocean-going group because it represents performers who entertain aboard cruise ships.

BLONDIE SERIES

1. *Blondie.* Columbia, 1938, Frank R. Strayer.
Penny Singleton (as Blondie), Arthur Lake (as Dagwood), Larry Simms (as Baby Dumpling, later Alexander), Gene Lockhart, Ann Doran, Jonathan Hale (as Mr. Dithers), Gordon Oliver, Stanley Andrews, Irving Bacon (as the mailman, Mr. Beasley), Danny Mummert, Kathleen Lockhart, Dorothy Moore, Fay Helm, Richard Fiske. 68 minutes.

2. *Blondie Meets the Boss.* Columbia, 1939, Frank R. Strayer.
Penny Singleton, Arthur Lake, Larry Simms, Jonathan Hale, Danny Mummert, Dorothy Moore, Don Beddoe, Linda Winters (Dorothy Comingore), Stanley Brown, Joel Dean, Richard Fiske, Inez Courtney, Eddie Acuff. 58 minutes.

3. *Blondie Takes a Vacation.* Columbia, 1939, Frank R. Strayer.
Penny Singleton, Arthur Lake, Larry Simms, Danny Mummert, Donald Meek, Donald MacBride, Thomas W. Ross, Elizabeth Dunne, Robert Wilcox, Harlan Briggs, Irving Bacon. 61 minutes.

4. *Blondie Brings Up Baby.* Columbia, 1939, Frank R. Strayer.
Penny Singleton, Arthur Lake, Larry Simms, Danny Mummert, Jonathan Hale, Robert Middlemass, Olin Howland, Fay Helm, Peggy Ann Garner, Roy Gordon, Grace Stafford, Helen Jerome Eddy, Irving Bacon. 67 minutes.

5. *Blondie on a Budget.* Columbia, 1940, Frank R. Strayer.
Penny Singleton, Arthur Lake, Larry Simms, Rita Hayworth, Danny Mummert, Don Beddoe, John Qualen, Fay Helm, Irving Bacon, Thurston Hall, William Brisbane. 72 minutes.

6. *Blondie Has Servant Trouble.* Columbia, 1940, Frank R. Strayer.
Penny Singleton, Arthur Lake, Larry Simms, Danny Mummert, Jonathan Hale, Arthur Hohl, Esther Dale, Irving Bacon, Ray Turner, Walter Soderling, Fay Helm. 69 minutes.

7. *Blondie Plays Cupid.* Columbia, 1940, Frank R. Strayer.
Penny Singleton, Arthur Lake, Larry Simms, Jonathan Hale, Danny Mummert, Irving Bacon, Glenn Ford, Luana Walters, Will Wright, Spencer Charters, Leona Roberts. 67 minutes.

8. *Blondie Goes Latin.* Columbia, 1941, Frank R. Strayer.
Penny Singleton, Arthur Lake, Larry Simms, Ruth Terry, Tito Guizar, Jonathan

Hale, Danny Mummert, Irving Bacon, Janet Burston, Kirby Grant, Joseph King, Eddie Acuff. 70 minutes.

9. *Blondie in Society.* Columbia, 1941, Frank R. Strayer.
Penny Singleton, Arthur Lake, Larry Simms, Jonathan Hale, Danny Mummert, William Frawley, Edgar Kennedy, Chick Chandler, Irving Bacon, Bill Goodwin. 77 minutes.

10. *Blondie Goes to College.* Columbia, 1942, Frank R. Strayer.
Penny Singleton, Arthur Lake, Larry Simms, Janet Blair, Jonathan Hale, Danny Mummert, Larry Parks, Adele Mara, Lloyd Bridges, Sidney Melton, Andrew Tombes, Esther Dale. 74 minutes.

11. *Blondie's Blessed Event.* Columbia, 1942, Frank R. Strayer.
Penny Singleton, Arthur Lake, Larry Simms, Jonathan Hale, Danny Mummert, Hans Conried, Olin Howland, Stanley Brown, Eileen O'Hearn, Norma Jean Wayne. 69 minutes.

12. *Blondie for Victory.* Columbia, 1942, Frank R. Strayer.
Penny Singleton, Arthur Lake, Larry Simms, Majelle White, Stuart Erwin, Jonathan Hale, Danny Mummert, Edward Gargan, Renie Riano, Irving Bacon, Harrison Greene, Charles Wagenheim. 72 minutes.

13. *It's a Great Life.* Columbia, 1943. Frank R. Strayer.
Penny Singleton, Arthur Lake, Larry Simms, Hugh Herbert, Jonathan Hale, Danny Mummert, Alan Dinehart, Douglas Leavitt, Irving Bacon, Marjorie Ann Mutchie. 68 minutes.

14. *Footlight Glamour.* Columbia, 1943, Frank R. Strayer.
Penny Singleton, Arthur Lake, Larry Simms, Ann Savage, Jonathan Hale, Irving Bacon, Marjorie Ann Mutchie, Danny Mummert, Thurston Hall, Grace Hayle, Rafael Storm. 68 minutes.

15. *Leave It to Blondie.* Columbia, 1945, Abby Berlin.
Penny Singleton, Arthur Lake, Larry Simms, Marjorie Weaver, Jonathan Hale, Chick Chandler, Danny Mummert, Arthur Space, Eddie Acuff, Marjorie Ann Mutchie, Eula Morgan, Fred Graff, Jack Rice, Maude Eburne. 75 minutes.

16. *Blondie Knows Best.* Columbia, 1946, Abby Berlin.
Penny Singleton, Arthur Lake, Larry Simms, Marjorie Kent, Steven Geray, Jonathan Hale, Shemp Howard, Jerome Cowan, Danny Mummert, Ludwig Donath, Arthur Loft, Edwin Cooper, Jack Rice, Carol Hughes, Kay Mallory, Alyn Lockwood. 69 minutes.

17. *Life with Blondie.* Columbia, 1946, Abby Berlin.
Penny Singleton, Arthur Lake, Larry Simms, Marjorie Kent, Jonathan Hale, Ernest Truex, Marc Lawrence, Veda Ann Borg, Jack Rice, Bobby Larson, Douglas Fowley, George Tyne, Edward Gargan, Francis Pierlot, Ray Walker. 69 minutes.

18. *Blondie's Lucky Day.* Columbia, 1946, Abby Berlin.
Penny Singleton, Arthur Lake, Larry Simms, Marjorie Kent, Robert Stanton, Angelyn Orr, Jonathan Hale, Paul Harvey, Jack Rice, Bobby Larson, Charles Arnt, Margie Liszt, Frank Orth, Frank Jenks. 69 minutes.

19. *Blondie's Big Moment.* Columbia, 1947, Abby Berlin.
Penny Singleton, Arthur Lake, Larry Simms, Marjorie Kent, Jerome Cowan, Anita Louise, Danny Mummert, Jack Rice, Jack Davis, Johnny Granath, Hal K. Dawson, Eddie Acuff, Alyn Lockwood, Robert Stevens, Douglas Wood. 69 minutes.

20. *Blondie's Holiday.* Columbia, 1947, Abby Berlin.
Penny Singleton, Arthur Lake, Larry Simms, Marjorie Kent, Jerome Cowan, Grant Mitchell, Sid Tomack, Mary Young, Jeff York, Bobby Larson, Jody Gilbert, Jack Rice. 61 minutes.

21. *Blondie in the Dough.* Columbia, 1947, Abby Berlin.
Penny Singleton, Arthur Lake, Larry Simms, Marjorie Kent, Jerome Cowan, Hugh Herbert, Clarence Kolb, Danny Mummert, William Forrest, Eddie Acuff, Norman Phillips, Kernan Cripps, Fred Sears. 69 minutes.

22. *Blondie's Anniversary.* Columbia, 1947, Abby Berlin.
Penny Singleton, Arthur Lake, Larry Simms, Marjorie Kent, Adele Jergens, Jerome Cowan, Grant Mitchell, William Frawley, Edmund MacDonald, Fred Sears, Jack Rice, Alyn Lockwood, Frank Wilcox. 75 minutes.

23. *Blondie's Reward.* Columbia, 1948, Abby Berlin.
Penny Singleton, Arthur Lake, Larry Simms, Marjorie Kent, Jerome Cowan, Gay Nelson, Ross Ford, Danny Mummert, Paul Harvey, Frank Jenks, Chick Chandler, Jack Rice, Eddie Acuff, Alyn Lockwood, Frank Sully, Myron Healey, Chester Clute. 65 minutes.

24. *Blondie's Secret.* Columbia, 1949, Edward Bernds.
Penny Singleton, Arthur Lake, Larry Simms, Marjorie Kent, Jerome Cowan, Thurston Hall, Jack Rice, Danny Mummert, Frank Orth, Alyn Lockwood, Eddie Acuff, Murray Alper, William Phillips, Greta Granstedt, Grandon Rhodes. 68 minutes.

25. *Blondie's Big Deal.* Columbia, 1949, Edward Bernds.
Penny Singleton, Arthur Lake, Larry Simms, Marjorie Kent, Jerome Cowan, Collette Lyons, Wilton Graff, Ray Walker, Stanley Andrews, Alan Dinehart III, Eddie Acuff, Jack Rice, Chester Clute, George Lloyd, Alyn Lockwood, Danny Mummert. 66 minutes.

26. *Blondie Hits the Jackpot.* Columbia, 1949, Edward Bernds.
Penny Singleton, Arthur Lake, Larry Simms, Marjorie Kent, Jerome Cowan, Lloyd Corrigan, Danny Mummert, James Flavin, Dick Wessel, Ray Teal, Alyn Lockwood. 66 minutes.

27. *Blondie's Hero.* Columbia, 1950, Edward Bernds.
Penny Singleton, Arthur Lake, Larry Simms, William Frawley, Iris Adrian, Edward Earle, Danny Mummert, Joe Sawyer, Teddy Infuhr, Alyn Lockwood, Frank Jenks, Dick Wessel, Jimmy Lloyd, Robert Emmett Keane, Mary Newton, Pat Flaherty, Ted Mapes, Frank Wilcox, Frank Sully. 67 minutes.

28. *Beware of Blondie.* Columbia, 1950, Edward Bernds.
Penny Singleton, Arthur Lake, Larry Simms, Marjorie Kent, Adele Jergens, Dick Wessel, Jack Rice, Alyn Lockwood, Emory Parnell, Isobel Withers, Danny Mummert, Douglas Fowley, William E. Green. 66 minutes.

Boyfriend Ted Nickerson (Frankie Thomas) sends a message for help via Morse Code while Nancy (Bonita Granville) watches apprehensively in *Nancy Drew, Reporter*.

NANCY DREW

Nancy Drew, Detective
(1938)

Screenplay by Kenneth Gamet, based on the "Nancy Drew" stories by Carolyn Keene. Camera, L. William O'Connell. Editor, Frank Magee. Directed by William Clemens. Λ First National Picture. 67 minutes.

Nancy Drew	BONITA GRANVILLE
Carson Drew	JOHN LITEL
Challon	JAMES STEPHENSON
Ted Nickerson	FRANKIE THOMAS
Inspector Milligan	FRANK ORTH
Effie Schneider	RENIE RIANO
Mary Eldridge	HELENA PHILLIPS EVANS
Hollister	CHARLES TROWBRIDGE
Keifer	DICK PURCELL
Adam Thorne	ED KEANE
Dr. Spires	BRANDON TYNAN
Miss Van Deering	VERA LEWIS
Miss Tyson	MAE BUSCH
Spud Murphy	TOMMY BUPP
Mrs. Spires	LOTTIE WILLIAMS

She can get a balky outboard motor going again with a bobby pin. She can scale a trellis to a second-story window. She can shoot a rabbit at 100 yards. And in a pinch, she can swim a quarter-of-a-mile with all her clothes on.

While little boys curled up with books about Tarzan and Tom Swift in pre–World War II days, little girls thrilled to the adventures of Nancy Drew.

The 16-year-old sleuth* is the creation of Carolyn Keene, the *nom de plume* of Harriet S. Adams, a grandmotherly widow whom *Newsday* columnist Mike McGrady once dubbed the "world's most successful unknown author." Writing under a pseudonym, Mrs. Adams has turned out 46 *Nancy Drew* books. Since 1930, they have sold about 40 million copies and been translated into 17 languages. They have helped shape the dreams of generations of growing boys and girls and inspired a movie series starring Bonita Granville.

And the end is nowhere in sight. Not only are new titles still churning out—the latest is *The Secret of Mission Bay* (1972)—but old ones are still doing a brisk business. Mrs. Adams reports that *Nancy Drew* books sold 1.5 million copies last year compared to 1 million for *The Hardy Boys*. The two series are today's best-selling juveniles. But the competition is really academic. They—along with several other books for the children's market—are all produced by the Stratemeyer Syndicate, a seven-man concern Mrs. Adams runs with her partner, Andrew E. Svenson.

It was Mrs. Adams' father, Edward Stratemeyer, who started the syndicate and from it produced the *Hardy Boys* and *Nancy Drew* series. "He thought juvenile trends followed adult books trends by about five years," Mrs. Adams said. "When adult book mysteries came into vogue, he took note. And within five years, he started juvenile mysteries. He created the Hardy Boys in 1927. And Nancy Drew in 1930."

Stratemeyer, a free-lance writer whose efforts ranged from pulp serials to historical novels, began writing magazine short stories in the 1880s. An admirer of juvenile author Horatio Alger, Stratemeyer edited 18 of Alger's "rags to riches" stories after the author's death and completed his last story.

But it wasn't until 1910, that Edward Stratemeyer came into his own. That was the year he founded the Stratemeyer Syndicate to supply publishers with stories for boys and girls. It became a literary gold mine.

The magic formula for mass-producing books was a simple one. Stratemeyer turned out bare-bones plots and outlines. Ghost-writers fleshed them out—although Stratemeyer wrote some himself and edited them all. He started with such soon-to-be-immortal heroes as the Rover Boys, the Motor Boys and Tom Swift. He went on to create such perennial favorites as the Bobbsey Twins and the Hardy Boys. There were also such lesser-known characters as Bomba the Jungle

*She becomes 18 years old in revised editions.

Boy, Bunny Brown, Curlytops, Don Sturdy, Honey Bunch, Roy Stover and the X Bar X Boys.

Stratemeyer wrote the books under no less than 46 pen names—Victor Appleton *(Tom Swift)*, Franklin W. Dixon *(Hardy Boys)*, Laura Lee Hope *(Bobbsey Twins)*, Arthur W. Winfield *(Rover Boys)*, et al. "He used pen names," Mrs. Adams said, "because he wrote books for boys, books for girls and books for different age groups. And normally a person writes for only one classification." She said she did not know just how he went about coining the pseudonyms, except that he tried to make the names euphonious—catchy, easy to say, and easy for children to remember.

Over his long career, he personally authored 250 books and had a hand in doing 700 others. The total of 950 books is utterly mind-boggling when one considers that many full-time writers produce no more than 10 or 20 books in a lifetime. It dwarfs prolific Isaac Asimov's awesome total of something over 100 titles. But, at the same time, it is somewhat unsettling to realize that a single man had such enormous influence over the reading habits of so many children.

There was occasional criticism of the books' low literary value and obviously impossible plots. Some librarians became dismayed because they thought the books diverted children from the classics. But their protests didn't interfere with sales. Stratemeyer won the nicknames "the Henry Ford of the juvenile industry" and "the father of the 50-centers." That was the going price for his books through most of his lifetime. Today, they sell for $1.50.

Stratemeyer wrote three *Nancy Drew* novels before his death in 1930 at the age of 78. Then, his daughter, Mrs. Adams, a Wellesley graduate and later the wife of an investment broker and mother of three, took over.

She and her staff work on the fifth floor of an old office building in East Orange, New Jersey. For years, Mrs. Adams put in a full nine-to-five day. A vaporizer sits in one corner of her tastefully appointed office, spewing forth great clouds of steam. One visitor said the vaporizer seemed equally effective for clearing up a hangover or for taking the crease out of permanent press pants. Actually, she uses it to put moisture into the hot, dry air sent up by the building's antiquated heating system.

Her usual approach to doing a book begins when she sketches a brief description of plots and subplots. Then she jots down an outline. When she is ready to begin, she turns to a Dictaphone machine. Her books project a simple, unadorned writing style—Mrs. Adams likes the word "peppy"—and her characters remain honest, wholesome, all-American types.

"They have to be smart," she said. "But always tactful, especially in their detective work. They never argue with grown-ups. If they disagree with them, it's always afterward when they're by themselves. They're never disrespectful. And they always tell the truth."

Edward Stratemeyer (left), creator of *Nancy Drew*—as well as such popular juvenile fictional series as the *Hardy Boys,* the *Rover Boys, Bomba the Jungle Boy,* and the *Bobbsey Twins.* When he died in 1930, his fantastic total of 950 books had earned him the nickname of the "Henry Ford of the juvenile industry." Harriet Adams (right), who carried on her father's career. She wrote 46 of the 49 *Nancy Drew* stories. Since 1930, they have sold about 40 million copies, been translated into 17 languages and been the basis of a four-picture Warner Brothers series.

Bonita Granville at age 14 in 1937—one year before she starred in the *Nancy Drew* series. At right, she is shown in 1969 with her husband Jack Wrather, industrialist and TV producer. Mrs. Wrather is now the mother of four and assistant producer of the "Lassie" television series.

Nancy hasn't changed much over the years. But her readers have. In the 1930s, most of her fans were between 10 and 15. Today, youngsters have grown older earlier through the influence of television. Girls pick up Nancy Drew at about 8 and put her down by 12. "I think that's regrettable," Mrs. Adams said. "Childhood is so short today. All those pressures—school, athletics, singing lessons, dancing lessons, skiing lessons, even. Oh, yes, and straight A's in everything."

What is it that draws the sub-teen crowd to Nancy Drew? Certainly not her style. Nancy is far from a mod swinger. She has not even allowed her boyfriend, college sophomore Ned Nickerson ("Ted" in the the movies because somehow producers felt it sounded clearer), a single kiss in more than 40 years.*

"We get a good deal of mail," Mrs. Adams said. "People wondering when Nancy is going to marry Ned. But our feeling about this is that when a girl gets to thinking about this, well, it's time she stopped reading Nancy Drew."

The truth is Nancy isn't likely to get married until the series ends. "My father tried that with one heroine," Mrs. Adams said. "Sales went right down. The instant a girl marries—no matter what her age—it puts her in a class with her own mother."

If Nancy is destined to lead a literary life of celibacy, she nevertheless is a quick-witted, self-reliant teen-ager who has won the confidence of her widowed father, attorney Carson Drew. While her girlfriends are out buying the latest Frank Sinatra records, this pert, well-to-do youngster from suburban River Heights somewhere in Middle America is out catching crooks. Her Dad gives her free rein—as many girls wish their real-life fathers would—and time and time again, she proves she can take care of herself even in the most trying circumstances.

There are other reasons for her popularity. Arthur Prager, writing about the golden age of children's literature in his book, *Rascals at Large,* says girls found it easy to identify with Nancy. "She is an example of the fantasy world in which pre-pubescent girls live in daydreams," writes Prager. "A boy can imagine that he is swinging from tree to tree, ululating the victory cry of the bull ape. But he knows in his heart it will never happen. Nancy, on the other hand, is within reach."

Also, said Prager, the stories have a timeless quality. "I looked for anachronisms in our 1930 first edition of *The Secret of the Old Clock,*" he said. "Except for Nancy's roadster with its running boards and rumble seat, there were none. Like the Land of Oz, Nancy Drew Country is another time dimension, untouched by the outside world."

This is only partially true. Nancy has, in fact, had to bow to changing times

---

*Curiously, Nancy's best girlfriend has rather masculine inclinations. She is George Fayne, a "tall, athletic girl who loved her boyish name." The relationship is portrayed as platonic.

in several respects. First, the story line of the books has become more complicated. The original books had only one plot. The later ones have a plot and subplot that mesh. Mrs. Adams spends three-quarters of her time updating old books. For every new book she writes, she revises three older ones.

But the biggest change is the elimination of ethnic stereotypes that would not fit into today's juvenile books. There is Uncle Rufus, the Voodoo practitioner, and Negroes like Mandy and Beulah, who said "Lawsy Me," "Yassuh" and "Scuse me, sah." Irish and Italians spoke in dialect, too. And some of the most obnoxious characters were Jews.

Pressure from school and minority groups have prompted the changes. "These things were not meant to show prejudice at the time," said an editor at Grosset and Dunlap, Mrs. Adams' publisher. "But younger readers are so impressionable. We just have to be extremely careful about including anything of that kind."

And so in the 1960s, Mrs. Adams began a "modernizing" campaign. She has rewritten 22 of these earlier books. Negroes have become articulate. So have Irish and Italians. According to author Prager, Mrs. Adams has cleaned up "vulgar, pushy Johnny and Kitt Blair, who had changed their name from Sellerstein, and smirking, cringing, disbarred lawyer Abe Jacobs."

Asked about these changes, Mrs. Adams said she doesn't remember Jacobs and the Sellersteins. But, she said, the Voodoo man is a true-to-life character. "Nobody was making fun of him," Mrs. Adams said. "He's a part of New Orleans —even today . . . Children of the 1930s grew up with dialect [in the books they read]. In the older days, there weren't so many rules and organizations and committees that wouldn't allow things . . . Now you can't do it."

With or without the changes, many of the stories offer the fascination of a tingling mystery geared to the level of a pre-teenager. There are no guns. And no murders take place. But the plots, which have their origin in the Mary Roberts Rinehart mystery-adventure Gothic pattern, follow a neat and predictable line.

In his book *The Unembarrassed Muse,* Russell Nye sums up the themes like this: "Nancy by accident stumbles into a mysterious situation, probes it and is warned to stay out. However, she continues to investigate, follows a series of puzzling clues, and after some dangerous moments, solves the affair, which usually involves money, wills, valuables, hidden jewels, lost documents, old maps, forgeries, embezzlements, and the like."

Nye adds: "'Each narrative involves a chase, a kidnaping or both. There is a hideout, a mysterious box or stairway or chamber or code and some violence (lightning, dynamite, landslides, fires, storms, auto wrecks, wild animal attacks) which she barely escapes."

In 1938, Warner Brothers became interested in the novels' movie possibilities and began casting about for a teen-ager to star in a series. The studio eventually picked Bonita Granville, a pint-sized, blue-eyed blonde who had previously parlayed meanness into Hollywood success.

Born in New York City in 1923, she was the daughter of show people and had joined her parents' vaudeville act at the tender age of three. But it was not her talents as much as her resemblance to actress Ann Harding that won Bonita her first film role. Strictly on look-alike appearances, she was picked to play Miss Harding's daughter in *Westward Passage* (1932). She went on to small parts in *Silver Dollar* (1932), *Cavalcade* (1933) and *Ah, Wilderness* (1935). However, it was her searing performance as the shrill, malicious schoolgirl in *These Three* (1936) —a watered-down version of Lillian Hellman's play, "The Children's Hour"— that won her widespread attention. She won an Oscar nomination. From then on, it was Bonita the brat.

As she advanced into her teens, fan magazines began reporting her social life. She went steady with Jackie Cooper while she attended school on the Metro-Goldwyn-Mayer lot. Lana Turner and Mickey Rooney were classmates. Others in her dating group were Peter Lind Hayes and Mary Healy (later husband and wife), Judy Garland and Dick Paxton.

Sidney Skolsky reported that Bonita's favorite radio program was "Those We Love." In a 1941 "Tintype" column, he wrote:

> She is five feet, two inches tall, weighs 105 pounds and her hair is naturally curly, golden . . . She goes to the movies with Jackie Cooper and they hold hands watching themselves on the screen . . . No matter what time she and her friends return home from a party, she has to make coffee for them. This is all she can make—coffee. They take their shoes off so as not to wake up the household. This makes them feel "smart." . . . Her favorite drink is Coca-Cola with a dash of cinnamon . . . She drinks coffee without cream or sugar. She always takes the first sip with a spoon . . . She loses pocketbooks and is always finding pocketbooks—but they aren't the pocketbooks she lost. She wants to marry young. But she thinks 21 is early enough.

In another interview, she talked about playing "meanies" on the screen. She said they are very definite characterizations, which she divided into four types— vicious, psychopathic, mischievous, and sympathetic. Some years later, she added a fifth type—sniveling. She said she liked being cast as meanies. "It started my career," she told the author in a telephone interview from Beverly Hills. "And I enjoyed doing roles as heavies. It was always easier for me than just playing myself."

But it was hard work, too.

"In *Beloved Brat* [1938], I remember I went into a tantrum because the ritzy

Bonita Granville helps John Litel, her movie
Dad, on with his shoes in *Nancy Drew, Detective*
(1938), first of the series.

City Editor Thomas Jackson seems to have his hands full as Nancy and her
classmates descend on the River Heights newspaper office. Charles Halton,
right, looks on approvingly. The kids, from left, are: Florence Halop, Lois
Verner, Joan Leslie (soon to be a star for Warner's), Jack Wagner and Charles
Smith.

butler wouldn't let me keep a colored boy in my room," she said. "I had to be dragged up a flight of stairs by the hair. And we did the scene 15 times."

It was no surprise that Bonita soon tired of playing rotten little kids. "I'm growing up," she told one movie reporter. "A girl likes to have people think of her as a young lady and not as a kid who beats her head on the floor every time she can't have her own way."

Warner Brothers came to her rescue by casting her in the *Nancy Drew* series. It never achieved the popularity of *Andy Hardy* or *Charlie Chan*. She made only four of these pictures—from 1938 to 1939, when she was 15 and 16. But she played them with the skill and ease of a veteran and this helped turn them into fast-moving, entertaining fare for the matinee trade.

Adding to their quality were plots that were well above the run-of-the-mill programmer. For example, the series opener, *Nancy Drew, Detective* (1938), revolves around a kidnapping, strange goings-on in a sanitarium and a message for help transmitted from an X-ray machine.

The movie opens as a wealthy spinster pledges a $250,000 gift to the Brinwood School for Girls. The next day, she suddenly disappears. Hollister (Charles Trowbridge), her business manager, announces that she has gone to an undisclosed rest home. The faculty feels the old lady has really changed her mind about the donation. But Nancy Drew suspects something odd is going on. So she sets out to find the old lady to prove to her classmates that she was sincere in making the donation.

As she searches for the sanitarium, she passes Dr. Spires' (Brandon Tynan) home just as kidnappers throw him in a car. Some hours later, the doctor returns. Ignoring the gang's warning not to talk, he tells Nancy's father (John Litel) that he was blindfolded, and taken to the country to treat an old woman. Nancy's father reports the case to Inspector Milligan (Frank Orth). The next day, mobsters beat up the doctor, then follow the Drews and warn them to forget what they know.

But Nancy refuses to be scared off. She stays on the case and finds an injured carrier pigeon with the cryptic message—"Shoulder okay. Blue Bells." She and her boyfriend, Ted (Frankie Thomas, a talented youngster from the New York stage), release the bird, follow it to a country estate and call the police. But much to the teen-agers' embarrassment, the estate merely turns out to be the home of the old lady's business manager.

A few days later, Nancy and Ted go to Sylvan Lake with Ted's parents. By chance, she sees the kidnap car again. It drives off before she can follow it. But ever-resourceful, she and Ted go aloft in a plane and spot the car in an old estate. They go to the estate and find it is a sanitarium for old ladies. Nancy disguises herself as an old woman. Ted dresses as a nurse. Then, after overhearing the password, they get inside the grounds by whispering "Blue Bells" to the guard.

The sanitarium turns out to be the kidnappers' hideout. Nancy and Ted find the old lady. But the crooks capture them, hold all three for ransom and lock them in an old storeroom. There, Ted finds an X-ray machine, which he ingeniously rigs up as a makeshift wireless. He causes interference with radios for miles around and sends out a call for help in Morse code. The cops receive his dot and dash message and rush to the sanitarium. They arrive just in time to catch the gang. And Nancy Drew has solved her first screen case.

After the *Nancy Drew* series, Miss Granville went on to play in such major films as *H. M. Pulham Esquire* (1941), *Now Voyager* (1942) and *Hitler's Children* (1942),* in addition to appearing in two other series—*Dr. Kildare* and *Andy Hardy*. She retired soon after her marriage in 1947 to industrialist Jack Wrather, whose far-flung interests were to include Disneyland Hotel, Tele-Prompter and the "Lone Ranger" and "Lassie" shows. However, after having four children, Miss Granville returned to the business world to become associate producer of the "Lassie" television series.

Yet, despite her successful career as a TV executive, her image as a child-star persists. Occasionally, she comes east to promote the "Lassie" series and, inevitably, reporters talk to her as if she were still playing Nancy Drew. At 49, the world of X-rated movies is a world she never knew.

"I don't go to the movies," she says. "They're indecent. They appeal to the baser tendencies, to temptations. Young people aren't able to cope with them, all this sex starting too early. It's thrown at them under the guise of art. But it's really immoral, amoral stuff made just for the money they can make."

"More than that," she adds, "it's done something to our generation. It's destroyed romance and imagination that goes along with sex. And that's pretty important because otherwise, sex becomes mechanical. Don't get me wrong. I'm a great believer in sex. But that's not the way to go about it."

And how does the "now generation" compare to the youth of her era?

"I'm against all this permissiveness. This rioting and revelling," she said, referring to the campus rebellions of the 1960s. "When I was a girl in school, we didn't have all the advantages these kids have today. The schools, the books. Even the television, which can be such a marvelous tool. I believe in freedom of speech as much as anyone else. But there's a limit. These young people today . . . Where are their good purposes?"

Bluestockinged Nancy Drew, never kissed in more than four decades, might have agreed.

---

*Miss Granville said this was her favorite of all her movies. "It put me into the star category," she said.

NANCY DREW SERIES

1. *Nancy Drew, Detective.* Warner Brothers, 1938, William Clemens.
   Bonita Granville (as Nancy Drew), John Litel (as Carson Drew), James Stephenson, Frankie Thomas (as Ted Nickerson), Frank Orth, Renie Riano, Helena Phillips Evans, Charles Trowbridge, Dick Purcell, Ed Keane, Brandon Tynan, Vera Lewis, Mae Busch, Tommy Bupp, Lottie Williams. 60 minutes.

2. *Nancy Drew—Reporter.* Warner Brothers, 1939, William Clemens.
   Bonita Granville, John Litel, Frankie Thomas, Mary Lee, Sheila Bromley, Larry Williams, Betty Amann, Thomas Jackson, Dickie Jones, Olin Howland, Frank Orth, Charles Halton, Joan Leslie, Florence Halop, Lois Verner, Jack Wagner, Charles Smith. 65 minutes.

3. *Nancy Drew—Trouble Shooter.* Warner Brothers, 1939, William Clemens.
   Bonita Granville, Frankie Thomas, John Litel, Aldrich Bowker, Charlotte Wynters, Edgar Edwards, Renie Riano, Roger Imhof, Erville Alderson, Willie Best, John Harron, Cliff Saum, Tom Wilson. 70 minutes.

4. *Nancy Drew and the Hidden Staircase.* Warner Brothers, 1939, William Clemens.
   Bonita Granville, Frankie Thomas, John Litel, Frank Orth, Renie Riano, Vera Lewis, Louise Carter, William Gould, George Guhl, John Ridgely, DeWolf Hopper, Creighton Hale, Frank Mayo, Fred Tozere, Don Rowan, Dick Elliott. 78 minutes.

Lupe Velez, the Mexican Spitfire, whose life ended tragically at age 34.

MEXICAN SPITFIRE

Mexican Spitfire

(1939)

Screenplay by Charles E. Roberts and Joseph A. Fields. From a story by Fields. Musical director, Paul Sawtell. Photography, Jack Mackenzie. Art director, Van Nest Polglase. Editor, Desmond Marquette. Production executive, Lee Marcus. Directed by Leslie Goodwins. Produced by Cliff Reid for RKO. 67 minutes.

Carmelita	LUPE VELEZ
Uncle Matt ⎱	
Lord Epping ⎰	LEON ERROL
Dennis Lindsay	DONALD WOODS
Elizabeth Price	LINDA HAYES
Aunt Della	ELISABETH RISDON
Chumley	CECIL KELLAWAY
Butler	CHARLES COLEMAN

Of all of Hollywood's actresses, she was the most vivacious. She was the one with the most verve and energy, the one bubbling over with the sheer exuberance of life. And so her suicide in 1944 came as both a surprise and a shock.

They found Lupe Velez clad in pale blue pajamas on her bed in her suburban

Laurel Canyon mansion outside Hollywood. Mrs. Beulah Kinder, her housekeeper and personal secretary, discovered the body. She said a half-empty bottle of sleeping pills was nearby. "She looked so peaceful," the housekeeper said. "I thought she was asleep."

At 34, the raven-haired Mexican star was at the peak of her flamboyant career. Lupe was one of the film capital's loveliest stars. She was just over five feet, weighed 108 pounds and her glistening black hair set off her wide, dark eyes and her beautiful tawny complexion.

But she chose to end her life because she couldn't face the shame of bearing a child out of wedlock from a man she felt bore her no love. Nor could she bring herself to have an abortion. Soon after her death, a medical examiner disclosed that she would have given birth in about five months.

Five days before her suicide, she had quarreled bitterly with Harold Ramond, an obscure French actor. She had once called Ramond "the one love in my life." One of two notes on a small table near her bed where she lay, her long hair streaming across a satin pillowcase, was addressed "To Harold."

It read: "May God forgive you and forgive me, too. But I prefer to take my life away and my baby's before I bring him with shame or kill him. How could you, Harold, fake such great love for me and my baby when all the time you didn't want us. I see no other way out for me. So good by and good luck to you. Love, Lupe."

Another note written to Mrs. Kinder concluded: ". . . Say good by to all my friends and the American press that were always so nice to me. Lupe."

Estelle Taylor, former wife of Jack Dempsey, said that Miss Velez had hinted at suicide the night before. Miss Taylor had paid Lupe an extended visit from 9:30 P.M. to 3:30 A.M. Lupe, Miss Taylor said, was depressed and distraught. She paced the floor. "Lupe told me about the baby," Miss Taylor said. "She said she had plenty of opportunity to get rid of it. But she said, 'It's my baby. I couldn't commit murder and still live with myself. I would rather kill myself.' "

Weeks earlier, before her fight with Ramond, Lupe had announced that they planned to marry. Later, she said it was all off. Ramond appeared shaken and confused when reporters reached him. He said he never dreamed she would take her life.

"The last time I talked to Lupe, I told her I was going to marry her any way she wanted," the handsome continental said. "She said then that she wasn't going to have a baby. So we parted." However, Ramond admitted that he had once asked her to sign an agreement that he was only marrying her to give the baby a name. "But I didn't mean that," he said. "We had had a fight. And I was in a terrible temper."

Although Ramond, who quickly faded from the Hollywood scene, was Lupe's last boyfriend, he was far from the only one. Lupe's first great American love was

Errol played a triple role, appearing as the bumbling, bow-legged Lord Basil
Epping, as Uncle Matt, and as Uncle Matt masquerading as Lord Epping.
Here Lupe's embrace gives Lord Epping an uncomfortable moment as Lyle
Talbot looks on.

Lupe does a Spanish dance in *Mexican Spitfire's Blessed Event* (1943), last in
the eight picture series. She was a dancer before beginning her film career.
Dancers are George Rogers and Don Kramer.

Gary Cooper, then a shy, young actor moving up from silent westerns. They made *The Wolf Song* (1929) together and became constant companions. They were seen together at nightclubs, premieres, restaurants. He spent weekends at her palatial home, sometimes staying for months. But they had frequent spats. And in the end, her mercurial nature did not fit Cooper's concept of wedded bliss. So their tempestuous romance never reached the altar. But Cooper never forgot her. Once, he was asked what the biggest thrill he got from his movie career. "Lupe," he said.

A list of her escorts would be sprinkled with names of the movies' top stars. There were Ronald Colman, Ricardo Cortez and Jack Gilbert, among many others. She was a flashy figure in public—often seen glistening in diamonds or wrapped in a luxurious $25,000 chinchilla coat.*

Then, in 1933, she married Johnny Weissmuller. But she never learned to control her fiery temper. Nor was Weissmuller exactly a choir boy. Their frequent nightclub brawls and separations kept tabloid writers busy during five stormy years of marriage.

She tried to laugh off her troubles. The way to be happily married, "ees to fight once a week," she told reporters. But once, she stomped out of the house in the middle of the night and sailed for Europe. On another occasion, she kicked a girl out of a party "for making eyes at my Johnee." On the other hand, she said her screen Tarzan sometimes acted like a Tarzan at home—breaking furniture in violent fits.

The marriage just didn't work. And when they were divorced in 1938, she made the widely quoted crack, "Marriage—eet stinks."**

Born Guadaloupe Velez de Villalobos in San Luis de Potosi, Mexico, in 1910, she was the daughter of an army colonel and an opera singer. A theatrical life appealed to Lupe at an early age. She was a trouper before she was grown. At 13, she appeared as a dancer in Mexico City. Soon, she was playing in Mexican movie shorts and musical comedies.

When she came to Los Angeles and danced in a stage show, her dark beauty caught the eye of Douglas Fairbanks. After she had served an apprenticeship in Hal Roach two-reelers, Fairbanks hired her for the role of a wild mountain girl in the silent film, *The Gaucho* (1927). She was an immediate hit. Soon afterward, Florenz Ziegfeld brought her to New York to appear in his musical, "Hot-Cha."

The show was far from first-rate. But she teamed with Bert Lahr and he had

*Her estate was estimated at $100,000–200,000.
**Before their breakup, she was asked for a list of the ten most interesting men. After Weissmuller, she put President Franklin D. Roosevelt ("because if I was his wife, I'd never have to worry about publicity"), Clark Gable ("the nicest man I know"), singer Lawrence Tibbett, comedian Ed Wynn, author Ernest Hemingway, symphony conductor George Enesco, union boss John L. Lewis ("because he ought to be able to handle women the way he handles labor problems"), boxer Jack Dempsey and humorist George S. Kaufman.

a ball ad-libbing their comedy scenes. "Working with Lupe was quite an experience," Lahr said. "She couldn't laugh. She cackled—like a duck. I'd say things under my breath to her on the stage and she'd start to cackle."

Lupe was a free spirit off stage, a liberated woman before her time. And her free-wheeling life style intrigued Lahr. "Lupe never washed," he said. "When she'd go to the Mayfair or somewhere, she'd just put on a dress. Nothing under it—nothing. So when I'd be clowning with her on the stage and I'd notice her dirty hands, I'd say, 'You've got your gloves on again.' It would break her up."

But the stage was only a way station for Lupe. Movies were her first love. Although she did two more musicals, she eventually returned to the West Coast to make such pictures as *East Is West* (1930), *The Squaw Man* (1931), *Cuban Love Song* (1931), *Palooka* (1934) and *Hollywood Party* (1934).

Ironically, she is best remembered for the B-movies she did after she slipped from major productions. The most famous of these is the *Mexican Spitfire* series. It had two things going for Lupe. For one thing, the studio, RKO, took the unusual step of naming the series after her real-life volcanic personality. It was, in fact, originally titled *Hot Tamale*. For another, RKO teamed her with Leon Errol, a veteran stage and screen comedian. He made a perfect foil for her.

Errol's background was not as colorful as Lupe's. But his stage ambitions brought him half-way round the world. Born in Australia, he was prepared for a career as a doctor. But while he was a pre-med student at Sydney University, he wrote and acted in amateur stage musicals. He first appeared as a red-nosed comic in a college operetta and was an instant success. His parents came to see him and afterward his father summoned Leon to his office. He accused his son of disgracing the family. He said that Leon's mother had wept at his performance. Crestfallen, the younger Errol went home to face his mother only to find that she had cried tears of laughter. When his father learned this, he reluctantly permitted Leon to continue doing shows. Eventually, his father despaired of further attempts to turn him into a doctor. After putting in his early training in touring road shows, young Errol came to the United States with his heart set on an acting career.

San Francisco beer hall audiences couldn't understand his accent. But they laughed heartily at his eccentric dancing. So he performed for seasons without speaking. And it was this experience that contributed to his masterful pantomime skill. His most famous impression was that of a happy rubber-legged boozer, pitching to and fro like a seasick sailor, occasionally folding like an accordion.

When he died in 1951 at age 70, the now defunct *New York Herald-Tribune* described the climax of his famous routine. "Errol's entire skeleton would seem to disintegrate within him," the paper said. "He would collapse in a slow heap, like gelatin that has lost its stiffness from being too long in the sun."

The comedian said he got the idea by watching a sick dog. The old pooch, who

Lupe, as Carmelita, sits astride Leon Errol playing Uncle Matt in *Mexican Spitfire's Elephant* (1942). The vivacious Lupe and the rubber-faced Errol made a perfect comedy team.

Lord Epping does his best to soothe a tearful Marion Martin in *Mexican Spitfire's Elephant*. The statuesque Miss Martin rose from the Ziegfeld chorus to become a B-film fixture as the sexy blonde or other-woman type. She appeared in three of the *Spitfire* series.

belonged to a fellow actor, was on his last legs. One night in his dressing room, Errol watched him sag to the floor. Taking pity on the animal, he propped him up against the wall. "He'd stand there for a few seconds," Errol said, "and then slowly and almost imperceptibly, his joints would give in. He'd sort of melt to the floor."

After playing in musical stock and burlesque, he came to New York. Ziegfeld put him in his 1911 "Follies" and Errol became one of the outstanding Broadway comedians of pre–World War I days. One of his memorable performances was in the musical "Sally" in which he starred with the great Marilyn Miller. It ran 568 performances. Errol went on to direct and stage some of the "Follies," and appeared with such other musical comedy stars as Fanny Brice, Mae West, Bert Williams, Ed Wynn and W. C. Fields.

In 1924, he went to Hollywood and later made two-reel comedies, which he continued doing on and off throughout his entire career. A favorite character part was that of a henpecked husband and he appeared opposite Dorothy Granger in many of these roles in short subjects. But he also did feature-length films. He played in nearly 60 such productions, including *Sally* (1925), *One Heavenly Night* (1930), *Her Majesty Love* (1931), *We're Not Dressing* (1934), *Never Give a Sucker an Even Break* (1941) and *The Invisible Man's Revenge* (1944). From 1946 to 1950, he appeared with Joe Kirkwood, Jr. in the *Joe Palooka* series, playing Knobby Walsh, the fighter's manager.

But most movie fans remember Errol as Lord Epping, the bluff, absentminded, featherbrained character in the *Mexican Spitfire* movies. The first picture in this comedy series was *Girl from Mexico* (1939), a story of the search for a Mexican singer to star on a radio show. Errol's comedy role was a small one and the movie got only lukewarm reviews. But the sequel, *Mexican Spitfire* (1939), gave him free rein and his slapstick, combined with Lupe's whirlwind personality and assault on the King's English, added up to side-splitting farce.

The picture opens as Dennis Lindsay (Donald Woods), an advertising man, and Carmelita (Velez) are returning from their Mexican honeymoon. They are met by Dennis' haughty Aunt Della (Elisabeth Risdon), who disapproves of the match, his Uncle Matt (Errol), who is fond of them both, and Elizabeth Price (Linda Hayes), Dennis' jealous ex-fiancee. Elizabeth, egged on by her aunt, sets out to break up the marriage.

While Dennis goes to meet a British client, whiskey baron Lord Epping (also played by Errol), Elizabeth gets Carmelita drunk. Then, she persuades the tipsy bride to visit Dennis' office, where Carmelita promptly makes a fool out of herself in front of Lord Epping. Thinking fast, Dennis passes her off as his secretary. But this only complicates matters. After Dennis invites Lord Epping to dinner, he realizes he can't introduce Carmelita as his wife. So, to avoid the embarrassment of explaining Carmelita, Dennis gets Elizabeth to pose as his wife.

That only infuriates Carmelita. However, she soon gets a chance to vent her spleen. When she learns Lord Epping can't make it, Carmelita gets Uncle Matt to make up as the titled Englishman. This he does by donning wig, whiskers and spectacles. In fact, by spouting "donchaknows" and "cawnts," he seems a dead-ringer for the old codger.

Impersonating Lord Epping, Uncle Matt arrives and starts insulting Elizabeth, Aunt Della and everyone present—to Carmelita's delight and Dennis' dismay. Accidentally, he spills wine on his shirt. And while he is in his own room changing, the real Lord Epping arrives.

Utter confusion reigns. The two Lord Eppings (both played by Errol) somehow avoid meeting. There's a lot of in-one-door-and-out-the-other business as they baffle everyone with their contradictory pronouncements. The mistaken identity bit may be as ancient as vaudeville, but it works beautifully here.

This was Errol at the height of his low-comedy talent. "His Lord Epping is a lean cousin of Colonel Blimp," said reviewer Theodore Strauss of the *New York Times,* "a beetle-browed, beef-eating old duffer with legs as brittle as peppermint sticks and a way of blowing his vowels through his fluffy moustache in a terrifying manner. He grasps at ideas in fits and starts and glares down his nose at bounders to whom he hasn't been introduced properly. If this is libel, let the English laugh loudest."

Epping finally leaves in a rage. Carmelita feels that Dennis never wants to see her again. So she and Uncle Matt skip to Mexico—he to avoid arrest for imper-sonation, she to get a quick divorce.

But Lord Epping has also gone to Mexico and Uncle Matt learns he still wants to have Dennis handle his Americana whiskey campaign. Sure enough, Uncle Matt saves the day and gets the signed contract. With Carmelita, he hurries back to New York. There, they find Dennis having a bachelor dinner on the eve of marrying Elizabeth. But Carmelita gets a telegram telling her that her Mexican divorce is illegal. She's still Dennis' wife, which now suits both Dennis and her fine. However, nobody else knows this. When Carmelita wakes up the next morning at the Lindsay home and finds guests assembling for the wedding, she has a knock-down, drag-out, hair-pulling battle with Elizabeth. It all ends in a wild, pie-throwing, free-for-all.

Mexican Spitfire got top reviews and RKO began grinding out the series at about two films a year. In time, they succumbed to the fatal series flaw. Plot situations became repetitive. The audience eventually became so familiar with the characters that it could anticipate the action well in advance. Errol's uproarious antics became the main prop holding up the pictures. That he could still amuse audiences from such thin material was a testimony to the brilliance of his mim-icry. But as Errol's star began rising, Lupe's career began going downhill.

"While Errol appears on the screen the proceedings are at their funniest," said one critic after watching *Mexican Spitfire Sees a Ghost* (1942), sixth in the series. "But it is another matter when other members of the company are required to carry on by themselves." Said another reviewer: "It is Lupe who claws her way through the role. But it is Errol who makes each film a personal comic excuse." Said a third: "All but the title of the series has been stolen from Miss Velez by the act Errol does so well."

In the end, it really didn't matter. One desolate dawn, Lupe found herself alone and pregnant. And it was her bitter love life, not her fading screen career, that impelled her to open that vial of pills and swallow enough of those brain-numbing tablets to blot out all memory.

And so she passed quietly from the Hollywood scene. She was 34, a woman in the full flower of her beauty. She took with her an unborn child whose sex would never be known. Nobody thought about it then, but it was ironic that the last series picture she would make was called *Mexican Spitfire's Blessed Event.*

Lupe shows Leon a statuette of a broken-down nag in *Mexican Spitfire's Blessed Event.* By the series' end, Lupe's career was waning. Leon's was rising.

MEXICAN SPITFIRE SERIES

1. *The Girl from Mexico.* RKO, 1939, Leslie Goodwins.
   Lupe Velez (as Carmelita), Leon Errol (as Uncle Matt), Donald Woods (as Dennis Lindsay), Linda Hayes (as Elizabeth Price), Elisabeth Risdon (as Aunt Della), Donald MacBride, Edward Raquello, Ward Bond. 69 minutes.

2. *Mexican Spitfire.* RKO, 1939, Leslie Goodwins.
   Lupe Velez, Leon Errol (as Uncle Matt and Lord Epping), Donald Woods, Linda Hayes, Elisabeth Risdon, Cecil Kellaway, Charles Coleman, Grant Withers, Tom Kennedy, Gus Schilling, Ferris Taylor. 67 minutes.

3. *Mexican Spitfire Out West.* RKO, 1940, Leslie Goodwins.
   Lupe Velez, Leon Errol, Donald Woods, Elisabeth Risdon, Cecil Kellaway, Linda Hayes, Lydia Bilbrook, Charles Coleman, Charles Quigley, Eddie Dunn. 76 minutes.

4. *Mexican Spitfire's Baby.* RKO, 1941, Leslie Goodwins.
   Lupe Velez, Leon Errol, Charles (Buddy) Rogers, ZaSu Pitts, Elisabeth Risdon, Fritz Feld, Marion Martin, Lloyd Corrigan, Lydia Bilbrook, Tom Kennedy. 69 minutes.

5. *Mexican Spitfire at Sea.* RKO, 1941, Leslie Goodwins.
   Lupe Velez, Leon Errol, Charles (Buddy) Rogers, ZaSu Pitts, Elisabeth Risdon, Florence Bates, Marion Martin, Lydia Bilbrook, Eddie Dunn, Harry Holman, Marten Lamont. 73 minutes.

6. *Mexican Spitfire Sees a Ghost.* RKO, 1942, Leslie Goodwins.
   Lupe Velez, Leon Errol, Charles (Buddy) Rogers, Elisabeth Risdon, Donald MacBride, Minna Gombell, Don Barclay, John Maguire, Lilian Randolph, Marten Lamont. 70 minutes.

7. *Mexican Spitfire's Elephant.* RKO, 1942, Leslie Goodwins.
   Lupe Velez, Leon Errol, Walter Reed, Elisabeth Risdon, Lyle Talbot, Lydia Bilbrook, Marion Martin, Jack Briggs. 63 minutes.

8. *Mexican Spitfire's Blessed Event.* RKO, 1943, Leslie Goodwins.
   Lupe Velez, Leon Errol, Walter Reed, Elisabeth Risdon, Lydia Bilbrook, Hugh Beaumont, Aileen Carlyle, Alan Carney, Wally Brown, Ruth Lee, George Rogers, Don Kramer. 63 minutes.

Glenda Farrell as Torchy Blane, the nervy girl reporter who pre-dated women's lib.

TORCHY BLANE

Torchy Blane in Chinatown
(1939)

Screenplay by George Bricker from a story by Murray Leinster and Will Jenkins. Based on characters created by Frederick Nebel. Camera, Warren Lynch. Editor, Frederick Richards. Art Director, Charles Novi. Dialogue director, Harry Seymour. Assistant director, Arthur Leuker. Directed by William Beaudine. Produced by Bryan Foy. Released by Warner Brothers. 58 minutes.

Torchy Blane	GLENDA FARRELL
Steve McBride	BARTON MACLANE
Gahagan	TOM KENNEDY
Captain Condon	PATRIC KNOWLES
Senator Baldwin	HENRY O'NEILL
Mansfield	JAMES STEPHENSON
Janet	JANET SHAW
Fitzhugh	ANDERSON LAWLER
McTavish	FRANK SHANNON
Sergeant	GEORGE GUHL
Staunton	RICHARD BOND
Captain McDonald	EDDY CHANDLER

"Did you break this murder story," a stern-looking McBride asks. "I sure did, you big palooka," cracks Torchy. "You can't muzzle the press." In the middle is big, birdbrained but lovable Sergeant Gahagan (Tom Kennedy).

Torchy winks at a smiling Gahagan as she shows him a badge she has borrowed. Even in the 1930s, Torchy was scrambling for her stories alongside the so-called stronger sex—and got them.

A parade is winding down Main Street. Thousands line the streets, leaving the Haywood National Bank all but empty. The lone customer pushes up to the teller's window. "This is a stickup," he says quietly.

With a band going by outside, no one notices him filling a satchel with $90,000, then dashing to the door. With a spirited Sousa march blaring, no one hears his exchange of gunfire with a bank guard, or sees a teller go down, mortally wounded with a bullet in the chest.

Within minutes, police are on the scene, sealing off the bank. But one persistent person pushes to the edge of the crowd.

"Wait a minute," a cop barks. "You can't go in there, lady." Another says: "There's been a holdup and a murder."

"You're wrong, boys," a pretty, sharp-tongued blonde snaps. "Holdups and murders are my meat. I'm Torchy Blane of the *Star.*"

With that, the nervy gal pushes by the dumbfounded men in blue and skips into the bank to get her story.

A generation before women's lib was born, Torchy Blane was going after fast-breaking cityside stories—asking no quarter and giving none. More often than not, this whirlwind newshen scooped her male colleagues. She was no sob sister, no society dame after the woman's angle. She was an honest to goodness pencil pusher who scrambled for her story along with the so-called stronger sex —and got it.

Yet beneath her hard-boiled exterior was a soft-boiled heart. She was head over heels in love with Detective Lieutenant Steve McBride, played by Barton Mac-Lane.* Torchy was clever enough to solve a murder right under his Irish nose, but not smart enough to lead him to the altar. A sensational murder or a big story always popped up to postpone the wedding bells. So in the end, Torchy got everything but her man.

McBride, of course, really loved Torchy. But he liked her to stay far away from him when he was on a case—and for good reason. He sometimes turned up in time to rescue Torchy, but he never solved anything. As a detective, he made a prize exhibit for women's lib. If the truth be known, said *New York Post* reviewer Archer Winsten, "McBride is putty in the hands of this remarkable force of nature [Torchy]."

The actress who made this bubbly, super–star reporter come alive on the screen was Glenda Farrell. She played Torchy in seven** of the nine films of the series,

---

*A football player at Wesleyan University in Middletown, Connecticut, MacLane was called to Hollywood to appear in *The Quarterback* (1926) with Richard Dix. Thereafter, he played a succession of "heavies," broken by his role in the *Torchy Blane* series. More recently, he appeared on the television series, "The Outlaws." He died in 1969 at the age of 66.

**In *Torchy Blane in Panama* (1938), Lola Lane played Torchy and Paul Kelly was Lieutenant McBride. In *Torchy Plays with Dynamite* (1939), last of the series, Jane Wyman was Torchy and Allen Jenkins appeared as McBride.

which ran from 1936 to 1939. And perhaps no other actress ever fit as well into a series role.

Director Frank McDonald credited her with being responsible for a good part of the series' success. One of the reasons he singled out was her exciting, fast-talking delivery. Miss Farrell could spout lines in rat-a-tat style. She could race along a mile-a-minute and still get dramatic inflection into her voice. *In Torchy Gets Her Man* (1938), sixth picture in the series, she read a 400-word speech in 40 seconds.

Miss Farrell stood head and shoulders above any of the other leading ladies in machine-gun style delivery. Lee Tracy, Pat O'Brien and Jimmy Dunn popularized the technique. In the distaff department, Joan Blondell—one of Glenda's off-stage pals—could hold her own as a speedy speaker. So could Patsy Kelly and Constance Bennett. But when it came to finding an actress who could let loose with a long sentence in two seconds flat, most directors would have picked Glenda.

However, the role of Torchy was more than just a showcase for her fast-talking talent. It gave her a chance to break a Hollywood stereotype. Until Torchy Blane appeared on the screen, most movies portrayed women reporters as gushy, homely old maids or sour, masculine-looking feminists.

"They were caricatures of newspaperwomen as I knew them," Miss Farrell said. "So before I undertook to do the first Torchy, I determined to create a real human being—and not an exaggerated comedy type." She said she watched them work on visits to New York City and met with those who visited Hollywood. "They were generally young, intelligent, refined, and attractive. By making Torchy true to life, I tried to create a character practically unique in movies."

Glenda Farrell—that's her real name—was born in 1904 in Enid, Oklahoma, the only child of an Irish father and a German mother. She wanted to be an actress from early childhood. At seven, she debuted as Little Eva in a local production of "Uncle Tom's Cabin." After a convent education, she joined a stock company and toured the country. She came to Broadway in the mid-1920s and scored a hit in several successful plays, including "Skidding" (1928), which inspired the *Andy Hardy* movie series. In other productions, she shared the spotlight with Clark Gable and George Brent.

Then, she went to Hollywood where she scored an immediate hit in *Little Caesar* (1930) as Douglas Fairbanks, Jr.'s sweetheart and dancing partner. (She is often erroneously credited as Edward G. Robinson's moll. But in the film, Robinson actually despised her for taking his pal, Fairbanks, away from the rackets.)

It was a whole new world for Glenda. Reminiscing about those giddy days a few months before her death at age 67 in 1971,* she recalled the early era of sound movies.

*She is the only member of her profession to be buried in the cemetery of the U.S. Military Academy at West Point. She has that distinction because she was the wife of Colonel Henry Ross, Class of 1926, and specially chose the site.

In *Torchy Runs for Mayor* (1939), Glenda and John Butler are spotted as they slip into the cellar entrance of a building.

Lola Lane, making her only appearance as Torchy in *Torchy Blane in Panama* (1938), gets set to jump to catch up with McBride steaming below on an ocean liner. Miss Lane made a game effort but fans felt she couldn't hold a candle to Miss Farrell. And Glenda returned to the series.

"Not many actors could talk," she said. "So they shoved the ones who came from Broadway into everything. It all went so fast. I used to ask myself, 'What set am I on today? What script am I supposed to be doing—this one or that one?' "

She was up at 5:00 A.M., at the studio by 6:00 A.M. She worked six days a week, sometimes getting home at 9:00 P.M., sometimes midnight. "All I shouted for was a day off. We got it Sunday. But I had to stay in bed that one day to get ready for the next six days of shooting. I wonder if Jack Warner really appreciated his movie-acting family?"

At Warners, where she made 22 pictures that first year, Glenda never achieved real stardom. But that didn't bother her. For one thing, Warners had a kind of repertory theatre approach to its contract players. The studio rotated many of them between leading and supporting roles and bit parts. "So you weren't Kay Francis," she said. "You were still well paid and you didn't get a star complex."

Miss Farrell wisecracked her way through 122 movies, appearing often as a dizzy, fun-loving, gum-chewing broad. Some of her most memorable pictures were the *Gold Diggers* series, in which she teamed with Miss Blondell. She also played cynical, hard-boiled types. But if her lines were too rough, she blue-penciled them.

Among her most famous films were *I Am a Fugitive From a Chain Gang* (1932), *Hi, Nelli!* (1934), *Johnny Eager* (1941), *Susan Slept Here* (1954) and *Middle of the Night* (1959). All during this period, she never lost touch with the theatre. She returned to Broadway to appear in such plays as "Separate Rooms" (1940), "Home Is the Hero" (1954) and "Forty Carats" (1968). She also did occasional television roles and won a 1963 Emmy for best supporting actress for her performance in "A Cardinal Act of Mercy," on the "Ben Casey" show.

But she will be remembered longest for her movie days. "She invented and developed that made-tough, uncompromising, knowing, wisecracking, undefeatable blonde," said author Garson Kanin. He recalls that certain types were described—sometimes in screenplays—as "a young Glenda Farrell," or "an old Glenda Farrell" or a "French Glenda Farrell." Said Kanin: "She was widely imitated, and lived long enough to see her imitators imitated."

Of all her pictures, probably the *Torchy Blane* series best showcases her vivacious, flippant screen personality. So let's take a look at Glenda in *Torchy Blane in Chinatown,* seventh in the Warner series.

The picture opens with three English adventurers in the office of Lieutenant McBride. They have just returned from China with priceless jade burial tablets. They intend to sell them to Senator Baldwin (Henry O'Neill), a rich collector of rare jade. But the tablets have been stolen and the Chinese family involved has apparently followed the Englishmen to the States. The travelers have gotten a mysterious note in Chinese signed "The Golden Dragon."

"They've threatened my life, whoever they are," says Fitzhugh (Anderson Lawler). "They've set tonight at midnight for the hour of execution."

Fitzhugh, who has come to McBride for protection, asks to be kept in jail overnight. "We're going to protect you, all right," McBride says. "But at the same time, we're going to catch those guys threatening your life." As McBride begins detailing how his police will guard Fitzhugh at the Adventurers Club, where he is staying, there is a sharp knock on the door.

"See who that is," McBride tells his assistant, the superdumb cop Gahagan (Tom Kennedy), who occasionally likes to quote poetry. "And if it's who I think it is, throw her out."

The camera cuts to a room at the Adventurers Club. Midnight is fast approaching and the final minutes are ticking off. When a Chinese waiter comes in to serve drinks, McBride, suspecting poison, pours the drinks on the floor and arrests the waiter. Then, confident he has outwitted the assassins—his watch says midnight has passed—he leaves to take the suspect to headquarters.

Fitzhugh also leaves. But a black limousine swings by as he steps into his car. The limousine's windows roll down and a machine gun fires into Fitzhugh's car. McBride rushes over—too late. The limousine has roared off. Blood is cascading from Fitzhugh's car.

"Yeah, they got him all right," McBride says. "Blew his head right off."

Just then, Torchy shows up. She hasn't been intimidated by the brush-off she got earlier in the day. She's tapped her own source of information to find out how McBride intended to outwit the assassins. Now she's seen how he, in fact, fell right into their trap.

"Torchy Blane!" McBride gasps, realizing she's about to spread his blunder all over page one. "What are you doing here? You're not going to gum things up. You're not going to print a line in the paper until I find out who did it."

"A man's just been killed," Torchy protests. "The public's got a right to know."

"The public will know everything just as soon as we've got the murderers," says McBride. "Gahagan. Get her out of my hair."

As a platoon of flatfoots are removing Torchy from the scene, a church clock tolls midnight. "My watch says 12:15," says McBride.

"I'm afraid your watch is fast," says Dr. Mansfield (James Stephenson), one of the two remaining English travelers. Also present is the third companion, Captain Condon (Patric Knowles). When Condon reaches for his pocket watch, he pulls out another note. It says, "The Golden Dragon is never tardy. Dr. Mansfield, you're next."

Meanwhile, Torchy has shaken her police escort and gotten to a phone. "Hold a nice spot for me on page one," she tells her city editor. "I'm going to show that big palooka [McBride] he can't get away with it."

A few hours later, Torchy runs into McBride at the home of Senator Baldwin, owner of America's largest jade collection and the man who paid Fitzhugh to bring back the Chinese tablets. Torchy hands the detective a copy of a paper hot off the press. "This will teach you to try to muzzle the press," Torchy says.

The headline reads, "Fitzhugh, Soldier of Fortune, Murdered." The story goes on to say: "A murder occurred at 62nd Street last night which has investigating officers, headed by Det. Lt. Steven McBride, running around in circles so fast they are about to meet themselves coming."

"Someday I'm going to—," says McBride. But before he can unleash his stormy temper, another note crops up. This one orders the senator to hand over $250,000. It says instructions will be sent "after we remove Mansfield from this world—tomorrow."

The next day, when Dr. Mansfield attends the funeral of his countryman, police are swarming all over the cemetery. It looks like this time McBride has covered all bets, and no one is going to get near Mansfield. That is, until Mansfield puffs on a cigarette. Suddenly, he begins coughing convulsively. McBride picks up the cigarette. It has the sign of the Golden Dragon. "It's poison," he says.

The doctor, barely conscious, gasps that he has an antidote in his home. Police rush him there. But when they find the bottle with the antidote, it contains only water.

"What a story!" says Torchy.

Gahagan shakes his head. He can't understand how anyone—even a reporter —can think of his job at a moment of personal tragedy. "It's a shame, Torchy," Gahagan clucks. "Ain't anything sacred?"

But things are still popping fast. When Gahagan and McBride step out to call headquarters, the doctor's body disappears. Left behind is a note ordering Senator Baldwin to send his daughter's fiance, Staunton (Richard Bond), at 1:00 A.M. the next morning, to the summer house on Baldwin's Long Island estate. That's when the senator is throwing a party announcing his daughter's engagement.

McBride suggests the party go on as planned. But Captain Condon, Englishman number three, persuades the senator to let him take his prospective son-in-law's place and show up at the rendezvous with phony bills.

McBride again floods the area with his men. But as Condon goes to the summer house, a time bomb explodes in the senator's mansion. McBride and police rush inside. No one is hurt and he realizes he's been duped again. "They've planted this explosion to cover up whatever they're doing to Condon," McBride shouts.

What "they"—whoever they are—are doing to Condon is kidnapping him and warning the senator not to switch places again. The next meeting, they tell him, will be at the last buoy in New York harbor. The senator's son-in-law is to bring $250,000 at midnight tomorrow or the senator's daughter will be killed.

At the appointed hour, young Staunton goes out alone in a speedboat to the buoy. McBride's men are nowhere to be seen.

Minutes later, another motor launch approaches. Three masked men are aboard. As it draws near Stanton, they order the money thrown aboard. The son-in-law tosses a bag which the men immediately open. But before the extortionists can get away, a submarine rises from the depths of the bay. Aboard are Torchy and McBride and a naval crew that rakes the boat with gunfire.

However, the honor of unmasking the crooks falls to Gahagan, who has gotten a rowboat and pulled oars all the way from shore. Who are the culprits? None other than Captain Condon and the supposedly dead Fitzhugh and Dr. Mansfield.

That's no surprise to Torchy. It was just too coincidental that the first man's head was shot off (and another corpse substituted) and the second dead man's body vanished. "So I went to the morgue and took the fingerprints of the guy supposed to be Fitzhugh," says Torchy. "They didn't check out."

So Torchy has saved the day. But there is honor for everyone. The submarine caper was McBride's brainstorm.

"There's an old Chinese saying," says Torchy as she embraces and kisses her love-hate affair boyfriend. "What's sauce for the goose is sauce for the gander."

"And it's a wise goose that doesn't stick his neck out," says McBride.

"Don't worry about me," Torchy winks. "I can always duck."

TORCHY BLANE SERIES

1. *Smart Blonde*. Warner Brothers, 1936, Frank McDonald.
Glenda Farrell (as Torchy Blane), Barton MacLane (as Steve McBride), Winifred Shaw, Craig Reynolds, Addison Richards, Charlotte Wynters,* Jane Wyman, David Carlyle (later Robert Paige), Joseph Crehan, Tom Kennedy (as Gahagan), John Sheehan, Max Wagner, George Lloyd. 57 minutes.

2. *Fly-Away Baby*. Warner Brothers, 1937, Frank McDonald.
Glenda Farrell, Barton MacLane, Gordon Oliver, Hugh O'Connell, Marcia Ralston, Tom Kennedy, Joseph King, Raymond Hatton, Gordon Hart, Anderson Lawler, Harry Davenport, Emmett Vogan, George Guhl. 60 minutes.

3. *The Adventurous Blonde*. Warner Brothers, 1937, Frank McDonald.
Glenda Farrell, Barton MacLane, Anne Nagel, Tom Kennedy, George E. Stone, Natalie Moorhead, William Hopper, Anderson Lawler, Charles Foy, Bobby Watson, Charles Wilson, Virginia Brissac, Leyland Hodgson, Raymond Hatton, Frank Shannon, James Conlin, Granville Owen, Walter Young, George Guhl, Al Herman. 60 minutes.

4. *Blondes at Work*. Warner Brothers, 1938, Frank McDonald.
Glenda Farrell, Barton MacLane, Tom Kennedy, Rosella Towne, Donald Briggs, John Ridgely, Betty Compson, Thomas E. Jackson, Frank Shannon, Jean Benedict, Carole Landis, Suzanne Kaaren, Theodore Von Eltz, Charles Richman, Robert Middlemass, Kenneth Harlan, George Guhl, Joe Cunningham, Ralph Sanford, Milton Owen. 63 minutes.

5. *Torchy Blane in Panama*. Warner Brothers, 1938, William Clemens.
Lola Lane (as Torchy Blane), Paul Kelly (as Steve McBride), Tom Kennedy, Anthony Averill, Larry Williams, George Guhl, Betty Compson, Frank Shannon, Joe Cunningham, John Ridgely, Hugh O'Connell, Jimmy Conlin, George Lloyd, George Regas, John Harron, James Nolan. 58 minutes.

6. *Torchy Gets Her Man*. Warner Brothers, 1938, William Beaudine.
Glenda Farrell, Barton MacLane, Tom Kennedy, Willard Robertson, George Guhl, John Ridgely, Tommy Jackson, Frank Reicher, Edward Raquello, Ed Keane, Nat Carr, Frank Shannon, Joe Cunningham, Herbert Rawlinson, John Harron, Loia Cheaney, Greta Meyer, Cliff Saum. 62 minutes.

7. *Torchy Blane in Chinatown*. Warner Brothers, 1939, William Beaudine.
Glenda Farrell, Barton MacLane, Tom Kennedy, Henry O'Neill, Patric Knowles,

*Charlotte Wynters was Mrs. Barton MacLane.

James Stephenson, Janet Shaw, Frank Shannon, George Guhl, Anderson Lawler, Richard Bond, Eddy Chandler. 59 minutes.

8. *Torchy Runs for Mayor.* Warner Brothers, 1939, Ray McCarey.
Glenda Farrell, Barton MacLane, Tom Kennedy, John Miljan, Frank Shannon, Joe Cunningham, George Guhl, Joe Downing, Irving Bacon, John Butler, Charles Richman, John Harron, Walter Fenner, Millard Vincent, Joe Devlin. 58 minutes.

9. *Torchy Plays with Dynamite.* Warner Brothers, 1939, Noel Smith.
Jane Wyman (as Torchy Blane), Allen Jenkins (as Steve McBride), Tom Kennedy, Sheila Bromley, Joe Cunningham, Eddie Marr, Edgar Dearing, Frank Shannon, Bruce MacFarlane, George Lloyd, Aldrich Bowker, John Ridgely, Larry Williams, John Harron. 59 minutes.

The Dead End Kids, Hollywood's original juvenile delinquents, whose name added a term to the dictionary. Front, from left, Gabe Dell and Billy Halop (hands on Dell's knee). Rear, from left, Leo Gorcey, Bernard Punsley, Bobby Jordan and Huntz Hall.

THE
DEAD END KIDS

Angels with Dirty Faces

(1938)

Screenplay by John Wexley. From an original story by Rowland Brown. Camera, Sol Polito. Editor, Owen Marks. Song "Angels with Dirty Faces" by Fred Fisher and Maurice Spitalny. Music, Max Steiner. Dialogue director, Jo Graham. Director, Michael Curtiz. A Warner Brothers release of Sam Bischoff's production. 97 minutes.

Rocky Sullivan	JAMES CAGNEY
Jerry Connolly	PAT O'BRIEN
James Frazier	HUMPHREY BOGART
Laury Ferguson	ANN SHERIDAN
Mac Keefer	GEORGE BANCROFT
Soapy	BILLY HALOP
Swing	BOBBY JORDAN
Bim	LEO GORCEY
Patsy	GABRIEL DELL
Crab	HUNTZ HALL
Hunky	BERNARD PUNSLEY
Steve	JOE DOWNING

Edwards	EDWARD PAWLEY
Blackie	ADRIAN MORRIS
Rocky (as a boy)	FRANKIE BURKE
Jerry (as a boy)	WILLIAM TRACY
Laury (as a child)	MARILYN KNOWLDEN
Warden	WILLIAM WORTHINGTON
Death Row Guard	JACK PERRIN
Priest	EARL DWIRE

And the St. Brendan's Church Choir

They were Hollywood's original juvenile delinquents—rowdy, shrill, undisciplined, eternally scrapping roughnecks from New York's teeming East Side tenements.

The public thought they were urchins who came right off the streets. But some were really professional child actors or from stage families. And the origins of others were far from humble.

Remember the six original Dead End Kids?

• Leo (Spit) Gorcey, the gang's toughest member, was an actor's son. Gorcey, who got star billing although he never took dramatic lessons, continued making gang films through the 1940s and 1950s before retiring to his North California ranch. He died in 1969 at 53.

• Huntz (Dippy) Hall, the rubber-faced, crooked-nosed comic, was the son of an air-conditioning engineer. The fourteenth member of an Irish family of 16, Hall's real first name was Henry. But a brother called him Huntz because he thought he looked German. The nickname stuck. Hall attended Professional Children's School, later appeared on radio serials. After his movie career ended, Hall traveled the nightclub circuit. He did occasional guest star roles on TV shows ("Flipper," "Gentle Ben") and co-directed a movie for television *(Lost Island)*. In 1971, he played a continuing part in the comedy TV series "The Chicago Teddy Bears," starring Dean Jones. But the show was short-lived. Hall now lives in California and can boast of a son who went to Yale.

• Billy (Tommy) Halop, the dark, curly-haired, handsome lad, was a lawyer's son. The gang's first leader, Halop broke away to try to become a star. Among other films, he played in *Tom Brown's Schooldays* (1940) with Jimmy Lydon and Freddie Bartholomew. But he never really made it. Eventually, he became a male nurse, attracted to the field by his wife's long confinement with multiple sclerosis.

• Bobby (Angel) Jordan, the innocent-faced, long-haired scrapper, was the son of a garage-owner. Jordan, who had a varied career, including sporadic television appearances, died in 1965 at the age of 42. He was the youngest of the kids.

• Bernard (Milty) Punsley, the fat guy of the troupe, and the smartest, was a salesman's son. He went on to graduate from the University of Georgia's medical school. Today, he is a successful doctor (specializing in obstetrics) in Beverly Hills.

• Gabriel ("T.B.") Dell, the tousle-haired ruffian, was the son of an immigrant Italian doctor. Dell later knocked around in stock, put in a couple of seasons on TV with Steve Allen, then played in the movie *Who Is Harry Kellerman?* (1971) and in ten straight off-Broadway flops. He attracted attention when he took over for Alan Arkin in the hit play "Luv." And in 1972, *The New York Times* said he was an "excellent foil" for Joan Rivers in the Broadway comedy "Fun City." But, alas, it, too, joined his long list of lemons. Later that same year, Dell guested as bartender Harry Grant in the ABC summer TV series "The Corner Bar."

Today, the Dead End Kids' hooliganism would turn off many movie-goers. It would be too close to the grim realities of the crime-ridden, poverty-stricken ghettos. The ghettos were there in the 1930s. But mainstream America, mired in a seemingly endless Depression, was oblivious to their problems. Audiences were more interested in the exciting kind of entertainment the Dead End Kids brought to the screen. Movie crowds found the kids' aggressive antics roguishly appealing.

In fact, the gang made such a striking impression in 1935 in Sidney Kingsley's stage melodrama "Dead End," and later in Samuel Goldwyn's movie version, that they added a new idiom to the language. "Dead End Kids" came to mean deprived youth growing up in city squalor—one step away from a life of crime.

But their success had ironic overtones. The boys were quickly typecast. Producers wouldn't let them grow up. When their Dead End series ran its course as A-movie productions, the only way they could stay in Hollywood was to form another gang and do B-pictures. "We were the first generation gap," said Dell. "Breaking out of that early image was difficult, real hard."

So permanent was their image, in fact, that they found it hard to step out of character even off the set. "Everywhere we went, genuine tough guys would challenge us," Hall said. "I've been slugged at least 25 times by guys who wanted to find out if I'm as tough as I made out. I've had more black eyes than a prize fighter."

Perhaps as a result of their publicity, or for other reasons (they reportedly made more than $1.5 million in their first six years), some of them had trouble staying out of the gossip columns. Gorcey carried a gun, was accused of shooting at— but missing—the second of his five wives.* Once, he served five days in the Los

---

*In his candid autobiography, *Dead End Yells, Wedding Bells, Cockle Shells and Dizzy Spells,* Gorcey describes another domestic battle royal—this one with wife number one. It took place as they were taking a bath together. For no good reason, Gorcey decided to squirt water in her eye. She retaliated by spitting at him. His next move was to fill a glass with cold water and toss it in her face. She calmly put on her robe, left the bathroom and returned minutes later to splash a bucket of cold water over his face. Infuriated, he leaped from the tub, raced nude to the backyard, turned on the garden hose full blast and chased her through every room in the house squirting her all the time. In fact, Gorcey rivaled Mickey Rooney in his bad luck in marriage. "Kids have a habit of marrying their first date and spending an awful lot of time wondering what the other dates would have been like," Gorcey once said. "I never made that mistake. I married them all."

Joel McCrea pulls Halop off Gorcey as they tussle in the film version of *Dead End* (1937). The kids were so impressive, Warner Brothers extended their contract and put them in a series of crime melodramas.

The kick in that cocktail is potent enough to spin Gorcey's bowtie. Scene is from *Paris Playboys* (1954).

Angeles County Jail for driving 90 miles an hour within the city limits. Hall was arrested on marijuana possession charges. Both he and Halop were apprehended on separate drunk driving charges. Jordan was jailed for a few days when he couldn't keep up alimony and child-support payments.

Despite their own spotty record, Hall came to regret the effect he thought their pictures may have had on kids of his generation. After *Dead End*, producers lost sight of the fact that the gang's rowdyism was part of a larger portrayal of social evils. Instead, their brash actions were exploited for their own sake. Their pictures eventually became a pointless melange of loosely related brawls and wisecracks.

In a surprisingly candid interview with Hedda Hopper in 1944, Hall said that over the years he felt their impact had been a negative one. To the extent that movies can influence impressionable children, he thought they contributed to the creation of bullies, exhibitionists, vulgarians and brats. The effect of movies on youngsters has never been proved. But it was reported that Nazi propagandist Joseph Goebbels edited the *Dead End Kids* films and showed them to illustrate the degradation of youth in "decadent democracies."

Some don't share Hall's harsh criticism. Those who differ with him point out that although the gang didn't wipe out slums, it did contribute an acting style that injected primitive realism into drama—long before the method school. There were also elements of classic slapstick in their humor. The kids had a refreshing vitality and each had his own personality. In fact, Hall once conceded that with a different emphasis, they could have been portrayed as All-American boys— rough and ready city kids but essentially decent and good-hearted rascals.

Did Hall change his mind over the years? In 1972, nearly 30 years later, Hall recalled the Hedda Hopper interview. He said her story was accurate and he still agreed with his assessment then. "I think, to a point, they [the *Dead End* films] did influence some kids to be bullies," Hall said. In a telephone interview from his Los Angeles home, he added: "But those pictures really weren't made for American kids. They were made for American adults. They were some of the first social dramas. The public was seeing the dirty laundry, the slums, the garbage. It hurt."

Despite the gang's controversial career, no one can deny the enormous success the *Dead End* story had both as a movie and as a play. Much of it can be attributed to the happy chance of casting. When the call went out, Halop was the first to be chosen. By then, he was an established child star. At 12, he had played Romeo in a radio version of the Shakespearean drama. He later created the character of young western hero Bobby Benson in an early radio serial and appeared at Madison Square Garden with Col. W. T. Johnson's rodeo.

Gorcey was a less logical choice. He was an apprentice in his uncle's plumbing shop when the casting call went out. His father, Bernard Gorcey, who had played Papa Cohen in "Abie's Irish Rose" (and later appeared as sweetshop-owner Louie

Dumbrowsky in the gang's later series), urged Leo to try out. The younger Gorcey was 18, older than the part called for. But he was on the small side. So age didn't deter him.

"I got a very close shave and put on kids' knickers," Gorcey said. "I got the part. I began with a couple of lines and wound up as Spit."* The name referred to a rather crude habit he reverted to when he was disgruntled. One reviewer described Spit as a "venomous expectorator for whom the eye of an enemy was like a flying quail for a huntsman."

From the start, his hard-boiled exterior carried over into real life. He signed for $35 a week. When critics picked him as the best in the group, he asked for more money. He was told there was an army of kids in New York who could play the part. "Yeah," Gorcey snapped. "Go find one." He got a $15 raise.

Not every director would share this appreciation of Gorcey's talent. In *They Made Me a Criminal* (1939), Gorcey had a single line to say to John Garfield. The line was "One bourbon coming up." But director Anatole Litvak thought Gorcey's performance was so bad, he photographed the sequence 12 times. Still, he was not satisfied. Finally, in his frustration, Litvak lost his cool. "Gorcey," he yelled. "As an actor you stink."

Gorcey never really thought much of his acting ability. But the remark was heard by everyone on the set and this embarrassed him. He pushed up very close to Litvak and said at the top of his lungs, "Don't *ever* scream at me. Don't *ever, ever* scream at me. Don't *ever, ever, ever* scream at me." Then he went to the nearest bar. Back at the set an hour later, Gorcey went through five more unsuccessful takes. Finally, Litvak crushed out a cigarette and walked over to him. He whispered in his ear, "Gorcey, as an actor you stink. And I'm not shouting."

In Hollywood, the kids made *Dead End* with such stars as Humphrey Bogart (whom they liked) and Sylvia Sidney (whom they didn't). Also in the cast were Joel McCrea, Claire Trevor, Marjorie Main and Ward Bond. The well-known story tells how tenements breed gangsters and how the vicious cycle continues in each generation, boxed in by an environment that cuts them off from everything but life's sordidness. The kids stole the picture and Warner Brothers picked up their contracts and put them in a series of crime melodramas. The same group, more or less, appeared in *Crime School* (1938) with Bogart, *Angels Wash Their Faces* (1938) and *Hell's Kitchen* (1939) with Ronald Reagan. They also made movies on their own, although only in roles as tough juveniles.

But the group's career as a unit was a brief one. Gorcey and Halop had vied for the role of gang leader without being able to resolve their differences. So there

*Charles R. Duncan played Spit in the opening performance. Gorcey, who was billed as one of three Second Avenue Kids, took over later in the run.

It's whitewash time. Humphrey Bogart, playing a reform school warden, does the supervising in *Crime School* (1938). Putting in the elbow grease are, from left, Jordan, Hall, Punsley, Halop, Dell and Gorcey.

Here's what the kids looked like when they became the Bowery Boys. From left: Billy Benedict, Hall, Bernard Gorcey, Leo Gorcey, Bennie Bartlett, David Gorcey. Bernard was Leo's father—he played sweetshop proprietor Louie Dumbrowsky—and David was Leo's brother. Publicity shot comes from *Angels in Disguise* (1949).

was a parting of the ways. "Halop, Huntz, Gabe and Bernard signed up for a series at Universal called *Little Tough Guys,*" Gorcey recalled. "Bobby Jordan signed with Monogram to do a series called the *East Side Kids.* I joined him for the second picture. Later, Huntz and Gabe joined us at Monogram."

Stanley Clements, Billy Benedict, Bennie Bartlett and David Gorcey, (Leo's brother), subsequently came into the fold and after a while the Monogram gang became known as the *Bowery Boys.* But the low-budget pictures did not add to their reputations. Most of these flicks—many of which still appear on television —were aimless, plotless and all but humorless.*

Unquestionably, the boys will be remembered for their Warner Brothers days when they played the Dead End Kids. They were perhaps at their best in *Angels with Dirty Faces,* which Hall rates as their best picture. The taut crime melodrama revolves around James Cagney and Pat O'Brien, who play two poor city kids. One becomes a priest and the other a gangster. Much to the priest's surprise and chagrin, it is the gangster who wins the admiration of the Dead End Kids.

As the film opens, two New York City slum kids, Rocky Sullivan (Frankie Burke, played as an adult by Cagney) and Jerry Connolly (William Tracy, later O'Brien), break into a freight car to steal some fountain pens. But a railroad inspector spots them. Suddenly, police rush in. Jerry gets away only because he is a step faster. The cops nab Rocky and send him to reform school.

And so the pattern of their lives is set. Rocky goes on to a life of crime. Jerry becomes a priest.

Fifteen years later, Rocky is released from prison. He has just served a sentence for his attorney, James Frazier (Humphrey Bogart), who has promised him $100,000 when he gets out.

When Rocky returns to his former neighborhood, he renews his acquaintance with a pretty neighborhood girl, Laury (Ann Sheridan). He also finds Jerry, pastor of his own church, trying to make citizens out of tenement kids. Jerry asks Rocky to help. But Rocky says the straight world isn't for him. "Ain't got no heart left, Jerry," he says. "Had it chopped out of me in jail. But maybe it was worth it. I get plenty of dough and know where more is coming from."

As Rocky walks through the familiar streets, a gang of toughs (the Dead End Kids) pick his pocket and steal his wallet. They run to a basement hideout that turns out to be one of Rocky's old haunts. He easily follows them. When he walks in and tells them who he is and shows them his initials on the wall, he immediately wins their admiration.

---

*Not so, argues Larry Budner of Ramsay, New Jersey, a *Bowery Boys* buff who is writing a book on the gang. "Monogram, of course, was not Warner Brothers," says Budner. "And, consequently, their movies usually lacked any creative spirit. But every third or fourth film, depending on the director or writers, sparkles occasionally with wit and humor . . . They were all filmed in one or two weeks. But the point is, they have survived (via TV) for 20 years."

James Cagney, playing Rocky, a gangster whom the kids idolize, starts throwing a few elbows after he becomes fed up with the gang's rowdy tactics in a church basketball game. His strategy, in *Angels with Dirty Faces* (1938), brings quick results. Halop clutches his chest. That's Punsley with hand on hip and Dell behind him. Gorcey peeks up beneath Halop and Cagney.

"All the evidence is in that record book," says Ronald Reagan, two decades before he became governor of California. He's trying to help Bonita Granville and the Dead End Kids get one of their pals out of trouble. Others, from left, are Gorcey, Dell, Jordan, Hall and Halop. Seated is Henry O'Neill. Scene is from *Angels Wash Their Faces* (1939).

The boys are so many gangsters in the making. And though Rocky is a confirmed mobster, he persuades them to go to Jerry's gym. One of the picture's lighter moments comes when Rocky referees a basketball game between the gang and a church group and knocks the Dead Enders silly each time they try to play dirty.

But the good times are short-lived. Frazier is now allied with influential politician Mac Keefer (George Bancroft) and they decide to double-cross Rocky. Keefer sends thugs out to gun Rocky down after Rocky demands his $100,000 and a spot in Frazier's business. However, Rocky outwits the hoodlums and one of Keefer's own gunmen ends up in the morgue. Then, Rocky holds up Frazier, takes his money from Frazier's safe along with records linking high city officials with racketeers. Keefer sends the cops after Rocky. But Rocky has stashed away the loot and records with the Dead End Kids. The cops have no choice but to release Rocky.

Now that Rocky has leverage, Frazier becomes more amenable. He helps Rocky become a partner in Keefer's nightclub. As Rocky's star rises, he begins taking out Laury. He also rewards the Dead End Kids handsomely for taking care of his loot and they start gambling away their newfound wealth. When Father Jerry learns that the kids are starting to follow in Rocky's footsteps, he trails them to a pool hall. There, he appeals to them to turn to the straight and narrow. He gets a fast brushoff.

"Look, Father," Soapy (Billy Halop) says. "We don't fall for that pie-in-the-sky stuff anymore."

However, Father Jerry is just as stubborn as Rocky. Instead of giving up, the priest vows to put an end to the city's corrupt forces. He launches a clean-up campaign against Rocky and his crooked politician friends. Frazier promises a new boys' club for the priest's neighborhood. But the offer only outrages the outspoken clergyman.

"This very afternoon, I was approached with a sugar-coated proposition," the priest says in a special radio broadcast. "A bribe was offered me by this corrupt officialdom—$100,000 for the building and equipment of a recreation center in my parish. They wanted me to agree to refrain from further attacks . . ."

The camera cuts to show the syndicate big shots cursing as they listen to the radio with Rocky. "But," the priest continues, "the building of an isolated playground to shield my boys from crime is not rooting out the crime itself . . . We must rid ourselves of the criminal parasites that feed on us. We must wipe out those we have ignorantly elected and those who control and manipulate this diseased officialdom behind locked doors . . ."

On the eve of a grand jury investigation, Rocky overhears Frazier and Keefer planning to assassinate the priest. Rocky won't go along with them. In the midst of a bitter argument, Rocky guns them both down. As the smoke clears, sirens scream through the streets. Police chase Rocky in a gun battle that leads to a warehouse. Trapped and surrounded, Rocky gets ready for a last stand. When Jerry goes in after him, he turns on the priest and uses him as a shield. He rushes out with his gun blazing—only to be wounded by a hail of bullets.

Rocky goes on trial for murder and a judge sentences him to the electric chair. Still, Rocky remains a hero to the street boys. So Jerry goes to see Rocky on death row and asks him for one more favor—to die as a coward so he won't be a martyr to Soapy and the other kids. "I want them to despise your memory," Jerry says.

At first, Rocky turns him down. "You're asking too much," Rocky says. But as he enters the death chamber, Jerry whispers one more plea. Minutes later, as Rocky is being strapped into the chair, he starts struggling. "I don't want to die," he pleads, "I don't want to burn."

The newspaper headlines say Rocky went to the chair yellow. And the spell is broken. Gravely disillusioned, the Dead End Kids trudge off to church, where the priest asks them to say a prayer "for a boy who couldn't run as fast as I could."

Jerry's ruse has worked. Yet in the end, we know it is Rocky who has been the true hero. It is the gangster, after all, who was the one with moral fiber and courage. And it is the priest who has deceived his young flock.

Headlines that say "Rocky Dies Yellow" leave the gang disillusioned. Halop holds the paper while looking on disconsolately, from left, are Dell, Jordan, Hall (with beanie), Gorcey (also with beanie), and Punsley. That's Pat O'Brien in background. Scene is from *Angels with Dirty Faces*.

1. *Dead End.* United Artists, 1937, William Wyler.
    Sylvia Sidney, Joel McCrea, Humphrey Bogart, Wendy Barrie, Claire Trevor, Allen Jenkins, Marjorie Main, Billy Halop (as Tommy), Huntz Hall (as Dippy), Bobby Jordan (as Angel), Leo B. Gorcey (as Spit), Gabriel Dell (as T.B.), Bernard Punsley (as Milty), Charles Peck, Minor Watson, Charles Halton, James Burke, Ward Bond, Elisabeth Risdon, Esther Dale, George Humbert, Marcelle Corday. 90 minutes.

2. *Crime School.* Warner Brothers, 1938, Lewis Seiler.
    Billy Halop (as Frankie Warren), Bobby Jordan (as Squirt), Huntz Hall (as Goofy), Leo Gorcey (as Spike), Bernard Punsley (as Fats), Gabriel Dell (as Bugs), Humphrey Bogart, Gale Page, George Offerman, Jr., Weldon Heyburn, Cy Kendall, Charles Trowbridge, Milburn Stone, Harry Cording, Spencer Charters, Donald Briggs, Frank Jaquet, Helen MacKellar, Al Bridge, Sybil Harris, Paul Porcasi, Jack Mower, Frank Otto, Ed Gargan, James B. Carson. 90 minutes.

3. *Angels with Dirty Faces.* Warner Brothers, 1938, Michael Curtiz.
    James Cagney, Pat O'Brien, Humphrey Bogart, Ann Sheridan, George Bancroft, Billy Halop (as Soapy), Bobby Jordan (as Swing), Leo Gorcey (as Bim), Gabriel Dell (as Patsy), Huntz Hall (as Crab), Bernard Punsley (as Hunky), Joe Downing, Edward Pawley, Adrian Morris, Frankie Burke, William Tracy, Marilyn Knowlden and the St. Brendan's Church Choir. 97 minutes.

4. *They Made Me a Criminal.* Warner Brothers, 1939, Busby Berkeley
    John Garfield, Billy Halop (as Tommy), Bobby Jordan (as Angel), Leo Gorcey (as Spit), Huntz Hall (as Dippy), Gabriel Dell (as T.B.), Bernard Punsley (as Milt), Claude Rains, Ann Sheridan, May Robson, Gloria Dickson, Robert Gleckler, John Ridgely, Barbara Pepper, William Davidson, Ward Bond, Robert Strange, Louis Jean Heydt, Frank Riggi, Cliff Clark, Dick Wessel, Raymond Brown, Sam Hayes. 92 minutes.

5. *Hell's Kitchen.* Warner Brothers, 1939, Lewis Seiler and E. A. Dupont.
    Billy Halop (as Tony), Bobby Jordan (as Joey), Leo Gorcey (as Gyp), Huntz Hall (as Bongo), Gabriel Dell (as Ace), Bernard Punsley (as Ouch), Margaret Lindsay, Ronald Reagan, Stanley Fields, Frankie Burke, Grant Mitchell, Fred Tozere, Arthur Loft, Vera Lewis, Robert Homans, Charley Foy, Raymond Bailey. 82 minutes.

6. *Angels Wash Their Faces.* Warner Brothers, 1939, Ray Enright.
Ann Sheridan, Ronald Reagan, Billy Halop (as Billy Shafter), Bonita Granville, Frankie Thomas, Bobby Jordan (as Bernie), Bernard Punsley (as Sleepy), Leo Gorcey (as Leo Arkelian), Huntz Hall (as Huntz), Gabriel Dell (as Luigi), Henry O'Neill, Eduardo Ciannelli, Berton Churchill, Minor Watson, Margaret Hamilton, Jackie Searle, Bernard Nedell, Cy Kendall, Dick Rich, Grady Sutton, Aldrich Bowker, Marjorie Main, Robert Strange, Egon Brecher, Sibyl Harris, Junior Coghlan, Frankie Burke, John Hamilton, John Ridgely, William Hopper, Elliott Sullivan, Charles Trowbridge, John Harron, Howard Hickman, Sarah Padden. 76 minutes.

7. *The Dead End Kids On Dress Parade* (also known as *On Dress Parade).* Warner Brothers, 1939, William Clemens.
Billy Halop (as Cadet Major Rollins), Bobby Jordan (as Cadet Ronny Morgan), Huntz Hall (as Cadet Johnny Cabot), Gabriel Dell (as Cadet Georgie Warren), Leo Gorcey (as Slip Duncan), Bernard Punsley (as Dutch), John Litel, Frankie Thomas, Cissie Loftus, Selmer Jackson, Aldrich Bowker, Douglas Meins, William Gould, Don Douglas. 62 minutes.

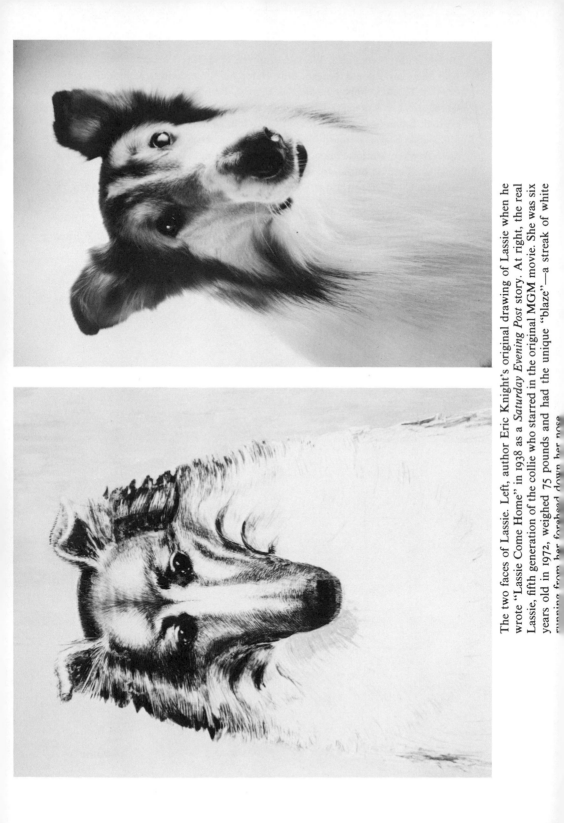

The two faces of Lassie. Left, author Eric Knight's original drawing of Lassie when he wrote "Lassie Come Home" in 1938 as a *Saturday Evening Post* story. At right, the real Lassie, fifth generation of the collie who starred in the original MGM movie. She was six years old in 1972, weighed 75 pounds and had the unique "blaze"—a streak of white running from her forehead down her nose.

LASSIE

Lassie Come Home

(1943)

Screenplay by Hugo Butler based on Eric Knight's novel. Musical score, Daniele Amfitheatrof. Art Director, Cedric Gibbons. Camera, Leonard Smith. Editor, Ben Lewis. Special effects, Warren Newcombe. Directed by Fred M. Wilcox. Produced by Samuel Marx for Metro-Goldwyn-Mayer. 88 minutes.

Joe Carraclough	RODDY MCDOWALL
Sam Carraclough	DONALD CRISP
Dally	DAME MAY WHITTY
Rowlie	EDMUND GWENN
Duke of Rudling	NIGEL BRUCE
Mrs. Carraclough	ELSA LANCHESTER
Priscilla	ELIZABETH TAYLOR
Dan'l Fadden	BEN WEBSTER
Hynes	J. PATRICK O'MALLEY
Jock	ALAN NAPIER
Andrew	ARTHUR SHIELDS
Snickers	JOHN ROGERS
Buckles	ALEC CRAIG

ROY PARRY
GEORGE BROUGHTON
and Lassie

Don't pity the pooch who works in the movies. It's anything but a dog's life —especially if the dog is Lassie.

Take the famous collie's bedroom. It's probably the equal or superior to those of many of her *homo sapiens* fans. At her owner-trainer Rudd Weatherwax's home in the San Fernando Valley, Lassie sleeps in a standard-size room. She has a king-sized bed in the bedroom once occupied by Weatherwax's now grown daughter, and her own chest of drawers. Everything is carefully chosen, down to the colors and wall decorations. "A persimmon carpet matches the bedspread, and an oil portrait (of Lassie) painted on black velvet hangs on one wall," an awed visitor once reported. He added: "A hi-fi set throbs soft Hawaiian music."

Lassie travels first class, too. When she flies, Weatherwax buys an extra ticket —at half-fare because Lassie is under 12—and she lies in the aisle or naps in a window seat. When Lassie goes by car, she rides in an air-conditioned station wagon.

At hotels, she shares a room or suite with her trainer.* Meals are usually pretty fancy, too. Lassie eats about one and one-half pounds of steak and four scoops of cottage cheese—although at home she usually gets only a stew of vegetables and beef, supplemented by cottage cheese and vitamins.

If all this tender, loving care seems incongruous, remember the object of this attention is insured for $1 million. Lassie has been in the public eye since 1943, when she debuted in the movie, *Lassie Come Home.* Since then, Lassie has appeared in seven pictures, been the star of a television series that has run 19 years and made an estimated $3 million. In earnings, that puts her ahead of such top Hollywood dogs as Rin-Tin-Tin,** Strongheart, Mack Sennett's dog Ben, Asta of *The Thin Man,* Pete of *Our Gang,* and Daisy of the *Blondie* series.***

Ironically, this superdog cost Weatherwax only $70. Lassie's first owner sent her to Weatherwax to break her of her habit of barking and chasing cars. The

*Windows, however, can be a problem. Lassie is so finely trained that if Weatherwax inadvertently gestures in a certain way, the dog may dash toward the nearest window and jump out. To avoid disaster, Weatherwax keeps the shades drawn and gestures to a minimum.

**That is, if you figure all five generations of dogs who played Lassie and the TV profits that went to those who acquired her rights. If you compare the original Rin-Tin-Tin and the original Lassie and their trainers, says Weatherwax, then Rin-Tin-Tin is far and away the all-time money maker. "Lee Duncan, his trainer, got $1,500 a week plus five per cent of the gross," said Weatherwax, "And those were the silent days before taxes."

***Weatherwax also trained Asta and Daisy, as well as Corky, a mutt who worked with Wallace Beery in *The Champ* (1931) and with Jackie Cooper in *Peck's Bad Boy* (1934). In all, he trained more than 1,500 dogs for theatrical work and for private people. Other animals of movie and TV fame— which Weatherwax did not train—include Cheta the chimpanzee, Flipper the dolphin, Clarence the cross-eyed lion, Francis the talking mule and many, many horses.

owner found the peace and quiet so pleasant that he wouldn't take her back. Instead he gave Weatherwax the dog in lieu of paying his $70 training bill.

So Weatherwax, who once played bit parts in pictures, added Lassie to his kennel of pooches. "I never broke the original Lassie of chasing cars," Weatherwax said. "But we used this habit in filming. When we had a scene where Lassie was supposed to try to make an escape, we brought a motorcycle to the set. As soon as we'd start it, man, Lassie'd tear the place down to get at it."

The original Lassie lived 19 years and has been succeeded by four other dogs —all her children and grandchildren. And all males.

As Weatherwax explains it in his training book, *The Lassie Method,* Lassie's career began when Metro-Goldwyn-Mayer wanted a collie for Eric Knight's* novel of a dog who walks 1,000 miles to return to her master. However, the studio wanted a female and Weatherwax's dog, named Pal, also had a white blaze on his muzzle. The marking was then unpopular with collie fanciers, who favored a russet mask.

So MGM turned down Pal. But it hired Weatherwax to help pick Lassie from among 1,000 collies it screened. When the movie went into production, Weatherwax turned up with Pal, who was doubling for the female the studio had hired. Makeup men hid Pal's blaze with cosmetics.

"The female was a decent performer," Weatherwax recalled. "But it was the end of summer and she was shedding heavily. She looked small and gaunt, nearly naked. The male collie also shed, of course. But because his coat is much fuller, the change is not so marked. And he always retains enough coat to photograph well.

"Since it would have been prohibitively expensive to stop the film and reschedule for a later date, we shot some tests of Pal. He did spectacularly well, and people began to mutter, 'Why didn't we pick this dog in the first place?' "

Then one day Pal came through with flying colors in a difficult scene where he had to swim 100 yards, roll over and pretend to collapse. Then and there director Fred Wilcox decided Pal was to be Lassie. "The makeup came off for good," said Weatherwax.

Lassie—we shall now give Pal his movie name and sex to avoid confusion— wasn't a blue-ribbon winner. In fact, Weatherwax couldn't get her to respond to

---

*"Lassie Come Home" first appeared as a short story in a 1938 issue of the *Saturday Evening Post.* It achieved wide popularity and an editor at the John C. Winston Publishing Company suggested that Knight expand it into a book. It turned out that Knight had already done that and then shortened it for magazine publication. So Knight merely restored the cuts and added some new adventures to produce his novel. It has now sold more than a million copies and been translated into 24 languages. Knight, borne in 1897 in Yorkshire, England, owned his own come-home collie as a boy. Knight came to the United States as a teen-ager and launched a career as a newspaperman. For a while, he was film critic for the *Philadelphia Public Ledger.* Eventually, he started writing novels full-time and wrote, among others, *The Flying Yorkshireman* and *This Above All.* He was killed in a 1943 plane crash over Dutch Gui[n]ea while serving in the U.S. Army during World War II.

simple commands. For a long time, she wouldn't even shake hands. But Weatherwax stayed with her. He used all the patience and kindness he could muster. After a while, Lassie began to obey instructions. In time, she learned to respond during filming.

Still, the job of directing an animal actor is not an easy one. On the set, Weatherwax, out of camera range, must gesture and whisper commands. His orders are later erased from the sound track. Dogs take instruction only when facing their master. Weatherwax sometimes has to crawl beneath tables and chairs so Lassie can always see his face.

Studio press releases claimed Lassie became adept at acting. They said she learned to portray mood and emotion, even showed an intuitive talent for doing just what was asked—and more. For example, in one scene, Lassie was supposed to dig under a kennel-yard gate to escape. "His ad libs were amazing," said Weatherwax—who always refers to Lassie as "he" to uphold his dog's masculine dignity.

"I said, 'Lassie, you're going to come out of there to me.' He looked puzzled a moment, whined, then jumped up and tugged at the lock, bit the wire, then dug. Perfect. We had shown him only where to dig. There were no cuts or splices in this scene. And I had to explain it only once. When it was over, he looked up at me as if to say, 'This all seems pretty crazy. I could have run around the fence

Rudd Weatherwax, Lassie's owner and trainer, working out with the original collie who made *Lassie Come Home* (1943). Lassie, whose off-screen name was Pal, was really a male.

and come out. But if that's what you want, okay. What do we do now, boss?' "

As responsive as Lassie was in this instance, she was at other times far from a perfect actor. Years later, Weatherwax told a reporter that the original Lassie was too aloof and didn't get along well with children. Once, director Wilcox conceded that sometimes he had to resort to trickery to get Lassie to play scenes just so.*

For example, sometimes food was used as a lure. When you saw Lassie scratching at a door, Weatherwax was usually at the other side—holding a dog biscuit and whispering, "Come and get it." When you saw Lassie gazing affectionately at Roddy McDowall, she was really looking past the young actor to Weatherwax's pants pocket, bulging with reward biscuits. When Lassie covers Roddy's face with kisses, she was licking off the ice cream on Roddy's cheek.

Sometimes, favorite playthings were used as gimmicks. To get Lassie to open a door, Weatherwax put a rubber ball over the knob. Then, he told Lassie, "Get the ball." When Lassie stood up and stretched her full frame across a door—apparently trying to get out—she was really trying to reach her trainer. Weatherwax was on a catwalk above her, dangling a net rag Lassie loved to play with.

Occasionally, doubles are used for Lassie. This is particularly true in television, where production time is drastically reduced. When the "Lassie" television series began in 1955, Weatherwax began using Lassie's sons, the pick of Lassie-sired litters, as stunt dogs and for special effects. For example, one son, Old Laddie, excelled at jumping through windows (made of resin and sugar so they shatter but don't cut). Pal, Jr. had a menacing snarl. Young Laddie, youngest of the group, did some of the difficult running scenes with horses and much of the stand-in work while crews set up lights.

"Lassie could do it all," said Weatherwax, "But we want to take the very best care of him. And sometimes after a run, he's panting so hard that it's too much for the sound track."

Periodically, writers report Lassie is really several identical-looking dogs. This infuriates Weatherwax. "There is only *one* Lassie," he says. "And it has always been that way. There have been, though, five *generations* of Lassies—each being the son of a previous dog. I don't put Lassie before the cameras until he is two years old. I work him for five years and then retire him, moving his son into the role."

Here is a rundown Weatherwax gives on the Lassie dynasty: "The original Lassie had a long and full life with us, living to the age of 19. His son, the second Lassie, lived to be 18. The third Lassie died prematurely of cancer when he was

*Nevertheless, Lassie has won three TV Patsy awards (1958, 1959 and 1964) recognizing top animal performances.

In *Lassie Come Home* (1943), Sam Carraclough (Donald Crisp) tells his son Joe (Roddy McDowall) that he'll have to sell their dog. Hard times have descended upon their Yorkshire town and Carraclough can no longer afford the collie.

A sad-faced Joe spends his last day with his pet.

seven. The fourth Lassie is retired. And the fifth and present Lassie is seven years old [in 1972]."

Because of the demands on their time and the difficult tasks they must perform, many people wonder if movie animals are exploited. The studios say they are not and that if anything they get better care—if only because so much money is invested in them. Whether this is true or not, it is a fact that in 1940, the industry's production code began requiring studios to "invite" a field representative of the American Humane Association on the set to see if animals were properly handled. This came about because of public reaction to studios' widespread mistreatment of animals through the 1930s. It culminated in the killing of a horse in *Jesse James* (1939). "The horse plunged off a cliff into a lake and wound up with a broken back," said Harold Melniker, director of the AHA's Hollywood office. "The story got into the newspapers. There was an uproar."

The new code amendment also banned the infamous "Running W." This was a wire device fixed to a stake. It yanked the front feet of a horse at full gallop and made him go head over heels. "It was a spectacular fall," Melniker said. "But it killed or crippled many animals." Errol Flynn said that in *Charge of the Light Brigade* (1936), about 50 horses were mechanically tripped for the charge. Some were killed.

After the Running W was outlawed, studios had to use horses specially trained to fall and shoot in areas with softened ground to cushion the impact. However, in 1968, after Jack Valenti became president of the Motion Picture Association, the code was revised and dropped specific "do's" and don'ts" regarding treatment of animals. Its new version simply says: "Excessive cruelty to animals shall not be portrayed and animals shall not be treated inhumanely."

Because there are no specific requirements to have AHA representatives on the lot, Melniker says some producers—especially when shooting overseas—have again begun overstepping the line in efforts to cut corners. He said, for example, that a donkey was shot to death in *Patton* (1970). Animals, he added, have been killed in other movies made in Europe and the Running W has been brought back. "All the AHA asks," he said, "is that all animal deaths be simulated and animals not be forced to perform beyond their capabilities. If a horse must fall or jump or play dead, the requirement is simply that a horse trained to do those things be used."

In 1943, when *Lassie Come Home* was made, the original code was in force. But it imposed no special problems for MGM and the filming was carried off with imagination, skill and realism. Without oozing sentiment, it came through as a sincere and poignant tale of a dog's heroic odyssey. Audiences took to its honest evocation of warmth and tenderness. It became an immediate family favorite. Today, its appeal remains universal. In 1971, when MGM re-released it, both adults and children lined up for pre-Christmas weekend matinee runs.

The story tells of a handsome brown and white Yorkshire collie who grows up in the mining town of Greenall Bridge during the Depression. Lassie is the prize possession of Sam Carraclough (Donald Crisp), a miner. But Lassie is more attached to the miner's son, Joe (McDowall). The two are inseparable. Lassie carries his books to school and every day at four o'clock, she runs to school to meet him. So punctual is she that the shopkeepers all say, "You can set your clock by her."

However, hard times begin pressing in on Carraclough. The mine has closed. He is on the dole and he finds he can't afford to feed Lassie and his family. And so he is forced to sell Lassie to a neighborhood aristocrat, the Duke of Rudling (Nigel Bruce), who wants to groom her as a show dog. The duke's blue-eyed granddaughter, Priscilla (Elizabeth Taylor in her first MGM picture), takes to the collie. But Lassie longs for Joe. She escapes twice from the duke's disagreeable Cockney trainer (J. Patrick O'Malley)—digging underneath her kennel the first time and scaling the fence the second time.

Finally, the duke has her shipped off to his Scotland estate. Lassie breaks free again and sets out on an adventure-filled journey through lakes, wild terrain and heather.

At the outset, she has a close brush with death. A sheepherder trains his shotgun on her. But something stops him from pulling the trigger. His companion, however, sets loose his killer dog and he and Lassie go at each other in savage combat. When it is over the sheep dog cowers away. Looking at Lassie fade away in the dusk, one of the men says, "She's a brave dog. And she's a-going somewhere."

To do this memorable scene, handlers muzzled both dogs. "They looked as if they were really fighting," said director Wilcox. "They made their own sound effects—part of them during the camera action and partly at another session when we had them make just a sound track."

Lassie goes on to swim a fast-running river. Bleeding, exhausted and starving, she drags herself to the cottage of a kindly old couple (Dame May Whitty and Ben Webster). They are glad to adopt her. But as time passes, they notice that every afternoon at four, she raises her head, looks longingly out the window, whines and goes to the door. They realize that the restless dog wants to move on. "She's on her way somewhere," the old lady says. "And she wants to be on her way. Only she's too polite and understanding. And she doesn't want to hurt us."

The scene, in which Lassie seemed to catch just the right mood, took some ingenuity to work out. According to director Fred M. Wilcox, who became so attached to Lassie that he took the dog home during the filming,

It was easy to get Lassie to do the slow-motion head-lift. It wasn't hard to get him to make a noise vaguely like whining. But it wasn't realistic enough. We filmed the action many times, spoiling the dog's extraordinary one and two-take record. Then, we hit on a scheme. Standing by the camera I commanded him to "Stay there." I spoke very firmly. Then, one of the men pretended to push me around.

Lassie didn't know what to do. He had been told to stay put within the camera lines. But, at the same time, I, his friend, seemed to be needing help. He lifted his head slowly, whined with real concern—over what was being done to me—paced restlessly around the room, obviously a worried dog. He went to the door, still whining. He looked back, as I got another shove, wrinkled his brow, and put on a most heart-breaking expression. That did it. We had set up in his mind a feeling of great frustration, which was what the script called for.

Next, Lassie meets up with a friendly traveling peddler (Edmund Gwenn) and helps him and his little pug-nosed dog Toots put on a show to sell pots and pans to villagers. When thieves try to rob him, Lassie helps the peddler fight them off. Though the scene was a gripping one, director Wilcox said it was not a difficult one to stage. "Lassie loves to play fight," he said. "We did the scene without a muzzle. He pretends to be ferocious. But he's such a gentle dog, we knew he wouldn't bite."

When it's time for Lassie to go, the peddler also then understands Lassie is on a mission. "Sometimes I think you didn't come along with me as much as you let me come along with you," he says. "On you go, then. And good luck."

Lassie's final adventure comes when he is the prey of dogcatchers and has to leap from a third-story window of a warehouse for his freedom. He ends up limping home, bedraggled and barely alive. The limp was achieved by attaching a piece of cork to one paw. "It didn't hurt him," Wilcox said. "But he was thrown off balance and favored that foot."

Sam Carraclough is stunned to see his dog home after an unbelievable struggle. But before he can clean and feed her, the duke comes calling. Carraclough is put on the spot. Will he give the dog back a third time? Surely this would break his son's heart. So, touched by the dog's devotion, he resolves to keep her.

Carraclough hides Lassie. The duke hears her panting in the next room and discovers her. However, he has no intention of standing in the way of such loyalty.

"Priscilla," he asks his granddaughter, "have you ever seen this dog before?"

"No," she answers.

"Well, neither have I," the duke says. "She's no dog of mine."

Then, to add to his humanitarian gesture, the duke offers Sam a job as his kennel-keeper.

Ah, but we have one more handkerchief to go. It's four o'clock and Lassie painfully pulls herself up and shuffles along the familiar way to Joe's school. We see Joe walking out with his chums. His face is long and solemn. Then, his eyes turn to the greensward where Lassie has sat waiting in days gone by. No brighter

His features strained with apprehension, Jon Provost pushes a log raft downstream with Lassie in the last feature-length *Lassie* movie—*Lassie's Great Adventure* (1963). The movie was a paste-up of TV shows.

Lassie with one of his television masters, Ron Holden (Skip Burton). The "Lassie Show," in its nineteenth year in 1972, is the longest running show on TV.

Bonita Granville Wrather, the former child actress and now associate producer of the "Lassie Show," poses with her star. "The hour glass signifies the time change made this year [1971–72 season] in scheduling the Lassie shows," Mrs. Wrather explains, "as Lassie is no longer on the network. The cap is a trademark of the show. The crew wears them when shooting the series."

face has ever shown up on the screen. When Joe sees Lassie, he runs to her and throws his arms around his beloved dog. "Oh, my Lassie come home," he cries.

Lassie went on to do about a picture a year through the early 1950s. Then, she reached what Metro thought was a dead end. The studio sold Weatherwax the rights to her title for a paltry $2,000. Gray hairs sprout on the heads of studio executives every time they are reminded of the deal. In 1954, Robert Maxwell bought the television rights, produced the "Lassie" show and built up a national following. Two years later, he sold the show to Jack Wrather for a cool $3.5 million. Even with that enormous price tag, Wrather still made a bundle. Lassie has grossed over $60 million. In fact, she has her own syndicated group of television stations called the "Lassie Network." In 1972, its 206 outlets represent 98 percent of all TV homes.

On the show, Lassie's earliest owners included Jan Clayton, June Lockhart and Cloris Leachman. Then, she had two masters, Tommy Rettig and Jon Provost, both of whom grew out of their roles. After several seasons working with the Forest Rangers, Lassie spent five years with actor Robert Bray, then two seasons with Jed Allen and Jack DeMave. In 1971, Skip Burton, playing the college-age son of ranch-owner Ron Hayes, became Lassie's master.

But it is Lassie's affection, courage and simple dedication that attracts viewers. "Surprisingly," said Bonita Granville Wrather, the former child star who is the show's associate producer, "most children identify with Lassie and not the humans in the program. That's because of the dog's adventures and her basic goodness. Everybody loves Lassie."

Well, almost everybody. One maverick is the British critic Cyclops. Writing in *Life* magazine, he said that what has happened to Lassie since Eric Knight's time shouldn't have happened to a dog:

> The sentimentalizing and inflating, the scouring away of the story's social context, the Disneyization of Lassie have left us with Super-Collie—the brain of Herman Kahn grafted into the body of the Hound of Heaven. The TV Lassie . . . patrols the American West as though she were a four-legged FBI. Super-Collie bears no more resemblance to Eric Knight's Lassie than Shaft bears to big-city private detectives, black or white. And she's bound to make you look at your own mutt and wonder if somebody put stupidity pills into the Gaines-burger.

But in the end, Cyclops winds up in the lonely minority. Not only has the "Lassie" Show won the industry's most coveted prizes, including a Peabody and two Emmys, but, more important, it has consistently been one of the nation's most popular TV programs. In 1972, millions of viewers remained loyal enough to make "Lassie" the longest-running show on television.

LASSIE SERIES

1. *Lassie Come Home.* MGM, 1943, Fred M. Wilcox.
   Roddy McDowall (as Joe Carraclough), Donald Crisp (as Sam Carraclough), Dame May Whitty, Edmund Gwenn, Nigel Bruce (as Duke of Rudling), Elsa Lanchester (as Mrs. Carraclough), Elizabeth Taylor (as Priscilla), Ben Webster, J. Patrick O'Malley, Alan Napier, Arthur Shields, John Rogers, Alec Craig, Lassie. 88 minutes.

2. *Son of Lassie.* MGM, 1945, S. Sylvan Simon.
   Peter Lawford (as Joe Carraclough), Donald Crisp (as Sam Carraclough), June Lockhart (as Priscilla), Nigel Bruce (as Duke of Rudling), William "Billy" Severn, Leon Ames, Donald Curtis, Nils Asther, Robert Lewis, Fay Helm, Eily Malyon, Helen Koford (who later changed her name to Terry Moore), Lassie, Laddie. 102 minutes.

3. *Courage of Lassie.* MGM, 1946, Fred M. Wilcox.
   Elizabeth Taylor, Frank Morgan, Tom Drake, Selena Royle, Harry Davenport, George Cleveland, Catherine Frances McLeod, Morris Ankrum, Mitchell Lewis, Jane Green, David Holt, William Wallace, Minor Watson, Donald Curtis, Clancy Cooper, Carl "Alfalfa" Switzer, Conrad Binyon, Lassie (as Bill). 93 minutes.

4. *Hills of Home.* MGM, 1948, Fred M. Wilcox.
   Edmund Gwenn, Donald Crisp, Tom Drake, Janet Leigh, Rhys Williams, Reginald Owen, Edmond Breon, Alan Napier, Hugh Green, Lumsden Hare, Eileen Erskine, Victor Wood, David Thursby, Frederick Worlock, Lassie. 97 minutes.

5. *The Sun Comes Up.* MGM, 1949, Richard Thorpe.
   Jeanette MacDonald, Lloyd Nolan, Claude Jarman, Jr., Lewis Stone, Percy Kilbride, Nicholas Joy, Margaret Hamilton, Hope Landin, Esther Somers, Lassie. 92 minutes.

6. *Challenge to Lassie.* MGM, 1949, Richard Thorpe.
   Edmund Gwenn, Donald Crisp, Geraldine Brooks, Ross Ford, Reginald Owen, Alan Webb, Henry Stephenson, Alan Napier, Sara Allgood, Lumsden Hare, Edmond Breon, Arthur Shields, Charles Irwin, Lassie. 76 minutes.

7. *The Painted Hills.* MGM, 1951, Harold F. Kress.
   Lassie (as Shep), Paul Kelly, Bruce Cowling, Gary Gray, Art Smith, Ann Doran, Chief Yowlachie, Andrea Virginia Lester, "Brown Jug" Reynolds. 65 minutes.

8. *Lassie's Great Adventure.* 20th Century-Fox, 1963, William Beaudine.
   Lassie, June Lockhart, Hugh Reilly, Jon Provost. 103 minutes.

Quick now. Cover the caption, and see how many you can name in this *Our Gang* lineup. From left, Baby Patsy May, Eugene (Porky) Lee, Darla Hood, George (Spanky) McFarland, Billy (Buckwheat) Thomas, and Carl (Alfalfa) Switzer.

OUR GANG

Readin' and Writin'
(1932)

A Hal Roach production. Photographed by Art Lloyd. Edited by Richard Currier. Directed by Robert McGowan. And starring the Our Gang Kids: Kendall (Breezy/Brisbane) McComas, Matthew (Stymie) Beard, Bobby (Wheezer) Hutchens, Dorothy de Borba, Sherwood (Spud) Bailey, Donald Haines and Carolina (Marmalade) Beard. Adult cast members: June Marlowe, May Wallace, Lyle Tayo, Harry Bernard and Otto Fries.

Their life was every kid's dream. They had a gang and a club house and a pooch. They got the best of dogcatchers, schoolteachers and cops. They went fishing, hunted for buried treasure, prowled in haunted houses.

The *Our Gang* kids were typical, fun-loving American youngsters, just being their mischievous selves. Perhaps that's why the comedies clicked and still retain a universal appeal today. "They [the shorts] were something for the kids that everybody ended up enjoying," said producer Hal Roach, their creator. "People loved them and loved to laugh at them."

The gang had a natural humor because the little guys never thought there was anything unusual about acting before a camera. "I was eight or nine years old before I realized all kids weren't in the movies," said George (Spanky) McFar-

Here's another group shot. If you can identify everybody, you're demonstrating nostalgia one-upsmanship. From left, Jackie Cooper, Allen Clayton Hoskins, better known as Farina, Norman (Chubby) Chaney, Matthew (Stymie) Beard, Bobbie (Wheezer) Hutchens, Petey the pooch, Jean Darling, Dorothy de Borba and Mary Ann Jackson.

The smiling urchin in the shoeshine getup is, of course, Spanky McFarland, perhaps the most famous of all the *Our Gang* kids.

land, the fat boy in the beanie who became perhaps the best known of all the gang regulars.

And so they gave us a child's view of a child's world. They held up a mirror to the salad days of life. They made us laugh at a simpler world where a chuckle could be fashioned from any situation.

When Stymie, the stereotyped Negro boy with the derby, tries to con a breakfast out of a rich boy, he goes about it with artless ingenuity.

"Did you know ham and eggs can talk?" Stymie asks.

"I don't believe it," the rich boy says.

"Cook it up," Stymie says, challenging him.

The rich boy puts eggs and ham in a pan and starts heating them on the stove. When they're done, he listens hard but doesn't hear a thing. The rich boy looks up skeptically. The only sound comes from the sizzling food. Stymie licks his chops. "They're saying 'Hello' to my stomach right now!" And he chomps down his breakfast.

When Spanky tries to become a caddy, a golfer asks him for his credentials.

"I shot a 74," Spanky says proudly.

"Was that for 18 holes?" the golfer exclaims.

"No. That was just for the first hole," says Spanky. "But I could do 64 on the second hole."

With these less than subtle jokes, a parade of *Our Gang* kids quipped, mugged and roughhoused their way through hundreds of one-and two-reelers and one full-length feature. Age was everyone's occupational hazard. They stayed in no longer than their eleventh or twelfth birthday. As they grew older, they had to step aside and be replaced by smaller fry. According to Roach, 176 youngsters played in the comedies during their 23-year production run from 1922 to 1944. They included Jackie Cooper, Dickie Moore and Johnny Downs. Nanette Fabray and Eddie Bracken had bit parts. Ironically, the most famous child actor of them all, Shirley Temple, turned out for the series but didn't make it.

There is a difference of opinion as to who was in the original group. But Kalton Lahue, in his book *World of Laughter,* identified the pioneer players as freckle-faced Mickey Daniels, tousle-haired Jackie Condon, cute Peggy Cartright and Negro Ernie (Sunshine Sammy) Morrison. They were soon joined by fat Joe Cobb, golden-haired Mary Kornman, tough guy Jackie Davis, Allen Clayton (Farina) Hoskins (the Negro toddler boy whose sex was a puzzle to movie audiences) and Pete, the canine with the black ring around his eye.

Today, kids enjoy the shorts on television without having any inkling that they were made generations ago. Some adults criticize the way Negroes were portrayed. However, it should be remembered that the gang was an integrated group in a day when black and white friendships were rarely depicted on the screen.

The gang, whose average age was 7, was supposed to be a cross-section of mainstream America. But Roach and his scouts didn't have to go far to find them. Mary Kornman, for example, was the daughter of a photographer on the Roach lot where filming of the Charley Chase, Laurel and Hardy and Harold Lloyd comedies was done. Studio scouts discovered most of the others around Hollywood. When gang units turned over—which was about every five years—hundreds of mothers flocked to volunteer their darlings for the openings. Most of them went away disappointed. Someone once computed the odds of making the troupe at a thousand to one. Of the many interviews the studio gave, only 41 children got contracts for major roles.

Pay started at $40 a week. But it went up fast. Spanky reportedly ended up with $1,250 a week. And he became just as independent as any grown-up actor. "Interviewers never got anywhere with Spanky," newspaperman Paul Harrison wrote. "He'll shake hands politely enough. But after that, he is about as garrulous as Garbo. It doesn't seem to be shyness. He's just bored."

When a director called him before the cameras, he often said, "Aw, nuts." When he was sure of his lines and ready for a take, he said, "Okay, toots." Instead of memorizing his lines from a script, Spanky usually learned them from the director, who explained each scene. Spanky often failed to deliver the sought-after expression. But he rarely blew his lines.

Spanky, part of a 1930s generation of *Our Gang* players, was in a unit with Carl (Alfalfa) Switzer, Billy (Buckwheat) Thomas, Scotty Beckett, Darla Hood, Baby Patsy May and Eugene (Porky) Lee. They usually had little time for play. Most of them got up before 8:00 A.M., got home at 5:00 P.M., and went to bed at 8:00 P.M. Youngsters under six were allowed to be at the lot six hours a day with half of the time set aside for playing. But after six, the "grown-up" actors put in a full, eight-hour work stint.

There was a school for the *Our Gang* kids and the teacher was Mrs. Fern Carter. "She was a wonderful person and a marvelous teacher," Darla Hood recalled. "She was with the series until the last year or so at Metro-Goldwyn-Mayer. A Mrs. McDonald was the MGM teacher for contract players such as Margaret O'Brien, Virginia Weidler and Elizabeth Taylor. And some big shot decided she could also teach the *Our Gang* kids and cut down on the studio payroll.

"It was a sad day when Mrs. Carter packed her belongings and they closed the Gang School House. She was missed by many."

Ironically, most of the kids faded into oblivion after they left *Our Gang*.* McFarland bounced from job to job—hotdog vendor, gas station operator, oil

---

*There were notable exceptions, previously mentioned. In addition, Robert Blake—who used his real name, Mickey Gubitosi, during his *Our Gang* days—portrayed one of the killers in *In Cold Blood* (1967) and starred in *Tell Them Willie Boy Is Here* (1969). And Jackie Davis became John H. Davis, M.D., of Beverly Hills. California.

Alfalfa, the fellow with the famous cowlick (covered by hat in this picture), holds, of all things, a beer bottle. Looking on disapprovingly is Spanky, with hands on hips. Others, from left, are Darla Hood, Eugene (Porky) Lee and Buckwheat Thomas.

It looks like our heroes are about to be turned into mincemeat by this club-wielding giant. But it turns out that this scary business is just one of Spanky's bad dreams. Kids in this sequence, from *Mama's Little Pirates,* are, from left, unidentified girl, Scotty, Spanky, Jerry Tucker and Stymie.

promoter. In 1972, he was a sales training supervisor for a television manufacturer in Texas. Joe Cobb worked as an assembler for an aircraft manufacturing plant in Inglewood, California. Darla Hood Granson was still in Hollywood doing TV commercials, mostly dubbing or voice-over work. She sang the mermaid ditty in the Chicken-of-the-Sea commercial. Mary Kornman was also married and living on a ranch near Hollywood. She and her husband rent horses to motion picture and TV studios for use in westerns.

Shirley Jean Rickert became a featured stripper who peeled under the name "Gilda." Johnny Downs emceed a daily kids' program over KFSD, San Diego, after a $1,500-a-week career in pictures. Tommy Bond, who was "Butch," became head of properties at KTTV in Hollywood. And Allen (Farina) Hoskins worked with young people with drug problems.

Some met untimely or tragic deaths. Switzer, the country bumpkin famous for his cowlick and squeaky voice, was shot to death in 1959 in an argument over $50. He was 33, working as a Los Angeles bartender and hunting guide in between bit parts. Buckwheat, who made the army his career for a while, was killed while flying food to Biafra in 1968. Beckett, a tyke with big brown eyes, died the same year at the age of 38, the victim of a possible overdose of alcohol or drugs.

Roach felt these were the exceptions. "Naturally, some got into trouble or had bad luck," he said. "They're the ones who got in the headlines. But if you took

That's Spanky chomping on that apple. And that's Buckwheat gazing at him with pleadingly hungry eyes.

176 other kids and follow them through their lives, I believe you would find the same percentage of them having troubles in later life."

Roach got the idea for a kids series in 1921, in the days when child actors were usually Little Lord Fauntleroy types. One day, according to one story, he looked out his window and saw a bunch of children arguing over wood they had snatched from a lumber yard. "Of course, they would throw the wood away when they had gone two blocks," Roach said. "But the argument seemed terribly important to them then. I watched for 15 minutes. And I got the idea of doing a series from the angle of kids' mentality."

And so *Our Gang* was born. The first short, "One Terrible Day," was released in September, 1922. It was well received from the start. Roach, at first, called the group the Little Rascals. But he liked the title of the third short, *Our Gang,* and it stuck.

The studio produced a dozen or more films every year. Writer-director Robert McGowan headed up the production staff until 1933 and thereafter did screen plays until 1939. The series had no trouble making the transition to talkies and many adult comedians appeared in them. They included Franklin Pangborn, Billy Gilbert and Edgar Kennedy.

In 1936, Roach did a full-length film, *General Spanky,* but it failed to draw enthusiastic reviews and no other feature picture was ever made. As for the shorts, their quality covered the spectrum. They ranged from deadly dull to mildly funny to hilarious. One of the best ones, *Bored of Education,* won an Oscar in 1936 for best short subject.

In 1938, when double features started making shorts unprofitable, Roach sold *Our Gang* to Metro-Goldwyn-Mayer, including the rights to the name. That's why it was changed to *The Little Rascals* when they began appearing on television.

MGM ground out shorts from 1938 to 1944. But few of them had the quality of the Roach pictures.

"For one thing," said Miss Hood, "at Hal Roach, all the big shows and production numbers were staged as dreams. That way, all the elaborate sets and costumes were easily explained. At MGM, the kids always gave the shows. And as they were almost Busby Berkeley productions, it seemed too unbelievable that a bunch of kids without money could have produced them. And then, instead of the kids talking like kids, the script writers made them sound too glib and worldly."

Some shorts added morals and that made them even more stilted. When World War II came, MGM lost interest and so the series died.

There were attempts to revive them. But all were unsuccessful. In 1956, Roach and Allied Artists disclosed plans to film a new series. But nothing came of it. Another producer's scheme to make a television series also fizzled.

Still, the old flicks survived. One entrepreneur, Charles King, bought 79 of them and reissued them for TV. For years, the comedies have been shown over and over again in cities throughout the country, serving to bridge the generation gap. They entertain not only children of today but their parents as well. For them it's a kind of nostalgic trip back in a time machine.

In *Readin' and Writin',* for example, the humor recalls the sinking feeling everyone can remember experiencing on going to school for the first time. It also tells the story of how the class smart aleck gets his comeuppance. The movie opens as the tots shuffle off to class from their respective homes—all but Brisbane (Kendall McComas). He shows an ornery streak from the start.

"Mother wants you to be president," his mom tells him as she kisses him goodbye.

"I don't want to be president," Brisbane says. "I want to be a streetcar conductor."

On the way to school, he stops off at the blacksmith's. While Brisbane pumps the bellows, he razzes the big guy. Bristling, the blacksmith tells Brisbane he once knew a fresh kid who ended up getting expelled from school.

"What did he do to get expelled?" Brisbane asks eagerly.

"He told a lot of new kids to do silly things," the blacksmith says.

"Is that all he done?" says Brisbane, a bulb lighting in his head.

The scene switches to school. Pretty blonde Miss Crabtree (June Marlowe) is welcoming her new pupils. She's in for a surprise from the start.

"What is your name, little girl?" Miss Crabtree asks.

"Pansy," one girl says.

"What does your father do?"

"Twenty years."

Meanwhile, Brisbane is busy laying diabolical plans. He tells one new girl that Miss Crabtree is deaf, advises another that the teacher likes to be called "Crabby." Then, he plants some booby traps in the classroom.

When the bell rings, the kids troop in. They all sit on the count of three and leap up screaming as one person. Brisbane has laid tacks on all the seats.

With some wires he has rigged to a hidden horn, he takes delight in setting off a blast every time the teacher talks. Minutes later, the little girl who thinks Miss Crabtree is deaf comes up to talk to her. Each thinks the other is hard of hearing and they end up shouting at each other. Then, Petey, one of the kids' dogs, jumps through the window and perches on Miss Crabtree's desk. While she's contending with him, Brisbane steals outside and chases a mule into the classroom. For punishment, Miss Crabtree asks him to learn a poem. When he refuses, she expels him. That's exactly what Brisbane wants. He gleefully trips out of class and saunters down to the ole swimming hole.

But when he gets there, he suddenly realizes he's all alone. His conscience begins talking. "What are you going to say to your ma when she finds out you're not in school . . . There's nobody to play with. The kids are all in school. There's no place to go. You can't go home."

Meanwhile, class is going on.

"What is an acre," Miss Crabtree asks.

"A bad tooth," One tot replies. "See, I got one right here."

"Here's a hard one. What is an escalator?"

"It's a great big thing that lives in a swamp. They make suitcases out of him."

"Bobby, what is two in one?"

"Shoe polish."

"What is three and one?"

"Oil."

"No, darling, you don't understand . . . Now if a hen laid an egg here. And I laid two here . . ."

"Hohoho! I don't think you can do it."

Silently, humbly, Brisbane creeps back in. "Miss Crabtree. I'm sorry I was a naughty boy," He says, crestfallen. "I don't want to be expelled. I want to be president, too."

He begs her not to make him stand before the class and recite the poem. But she insists. That's his punishment. So with tears flowing freely, Brisbane says, "I climbed to get the daffodil out on a limb so thin / I tumbled down like Jack 'n Jill and skinned my little shin."

The class enjoys a hearty laugh. However, their merriment is short-lived. A skunk finds its way into the classroom, and brings a quick and unceremonious end to the first day of school.

"Weren't they something," Roach said in the 1960s, after he had sold all the rights to his films and then saw his $6.5 million movie empire vanish. (It was a matter of a bankruptcy petition that came after Roach's son had taken over the studio and enmeshed it in the failing financial affairs of a stock manipulator named Alexander Guterma.)

"I've seen Cary Grant sit and watch those kids for half an hour at a time and marvel at their ability to convey an idea," the elder Roach went on wistfully. "They were natural little actors. Farina could cry great big tears in 20 seconds. You'd think his heart was breaking. And one moment later, he'd be back playing again . . . They were a special kind of child. Today you'd have to have a contest to find one like them. They talked and acted exactly like children really do. And that's what made *Our Gang* so popular."

1. *Small Talk*. Roach-MGM, 1929, Robert McGowan.
2. *Lazy Days*. Roach-MGM, 1929, Robert McGowan.
3. *Boxing Gloves*. Roach-MGM, 1929, Anthony Mack, supervised by Robert McGowan.
4. *Bouncing Babies*. Roach-MGM, 1929, Robert McGowan.
5. *Moan and Groan, Inc.* Roach-MGM, 1929, Robert McGowan.
6. *Railroadin'*. Roach-MGM, 1929, Robert McGowan.
7. *Shivering Shakespeare*. Roach-MGM, 1929, Anthony Mack, supervised by Robert McGowan.
8. *The First Seven Years*. Roach-MGM, 1930, Robert McGowan.
9. *When the Wind Blows*. Roach-MGM, 1930, James Horne.
10. *Bear Shooters*. Roach-MGM, 1930, Robert McGowan.
11. *A Tough Winter*. Roach-MGM, 1930, Robert McGowan.
12. *Pups Is Pups*. Roach-MGM, 1930, Robert McGowan.
13. *School's Out*. Roach-MGM, 1930, Robert McGowan.
14. *Helping Grandma*. Roach-MGM, 1930, Robert McGowan.
15. *Love Business*. Roach-MGM, 1930, Robert McGowan.
16. *Teacher's Pet*. Roach-MGM, 1930, Robert McGowan.
17. *Little Daddy*. Roach-MGM, 1931, Robert McGowan.
18. *Bargain Day*. Roach-MGM, 1931, Robert McGowan.
19. *Fly My Kite*. Roach-MGM, 1931, Robert McGowan.
20. *Big Ears*. Roach-MGM, 1931, Robert McGowan.
21. *Shiver My Timbers*. Roach-MGM, 1931, Robert McGowan.
22. *Dogs Is Dogs*. Roach-MGM, 1931, Robert McGowan.
23. *Readin' and Writin'*. Roach-MGM, 1931, Robert McGowan.
24. *Free Eats*. Roach-MGM, 1932, Raymond McCarey.
25. *Spanky*. Roach-MGM, 1932, Robert McGowan.
26. *Choo-Choo*. Roach-MGM, 1932, Robert McGowan.
27. *The Pooch*. Roach-MGM, 1932, Robert McGowan.
28. *Hook and Ladder*. Roach-MGM, 1932, Robert McGowan.
29. *Free Wheeling*. Roach-MGM, 1932, Robert McGowan.
30. *Birthday Blues*. Roach-MGM, 1932, Robert McGowan.
31. *A Lad an' a Lamp*. Roach-MGM, 1932, Robert McGowan.
32. *Fish Hooky*. Roach-MGM, 1933, Robert McGowan.
33. *Kid from Borneo*. Roach-MGM, 1933, Robert McGowan.
34. *Forgotten Babies*. Roach-MGM, 1933, Robert McGowan.

35. *Mush and Milk*. Roach-MGM, 1933, Robert McGowan.
36. *Bedtime Worries*. Roach-MGM, 1933, Robert McGowan.
37. *Wild Poses*. Roach-MGM, 1933, Robert McGowan.
38. *Hi'-Neighbor!* Roach-MGM, 1934, Gus Meins.
39. *For Pete's Sake*. Roach-MGM, 1934, Gus Meins.
40. *The First Round-up*. Roach-MGM, 1934, Gus Meins.
41. *Honky Donkey*. Roach-MGM, 1934, Gus Meins
42. *Mike Fright*. Roach-MGM, 1934, Gus Meins.
43. *Washee Ironee*. Roach-MGM, 1934, James Parrott.
44. *Mama's Little Pirates*. Roach-MGM, 1935, Gus Meins.
45. *Shrimps for a Day*. Roach-MGM, 1935, Gus Meins.
46. *Anniversary Trouble*. Roach-MGM, 1935, Gus Meins.
47. *Beginner's Luck*. Roach-MGM, 1935, Gus Meins.
48. *Teacher's Beau*. Roach-MGM, 1935, Gus Meins.
49. *Sprucin' Up*. Roach-MGM, 1935, Gus Meins.
50. *Little Papa*. Roach-MGM, 1935, Gus Meins.
51. *Little Sinner*. Roach-MGM, 1935, Gus Meins.
52. *Our Gang Follies of 1936*. Roach-MGM, 1935, Gus Meins.
53. *The Pinch Singer*. Roach-MGM, 1936, Fred Newmeyer.
54. *Divot Diggers*. Roach-MGM, 1936, Robert McGowan.
55. *The Lucky Corner*. Roach-MGM, 1936, Gus Meins.
56. *Second Childhood*. Roach-MGM, 1936, Gus Meins.
57. *Arbor Day*. Roach-MGM, 1936, Fred Newmeyer.
58. *Bored of Education*.* Roach-MGM, 1936, Gordon Douglas.
59. *Two Too Young*. Roach-MGM, 1936, Gordon Douglas.
60. *Pay as You Exit*. Roach-MGM, 1936, Gordon Douglas.
61. *Spooky Hooky*. Roach-MGM, 1936, Gordon Douglas.
62. *Reunion in Rhythm*. Roach-MGM, 1937, Gordon Douglas.
63. *Glove Taps*. Roach-MGM, 1937, Gordon Douglas.
64. *Hearts Are Thumps*. Roach-MGM, 1937, Gordon Douglas.
65. *Three Smart Boys*. Roach-MGM, 1937, Gordon Douglas.
66. *Rushin' Ballet*. Roach-MGM, 1937, Gordon Douglas.
67. *Roamin' Holiday*. Roach-MGM, 1937, Gordon Douglas.
68. *Night 'n' Gales*. Roach-MGM, 1937, Gordon Douglas.
69. *Fishy Tales*. Roach-MGM, 1937, Gordon Douglas.
70. *Framing Youth*. Roach-MGM, 1937, Gordon Douglas.
71. *The Pigskin Palooka*. Roach-MGM, 1937, Gordon Douglas.
72. *Mail and Female*. Roach-MGM, 1937, Fred Newmeyer.
73. *Our Gang Follies of 1938*. Roach-MGM, 1937, Gordon Douglas.

*Academy Award for best short subject.

74. *Canned Fishing.* Roach-MGM, 1938, Gordon Douglas.
75. *Bear Facts.* Roach-MGM, 1938, Gordon Douglas.
76. *Three Men in a Tub.* Roach-MGM, 1938, Nate Watt.
77. *Came the Brawn.* Roach-MGM, 1938, Gordon Douglas.
78. *Feed 'em and Weep.* Roach-MGM, 1938, Gordon Douglas.
79. *The Awful Tooth.* Roach-MGM, 1938, Nate Watt.
80. *Hide and Shriek.* Roach-MGM, 1938, Gordon Douglas.
81. *The Little Ranger.* MGM, 1938, Gordon Douglas.
82. *Party Fever.* MGM, 1938, George Sidney.
83. *Aladdin's Lantern.* MGM, 1938, Gordon Douglas.
84. *Men in Fright.* MGM, 1938, George Sidney.
85. *Football Romeo.* MGM, 1938, George Sidney.
86. *Practical Jokers.* MGM, 1938, George Sidney.
87. *Alfalfa's Aunt.* MGM, 1938, George Sidney.
88. *Tiny Troubles.* MGM, 1939, George Sidney.
89. *Duel Personalities.* MGM, 1939, George Sidney.
90. *Clown Princes.* MGM, 1939, George Sidney.
91. *Cousin Wilbur.* MGM, 1939, George Sidney.
92. *Joy Scouts.* MGM, 1939, Edward Cahn.
93. *Dog Daze.* MGM, 1939, George Sidney.
94. *Auto Antics.* MGM, 1939, Edward Cahn.
95. *Captain Spanky's Show Boat.* MGM, 1939, Edward Cahn.
96. *Dad for a Day.* MGM, 1939, Edward Cahn.
97. *Time Out for Lessons.* MGM, 1939, Edward Cahn.
98. *Alfalfa's Double.* MGM, 1940, Edward Cahn.
99. *The Big Premiere.* MGM, 1940, Edward Cahn.
100. *All About Hash.* MGM, 1940, Edward Cahn.
101. *The New Pupil.* MGM, 1940, Edward Cahn.
102. *Bubbling Trouble.* MGM, 1940, Edward Cahn.
103. *Good Bad Guys.* MGM, 1940, Edward Cahn.
104. *Waldo's Last Stand.* MGM, 1940, Edward Cahn.
105. *Goin' Fishin'.* MGM, 1940, Edward Cahn.
106. *Kiddie Cure.* MGM, 1940, Edward Cahn.
107. *Fightin' Fools.* MGM, 1941, Edward Cahn.
108. *Baby Blues.* MGM, 1941, Edward Cahn.
109. *Ye Olde Minstrels.* MGM, 1941, Edward Cahn.
110. *1-2-3 Go!* MGM, 1941, Edward Cahn.
111. *Robot Wrecks.* MGM, 1941, Edward Cahn.
112. *Helping Hands.* MGM, 1941, Edward Cahn.
113. *Come Back, Miss Pipps.* MGM, 1941, Edward Cahn.
114. *Wedding Worries.* MGM, 1941, Edward Cahn.

115. *Melodies Old and New.* MGM, 1942, Edward Cahn.
116. *Going to Press.* MGM, 1942, Edward Cahn.
117. *Don't Lie.* MGM, 1942, Edward Cahn.
118. *Surprised Parties.* MGM, 1942, Edward Cahn.
119. *Doin' Their Bit.* MGM, 1942, Herbert Glazer.
120. *Rover's Big Chance.* MGM, 1942, Herbert Glazer.
121. *Mighty Lak a Goat.* MGM, 1942, Herbert Glazer.
122. *Unexpected Riches.* MGM, 1942, Herbert Glazer.
123. *Benjamin Franklin, Jr.* MGM, 1943, Herbert Glazer.
124. *Family Troubles.* MGM, 1943, Herbert Glazer.
125. *Calling All Kids.* MGM, 1943, Sam Baerwitz.
126. *Farm Hands.* MGM, 1943, Herbert Glazer.
127. *Election Daze.* MGM, 1943, Herbert Glazer
128. *Little Miss Pinkerton.* MGM, 1943, Herbert Glazer.
129. *Three Smart Guys.* MGM, 1943, Edward Cahn.
130. *Radio Bugs.* MGM, 1944, Cyril Endfield.
131. *Tale of a Dog.* MGM, 1944, Cyril Endfield.
132. *Dancing Romeo.* MGM, 1944, Cyril Endfield.

OUR GANG PLAYERS

*1. George (Spanky) McFarland (89)
2. Billie (Buckwheat) Thomas (89)
3. Carl (Alfalfa) Switzer (60)
4. Darla Hood (48)
5. Eugene (Porky) Lee (40)
6. Mickey Gubitosi (later Robert [Bobby] Blake) (40)
7. Matthew (Stymie) Beard (33)
8. Bobby (Wheezer) Hutchins (31)
9. Billy (Froggy) Laughlin (29)
10. Tommy Bond (24)
11. Sidney Kibrick (23)
12. Dorothy de Borba (22)
13. Harold Switzer (22)
14. Darwood Kaye (20)
15. Allan Clayton (Farina) Hoskins (20)
16. Mary Ann Jackson (19)
17. Norman (Chubby) Chaney (18)
18. Jerry Tucker (18)
19. Scotty Beckett (17)
20. Alvin Buckelew (16)
21. Janet Burston (16)
22. Jackie Cooper (15)
23. Donald Haines (15)
24. Donald Proffitt (14)
25. Gary (Junior) Jasgar (13)
26. Leonard (Woim) Kibrick (9)
27. Rex Downing (8)
28. Sherwood (Spud) Bailey (8)
29. Shirley (Mugsy) Coates (8)
30. Joe Cobb (7)
31. Dickie DeNuet (7)
32. Marianne Edwards (7)
33. Bobby Mallon (7)
34. George (Derby) Billings (6)

*The figure in parentheses shows the number of talking *Our Gang* films in which each player appeared.

35.   Dickie Moore (6)
36.   Wally Albright (6)
37.   Kendall (Breezy/Brisbane) McComas (6)
38.   Freddie (Bully) Chapman (6)
39.   Billy (Ray) Smith (6)
40.   Marvin (Bubbles) Trin (6)
41.   Freddie (Slicker) Walburn (6)
42.   Jackie White (5)
43.   Robert Winkler (5)
44.   Dickie Hall (5)
45.   Douglas Greer (5)
46.   Jean Darling (5)
47.   Bobby (Cotton) Beard (5)
48.   Dorian Johnston (5)
49.   Valerie Lee (5)
50.   Tommy McFarland (5)
51.   Shirley Jean Rickert (5)
52.   Harry Spear (5)
53.   Jackie (Jane) Taylor (5)
54.   Willie Mae (Buckwheat) Taylor (5)
55.   Carolina (Marmalade) Beard (4)
56.   Joe (Corky) Geil (4)
57.   Dickie Jones (4)
58.   Mickey Laughlin (4)
59.   Bobby (Bonedust) Young (later Clifton Young) (4)
60.   Leon Tyler (3)
61.   Hugh Chapman (3)
62.   Patsy Currier (3)
63.   Edith Fellows (3)
64.   Philbrook Lyons (3)
65.   Budd MacDonald (3)
66.   Ray (Boxcar) Smith (3)
67.   Harold (Bouncy) Wertz (2)
68.   Delmar Watson (2)
69.   Bobs Watson (2)
70.   Robert Ferrero (2)
71.   Artye Folz (2)
72.   George Ernest (2)
73.   Barry (Ken) Downing (2)
74.   The Five Cabin Kids (2)
75.   The Five Meglin Kiddies (2)

76. Jannie Hoskins (2)
77. Georgia Jean LaRue (2)
78. Johnny Aber (2)
79. Philip Hurlic (2)
80. Cecelia Murray (2)
81. Juanita (Sally) Quigley (2)
82. Jackie Salling (2)
83. Yen Wong (1)
84. Billy Winderlout (1)
85. Kenneth Wilson (1)
86. Clyde Wilson (1)
87. Mary Ann Breckell (1)
88. Sheila Brown (1)
89. Sonny Bupp (1)
90. Tommy Bupp (1)
91. Joline Karol (1)
92. Beverly (Aurelia) Hudson (1)
93. Cordell Hickman (1)
94. Bobby (Gerald) Browning (1)
95. Bobby Anderson (1)
96. Maria Ayres (1)
97. Bobbie Burns (1)
98. Janet Comerford (1)
99. Patsy DiHemore (1)
100. Mickey Daniels (1)
101. Billy Finnegan (1)
102. Betsy Gay (1)
103. Maria Lisa Gumm (1)
104. Barbara Goodrich (1)
105. Teresa Mae Glass (1)
106. Marlene Mains (1)
107. Billy Mindy (1)
108. Philip MacMahon (1)
109. Gloria Mann (1)
110. Baby Patsy May (1)
111. Jack McHugh (1)
112. Annabella Logan (1)
113. Billy Lee (1)
114. Jackie Lynn (1)
115. Eva Lee Kuney (1)
116. Tony Kales (1)

117. Mildred Kornman (1)
118. Mary Kornman (1)
119. Cullen Johnson (1)
120. Leon Janney (1)
121. Harry Harvey, Jr. (1)
122. Hill Twins (1)
123. Darryl Hickman (1)
124. Raymond Rayhill Powell (1)
125. David Polonsky (1)
126. Josephine Roberts (1)
127. Betty Scott (1)

Selected Bibliography

BARBOUR, ALAN G. *A Thousand and One Delights*. Macmillan, 1971.
————. *The Thrill of It All*. Macmillan, 1971.
BUTLER, IVAN. *The Horror Film*. Barnes, 1967.
CARPOZI, GEORGE, JR. *The Gary Cooper Story*. Arlington House, 1970.
CHERTOK, HARVEY and TORGE, MARTHA. *Quotations from Charlie Chan*. Golden, 1968.
CLARENS, CARLOS. *An Illustrated History of the Horror Film*. Putnam, 1967.
CORNEAU, ERNEST N. *The Hall of Fame of Western Film Stars*. Christopher, 1969.
CROWTHER, BOSLEY.*Hollywood Rajah: The Life and Times of Louis B. Mayer*. Holt, Rinehart and Winston, 1960.
DOUGLAS, DRAKE. *Horror!* Macmillan, 1966.
ESSOE, GABE. *Tarzan of the Movies*. Citadel, 1968.
EVERSON, WILLIAM K. *A Pictorial History of the Western Film*. Citadel, 1969.
FENIN, GEORGE N. and EVERSON, WILLIAM K. *The Western*. Orion, 1962.
FENTON, ROBERT W. *The Big Swingers*. Prentice-Hall, 1967.
GRIFFITH, RICHARD. *The Movie Stars*. Doubleday, 1970.
HALLIWELL, LESLIE. *The Filmgoer's Companion: From Nickelodeon to New Wave*. Hill and Wang, 1965.
LAHR, JOHN. *Notes on a Cowardly Lion*. Knopf, 1969.
LAMPARSKI, RICHARD. *Whatever Became Of . . . ?* 1st, 2nd, 3rd Series. Crown, 1966, 1968, 1970.
MALTIN, LEONARD. *The Great Movie Shorts*. Crown, 1971.
MICHAEL, PAUL. *The Academy Awards: A Pictorial History*. Crown, 1968.
————, ed. *The American Movies Reference Book: The Sound Era*. Prentice-Hall, 1969.
MOSKOWITZ, SAM, ed. *Under the Moons of Mars*. Holt, Rinehart and Winston, 1970.
NYE, RUSSELL B. *The Unembarrassed Muse*. Dial, 1970.
PARISH, JAMES ROBERT. *The Great Movie Series*. Barnes, 1971.
PRAGER, ARTHUR. *Rascals at Large*. Doubleday, 1971.
QUIGLEY, MARTIN, JR. and GERTNER, RICHARD. *Films in America*. Golden, 1970.
REED, REX. *Conversations in the Raw*. World, 1969.
SCHICKEL, RICHARD. *The Stars*. Dial, 1962.
SENNETT, TED. *Warner Brothers Presents*. Arlington House, 1971.
SHELTON, ROBERT and GOLDBLATT, BURT. *The Country Music Story*. Arlington House, 1966.
SHIPMAN, DAVID. *The Great Movie Stars*. Crown, 1970.
TWOMEY, ALFRED E. and MCCLURE, ARTHUR F. *The Versatiles*. Barnes, 1969.

Magazines Consulted

Time, Newsweek, Life, Look, Playboy, The Saturday Evening Post, Collier's, Theatre Arts, Harrison's Reports, Films in Review, Film Culture, Sight and Sound, Screen Facts, Film Fan Monthly, Views & Reviews, Filmograph, Film Comment, Focus on Film, Audience.

Index

Ortego, Artie, 137
Orth, Frank, 327, 413, 421
Osborn, Ted, 257, 265
O'Sullivan, Maureen, 19, 20, 28, 31, 35, 36, 233
Our Gang, 464, 477
Ouspenskaya, Maria, 43, 48
Owens, Reginald, 199, 200

Palooka, 429, 431
Paluzzi, Luciana, 308
Pangborn, Franklin, 483
Park, E. L., 259
Parker, Cecilia, 367, 371, 375
Parks, Larry, 402
Parry, Roy, 464
Patton, 469
Pavlow, Muriel, 353
Pawley, Edward, 450
Paxton, Dick, 383, 419
Payne, Sally, 398
Pearson's Magazine, 292
Peck's Bad Boy, 464
Pendleton, Nat, 233, 239, 325, 331
Penman, Lea, 386
Penthouse, 247
Pepper, Barbara, 112
Pepper, Buddy, 383
Perrin, Jack, 450
Peter Ibbetson, 200
Peters, House, Jr., 107
Peterson, Dorothy, 383
Petrie, George, 222
Phantom, The, 83
Phantom of the Opera, 46
Phipps, Nicholas, 353, 354
Photoplay, 236
Pickford, Mary, 144, 346
Picture of Dorian Gray, The, 219
Pierce, James H., 26
Pinocchio, 225
Pittard, Bob, 384
Planet of the Apes, 93

Playboy, 315
Pleasence, Donald, 303, 311
Plues, George, 108, 176
Pollar, Gene, 26
Post, William, Jr., 195
Powell, Russ, 176
Powell, William, 233, 234, 236, 237, 400
Power, Tyrone, 181, 202, 221
Prager, Arthur, 417
Preisser, June, 383, 392
Price, Hal, 108
Price, Vincent, 72, 222
Pride and Prejudice, 28
Prisoner of Shark Island, The, 249
Provost, Jon, 473
Pryor, Maureen, 354
Public Cowboy Number One, 107–135
Punsley, Bernard, 449, 450, 456
Purcell, Dick, 413

Quon, Marianne, 264

Raht, Katherine, 386
Rains, Claude, 43, 46, 47, 69, 72
Ramond, Harold, 426
Randall, Jack, 111
Randolph, John, 93
Range Busters, 181
Range Riders, The, 118
Rascals at Large, 417
Rathbone, Basil, 55, 60, 195, 199, 202, 203
Rawhide, 181
Ray, Allene, 260
Raymond, Gene, 400
Readin' and Writin' 477–493
Reagan, Ronald, 454
Rebecca, 219
Reed, Donna, 331, 371
Reed, George H., 327, 331
Re-Enter Dr. Fu Manchu, 292
Reeves, George, 157
Renaldo, Duncan, 140, 142, 143, 179
Rendell, Robert, 199